BEING
ELVIS

Also by Ray Connolly

FICTION

A Girl Who Came to Stay

Trick or Treat?

Newsdeath

A Sunday Kind of Woman

Sunday Morning

Shadows on a Wall

Love Out of Season

NON-FICTION

John Lennon 1940–1980

Stardust Memories (anthology of interviews)

The Ray Connolly Beatles Achive

SCREENPLAYS FOR THE CINEMA

That'll Be the Day

Stardust

FILMS AND SERIES FOR TELEVISION

Honky Tonk Heroes

Lytton's Diary

Forever Young

Defrosting the Fridge

Perfect Scoundrels

TV DOCUMENTARIES

James Dean: The First American Teenager

The Rhythm of Life (three-part music series)

PLAYS FOR RADIO

An Easy Game to Play

Lost Fortnight

Tim Merryman's Days of Clover (series)

Unimaginable

God Bless Our Love

Sorry, Boys, You Failed the Audition

BEING ELVIS

RAY CONNOLLY

W&N
WEIDENFELD & NICOLSON

First published in Great Britain in 2016
by Weidenfeld & Nicolson

1 3 5 7 9 10 8 6 4 2

A CIP catalogue record for this book is available from the British Library.

HB ISBN 978 1 4746 0455 0
TPB ISBN 978 1 4746 0456 7

Typeset by Input Data Services Ltd, Bridgwater, Somerset

Printed and bound by CPI Group (UK) Ltd, Croydon, CR0 4YY

MIX
Paper from responsible sources
FSC® C104740
FSC
www.fsc.org

Weidenfeld & Nicolson
The Orion Publishing Group Ltd
Carmelite House
50 Victoria Embankment
London, EC4Y 0DZ
An Hachette UK Company

www.orionbooks.co.uk

For Louise and my grandchildren, Jack and Olivia

Picture Credits

Alamy: 2 below left (AF Archive), 7 above (Pictorial Press Ltd.), 11 above (AF Archive);

Getty Images: 5 (© Alfred Wertheimer), 6 below (CBS Photo Archive), 10 (Bettmann), 13 below (Bettmann), 15 above (Keystone), 16 (Gary Null/NBC/NBCU Photo Bank), 17 above (The Abbott Sengstacke Family Papers/Robert Abbott Sengstacke), 18 below (GAB Archive/Rederns), 19 (National Archives/Newsmakers), 21 (Gary Null/NBC/NBCU Photo Bank);

Getty Images/Michael Ochs Archives: 1, 2 below right, 3, 4 above (Colin Escott), 6 above, 12, 15 below, 18 above, 20 below 24;

Getty Images/LIFE Images Collection: 4 below (Don Cravens), 9 below (Don Cravens), 11 below (James Whitmore);

Photoshot: 2 above (© UPPA), 14 (© LFI);

Rex/Shutterstock: 7 below (SNAP), 8 (Everett Collection), 9 above (Everett Collection), 13 above (Sipa Press), 17 below (Everett Collection), 20 above (Sipa Press), 22 above (Sipa Press), 22 below (Reporters Inc.), 23 (Everett Collection)

CONTENTS

ACKNOWLEDGEMENTS

Years before I decided to write this book, I interviewed, in my job as a journalist and then a screenwriter, many of the people involved in the story of Elvis. They included Sam Phillips, Marion Keisker, the Reverend W. Herbert Brewster, Carl Perkins, saxophonist Boots Randolph, Roy Orbison, Mike Stoller, Rufus Thomas, Jerry Wexler, Paul McCartney, John Lennon, Ringo Starr, Chris Hutchins, Bob Dylan, Stanley Booth, B.B. King, Freddy Bienstock, Billy Swan, George Klein, 'Colonel' Tom Parker and my friend the late Mort Shuman. Then, of course, there was Elvis himself. So, I'm very grateful to all of them for sparing me their time and thoughts, as well as to YouTube for making so many interviews with those who knew him so easily accessible.

'Elvis, you're going to be a very big star. Here's some advice. Don't hide. Walk the streets, go to restaurants, but don't hide. Because, if you do, you're going to be the loneliest guy in the world.'

Jackie Gleason to Elvis, 1956

'It was murder for us as Beatles at the height of the hysteria. But there were four of us to share it. Elvis was on his own. There was only him. It must have been impossible.'

John Lennon to Ray Connolly, 1970

AUTHOR'S NOTE

One morning in August 1969, I found myself sitting in a New York office talking on the phone to Bob Dylan. I was the London *Evening Standard*'s rock critic at the time, and, as Dylan was soon to appear at England's Isle of Wight Festival of Music, I'd called in on his manager, Albert Grossman, to see if I could pre-book an interview with the great man.

The answer was, not unexpectedly, 'no'. But then, and I can only assume Grossman was thinking about festival ticket sales which were said to be slow, he suddenly suggested that Dylan may be prepared to chat to me on the phone. And, there and then, he asked his secretary to get 'Bobby' on the line.

Normally, before I did an interview, I liked to plan my questions. But on this occasion, I suddenly had a phone thrust into my hands, and there he was waiting for me, the most reclusive singer-songwriter in the world.

As it turned out, Dylan couldn't have been more friendly or patient with, I suspect, my pretty mundane enquiries, and before long, probably for want of anything better to say, I mentioned that I'd just been to Las Vegas to see Elvis Presley's stage comeback.

'Really?' Dylan's tone changed. 'You were there? How was he?' Then almost before I could answer he was saying, 'I read about it in *The New York Times*. Was he good? Was Scotty Moore [Elvis's first guitarist] with him? What did he sing? Were the Jordanaires backing him? Did he do any of the Sun stuff? "That's All Right"? What about "Mystery Train"? "Heartbreak Hotel"? What else? Did he do any new songs? Who was in the band? He had an orchestra on stage with him! Really?'

So it went on. Bob Dylan was asking me more questions than I'd asked him. No longer was he one of the most famous men in the world and me an interviewer caught off guard. We were equals, fans of the same person, talking excitedly as though we were both fifteen years old and had just discovered rock.

Towards the end of the conversation I happened to mention that Elvis had recorded one of Dylan's songs, 'Tomorrow Is a Long Time', which Dylan obviously knew. It was, he said, his favourite recording of any of the songs he'd written, which, I suppose, wasn't surprising, coming, as it did, from a fan.

A few days later I was back in London and had occasion to phone John Lennon. This, I should explain, was not an unusual occurrence, as I was seeing quite a bit of Lennon and Paul McCartney at that time. Once again, however, I mentioned that I'd just been to see Elvis, and once again I was facing a series of questions, identical almost to those asked by Dylan.

'Was Scotty Moore with him? And the Jordanaires?' It was a 'no' in both cases, by the way. 'What about his early Sun stuff? Did he do "Baby Let's Play House"? What about "I Got a Woman"? Was he good? Was he fat?'

I learned something from those two phone calls: mainly that, deep down, rock stars are really just grown-up fans. No matter how famous and celebrated Bob Dylan and John Lennon had become by that time, they were still fans of the man who had got them started in music in the first place, still fascinated by the sounds that had captured their youth. Their teenage imaginations, like those of Paul McCartney, Keith Richards, Bruce Springsteen and hundreds of others, had been ignited by Elvis.

As, taking my career in another direction, had mine.

Ray Connolly

FOREWORD

'How are people going to remember me when I'm gone?' he wanted to know. 'Will they soon forget me?'

It was May 1977 in a hotel in the small city of Binghamton, New York. And, lying lonely and depressed in his suite, temporarily abandoned after his latest girlfriend had become bored with the treadmill of touring, Elvis Presley had sent for his soprano backing singer Kathy Westmoreland to keep him company. He couldn't bear to be alone, to sleep alone. His entourage didn't like him sleeping alone either. They worried when there was no one to watch over him.

Kathy, a former lover and friend, who had been with him on stage for seven years, sat with him that night and the next, listening as he talked about his mother, his weight, his health and his daughter, consoling him as he agonised about the tell-all book which three of his former employees would soon be publishing, and shaking her head as he worried that he would quickly be forgotten after his death.

He had, he told her, 'never done anything lasting . . . never made a classic film'. No matter how much pleasure his singing had given, or how he'd helped change the direction of popular music, all he saw was his failure to become 'a real movie star'. And it tormented him.

Only forty-two, but sick with a host of internal problems, addicted, exhausted and desperately disappointed, he was already talking about himself in the past tense. Kathy should wear something white at his funeral, he tried to joke to her at one point. She laughed and promised she would, and then she held his hand until he fell asleep. The sleep he always craved, but which, so often, was so hard for him to find.

That was Elvis Presley, now recognised as the most loved entertainer ever, but then a sick man fretting out the final few months of the tragedy that his life had become.

Yet what a life it had been. During virtually the whole of his adulthood everyone had smiled whenever he had entered a room. When he made a joke, everybody laughed with him, only louder; and when he made a request, his aides hurried to oblige. Everybody wanted to please him, from the coterie of guys who daily walked the tightrope between servitude and friendship as they attended him, to the ever-extending clan of relatives who were dependent upon him for employment and homes. And then there were the many girlfriends whose affections he rewarded with gifts of cars and diamonds.

Yes, what a life. Whatever he wanted, he could buy, and so he did . . . houses, fleets of Cadillacs, aeroplanes, guns – and some doctors, too. And, although he always liked to be the one who gave, when he chose to ask a favour it was almost invariably granted. Two presidents of the United States took his calls, while senators, state governors, movie, rock and sports celebrities queued backstage to smile, shake his hand and be photographed with him. He was a magnet. Everybody came to him; while his local Memphis police, hospital authorities and press looked away when they thought it politic to do so.

Of course they did. He was Elvis the boy-man, who, in the mid-fifties, had gone, in the space of thirty months, from high school graduation to the top of the world's record charts, and who, through television, had gone on to provoke national and then international outrage and devotion.

With music the shortest route to the emotions, singing stars regularly come and go in short flushes of excitement, but there was something about his voice, his attitude, his shy smile, his boyish beauty, the movements of his body as he sang, his sex appeal and his story that stuck in the public's imagination. It still sticks, making him the ultimate, and, forty years after his death, the most enduring of American icons.

As a boy, he'd dreamed that success would free him and his family from poverty. But then he'd discovered that fame on his level imprisoned as well as released. He wasn't the first rock and roll singer, but he was the first rock superstar, a status which meant that not only was there no one from whose experience he could learn, but also there was no one with whom he could share the burden of being himself – of being Elvis. Throughout his life he would often say that he'd always felt lonely. That was understandable. No one, other than he, knew what it was like to be under the relentless glare of devotion and attention, to be the alchemist who could turn music into so much love and so much gold.

His ambition had been to become rich and famous. His extraordinary two-and-a-half-octave voice, with another level in falsetto, had achieved that and more for him. But when he left the stage, when the cameras were turned away and the spotlight was switched off, what then? Where did he fit in? Nowhere. Impossible to categorise, outrageous celebrity locked him out of any semblance of the real world. And, as the years passed, he retreated to his court, whether it be at his Graceland mansion home in Memphis, or in Hollywood or Las Vegas, where his courtiers would cosset him in his fears, insecurities and depression.

By the time of that night in Binghamton with Kathy Westmoreland, just fourteen weeks before his death, he was mentally broken, emotionally spent. How could he have fallen into this state of despair? What had gone wrong for the man blessed with so many gifts and talents? From the outside he seemed to have it all. But, looking out at the adoring fans one night some months earlier, he had said bleakly to one of his staff: 'Those people don't love me in a personal way. They don't know what's inside me.'

They couldn't. But, had they been able to see inside his mind, what would they have found? Most likely a multiple pile-up of warring desires, duties and pressures. By then his past had been in endless conflict with his present for over twenty years, his dreams blunted by brutish reality as his artistic ambitions lost out to his needs and to the demands of his manager and himself for an endless supply of money. On film and stage he displayed a charming bravura. But that was a mask behind which he hid his fears and weaknesses.

Would his fans stay loyal the older he got, he wondered aloud in those final months. He dreaded their desertion, and what they would think when they learned about his darker secrets. Then there were his more private worries. What about his pathological spending sprees? He knew, in his more sanguine moments, that they were ruining him, but he couldn't control them. Would he soon run out of money? His father thought it possible. Unable to stop himself, he'd either spent much of his fortune or given it away. And then there was his greatest fear, the recurrent nightmare: that he would soon be forced to sell his home, Graceland, and would one day end up back where he'd started, dirt poor again, remembered only as a washed-up has-been, or, worse, a pathetic joke.

From the very beginning, the enigma that was Elvis, the poor white boy from segregated Mississippi, who chose to sing the black music of his musical heroes, had been a highly combustible mix. Born into the bleakest thirties rural poverty, he earned hundreds of millions of dollars in his career, yet, at the end of his life, and with no investments to fall back on, he was dependent on loans from his bank to cover his spending from tour to tour – and pay his manager's gambling debts.

Then there were his complex religious beliefs. A lifelong Bible-reading Pentecostal Christian he also dabbled in numerology and mysticism; and, though he often prayed and was lavishly generous towards charities, he was also a serially unfaithful and promiscuous lover and husband, while demanding total fidelity from the many women in his life. Rock and roll had made him a star, but he had originally wanted to be part of a gospel-singing quartet and all his life he preferred spirituals and hymns to any other kind of music.

Contradictions were everywhere. At the same time as being the most scandalous and sexy young singer in the world he was, as a young man, also extraordinarily close to his mother; once the long-haired rebel, he became a model soldier and would later sing paeans of patriotism in concerts; and while on the surface he was always the supremely confident world star, in his dressing room he was so nervous he would need an injection of amphetamines before each performance to give him the courage to even get out on stage.

Then, when he wasn't on stage, when he was the audience at private screenings, he was the movie buff who for years booked cinemas after hours so that he could watch films he loved, old and new, cinematically literate enough to hate and be embarrassed by most of his own pictures.

That he was self-destructive there is no doubt. But were there explanations for it beyond his self-absorption? The most popular singer in the world, for whom any top songwriter would have been thrilled to write, why did he waste his voice and talent on so many hackneyed melodies and clichéd lyrics in songs for the films he loathed so much? And what was a sick man who was hopelessly addicted to prescription drugs doing on tour and being filmed in a television special just weeks before his death anyway? Could he really have been so desperate for money? Or could it have been that his manager, the self-styled 'Colonel' Tom Parker, was even more desperate?

As for that addiction to prescription drugs: exactly when did that start? Was it earlier than anyone suspected; during his spell in the US Army, or, as now seems likely, even before that? And how could a star with such a worldwide following be so supine and spend so many years unable to stand up to and defy his bullying manager? Had his mother been right when from the beginning she'd talked about Parker as 'the very Devil himself'?

'I'm so tired of being Elvis Presley,' he would say in the last months of his life. It's sometimes easy to understand why. But did it really have to be like that? And exactly where and when in Elvis Presley's life were the seeds of his successes, excesses and weaknesses sown?

1

'Since I was two years old all I knew was gospel music.'

His beginnings could hardly have been more humble; his expectations more limited. Born at around half past four in the morning of 8 January 1935, in a two-room shack in Tupelo, Mississippi, a couple of oil lamps provided the only light, and a log stove boiled the necessary water. Thirty minutes later a twin brother followed: Elvis Aron and Jesse Garon, their names had already been chosen. But Jesse was stillborn. The young parents, Vernon and Gladys Presley, had expected twins – they were in both of their families – but they hadn't been able to afford the cost of medical help when Gladys was pregnant. A doctor had only been called by a neighbour when Gladys began having complications with the birth. His fee was fifteen dollars. It would be paid by a charity.

Jesse was buried in an unmarked grave in the Priceville Cemetery in Tupelo a day or so later, but by this time Gladys, who had lost a lot of blood, had been taken, with her surviving baby, to a hospital. When Elvis was older, he would wonder if he and Jesse had been identical twins, and why his brother had died and not him, because, as they told him in church, there had to be a reason for everything. Sometimes he used to imagine the two of them as brothers, playing happily together; then at other times, perhaps, he would worry that they might have been rivals, like Cain and Abel in the Bible. On a couple of occasions after he became famous, he asked people to try to find out exactly which plot of land Jesse had been buried in at the cemetery. But they never could; no papers marked the spot. He was sometimes told that when one twin dies, the survivor grows up with all the additional qualities of the other. His mother encouraged him to think that: to believe that he was special. She was convinced that he was special.

Tupelo, Mississippi, then, as now, the poorest state of the Union, was a scabby little town of about six thousand people in the thirties, and the Presleys' little home was a frame house on blocks with no electricity and no running water on a dirt road above the creek and highway, close to the woods and farms. At school, Elvis was told that Tupelo was the Choctaw Indian name for that area, and, in the thirties, there were quite a number of Presleys in and around Tupelo. There was quite a lot of religion, too. So it was unsurprising that his parents, Vernon Presley and Gladys Smith, had first met at the Pentecostal First Assembly of God church in East Tupelo.

Gladys was the fourth of nine children. Her mother, Doll Smith, was a long-term, semi-professional invalid, and, as a girl, Gladys looked after her, in addition to taking care of her younger brothers and sisters. Doll died the year after Elvis was born and her husband, Bob Smith, followed soon afterwards. He'd been a sharecropper, taking his family from farm to farm in the neighbourhood looking for work. The local gossip said that Bob did a little moonshine on the side to try to make ends meet, but they never did meet. The Smiths seemed predisposed to die young.

Vernon's father was Jessie D. Presley, who, the rest of the family would say, was a good-looking, bad-tempered, womanising, hard-drinking man who did some farming, and who gave teenage Vernon some tough years in the thirties. Jessie's wife, Minnie-Mae, Elvis's grandmother, a long lean woman, had some bad times with him, too. He left her before Elvis knew him, so she went to live with her son Vernon and his wife Gladys, and their boy. Elvis always called her Dodger, after she once dodged a baseball he'd accidentally thrown in her direction.

Vernon, who liked to joke that he'd been raised on a cotton patch, had been only seventeen when, just a couple of months after they met, he and Gladys, then twenty-two, had run away to the next county to get married. That was in 1933. They both lied about their age, making him older and Gladys younger on their marriage licence. She was working in the Tupelo Garment Center at the time, sitting at a sewing machine for two dollars a day, while Vernon did whatever work he could find. It was the Depression, so that wasn't easy. Once married, they lived with Vernon's parents for a little while, and then borrowed $180 from a local money-lender called Orville Bean to build a house next door to the older Presleys on an empty lot that Bean owned. Vernon had done some work as a carpenter, so he put the house up himself with help from his father and a brother.

To most people it wouldn't have sounded much of a place to live, with no ceiling, no separate kitchen and an outside toilet, for which Gladys had to carry the water from a communal pump down the road and save it in a two-gallon tank. But when Elvis was little he would listen as his mother would tell him how happy and proud she'd been when they'd first moved in. A lot of people didn't have a house of their own then, she would say. They had chickens in the yard, and, when she was expecting, she and Daddy had sat out on the porch in the hot summer evenings and made plans. After the death of Jesse, Elvis turned out to be Gladys's only plan.

According to family history, most of their ancestors had originally been Scots or Irish or a mixture of the two, but Gladys would tell how before the Civil War, her great, great, great grandmother had been 'a full blooded Cherokee Indian called Morning Dove White'. Elvis liked the idea of that, and would later picture Morning Dove as one of those pretty little Red Indian girls they had in the Western movies. Probably only when he was a star and working in Hollywood did he realise that the actresses playing Red Indian maidens were as likely to come from Baltimore or Chicago as an Indian reservation.

Gladys didn't go back to the Garment Center after she came out of hospital, but the following September she would lay Elvis down on a sack beside her when she went cotton picking and drag him along the rows after her. He used to like that story, too, and, when he was a little older, it's told he would help her with the cotton, picking the bolls off the stems. It was hard, dry, scratchy work, but all the families around East Tupelo did it.

A vague, early memory would have found him and Gladys riding regularly seventy-five miles on a Greyhound bus across Mississippi when he was three years old. Just to be going on a long bus ride would have been thrilling, and he would have known that he and Mama were going to see his Daddy. What he wouldn't have understood was that the place where Vernon was staying was the State

Penitentiary at Parchman, a work farm in the middle of miles of pancake-flat fields near the Mississippi River.

The version of events explaining his father's incarceration that the family told, on the very rare occasion that the shameful story was even mentioned, was that he and Gladys's younger brother, Travis Smith, together with a friend, had got drunk and changed a cheque written out by Orville Bean. He was the man who had loaned Vernon the money to build his little house. According to Bean, out of the kindness of his heart he'd given them a cheque for four dollars for a pig they were selling, but they'd then changed it to either fourteen or forty dollars (no one can remember which) and taken it to a bank in Tupelo to be cashed. Not surprisingly, they'd been caught and the police had been called.

Elvis's great uncle, Noah Presley, who would later become a mayor of East Tupelo and drive the school bus, pleaded with Bean not to press charges and offered to pay back double the money. But Orville wanted his pound of flesh.

After six months on remand in Tupelo jail, Vernon had been sentenced to three years in Parchman Farm, although he got out after just nine months, when neighbours and friends petitioned for his release. Even Orville Bean wrote a plea, although by then he'd evicted Gladys from her home when she couldn't keep up the twelve-dollars-a month rent. That was Orville's rule. He loaned you the money to build a house on his land, but if you stopped repaying him, he took your home off you.

After that, Gladys, who was reliant on welfare, took Elvis and moved in with relatives, going from one family to another, until Vernon rejoined them, and they rented another place of their own. Years later Elvis could count over seven different homes they'd had during the time they lived in Mississippi, and then several more after the family moved to Memphis when he was thirteen. Some people, those who didn't have money problems, gossiped that the Presleys were the sort of family who always moved when the rent became due. To Elvis, that was unfair. His mother was as honest as the day.

She was also very nervous; timid even. But she was dutiful and hard working. While Vernon, who could never hold down a job for long, would regularly borrow money to get by, Gladys always tried to make sure it was paid back and that all the bills were settled. Elvis would watch their struggle throughout his boyhood, and hear his father read the Bible and say a nightly prayer that they could somehow be relieved of their poverty.

'Yes, we was poor,' Vernon would admit years later. 'But we weren't trash.'

Life might have been hard for the Presleys, but Elvis wasn't a sad little boy. He didn't know that they were poor. Nobody else they knew had much of anything, so he wasn't aware of rich people and of how different their lives were. And his parents always held him close: just the three of them.

Wherever they were living they all slept in the same room, and when Vernon was away, and later, after he was released from Parchman and would occasionally go off looking for work in other towns, Elvis would sleep in his mother's bed with her. Sometimes in the morning he and Gladys would lie there together, talking to each other in their own baby language. He called her Satnin. On other occasions she would read the Children's Bible stories to him, telling him of the adventures of Jonah in the belly of the whale and Joshua at the battle of Jericho. He would later record hymns about Jonah and Joshua.

When he was grown up he would sometimes hear Daddy say that they'd been so poor there were times when they 'didn't have anything but corn bread and water to eat for their supper'. But that wasn't how he remembered it.

'We'd have pork chops or country ham and cream potatoes. Stuff like that, with red eyed gravy,' he once told a reporter.

That wasn't every day, but, so far as he could recall, he never went to bed hungry, although 'we were pretty close to it sometimes'. And although he knew there may have been a degree of truth in the charge some people made that his father had no ambition, he would always defend him.

'They have no idea how hard it was for him,' he would say. 'He was wonderful for me. And, although he and Mama argued, she loved him.'

Vernon was a good-looking man when he was young, and Gladys, never wanting to wear shoes, would dance by herself to the music on the radio as her son watched. Before she'd married she loved to go dancing in Tupelo, and her impossible dream, she would tell the little boy, had been that she might become a dancer in the movies. Blessed with a good voice, she would sing all the time, too, as would Daddy, mainly hymns, with Elvis joining in with the two.

'I remember when I was little, people would listen to me singing around the housing project where we lived,' Elvis would say more than thirty years later. A favourite hymn for all the family was 'Peace in the Valley', with the story book pictures it painted: 'Well, the bear shall be gentle and the wolf will be tame, and the lion shall lay down by the lamb.' He loved that one, and as hymns became, and remained, a central part of his life, he would sing it in their little church that was just around the corner from where they lived. The family would all be there in their best clothes, three times on Sundays and all day during revivals, when Elvis would watch the preacher moving, pleading and praying to Jesus, with the congregation swaying in their seats, calling out and shifting their feet. Some people called them 'holy rollers', but he never did, and would become angry when he heard the phrase. He thought it was disrespectful of his religion.

Gladys liked to tell him how, when he was less than two years old, he would slide down from her lap in church, run into the aisle and try to sing with the choir. He was too little to know the words, she would say, but he could carry the tune, and would watch the faces of the singers and try to do as they did. Church then was both worship and entertainment for the family. There wasn't much of anything else.

'Since I was two years old all I knew was gospel music,' he would later recall when recording his sacred albums. 'We borrowed the style of our psalm singing from the Negroes. We used to go to these religious singings all the time. The preachers would cut up all over the place, jumping on the piano, moving every which way. The audience liked them and I guess I learned from them.'

Religion had a strong hold on him right from his earliest days. On one occasion when Gladys caught him stealing empty Coca-Cola bottles from neighbours' backyards and taking them to the grocery store to claim the penny on the bottle, she gave him a spanking. Worse than that punishment, though, was that she also hauled him round to the church where he had to confess his crime in front of the congregation.

Apart from being something of a physical curiosity in that on one foot his second and third toes were joined together, he was much like every other child with the usual illnesses of colds and flu, and measles and whooping cough. On one occasion, though, he was so sick with tonsillitis his parents thought there was a real danger that they might lose him. With no money for a doctor, and hospital being out of the question, they both got down on their knees by his bed and prayed for him. And the fever went away. After that Gladys was convinced that his survival had been a message from God, her proof that her boy really *was* special.

Everything worried her. She'd lost one child, and later miscarried another baby, and was terrified of losing Elvis.

'When I was little she never let me out of her sight,' he would remember.

One day while playing with some other children close to the nearby creek, he fell in. There was no danger, but he got a spanking when he got home with his wet trousers. So he knew he always had to be careful not to worry his mother. If he did, she'd threaten him with her broom. And, when other children bullied him, she'd threaten to use it on them, too. Normally she was a quiet woman, but 'when she was angry she could be heard', one friend would say, 'as far away as Cleveland'.

On occasion neighbours would gossip, saying, 'Gladys dotes on that boy so much she'll ruin him'. And she did spoil him, with what little she had to offer. Perhaps the tantrums he had were the result of that. Until he was in his teens he always had his own plate, cup, knife and fork and spoon, which he'd even take to school, to the amusement of some of the other children. For some reason he couldn't bear it if someone else used them, and would erupt in a fury if they did. He didn't know why it bothered him. It just did. All his life he would get mad over small things, although he knew he really shouldn't, and it was nearly always with the people he was closest to. 'You always hurt the one you love', ran the words of the old Mills Brothers song, and he could see the truth in that. Did he sometimes hurt his mother? Yes, but never intentionally.

By all accounts he was a passive, dutiful son, the biggest worry his parents had about him being his occasional bad dreams and sleep-walking. What he was doing or where he thought he was going in his sleep, he couldn't say. His mother would say he was looking for Jesse. Well, maybe. But she would just lead him back to bed and he'd settle down again.

2

'Don't you worry none, Mama. When I grow up I'm going to buy you a fine house and pay everything you owe at the grocery store, and buy two Cadillacs, one for you and Daddy and one for me.'

His first school was East Tupelo Consolidated. It was very small, with two grades in one room. Initially Gladys would walk him there every morning and back in the afternoons, though later he went with the other kids from round about. The story about her taking him to school every day until he was fourteen was just that – a story.

His parents hadn't had much education, Gladys never getting more than four months a year in class. She was determined, though, that Elvis would do better than she and Vernon had done, that he would graduate from high school and become somebody important with a good, regular job.

School was strict in those days, and Elvis was average and shy. He'd always been taught to be polite and courteous and say 'yes, ma'am' and 'no, ma'am', which he continued to do all his life, but he didn't ever say much else in class. When he was famous and saw old school photographs of himself with his classmates when he was six or seven, a skinny little kid in overalls, he must have wondered what future he might have been imagining. He had fair hair then – a light tawny colour that went blonder in the summer.

While he was at his first school, America joined the Second World War, and with US soldiers fighting in Europe and the Pacific, the children would sing 'God Bless America'. On one occasion, when he was seven, he did a duet with a little girl called Shirley. They sang 'You Are My Sunshine', with Elvis pretending to play on a toy guitar that someone had given him.

Did he imagine he was on the Grand Ole Opry, which the family and everyone else he knew would listen to on the radio on Saturday nights? It was a weekly treat, Daddy sometimes having to attach a radio to the battery in his car when the place they were living in didn't have electricity. Vernon nearly always had an old car of some kind, although frequently he'd hardly bought it before it broke down.

The Opry was probably where Elvis first heard Red Foley sing the old country weepy song 'Old Shep'. He had a dog of his own at one time called Rex, of which he became very fond, but it got the mange and had to be put down. So the idea of a boy growing up whose best friend is his dog would have resonated with him. A favourite right through childhood, 'Old Shep' became the first song he sang in public on children's day at the Mississippi-Alabama Fair and Dairy Show when he was ten.

The fair was a big day in Tupelo, with the children being taken to the Fairgrounds from all the local schools, and some being chosen to sing in a talent contest. They'd been rehearsing at his school when his fifth-grade teacher, Mrs Oleta Grimes, had heard him sing in morning prayers and suggested to the principal that he should be entered for the competition. She was Orville Bean's daughter, so perhaps she'd wanted to make up in some way for what had happened to his parents. Whatever the reason, on the big day he stood on a chair so that he could reach the microphone, and wearing pressed denims, an unfastened tie, and wire glasses, his short, fair hair parted to one side, he sang without accompaniment. A photograph shows him standing looking very serious, alongside the winners, two bigger children on his right, the girl dressed as Annie Oakley with a guitar and cowboy hat, while on his left is a little black boy in a bowler hat and waistcoat. To his recollection he came fifth in the competition, though some people liked to say he was second. Either way he got free rides in the amusement park as a result.

'But,' he would remember, 'I must have done something wrong, too. Probably going on the rides. Because Mama gave me a whipping that day, and I thought she didn't love me.'

Eleven years later, when he went out to Hollywood, he recorded 'Old Shep' for his second album. A lot of fans couldn't understand why it was there alongside 'Long Tall Sally' and two other Little

Richard rock and roll songs. They didn't know he'd been singing it nearly all his life.

Guitars came into his life when he was given his first proper one for his eleventh birthday. A guitar wasn't an unusual gift where he grew up, it being the working man's instrument of choice – cheap and easy to carry around. He'd really wanted a bicycle, but that was too expensive and Gladys was afraid he might get hit by a car on the road. He'd also asked for a hunting rifle, although he told his father that he didn't 'want to shoot no birds'.

The guitar was Gladys's idea. 'You could play it when you sing, Elvis,' she said, 'and you know people like to hear your singing.'

So he ended up getting a little Gene Autry type of instrument that cost his parents about $7.50 from a hardware store. The owner of the store later said Elvis threw a tantrum when he didn't get the rifle he wanted, but Elvis had no memory of that. Not on that day, anyway. Possibly he threw a tantrum on another day in the shop when he didn't get his own way. He would erupt into sudden rages of frustration all his life.

As it turned out, the guitar as a gift was more than inspired. Soon afterwards Daddy bought him a music book that showed him where to place his fingers on the frets to make basic chords and the pastor at their church, who was a relative, gave him a few tips on how to play. After that he more or less taught himself, and from that day on music and singing began taking up more and more of his time. And, as another photograph shows, he got a bike the next year anyway.

No one he knew had a television set, and by then he was desperate to see what TV was like. But he would have to wait, and for entertainment he would go down and watch an amateur afternoon show, *Saturday Jamboree*, at the local Tupelo radio station. It was held in the old court building, and sometimes he would be invited to sing. He did 'Old Shep' mostly, especially after he learned a few guitar chords.

'It sounded like someone beating on a bucket lid,' he would joke later about nearly all his early attempts at accompanying himself, but the guitar would have helped him keep the rhythm.

A country singer called Mississippi Slim would do country songs on the show on a regular basis, and, because he'd been to Nashville and made some records, he seemed very famous and glamorous to Elvis. He was the first star Elvis had ever met, and on one occasion

Mississippi Slim even backed the boy on his guitar. He must have been a kind man.

The world in general, however, still wasn't being kind to the Presleys, and when Elvis was twelve they had to leave where they were living in the predominantly white countryside around East Tupelo because, once again, they'd run out of money. Crossing over into the main part of the town, they ended up renting a house on the edge of what, in those days, was known as the Shakerag area, which was where a lot of the Tupelo coloured people lived. In those days segregation ruled in Mississippi, the white people having their schools and churches and hairdressers and much else, and the black population theirs.

East Tupelo had been a white working-class place where country music would have dominated people's entertainment. But living near Shakerag, a poor collection of shacks and shanties, and walking past the little churches and hearing the hymn singing coming from them, and, perhaps, further down the street, catching the music from the juke joints, would have been something new and exciting for a boy like Elvis. By this time he was discovering black rhythm and blues on the radio, too. His parents would scold him for listening to it, but it didn't stop him. Gladys always impressed on him not to forget that in the eyes of God he was no better than any other person, but then, in contradiction, she'd also be warning him not to get involved 'with any coloured girl'. It was just the way she'd been raised, he would say later when remembering it. But he never did.

Because they were now in Tupelo proper, he had to change schools and began attending Milan Junior High, where he was self-conscious about being the only kid in class still wearing overalls. That was all his parents could afford. Years later in the sixties when all young people were wearing jeans, he would be asked why he never wore them. The truth was that when he was a child, denim, the uniform of the poor, was pretty much all he ever had to wear. So, apart from when he wore jeans as a character in a movie, he never put them on. They reminded him of too many things he didn't like to think about.

Not surprisingly there were never many books in the Presley home apart from the Bible, so Gladys enrolled him at the Tupelo library. He went a few times, but what he really loved were the thick comic books of the time, with their full-length cartoon stories about Captain

Marvel and Flash Gordon. Boys at school would exchange them, but he always made sure he got his back, keeping them neat and tidy in a stack. He kept them for years, long after he became famous. He liked the movies, too, and would go to the Saturday serials that starred Roy Rogers and Gene Autry, although Daddy told him not to mention to anyone at church that he went to the picture house. Some people there were stricter than his parents and thought that watching movies was sinful.

Quite a number of things were considered sinful by the people at church, but luckily music wasn't among them, and by this time he was taking his guitar to school regularly, where one day some rougher boys stole it and cut the strings. They thought it was a joke. Elvis didn't, and everyone could see how upset he was. Perhaps a teacher said something, but the following day some other children made a collection among themselves and raised enough money for him to buy some new strings.

Probably it was the girls in class who organised it. Girls were often better that way. Elvis was only twelve, but he was already girl mad. He always liked girls and their company. At one time, while living in East Tupelo, he'd written out his name and that of a little girl on his parents' wedding licence, but had then changed his mind and given her a note saying that he now liked her friend more. And that was that. They'd been divorced.

Money was still always a problem at home, and from childhood he seems to have realised that it was going to be up to him to do something about it. On one occasion, on hearing his parents worrying because they couldn't afford to pay the rent or find a few dollars for the grocery bill, he said to Gladys: 'Don't you worry none, Mama. When I grow up I'm going to buy you a fine house and pay everything you owe at the grocery store, and buy two Cadillacs, one for you and Daddy and one for me.'

Gladys just smiled, but Daddy laughed and put his arm around the boy. 'Just so long as you don't steal one, son,' he said.

He didn't know when his parents first hit on the idea of leaving Tupelo. Vernon had been working away a lot, and had spent some time in Memphis, but by the time Elvis was thirteen Daddy had a job he liked, driving a wholesale grocery truck all around north Mississippi. Then one day he got fired again. He'd been caught bootlegging a little moonshine while on his deliveries. Moonshine was no big deal to people in the South, but it was illegal, and the boss said he had no choice but to let unlucky Vernon go.

So overnight the Presleys did what people always do when things can't get any worse. They sold what they could of their furniture, which was mainly second-hand anyway, and gave away the rest. Then they shoved whatever they could carry into a wooden trunk and strapped it on to the roof of the 1937 Plymouth that Vernon was then driving. And, with Mama in the front, and Elvis in the back with Grandma, they set off looking for work. They were flat broke again. Things just had to get better. Memphis, a hundred miles northwest, was the obvious place to go.

3

'I would just sit there in class and be looking out the window . . . I'd be thinking about being a star and singing. I was just dreaming all the time.'

All his changes were in Memphis. He left childhood behind when the family left Tupelo. It was November 1948, and he was nearly fourteen. Leaving everything and everybody he knew may have made his eyes sting as they drove away, but he sensed an excitement about Memphis from almost the moment they arrived. It was that sort of place. The only time he'd ever visited the city had been on a day out when Uncle Noah had brought some of the children up from Tupelo in the school bus to go to the zoo in Overton Park. Noah had then driven them around Riverside to show them the Mississippi River and the bridge to Arkansas. It had seemed like a big and threatening city to the children from a small town, and gloomy and tall where the old cotton warehouses were. But nowhere stays frightening for long when it becomes your home town.

Gladys was fretful at first and lonely in the city, but it didn't take Elvis more than a couple of weeks to get to know his way around. It wasn't as if they'd moved to Chicago or New York. Memphis might stretch quite a way out into the suburbs now, but in those days the area around the back of Front St, and then north and south of there, was only a few blocks this way or that. And that was the only part of Memphis he needed to know.

The first two or three places they stayed in were boarding houses; one room to cook, sleep and eat in, off a hotplate, with a shared bathroom and no tub. But then Vernon got a job at United Paint Company and Gladys went to work as a sewing machine operator, a job she'd had as a girl; and when, a little later, her brother, Travis Smith, and his wife, Lorraine, followed them up from Tupelo, also looking for work, the city began to feel more homely. Then, after a few months, the Memphis Housing Authority allotted them an apartment in Lauderdale Courts, which was a federally subsidised New Deal housing project for families. Some people would have turned up their noses at living in the projects, and the urban estate of three-storey brick buildings wasn't especially attractive. But two bedrooms, a sitting room, a kitchen and your own bathroom? It was the best home the Presleys had ever lived in. And when the housing officer called to see how they were getting along and praised Mrs Presley for how spick and span she kept everything, Gladys was tickled. She had always been house proud, but this was the first time since Elvis had been a baby that she'd had a home of which to be proud. For Elvis it was a good place to grow.

Racial segregation was the order in Memphis just as much as it had been in Tupelo, but while Lauderdale Courts and Elvis's school, Humes High, were in a white neighbourhood, nearby central Memphis was more of a black city than he'd expected, especially when he got down to Beale Street and beyond. He didn't realise it then, but its effect on him would be profound, in that it meant he would hear more of what was then called 'race' music on the radio. Gladys and Vernon still only wanted to hear hymns or country songs from Bill Monroe or Hank Williams, but as Elvis would say, he liked 'the real low down Mississippi singers' as well, people like Big Bill Broonzy and Big Boy Crudup. Had he never gone to live in Memphis and been exposed to so much blues and rhythm and blues in his formative years, his life and career would have been totally different. He couldn't have known it then, but Memphis would be the making of him.

Humes High School was about ten blocks from where he lived. He thought it looked like a prison when he first saw it. And not knowing where to go or how to fit in, and with a little lifetime stammer when he didn't quite know how to express himself, getting stuck on 'when', 'where' and 'why', and just about every word that began with a 'w', he was, he would say, 'bug-eyed nervous' at first. Having what some kids thought was a weird name didn't help either. 'Elvis' wasn't completely unknown as a Christian name in Tupelo, but there had probably never been an Elvis at Humes High before he got there – although after him there might have been one or two.

Some kids at school called him a teacher's pet, and made fun of the Mississippi way he talked, which was then very country, but he didn't know how else to behave or to speak. His favourite class was always English, and his teacher that year said he did well in recitation, although she criticised his grammar, which she thought 'atrocious'. But that was the grammar everyone had spoken in Tupelo. When he became famous and reporters sought out his former classmates and teachers, he would read about how he'd been a polite, shy boy. Perhaps he had been over-polite and too deferential towards people in any kind of authority, but, then, his parents were humble, too. That was the way you behaved when you were poor and didn't have much going for you.

He didn't take his guitar to school or sing at Humes at first because he didn't know what reaction he would get. Besides, his voice was breaking around then, and he couldn't tell what sound would come out when he opened his mouth to sing. That was a secret worry. He already knew that he wanted to be a singer, and it bothered him that his voice might not return when it had finished breaking.

Other than that, though, life was good for him around the Courts, which was what everyone called the subsidised apartment blocks. There were three or four other boys of about the same age living there, and they would hang out together, playing touch football or just wandering the streets for the fun of it. There were girls, too, and in the summer he would sometimes sit out on the grass in front of his apartment with one or another of them. There was a Betty and a Billie. Billie broke his heart for a day or two when she preferred a sailor. Now and again the kids would have parties in the basement and play spin-the-bottle when the lights went out. That was about as far as they got, but at fourteen, spin-the-bottle could be a lot of fun.

He'd known all about sex for years. Children who grow up in, or near, the country, where there are farms and animals, always know about these things, and in Tupelo he hadn't been the only one who was sleeping in the same room as his parents. Kids like him would hear things happening in the night, but then learn not to question too much. And sex was in a whole different order of things from spin-the-bottle.

Singing was more important to him, anyway, and, when he got

his voice back, he would sit on the stairs playing his guitar, singing to himself. A singer could get a great echo effect in a stairwell, which is what all the doo-wop groups he liked would be doing in New York and Philadelphia. Not that everybody wanted to hear him. There would be complaints – neighbours trying to get the baby to sleep, older people wanting some peace and quiet. And every time Daddy walked by he'd repeat, 'I never knew a guitar player who ever made a dollar', as if the record he was talking on had got stuck in a crack. But Gladys never stopped encouraging her boy.

Sunday was still a church day for the Presleys, as it seemed it was for most people in Memphis, with a church of some denomination or other on just about every corner. And they would go over to the First Assembly of God on McLemore Avenue. But what was getting more and more interesting to him were the gospel groups like the Blackwood Brothers Quartet and the Statesmen, who would sing at the revival meetings the family also attended. Singing with a small group was exciting to Elvis. It always would be.

With both his parents now working, there was more money coming in than there'd ever been in Tupelo, but it was still never enough, because it had to keep Grandma as well. So, when Daddy bought an old lawn mower, Elvis went around the streets knocking on doors offering to fix people's lawns. He didn't do badly, and he was proud when he could pay the grocery store bill. Vernon, who soon got a bad back picking up a five-gallon tin of paint, was pleased. 'Elvis, you always did have a generous heart,' he would say, as Elvis gave him whatever he'd earned. Gladys's reaction was always the same. 'That's nice. Just so long as you're doing your schoolwork, too.'

He was . . . as best he could. But he spent more time studying the records he heard on the radio than writing essays. And he really did study them, noting how a singer such as Billy Ward of the Dominoes might bend a note, what harmonies were used, and how a lyric could most effectively be sung.

Later he would sometimes feel as though he blinked and those early teen years passed by without him noticing. It was just school, hanging out, the radio, the movies, some church and his guitar. In a few years he would become closely associated with the guitar, but he would always happily admit that he was never anything more than a rhythm player – the instrument being mainly something to do with his hands while he was singing. Other guys, real guitarists, would always do the fancy picking on his records.

It was the same with the piano. The family never had a piano at home when he was young, but he'd learned a few gospel chords in church in Tupelo, and was allowed to fool around at the keys sometimes while he was at Humes High. There was obviously never any money for piano lessons so, as with the guitar, he was self-taught. He never learned to play any Rachmaninov or Chopin like some of the other kids at school, but he learned to hammer out by trial and error what he was hearing on the radio or at church.

For a long time the Presleys' only record player was a little wind-up RCA Victrola, and when he'd saved up enough money he'd go down to Charlie's record store on North Main St on a Saturday to play the juke box there and perhaps buy a record he liked. He could only afford them one at a time. They were 78s then, and at least two thirds of his collection were by black artists.

Later on he began buying 45s, and, after he married, Priscilla would wonder why he still had so many old 45s on the juke box at Graceland. She liked Peter, Paul and Mary, but, though he liked those people, too, his old records meant something more to him. He would return to them all his life; they carried him back. For most people, musical taste is frozen in their teens, and for Elvis teenage meant listening to local blues singer Rosco Gordon, the r and b group the Clovers and the doo-wop Orioles. For people a little younger, it would mean him singing 'Love Me Tender'.

As in every young life there are always extra-special days, and in his case it was getting his driving licence in Uncle Travis's ancient Buick when he was fifteen. Like all country boys he'd been driving for years – ever since he was sitting on Daddy's lap and steering the car when he was ten. But to be driving around Memphis, taking his mother out in Daddy's old Lincoln and showing her places – that was something special. Girls liked going driving, too.

Things began changing at school around that time. He'd never been a noisy or pushy kid, but from about sixteen onwards he began to discover himself. Or was it that others discovered him, as he re-invented himself the way he thought he ought to be? He'd seen other boys do that. One day they'd be meek and invisible, the next their hormones would start up, their skin would erupt into pimples and they'd be running wild. He got the pimples all right, a really bad case with open pores like moon craters. That was the downside of teenage. The upside was that he'd already begun working after class as an usher in the Loew's State movie theatre, which meant he could see the pictures for free and make some money at the same time. Gladys now had a job as a nursing assistant at St Joseph's Hospital, so it meant he finally had a little money to spend on himself. Most boys in class were wearing sweatshirts and jeans, but he would go down to the Tiger Shop or Ike's on North Main where the black musicians went, and buy himself brightly coloured clothes, maybe a pink shirt, a drape jacket and dress, pleated trousers. Snappy clothes would be a priority all his life.

In his mind he was already a famous singer – years before people began paying him to sing, before anyone had even *heard* him sing. And, as if to convince himself that he was a star before he was a star, he began dressing like one. Wearing bright stage clothes was his way of being noticed, when there was no earthly reason why anyone would want to notice him. It was the same with his hair. Gladys would tell him what good hair he had, so he grew it long, and, when he was old enough, grew sideburns, too, rubbing Royal Crown pomade into his quiff and whipping out his comb whenever he thought it might be messed up. No one else he knew had sideburns then, but he purposely chose to look like a young Confederate soldier who'd just stepped out of the Civil War.

It all came from the movies, usually Westerns. He would go at least twice a week and imagine himself as the star. Later he would joke that he'd simply wanted to look tough like a truck driver, but the truck drivers and he were all probably just trying to look like Tony Curtis. Was he vain? Of course, he was. Stars, and would-be stars, always are. Never able to pass a mirror without taking a quick look for reassurance, that was Elvis.

He was aware that the kids at high school thought he looked weird with his hair and fancy clothes, but it didn't bother him. On one occasion, some boys thought up a plan to knock some of the freakiness out of him, a 'let's git that squirrel' sort of thing, he would recall. Playfully ganging up on him in the locker room, they wanted to cut his hair and probably would have done, if a boy called Red West hadn't got in their way. Not many guys got past Red West, who, even as a teenager, was rock hard. After that day he and Elvis would stay friends, almost for life.

They'd met on the football team. Football was something Elvis had liked, but which he'd had to give up when he'd begun working at the movie theatre after school. Gladys had been glad about that. She'd been at the hospital when a boy had been brought in who had been badly injured in a football game. That had frightened her. Nothing had to hurt Elvis. The Saturday games in Guthrie Park with scratch teams that Elvis and Red would occasionally play in later were more of the friendly kind.

School notwithstanding, the singing never stopped. Elvis just loved to sing, but it was always in private or at parties, where, too timid to begin, he would make the other kids put the lights out before he'd start. After that there would be no stopping him. All kinds of music appealed to him, not just the r and b stars. And when he was seventeen he went across to Overton Park to listen to a concert given by a big orchestra, fascinated that the musicians could play for hours, and noticing that most of the time 'the conductor wouldn't even look at his sheet'. He already had records by the New York Metropolitan Opera and Mario Lanza, who was a big star then after being in the movies *The Great Caruso* and *The Student Prince*. It bothered him that he couldn't read music, and he worried that it might hold him back.

He still wasn't particularly popular at school, or, as he would describe it, 'dating anyone' there, but every April there was an annual minstrel show when any pupil who could play anything, or sing or dance or do acrobatics, could get up and perform in the auditorium. For some reason his home class teacher that year, Mildred Scrivener, entered him as a guitarist. He was listed sixteenth out of twenty-two on the programme, with his surname spelled 'Prestly', and coming on just before a boy who tap-danced. When he went on stage he could hear rumbling and whispering because most people didn't know he even sang, but he chose to do a Teresa Brewer hit 'Till I Waltz Again With You'. And they liked him.

'They liked me. They really liked me,' he said to Miss Scrivener as he came off. He was astonished. 'It was amazing how popular I became after that,' he would laugh later.

By now he was eighteen and almost at the end of his school career.

If it had been up to him he would probably have left school two years earlier. Vernon would have been happy about that, but Gladys wouldn't hear of it. So he'd carried on, working nights whenever he could, until on the evening of 3 June 1953, both his parents were in the audience at the Ellis Auditorium when he received his high school diploma, the first member of his family ever to graduate from high school. He was very proud that night, but pleased as much for his mother as for himself. It was due to her.

'Truthfully, I don't really know why they gave me a diploma,' he would later admit. 'I would just sit there in class and be looking out the window. I had no idea what the teacher was saying. I'd be thinking about Tony Curtis and Marlon Brando and being a star and singing. I was just dreaming all the time.'

Some classmates at Humes High went on to college, but only a couple of the boys he knew did. College wasn't an option for people from his background.

'I'd like to have gone to college, but we didn't have enough money,' he would say. College was for the better-off kids. Nobody at his school ever suggested anything like that to him. The teachers would have known it was impossible. They just wanted to educate him to the extent that he could find a way of making a living for himself. As a family, the Presleys were starting from nothing, and what Elvis earned had to help out at home. Since he'd been fifteen he'd been working every summer, taking any job he could get, and he'd been proud to be able to do that.

For a short while, he toyed with the idea of applying to join the Memphis police; the uniform and camaraderie, coupled with the notion of driving around in a police car like someone out of television's *Dragnet*, certainly appealed. But, school finished, he just wanted any job he could get. So, the week after graduating, he went down to the Tennessee Employment office, looking for full-time work.

4

'I don't sound like nobody.'

He'd read about the Memphis Recording Service in a newspaper as being a place where you could walk in off the street and make a recording on a disc to take home. He'd heard about Sam Phillips, too. He was the man who owned the company, and, by 1953, was getting to be a character around town. He'd been a radio engineer but had left his job to drive all over Memphis making private recordings of weddings, funerals and rotary club speeches. 'We record anything – any time – anywhere', Phillips promised in advertisements for his company in the city's newspapers. This was before anyone had home tape recorders, so he was on to something.

But Elvis also knew that the Memphis Recording Service was just a side business, something to help pay the rent while Phillips was starting his own record company. The new label was called Sun, for which Phillips would record some of the blues musicians off Beale Street, guys like B.B. King, Ike Turner and Howlin' Wolf, the fellows nobody else wanted to put on record. Then he would mainly lease the tapes to Chess, a much bigger label, in Chicago. Phillips was a white man from Alabama who loved the music that came out of Beale Street. So, for Elvis, he was definitely the man to get to know. But how? By knocking on Phillips' door, he decided.

The Memphis Recording Service was a single-storey shopfront building at 706 Union Avenue on the corner of Marshall Avenue, and he'd driven past it many times, hoping to see Phillips, or perhaps even Rufus Thomas, coming out. Rufus was a black Memphis disc jockey who'd made a record for Sun called 'Bear Cat', an answer song to Big Mama Thornton's 'Hound Dog', which Elvis had bought. But the boy had never spotted Rufus or Phillips.

So, a week or so after graduating, he found himself, one Saturday afternoon, walking up and down outside the studio, trying to see in the window a couple of times, then going away again when his courage failed him. Finally he realised that a blonde lady was watching him from behind the venetian blinds of her front office at Sun. He was too embarrassed to walk away again.

She smiled when he finally entered, as though she was rewarding him for being brave enough to open the door. She was in her mid-thirties and was wearing glasses. Sitting behind a big typewriter in the tiny front office, she looked like one of those kindly-but-firm teachers he'd known at Humes High.

There were other young men already waiting in the tiny office, some with guitars, presumably hoping to be discovered, too, so he had to wait his turn. When the secretary at last got around to him, he told her he wanted to make a recording for his mother's birthday, which was a little lie because Gladys's birthday was in April not July. But after taking down his name and the phone number of the family in the apartment next door, because the Presleys didn't have a phone, the secretary asked for $3.98 plus tax and took him through into the studio at the back. Later he would realise how small the place was, no more than the size of a very small bar. But it was his first time in any kind of recording studio, so it looked pretty impressive to him.

Standing him at a microphone, the secretary chatted for a few minutes, trying to put him at ease. 'So, what kind of singer are you?' she asked.

He didn't know how to answer that, so he just said: 'I sing all kinds.'

'But who do you sound like?' she wanted to know.

'I don't sound like nobody.'

'Do you sing hillbilly?'

'Yes.'

'So, who do you sound like in hillbilly?'

'I don't sound like nobody.'

By this time she had finished setting up. 'Okay. Start when you're ready,' she said, and, going to the end of the room, she went into the control booth and pressed whatever buttons she needed to.

By now he was so nervous his mouth was dry, but he managed to get through the love ballad 'My Happiness'. It had been a hit a few years earlier for Ella Fitzgerald and a couple of other singers. In those days several big stars would often record the same new song and fight it out for sales. Then, because he got both sides of a ten-inch acetate disc for his money, he sang 'That's When Your Heartaches Begin', which the Ink Spots, a black, four-part harmony group with guitars and bass, sang. Four years later he would record the song professionally for RCA and put it on the flip side of 'All Shook Up'. The voice of the Ink Spots' lead tenor, Bill Kenny, was a great influence on him, and for years he'd gone around singing Kenny's high part and doing the recitation of the bass singer as well.

All the time that he was at the microphone he could sense the secretary watching him. What he didn't know was that halfway through his first song she'd secretly switched the tape recorder on so that she could play it to Sam Phillips who was out recording a wedding. He learned later that the lady's name was Marion Keisker and that she'd helped Phillips set up the studio after they'd met while working together at a Memphis radio station, and that she'd fallen in love with him – a married man. A little after that, Elvis also learned that in order for her to remember what he looked like, she'd written 'Timothy Sideburns' alongside his name and the songs he'd sung. She didn't tell him that day, but she'd liked what she'd heard. She thought he had a pleading, plaintive kind of sound. 'Good ballad singer – hold' she'd written on a card for her filing system.

Elvis had naturally been hoping to meet the great Sam Phillips, but, even though he hadn't, he was excited to take his acetate home and play it over and over until, he would say, 'it must have been nearly worn through'. He kept it all his life. Years later when he heard it again, he was amused to hear how high his voice had been when he was eighteen.

Gladys was, naturally, very proud, and had him play the record to the few neighbours she knew. He thought that maybe Daddy was pleased, too, though Vernon never said much. It seemed to Elvis that just being on a record, even one he'd paid for himself, seemed evidence of some kind of intent. But what the lady at the recording studio had asked him kept playing on his mind. What kind of singer was he? He really didn't know. He liked Dean Martin and Bing Crosby and those crooner singers. But he also liked Hank Williams. His mother had cried all day when Williams' death had been announced on the radio. The problem was, pop and country music didn't seem to fit together. Not on the radio, anyway. There were separate stations for the two genres of music. And neither of them fitted in with the rhythm and blues bands he was listening to every night, or the black doo-wop groups he liked to copy. And then there was his first love, gospel music.

Around about that time he began dating a girl called Dixie Locke. She was fifteen and at a different school from the one he'd been to. He'd seen her at church with her friends, and had overheard the girls talking in loud voices about going skating at the Rainbow Rollerdrome the following Friday. Naturally he'd swallowed the bait and made sure he was there. Somehow he and Dixie got talking, as they'd both hoped they would, and he took her home in the old fifty-dollar car Vernon had bought him for his eighteenth birthday. A date was planned for the next week, but when he called at her house to pick her up, her parents refused to let her go out with him. With his loud clothes and long hair and sideburns, he didn't look like the kind of boy any respectable parents would trust with their daughter. So instead of going out he sat in with the family and played Monopoly.

Somehow, however, he must have impressed, because after a week or so Dixie's parents relented and the two soon began going to the movies together and sitting out by the canteen in Riverside Park listening to the juke box. They did all the stuff that teenagers do, though, it has to be said, it was a more innocent time.

Dixie was small with long, dark hair that came down to her shoulders, wore little white bobby socks and was forever laughing. She was loyal, too, and didn't mind if Elvis looked like some kind of freak. She'd go with him to listen to the gospel singing, and sometimes they'd go to a black Baptist church on East Trigg Avenue in South Memphis. The pastor there, Reverend Herbert Brewster, was famous for his sermons and for having written Mahalia 'Queen of Gospel' Jackson's first hit 'Move On Up a Little Higher'. Elvis already had some of Mahalia's records.

Because, in segregated Memphis, white people couldn't go inside a coloured church to a service any more than the two races could sit side by side in a diner, he and Dixie would stand as guests in a little porch behind a kind of gate at the side of the church and watch and listen. In Elvis's opinion it 'was always something wonderful'. If he could get to sing like some of the soloists that Reverend Brewster had, or like Clyde McPhatter, who sang with the Drifters doo-wop group, 'I wouldn't want for nothing else,' he would tell Dixie. She would laugh kindly and correct his grammar.

In fact, for a time, a career singing in a gospel group seemed possible, and he was thrilled when he was given a chance to audition for a young quartet who sang at the church he attended. They were called the Songfellows and they were good. Unfortunately they didn't think he was. They turned him down, because, they said, he couldn't sing harmony. He thought he could, but obviously his voice didn't fit. He was upset, and never forgot. When he began making records a little later, he made albums of all his favourite hymns with a male quartet singing with him.

His first job after school had been on an assembly line, but he didn't like it, and left after a few weeks to become an apprentice electrician at Crown Electric. That suited Gladys. She had always wanted him to be an electrician. 'I was serious about the job,' Elvis would remember. 'It paid three dollars an hour.'

Mainly though, when he wasn't learning how to do couplings and connections, he was driving a little black Chevrolet pick-up truck and delivering equipment around Memphis. This was handy, because it gave him the chance to call in at Sun a couple or more times and ask Marion Keisker if she knew of anyone who wanted a singer. She never did, but as Marion was always welcoming, he recorded another couple of tracks on an acetate for himself a few months later and reminded her of where she could still reach him by phone.

His drive never sagged. Summing up ambition when he was older he described it as 'a dream with a V8 engine', and it was something he never lacked, enquiring about work as a singer at several places around Memphis in that year after graduating. At a little nightclub called the Hi Hat he was told that he was never going to make it. Again he was upset.

Gladys would shake her head at the foolishness of those who turned him down, but Daddy would shrug as if to say 'well, what did you expect?' Vernon had a good voice, too, and Elvis would sometimes wonder if there was a part of Daddy that really didn't want his son to succeed, because he never had. But then Vernon had never tried either. He would tell Elvis that he should concentrate on being an electrician, because that was a good job.

Elvis wasn't so sure. 'Electricians have to keep their minds on what they're doing,' he would say. 'If they are the least bit absent minded, they're liable to blow up someone's house. I was always dreaming, my mind somewhere else.'

For over twenty years he would joke self-disparagingly about how he'd been 'driving a truck' and had somehow fallen almost accidentally into 'this crazy music business'. But that was an over-modest version of what happened. He was lucky, yes, there was no denying that. He came along at just the right time. But he was never planning to stay driving a little truck. That was just something he was doing until he found his way. Getting into music had been no accident. He never stopped working at it.

Then one stifling hot Saturday morning at the end of June 1954, almost a year to the day since he'd finished high school and first called in at Sun, Marion Keisker phoned him at work wanting to know if he could be over at Union Avenue by three. She would joke afterwards that he was there almost before she put the phone down.

He'd probably never said more than ten words to Sam Phillips before that Saturday afternoon, because when he'd called in at the Sun office, or accidentally-on-purpose hung around Taylor's café next door where all the Sun people would go between sessions, Phillips had always been busy with something else. That was Sam Phillips: always busy. He had the energy and drive of three men, and, although only thirty-two, he seemed to know so much, and be able to do so much more.

Over the years Elvis would read how when they first met, Sam thought he wore the 'same intimidated expression that some of the blues singers had when they first went into Sun, the look that said people like them had no business being in such a place'. Perhaps Elvis's demeanour did suggest that. Those black singers were just poor boys trying to make their mark, and so was he. But there was something else. Sam, whom he always called Mr Phillips, was a natural leader whose stature and gift with words demanded respect. In fact, he was probably the most impressive person any Beale Street blues singers or Elvis had ever met. And, though it was small, he owned his own record company. No wonder they all felt out of place.

Phillips liked to tell how he'd been brought up on a farm in Alabama and had learned about the blues from a blind old man his father had employed there called Uncle Silas Payne. Uncle Silas had been born into slavery, and Phillips now saw one of his missions in life as being able to 'give the poor Negro a voice in a place where he didn't have one'. But he also used to tell Marion that if he could ever find a white boy who could sing with the passion of a Negro 'he'd make a million dollars'. That was why she pestered him to listen to Elvis sing, and why she called Elvis in. Without her belief in him and her support none of what happened would have been possible, Elvis would always say; at least, not in the way it turned out.

Although Sun had already released a few records, the new label had only had one small local hit the previous year with a group called the Prisonaires, who'd come together in the Tennessee State Penitentiary – three murderers among them. The lead singer, Johnny Bragg, who'd been convicted of six rapes by the time he was seventeen, had a beautiful voice, and, after Sam enquired about the group, they'd all been driven to Memphis under armed guard to make their record – 'Just Walkin' in the Rain'. Two years later the song would be a big international hit for Johnnie Ray.

On that Saturday in 1954 when Elvis was called into Sun, Phillips had just got back from Nashville with another new song called 'Without You', which had been written by another prison inmate. He needed a singer for it, so Marion had suggested Elvis. And Phillips had decided it was worth a try. His technique in the studio was to keep attempting different things to see what worked. So Elvis spent the afternoon singing the new song in every way he possibly could. Phillips, immensely patient, just sat there listening and encouraging before always asking for it one more time.

Eventually Phillips said: 'Don't worry. It isn't you, Elvis. Maybe the song isn't what I thought it was. What else do you know? Just relax. Sing me something that means something to you.'

So Elvis went through everything he could think of – pop songs, spirituals, old favourites, just a few words of anything he remembered. He must have sat there for three hours, he reckoned, and all the time there was Sam Phillips watching him, concentrating.

Finally Phillips got up and thanked him. 'You did fine, Elvis, just fine. Let me think about it.'

And that was it. Elvis thought Phillips was probably just letting him down in as kindly a way as he could and went home thoroughly dejected. That had been his big break. Had he failed it? He thought he had.

As it happened, his mind was quickly taken off his apparent rejection when two members of the white Blackwood Brothers gospel quartet were killed in a plane crash in Alabama that week. They may have been gospel singers but the Blackwoods were real stars to the Presleys, and it was the first time Elvis had known a star who had died. Why could this happen, he kept asking himself as he drove Dixie and his parents to the funeral. There had to be a reason. He'd been told in church that God always had a reason. Then he sat and listened inside the packed auditorium as other choirs sang the hymns the Blackwoods had always performed.

Dixie went on vacation with her parents to Florida the next morning, and Elvis was left behind, upset over the plane crash, and afraid that Dixie would meet someone else while she was away – imagining what might happen if she did. He had always been, and would always be, the jealous, suspicious kind. He just couldn't help it.

Without her, and with nothing better to do, he went to the movies and was sitting in the dark when the usher's torch picked him out. There was Gladys in the aisle beckoning to him.

A guitarist called Scotty Moore had called the Presleys' neighbour, she told him, saying he'd been asked by Mr Sam Phillips to arrange an audition for Elvis. He had to call Scotty back, quick.

5

'What the hell y'all doin' in there?'

Sam Phillips

For most people in Memphis that Sunday, 4 July 1954, was a humid holiday weekend. Elvis didn't go to church that morning. The Presleys hadn't been attending as regularly as they did when they'd been in Tupelo. When Elvis went now it was usually in the evening, and by the time this Sunday evening came, he was busy changing his entire future. He was nineteen.

He'd never heard of Scotty Moore until he'd called back the previous night, when it had been suggested that he went over to the guitarist's home in north Memphis on the Sunday afternoon. When he got there, he couldn't but be impressed with how much Scotty had already managed to pack into his life. At twenty-three, Scotty had already served in the US Navy on an aircraft carrier in the Korean War, was now married for the second time, had two children by his previous wife, had his own little honky-tonk band called the Starlite Wranglers and lived in an apartment in what to Elvis was an attractive part of town. And, oh yes, like most guitarists in Memphis, he had a daytime job – fixing the hats at a dry cleaners. He was a busy man with a busy life, yet he was the quietest, neatest, most unassuming guy you could meet.

After he and Elvis had chatted for a while, a friend of Scotty's from down the street joined them. He was Bill Black, a double bass player. Elvis knew Bill's younger brother who'd lived in Lauderdale Courts, so he'd heard of him. But Bill didn't play that day. Instead he and Bobbie, Scotty's new wife, just sat in silence, looking at the pink pants and the white lacy shirt Elvis had put on hoping to impress, as Scotty went through a few songs with him.

'How did it go?' Gladys asked, when Elvis got home.

He didn't know. They hadn't thrown him out, but it could just as easily have been another dead end. So he was relieved the following day when he got a call at work from Marion Keisker asking him to go over to the studio to work with Scotty and Bill after he got off that night. It seemed the two musicians had agreed with Sam that the boy could sing, although, Elvis discovered later, they hadn't thought he was 'anything special'. And neither of them, nor Scotty's wife, had cared for what they'd called his 'wild clothes'. Not many people did.

At that point in his life Elvis had never sung or played with any other musicians, so Sam Phillips was curious to find out if indeed he could, and what he would sound like on tape. Phillips would later tell him that he could hear something in Elvis's voice, but that he didn't know what it was. Elvis didn't know either.

Air conditioning wasn't possible during recording sessions in the little Sun studio, so it was sticky when they all went to work that night – all three, as Scotty would admit, 'below average musicians'. With no drums, just Bill and his big, old, stand-up bass, trimmed with white tape, on one side, and Scotty, with his electric guitar, on the other, Elvis played rhythm guitar with the few chords he then knew. Phillips, meanwhile, was behind the glass in the control room, acting as both producer and engineer. Using every trick he'd learned when he'd worked in radio, he was willing to do and try anything to get the sounds he was looking for. And he never cared how long it took. Later, when Elvis moved to RCA, he discovered that union rules stipulated that a recording session couldn't last more than three hours. But Phillips wasn't paying any of them by the hour – or indeed in any other way yet. He didn't care about union rules, or any other kind of rules, just as he didn't care about mistakes or even a wrong note, so long as what he called the 'feel' was good. 'That's fine, Elvis,' he kept encouraging through his microphone as Elvis made his way through 'I Love You Because' and 'Harbour Lights' and several other pop ballads that Elvis assumed he wanted to hear.

Fairly soon, though, it became obvious that whatever Elvis was doing wasn't 'fine' enough. It wasn't different. And although Phillips didn't admit it, it was plain that he was disappointed, perhaps already deciding he'd made a mistake in calling everyone in. So, when, late in the evening, they all took a break, Elvis was half expecting Phillips to call it a night, because they all had to be up early for work the next day. The troubling thing was he just didn't know what Phillips wanted. Here he was, standing on the spot where all those blues records he liked had been made, and he kept looking around the little studio and imagining B.B. King and Howlin' Wolf right there with him. Had they got it wrong, too? He'd heard their records. He knew they hadn't.

His mind must have been wandering around the blues, because, as he waited while Scotty and Bill got a drink to cool down, and Sam was busy logging some tracks that they'd recorded, an old blues song began playing in the back of his head. He knew dozens of blues numbers, but this one had been on the radio a lot when he'd first arrived in Memphis. It was by a guy called Arthur Crudup – although everyone knew him as Big Boy Crudup. As if to break the tension, because he was always pretty wound up and never could abide a nervous silence, he began to sing to himself, kidding around: 'Well, that's all right, Mama, that's all right for you . . .'

Straight away, Bill got up, grabbed his bass, which was nearly as tall as he was, and began to slap away at it, as if he was beating on a drum. Picking up his guitar, Scotty joined in. Suddenly the three of them were jamming for the fun of it. It was the first jam session Elvis had ever been in, when Sam's voice came through from the control room, breaking it up. 'Hey, what the hell y'all doin' in there?'

'I don't know. Just foolin' around,' Scotty told him.

'Well, it don't sound too bad,' Sam came back. 'Find out what you're doing, find a place to start, and let me get it balanced right.'

And that's what they did. As they rehearsed it, this way and then that, it was agreed that Elvis would play the opening rhythm guitar chords and start singing before Bill and then Scotty came in. It was a simple, uninhibited arrangement. All the time, Sam, who was astonished that Elvis even knew the blues song, would be offering advice.

'Don't complicate it, Scotty. Keep it honest. If we'd wanted Chet Atkins, we'd have brought him over from Nashville. I want it fresh. And, Elvis, sing it plaintive and needy. That's what you're good at.'

They did six takes; three or four broke down when they didn't know their parts, then Sam chose one or two to keep and that was it.

'So, what the hell we got here?' Scotty asked, as they were about to leave.

Bill was amused. He usually was. He wasn't the best bass player in the world – Sam would joke that he thought he might be the worst – but he always had a sunny disposition. 'Damn!' he joked. 'If we ever get that played they'll run us out of town.'

They all knew what he meant. What they'd recorded wasn't black, it wasn't white and it wasn't pop. It wasn't blues and it certainly wasn't hillbilly. Unconsciously, they had fused a blues song with a country sound. The people who demanded that white singers did pure country weren't going to like it. That was for sure. As for the radio stations with disc jockeys who only played race records . . . ? They had no way of telling how they would react. It was just so different from anything any of them had ever sung or played or heard.

The job was only half done, of course. They needed a flip side for the record, so the next night they all went back to the studio again after work. They tried 'Blue Moon' to start with. Elvis had liked the Billy Eckstine version, but the verse seemed cluttered with too many words, so he just yodelled through the melody like an instrumental break. Marion said she thought it was dreamy. But Sam again wasn't happy, and after trying several other ideas for three or four hours, they broke up for the night. They didn't know what to do.

By this time, however, Sam had already played 'That's All Right' to the Memphis disc jockey Dewey Phillips. Despite their surnames being the same, Dewey was no relation to Sam, but they were good friends, especially when it came to music. If Dewey liked the record and played it on his nightly programme, *Red, Hot and Blue* on WHBQ, Sam would get some idea from the reaction as to whether it was worth releasing.

Elvis always listened to Dewey's show because he was the only disc jockey in Memphis to play both black rhythm and blues and white hillbilly. So, when he got a call from Marion telling him that Dewey was planning to play 'That's All Right' that night, he didn't know whether to be terror-struck or overwhelmed by embarrassment. Whatever it was, he turned the radio to the right spot on the dial and told Vernon and Gladys to keep listening from nine until midnight, and then went off to the movies by himself again. Without Dixie he spent a lot of time at the movies that week. In truth, he was afraid people would laugh when they heard the record. So there he was again, hiding in the dark, in the Suzore movie theatre, just a few blocks from where he lived, when, once again, Gladys came looking for him.

'Did Dewey Phillips play my record?' he asked, as she hurried him out.

'Play it? He's been playing it for over an hour and people are ringing in. They just called from the station to say Dewey wants you down there so he can talk to you on the radio.'

Talk on the radio! He'd hardly ever even spoken in class.

Whether it was drinking or talking, or whatever else he got up to, motormouth Dewey Phillips was known in Memphis for never doing things by half. Some people say he played 'That's All Right' eleven times on his show that night, and mostly back to back. Elvis didn't know. He was scared to death.

'I don't know nothing about being interviewed,' he said, as Dewey sat him down in the little WHBQ studio at the Hotel Chisca.

'Don't worry about that, Elvis. Just don't say nothing dirty, all right. Now, for information, first off . . . tell me a little bit about yourself. Where are you from, Elvis?'

Elvis told him about Tupelo.

'And where did you go to school?'

So he told him about Humes High and the church he went to, and that sort of thing. And after a little while Dewey just said, 'Thank you, Elvis.'

'Aren't you going to interview me?' Elvis asked, disappointed now.

Dewey said: 'I already did. You were going out live all the time you were talking. If I'd told you that you were on the air, you'd have been tongue-tied with nerves. The reason I asked about the school you'd been to, was because a lot of callers who like your record think you must be coloured, singing the way you do.'

Elvis understood. Dewey might not care about colour if he liked a record, but there were those who did. To get a crossover record that everyone liked, white as well as black, was what everyone wanted, Dewey as much as Sam Phillips. Elvis was learning about the colour of music.

The following day, as Marion Keisker found herself taking orders from Memphis record stores for copies of 'That's All Right', the task of recording a flip side became urgent. So that night they all began again, everyone throwing in songs and ideas, with Sam never being satisfied. It was only when Bill began crooning 'Blue Moon of Kentucky', which is about as country a song as any of them knew, that Sam began to nod.

'That's an idea. Let's try that.'

Firstly they tried it slow, the way Bill Monroe, who wrote the song, sang it. 'No, no. That isn't different enough. You could be any hillbilly singing like that, Elvis,' Sam called out.

So, they tried again, quickening the pace, and putting a new front on the song so that it started out like an attack. That was better. Sam was smiling again. 'Hell, now that's different. That's a pop song now, nearly 'bout, little boy,' he said to Elvis.

'Just don't nobody tell Bill Monroe what we've done with his song,' Bill laughed.

It turned out Bill Monroe hated what they'd done. 'That Elvis ruined my damn song,' he complained all over Nashville when he heard the record. In Memphis the little group didn't care. They all liked it. 'That's All Right' was a blues song with a country touch that came from Scotty's guitar licks, and the other side, 'Blue Moon of Kentucky', was a hepped-up country classic.

Before they left the studio that night, Sam cut Elvis an acetate of both tracks. It was very late when Elvis got home, but, as usual, Gladys was waiting up for him. She never went to bed until he got back. He just had to play his record again for her. With that echo Sam had put on to his voice Elvis sounded clearer, sharper, somehow more free than he'd ever heard himself.

Sitting there with his mother in a kind of hushed wonder, it must have seemed to him that at last he was becoming the Elvis Presley he'd been imagining he was for the last three years.

6

'What happened, what happened?'
'I don't know, Elvis, but whatever it was you were doing, get back out there and do it again.'

His world had changed. As soon as the record was pressed it was played on every station in Memphis. The rhythm and blues disc jockeys liked 'That's All Right' while the country ones went for the bluegrass 'Blue Moon of Kentucky'. The band had wondered where they might fit musically, but they found they were hitting both markets. For Elvis the biggest thrill was walking down North Main and hanging around Charlie's until he saw someone buy a copy, or play both sides on the juke box there. And with six thousand sales within a few days of release, the record was soon up to number three in the local chart.

He knew that didn't mean a thing to the world beyond, because no one outside Memphis had even heard it yet, but he would later discover that it was just as sweet as having a worldwide hit like 'Don't Be Cruel'. International fame would always be almost impossible for him to comprehend, because he wouldn't know the people buying his records. You couldn't taste that kind of celebrity the way you could when you got sudden fame in your home town, and where everyone was glad for you – except those folks who couldn't abide you or who were just plain jealous. And you always got some of those.

Dixie first heard 'Blue Moon of Kentucky' on the radio in her father's car as they drew near to Memphis on their way home from vacation in Florida. Elvis had sent her a telegram telling her what had happened, asking her to hurry home. She hadn't really understood what he meant. But . . . when her boyfriend came on the car radio!

She knew then. So much had happened in the two weeks that she'd been away and she'd missed it all. She would tell him over and over that she'd never known anyone who had made a record, that it didn't seem possible. Then, almost immediately, she began to realise that any plans they'd made might not now work out. She was only fifteen, but they'd already talked about marriage – well, to Elvis's recollection, *she* had more than him. Anyway, all those thoughts were now put on hold.

Sam Phillips' office at Sun was small, so when Sam wanted to discuss things with more than one person they would all meet in Taylor's café next door. And it was in there one day that Sam showed Elvis, Scotty and Bill musicians' union forms and insisted that they all quickly join, while also suggesting that the three of them should legally become a band. Scotty, he thought, should be the manager. The deal was that Scotty would get 10 per cent of whatever he got in bookings for them, while Scotty and Bill as musicians would get 25 per cent each of whatever was left, giving Elvis 50 per cent. Because Elvis was only nineteen, Vernon had to countersign the contract on his son's behalf.

Scotty and Bill were both working musicians while Elvis hadn't even sung in public yet, so he would have taken just about anything he'd been offered. He knew the record wouldn't have been made the way it was without the other two, with Scotty's guitar playing a kind of duet with his singing. But whether Elvis was experienced or not, Scotty reckoned the front man should be given more, so that was what Elvis got. Throughout his career Elvis never took much notice of contracts and payments. It was complicated and he didn't have the time or the interest. But, years later, he did know that although he'd earned a mountain of money, he'd also been ripped off many times for millions of dollars. He didn't particularly care. Back then, however, Scotty didn't steal from him. Not one penny.

Not that any of them were earning a penny yet. And although Elvis had made a record that was on the radio, he still had to go to work, driving all over town in his pick-up truck, and attending rehearsals with Scotty and Bill in a room over the dry cleaners where Scotty worked. It wasn't glamorous, but it was exciting. One lunchtime Marion took him to meet his first journalist, a reporter on the

Memphis Press-Scimitar. Because Elvis couldn't think what to say, she answered all the questions for him – although it didn't look that way when the newspaper came out.

A newspaper photographer took his picture that day for the first time, too. Elvis was as thin as a rail, wearing a Western-style jacket and a bow tie, and with his pimples in full rage. When he saw the picture in the newspaper he thought he looked pitiful.

'I had terminal acne when we started out,' he would say.

Dixie and Gladys told him not to worry, that he was good-looking, and he wanted to believe them. When you have a bad case of teenage acne you need all the encouragement you can get. He would, he determined, make sure he looked better next time.

From what he could see from the movies and the magazines, stars didn't have pimples – although he was sure some must, and it looked to him as though some of the actors wore eye make-up on screen, too. So he began sneaking some of Gladys's eye shadow on to his eyelids. Other boys would have thought it weird for a Memphis guy to wear eye shadow, but Elvis had been seeing things differently for years.

Somehow, and he couldn't imagine how, a couple of weeks later, Sam managed to get Scotty, Bill and him on to the bill at a concert at the Memphis Overton Park Shell amphitheatre. It would be their public debut, and Slim Whitman, who had just had a million-selling hit with 'Indian Love Call', was topping the line-up. As beginners, they shouldn't really have been there at all in such starry company. And Elvis was shaking to be facing hundreds of people for the first time, his nerves not helped when they got his name wrong again, this time the advertisements calling him *Ellis* Presley.

As the three walked out on stage for the afternoon show he could see his parents sitting with Dixie. For a moment the trio froze. The place looked so big and wide. Then Bill began thumping a rhythm on his bass and Elvis joined in on his guitar and they went into 'That's All Right'.

At first he was concentrating so hard he didn't notice, but, as the song went on, he became aware that there was a lot of shouting and yelling going on from some of the girls in the audience, which just got louder and louder when he went on to sing 'Blue Moon of Kentucky'.

He was confused. It was a wild sound. Were they laughing at him?

'What happened, what happened?' he asked Sam as they came off.

Sam was smiling. 'I don't know, Elvis, but whatever it was you were doing, get back out there and do it again.'

So they went back and sang the songs again – the only songs they all knew. And this time the girls went wilder.

After the show Scotty explained what he thought had happened. Most singers in those days stood flat-footed and still by the stand-up microphone and sang. But Elvis and the boys didn't have a drummer, so Elvis had been using his body to keep the rhythm, leaning forward on to the balls of his feet, and shaking his leg to keep time with the music. And because he was wearing some very loose-fitting, pleated trousers, his continual moving around, which he'd done when they'd been recording, too, looked, 'well . . . kind of provocative'. Bill put it another way. To him it looked as though 'something was going on inside his pants'. That was what got the girls excited.

Elvis had seen preachers and singers at revival meetings moving around like that, but later he swore that the first time he did it on stage and caused a reaction was unintentional. After that, yes, he worked at it. He learned quickly. He appeared with Slim Whitman a number of times after that day, and the star yodeller never stopped reminding him that Elvis had stolen the show off him that day in Memphis. Whitman wasn't just being kind. Elvis might have been crippled with stage fright, but something happened to an audience when he sang, and he would very quickly grow to expect it and love it.

All through those summer evenings of 1954 he was either seeing Dixie or trying out different songs at Scotty's place. Sam arranged a regular spot several times a week at a club called the Eagle's Nest, and then there was a date at the opening of Katz drugstore when they played on the back of a flat-bed truck – the way they would perform later in the movie *Loving You*. Because they were in a public parking lot, it wasn't a segregated performance, so it was the first time he'd seen black kids in the audience getting excited, too. He was paid $32.50 for the short appearance, which was nearly as much as he earned working all week for Crown Electric. Johnny Cash was in the crowd that day, and would say later that seeing Elvis on stage had pushed him to start his own career.

Other bookings were now coming along – clubs, school gymnasiums and even a free show in a hospital ward for paralysed people. It was all small, local stuff, but at the time it was one long thrill as sales of the record spread to Arkansas, Mississippi and Texas. And when Elvis saw his record in the Mid-South country chart in *Billboard* magazine he was giddy with excitement. 'Blue Moon of Kentucky' was the bigger hit outside Memphis, but for Elvis 'That's All Right' was his start, and he would sing it for the rest of his life when he appeared on stage.

If he could have had one time in his life over again, it would probably have been that summer of 1954. The worldwide hit records, the TV shows, the movies, the tours, the gold records, the money, the fame . . . yes, he enjoyed them all. But to be nineteen, to have a girl you love who loves you, for your parents to be proud and to have a hit record in your home town . . . could there have been anything better?

With a little more money now coming in from stage shows, he even bought himself a new guitar. Scotty and Sam had never been impressed with the cheap one he had, so he went into a place just up the street from Sun Records and got a Martin D-18. Scotty helped him choose it. It cost $175 and was the most expensive thing he'd ever owned, so he had the shop engrave his name on it. The shopkeeper who sold it gave him eight dollars for his old one and said he was going to throw it in the trash. He should have kept it.

For Elvis, every day something new was happening. He had often gazed in the window at Lansky Brothers on Beale Street, admiring the bright colours and styles that the black singers would buy, but he'd never had the nerve or the money to go in. Now he did, though there was precious little cash left after buying the guitar. It didn't matter. He was beginning to feel entitled just to be in there, and to be mixing with the famous Memphis people who also went there.

Rufus Thomas was a regular jokey character around Sun for years before he recorded 'Walking the Dog', and, as a big friend of Sam's, he was forever teasing Sam in front of Elvis about how he should get the boy to record his song 'Tiger Man' – something Elvis would finally do twenty years later. Elvis couldn't help but be flattered. Then one day Sam introduced him to B.B. King. What a summer!

By the beginning of September a follow-up record was needed. So one Saturday they all went back into the studio. Again they tried several songs, but in the end they settled for an old r and b favourite, Roy Brown's 'Good Rockin' Tonight', backed with a Patti Page hit, 'I Don't Care If the Sun Don't Shine', which Elvis had seen Dean Martin sing on TV. They still didn't have a drummer, so Sam asked one of Scotty's other band, the Starlite Wranglers, to come in and pat on a guitar case as though it was a bongo drum. Sam was ever inventive. Marion was always around, too, looking after Elvis, helping out in any way she could. And because 'I Don't Care If the Sun Don't Shine' only had one verse, she quickly wrote another for him to sing. When the publishers in New York discovered what she'd done they didn't object, but wouldn't let her name go on the record as a co-writer or allow her to share in any songwriting royalties. At the time she just laughed. She was just pleased to hear her words on the radio, but a little royalty cheque creeping into her bank account twice a year for the rest of her life would have been nice, too. The music business always did look after its own, as Elvis would soon learn.

In the meantime Elvis was rapidly proving that he was what might, in any other kind of music, be called a prodigy. Still only nineteen and with hardly any professional experience he was using the Sun studio as a laboratory where he could experiment with all his different voices and styles. It was as though his teenage years had been spent as a musical vacuum cleaner, during which he'd hoovered up all the influences he'd discovered on his stack of 78 records. Now, given the confidence of Sam's enthusiasm and Scotty's backing, he was breathing those influences out again – the doo-wop songs, the r and b, the country, the ballads, the pleading, begging and teasing, all subtly changed through the context of his own life and voice. By his second record his confidence was astonishing. He didn't know it, *couldn't* know it, but he was inventing the modern phenomenon of the guitar-wielding rock star.

The big thing on Saturday nights was still the Grand Ole Opry in Nashville, so when Sam pulled more strings and got the little band a

A serious little family. Looking as though they might have stepped from the pages of *The Grapes of Wrath*, Vernon and Gladys Presley pose with two-year-old Elvis in 1937. Already he was the centre of their lives.

With a couple of oil lamps providing the only light and the necessary water being boiled on a log stove, Elvis was born at around four in the morning in January 1935 in this two-room frame house in East Tupelo, Mississippi.

Blond-haired Elvis, aged six, in first grade at school, and outside another rented home. The Presleys were forced to move house many times throughout his childhood.

He saw her at church, and then met her at the Rainbow Rollerdrome in Memphis. Her name was Dixie Locke and here they are at her high school graduation in 1955. Later he would joke, ungallantly, that his burgeoning singing career saved him from marriage, but at the time he was serious about her.

Possibly the most iconic image in rock music, this photograph of Elvis on stage in Tampa, Florida in July 1955 – just a year after he'd first sung on stage – would be used on the sleeve of his first RCA album. A black-and-white photograph with pink and green lettering, it was an incendiary introduction to the singer, and the best album cover he would ever have.

Record producer Sam Phillips sits with Elvis in the café next door to Sun Records in Memphis in 1955. Elvis had the voice, the looks, the rhythm and the inbuilt charisma, but former radio engineer Phillips was the catalyst who knew how best to record him.

With drummer D.J. Fontana, bass player Bill Black and guitarist Scotty Moore alongside him in RCA's Nashville studio in April 1956, Elvis has just been presented with his first gold record for a million-plus sales of 'Heartbreak Hotel'.

Because his mother, Gladys, worried whenever he travelled by air, Elvis would take the train whenever possible. Here on his way back to Memphis after recording 'Don't Be Cruel' and 'Hound Dog' in New York in July 1956, he listens to acetates from the session on the little battery-driven portable record player he would carry around with him.

The first time Elvis sang on stage was at the Mississippi-Alabama Fair and Dairy Show in Tupelo, when, wearing glasses and bibbed denims, he came fifth in a children's competition when he sang 'Old Shep'. Eleven years later, now the most famous young man in America, he appeared at the same fair on Tupelo's 'Elvis Presley Day' wearing a shirt given to him by Natalie Wood.

Almost an onlooker at negotiations between his manager, 'Colonel' Tom Parker, and Ed Sullivan, Elvis messes with his hair after rehearsals for CBS's *The Ed Sullivan Show* in October 1956. When, earlier in the year, Elvis had first appeared on a rival NBC programme, Sullivan had said that he would never have the singer on his show. Within months the TV host had to eat his words.

At the end of his first year of international fame, Elvis went home to Memphis, where in December 1956 he called in to see Sam Phillips at Sun Studios. The visit ended with a jam session with Carl Perkins, Jerry Lee Lewis and Johnny Cash – the Million Dollar Quartet.

20th Century-Fox presents
RICHARD EGAN · DEBRA PAGET
and introducing
ELVIS PRESLEY
in his first motion picture
LOVE ME TENDER
MR. ROCK 'N' ROLL IN THE STORY HE WAS BORN TO PLAY!
CINEMASCOPE
CO-STARRING
ROBERT MIDDLETON · WILLIAM CAMPBELL · NEVILLE BRAND
with MILDRED DUNNOCK · BRUCE BENNETT
PRODUCED BY DAVID WEISBART
DIRECTED BY ROBERT D. WEBB
SCREENPLAY BY ROBERT BUCKNER
BASED ON A STORY BY MAURICE GERAGHTY
Copyright 1956 20th Century-Fox Film Corp.
COUNTRY OF ORIGIN U. S. A.

Elvis dreamed of being a film star and with unseemly haste 'Colonel' Parker rushed him to Hollywood in 1956 and into a contract with Hal Wallis at Paramount, who then immediately loaned him out to Twentieth Century Fox for the quickie Western, *Love Me Tender*. The movie would be only the first of Elvis's disappointments in Hollywood, but it gave him one of his biggest hits.

The constant attention of fans had driven Elvis and his parents from the first house Elvis had bought in Memphis. So in 1956 he bought Graceland and had large wrought-iron gates, complete with musical motifs, erected to keep the fans out. But the gates would also, metaphorically, lock him in.

booking on the show, they felt they'd reached the summit of success. Elvis had never been away from his parents for a single night before, and as the Presleys didn't own a suitcase, Marion lent him one.

It's two hundred miles from Memphis to Nashville and all the way there in Sam's Cadillac he was dreaming about the famous, beautiful old Ryman Auditorium from where the show was transmitted. Radio used to be special in the way it helped listeners conjure up pictures, and Elvis had built up the Ryman in his imagination as though it was a cathedral of music. When they got to Nashville, however, and he saw the decrepit, last-century theatre, he was disappointed.

He wasn't the only person to be disappointed. When the people who ran the Opry saw Elvis, Scotty and Bill and Scotty's one little amp their first words were: 'Where's the rest of the band?' Most country bands had at least five members, and Sam Phillips' recording brilliance had suggested a much bigger group.

'There is nobody else,' Scotty explained. 'Just us.'

It was Elvis's first time singing on the radio as a professional, and although he did his best, and even wore a tuxedo, the Opry-goers in the audience just didn't get it. They didn't sit on their hands, but they didn't scream and shout either and he felt out of place and foolish. The majority of the audience were older, middle-aged hillbilly fans, some of the men wearing cowboy hats and some of the women dressed like Doris Day in *Calamity Jane*, and he could see from the stage that they just didn't go for what he was doing. He would get used to that. Not everyone was going to like him. Some people would even hate him.

When they got off stage, Sam told them not to worry about it, but when some middle-management fellow who worked there meanly advised Elvis not to give up driving a truck just yet, he was cut. When he became a success, the Opry asked him back several times, but he never went.

Like the Presleys, who were listening at home, Marion and Scotty's wife, Bobbie, hadn't been invited to Nashville, either. But, on the spur of the moment, they'd followed, together with Bill's wife Evelyn, in Bobbie's car. And, after the show, they all trailed Phillips along Broadway as he looked in the bars until he found a piano player he'd heard about. He was always looking for new acts.

Elvis didn't stay long in the bar. It was a rough venue, with drinking and swearing, and the sort of women who, well . . .

Quietly he made an excuse and went outside and waited in the street. Eventually Scotty and Bobbie came looking for him, wondering if he was all right. Yes, he was, he explained, but it hadn't been the kind of place his parents would want to see him in.

They were astonished.

He was very young. The raunchy, provocative, sexy guy who jumped around on stage and who people would soon start calling the Hillbilly Cat and the King of Western Bop was one thing. Off stage he was a complete contradiction.

7

'Hi Babies, Here's the money to pay the bills.
Don't tell no one how much I sent.
Will send more next week . . . Love, Elvis.'

Western Union telegram

He left his job at Crown Electric at the beginning of October 1954, just three months after he'd made his first record. He hadn't had a 'regular' job, as Vernon would say, for very long. But from that moment he would always be a professional singer.

His employer, Mr Tipler, was very understanding. He liked Elvis and didn't want to lose him, but he could see the way things were going. In fact Tipler and his wife, another Gladys, were among the first Elvis Presley fans, going to support him and the band at the Eagle's Nest, with Mrs Tipler even sending Elvis to a salon she used, Blake's Coiffures. She'd been amused by how much time he spent sculpting the shape of his hair . . . wetting his comb in water before preening in front of a mirror. Blake's was a ladies' hairdresser, so Elvis had to make his appointments after hours, when they'd closed for the day. People would have thought him a sissy if he'd been seen going in there during the day with the women, but in 1954 men's barbers only knew one way to cut hair: and that was with clippers like an electric lawn mower. He'd hated the clippers when he'd reached his teens, and would hate them even more when he went into the army.

He'd always taken pains over his hair. Once in high school he'd had a Toni perm, as had his mother, but it had caused much amusement in class, so he'd been relieved when it grew out. On another occasion Mrs Tipler's beauticians gave him a blond rinse, but that didn't suit him either. He couldn't imagine his ancestor Morning Dove with fair hair. Besides, all the movie stars then seemed to have dark hair. So he'd gone back to his natural light brown, though with the grease he put on his hair, he made it look much darker.

Living at home, as he always would, he was still giving his pay to his father every week to help out, and neither Gladys nor Vernon were happy about him giving up his job. For Daddy a regular pay cheque was something he'd rarely known – and his back was bad again. Gladys had left her job at the hospital, of which she'd been very proud, when the family income had become too high for them to live in subsidised housing, and, since then, she hadn't had other work. And then there was Grandma, who had never worked while she'd been with them. So Vernon was cautious. 'What if it doesn't work out for you, son?' he would ask repeatedly.

Gladys never doubted Elvis's talent, but she was scared of him going out into the wider world. She was enjoying the attention he was getting, which to her mind was proving that she'd been right about him all along, but Elvis knew she was really hoping his singing would just be in and around Memphis. That was the extent of her horizons: but it was the smallest limit of his ambition. When she saw him going off to engagements out of town she was uneasy. And she would always warn him that she didn't want him falling in with bad company.

The world outside frightened her, and as his success grew, her fears increased. He'd noticed that she'd begun taking some pills that she was getting from the doctor and that they were making her fretful and overactive around the house – always running around and cleaning.

'What are those things for?' he asked her once when he caught her taking one.

'I'm putting on weight,' she told him. 'The doctor says these will help keep me slim. I want to be slim and pretty for you. I don't want you being ashamed of me in front of your new friends.'

He hated that she might even think like that. There was one thing she could be sure of, he told her. He would never be ashamed of her. And he never was. Later, when asked by reporters about his devotion to his mother he would be surprised that it should even be questioned. 'Doesn't everybody love their parents?' he answered. So Gladys kept on taking the pills, and drinking a little on the quiet. He pretended not to notice the drinking, because he never touched alcohol himself and didn't like drunks – Grandma having told him that his grandfather Jessie Presley had been an alcoholic. But sometimes he took some of his mother's slimming pills, which we would now call amphetamines, when he saw how much energy they gave her. He needed energy for what he was doing on stage nearly every night, and he liked what they did for him.

For Gladys everything was happening too quickly. She would have liked him to settle down and marry Dixie soon. She was very fond of the girl, and kids did marry young in the South.

But Dixie had seen how girls reacted to Elvis when he was on stage. She didn't say much, and didn't complain, and he would be embarrassed about it, and try to tell her that it was nothing, that they were screaming just for the fun of it, to amuse themselves – which was partly true. To which she would just smile and say: 'I know, Elvis. I know.' But then she'd go quiet and he could tell she was worrying. The truth of it was, although he pretended he didn't care for the screaming either, he loved it. How could he not? And he would play up to it. The more excited the girls became, the more he'd move around, jack-knife his legs, and tease them. On stage he would flirt with a whole audience of girls. And sometimes, when he was away, playing out of town perhaps, he began doing a little more than flirting with some of them, after which he'd feel guilty.

When, years later, he was asked about marriage he would joke: 'The closest I ever came to getting married was just before I started singing. In fact, my first record saved my neck.' But that was hindsight talking. He'd been really serious about Dixie.

Scotty and Bill also gave up their day jobs, when Elvis did. The two now called themselves the Blue Moon Boys, Scotty having abandoned his band, the Starlite Wranglers, when 'That's All Right' began to take off. Putting the Grand Ole Opry's reserve down as a learning experience, Sam had immediately booked the trio on to the *Louisiana Hayride* radio show in Shreveport, Louisiana, which was known for promoting younger talent. That meant they had to spend more and more time on the road, using Scotty's wife's car, because she had the only vehicle among them that was reliable.

Shreveport was a seven-hour drive from Memphis, where they

would book into the cheapest hotel they could find, Scotty and Bill in one double room, Elvis in another. He was getting eighteen dollars a show, and the two musicians got twelve dollars each, not a fortune for a programme that millions listened to all over the South and Southwest. But, as Sam said, you couldn't measure the value of the *Hayride* in helping get you known.

At first they only had the four or five songs they'd already recorded that they all knew how to play, but gradually they began adding new ones. They liked doing Chuck Berry's 'Maybelline', the Clovers' 'Fool, Fool, Fool' and LaVern Baker's 'Tweedlee Dee'. Elvis wanted that to be his next record, and they recorded it, but Sam wouldn't put it out and the recording was lost.

'Elvis,' he would say, 'there's no point in you covering songs that are already in the damn charts by other singers. You have to be different.'

Unfortunately, none of them, not Scotty, Bill, Sam nor Elvis, wrote songs.

'If my life depended on it, I couldn't write a song,' Elvis would sometimes say.

Not a good song, anyway, not one that didn't sound like something else that he'd heard before. So, there they would be at Sun, going through old records trying to find songs that everybody had forgotten about so that they could dress them up in a new way. That was the way they did their third single 'Milk Cow Blues' – a classic blues which had been written before Elvis had even been born. And that was how the rest of 1954 and the first months of 1955 went. Just singing and playing high school gymnasiums and little clubs, and then driving and driving, sleeping in the back of the car as they went from town to town, sometimes with just enough time to get a wash before they did the next show.

If Elvis had been asked to describe what it felt like in those first months, he might well have said that it was as if he was a pebble that had been thrown into a pond. At first the ripples were small but they somehow never reached the edge of the pond, because the pond just kept getting bigger; and the bigger the pond got the bigger the ripples became. When they'd begun in the summer they'd been excited just to get dates over in West Memphis, which is on the other side of the bridge into Arkansas. But after they'd played the *Louisiana Hayride* a couple of times, they were given a year's contract to appear on the show every Saturday night. That was when the screaming started to get really loud.

It was also when they added drums to the band. D.J. Fontana was the house drummer on the *Hayride* and he soon began backing them when they were down to Shreveport for the show. He liked to joke that because he'd sometimes played in strip joints he was familiar with keeping rhythm by following the bumps and jerks of a backside – 'but not one like Elvis's'. But often, when the screaming got so loud he couldn't hear Elvis singing, that was all he had to go on.

Around Christmas 1954, Scotty decided he didn't want to manage the group any more. He preferred to concentrate on being a musician, so a friend called Bob Neal, who'd been a disc jockey in Memphis, took over arranging their dates. At the same time Elvis bought himself a new car – new to him, anyway. It was a 1951 Lincoln, and he asked a paint shop to write 'Elvis Presley – Sun Records' on the sides. Then they would strap Bill's big string bass on top and off they would go, working as many nights as they could, wherever anyone wanted them.

After a show Elvis would be constantly jabbering away, changing the stations on the car radio as he looked for records he liked, his hands and feet still going. Often, after they'd driven thirty miles or so away from a venue, which they considered a safe distance, he'd ask the other guys to stop the car so that he could walk for a while and cool down. One of them would always walk with him for safety in case any boyfriend or husband wanted to take a shot or a punch at him because of some over-excited girlfriend or wife. The first time his act got him into trouble was one night at an army base near Texarkana, when they were playing in a hot and smoky club. After the first set Elvis had gone out on to a flight of steps for some fresh air, when a husband followed him and swung a punch, sending him tumbling down the stairs.

'What did you do that for?' Elvis said, hitting back.

The husband took another shot. 'While you were singing, my wife got too excited. I've never seen her like that before. No one's allowed to do that to my wife.'

Luckily a couple of other soldiers quickly moved in and separated the two. But that was why Scotty, Bill and now D.J. never left Elvis's side after a show. He was becoming a handsome young man, and that aroused jealousies.

Whether his hyperactivity after a show had been in part chemically induced, he would never really know. Not counting the pills he may have borrowed from his mother, those were the days when anyone could buy Benzedrine over the counter to help stay awake when driving. Almost everybody who was touring in those days was taking it. Elvis took his share.

Day by day the word was getting around the South that the boy from Memphis was something special, and his pay was improving. But it wasn't regular. Royalties from the records he'd sold were very slow in coming in, and bills still had to be met at home. So, if he got paid for a date in cash, he would send the money home by Western Union. Gladys used to save the money orders in a box when they arrived.

One was from Houston, dated November 1954, and read: 'Hi Babies, Here's the money to pay the bills. Don't tell no one how much I sent. Will send more next week . . . Love, Elvis.'

He wasn't yet twenty, and he was already supporting his family.

While he was away, Dixie would go over to see Gladys, and when Elvis called home, and the Presleys now had a telephone, she would frequently be there. She and Gladys would go shopping together, and talk about what Elvis was doing and where he was. But, always afraid that she might start seeing someone else while he was away, if Dixie wasn't at home when he called, Elvis always wanted to know if she'd been round to see Gladys and what she'd said. Although he was no angel himself, he couldn't stop being suspicious and jealous. Then, when he went home to Memphis to do some recording, he and Dixie would fall out, only to make up again when he had to leave.

Mainly, though, Memphis was a treat for him now. Everyone seemed to know him. He'd go shopping on Beale Street and strangers would shake his hand and ask for autographs. He was white but he was accepted there. What he didn't notice, or simply took for granted, in those first months, was how much Scotty and Bill were already beginning to treat him as if he was their own Boy Wonder. The centre of attraction on stage and off it, their joint world was totally revolving around him. When he'd first gone to Scotty's place that fourth of July afternoon just six months earlier, all he'd been hoping for was to impress. Now, as far as the music they were playing was concerned, he was telling them both what he wanted them to do, the order of the songs he wanted to sing and what new songs they had to learn. They talked about music and tried out different ideas on the road, of course, and he listened to whatever any of them suggested, but he, the baby and least experienced of the band, was making all the decisions. And as he was more into rhythm and blues than Scotty, that was where 'Money Honey' and 'I Got a Woman' came from. In the studio it was different. If he wanted to record anything he had to convince Sam, and that wasn't always easy.

Every night, as the weeks and months went by, the act was getting wilder. Bill was a joker, fooling around, shouting out and pretending to ride his double bass as if it were a horse, while Elvis would be twitching and moving away in front, acting out the rhythm with his whole body . . . getting the girls going. And then there would be Scotty in between them, never moving or saying a word, just concentrating on his guitar as if none of the crazy stuff that was happening alongside had anything to do with him. Sometimes Elvis would come out on stage, hear the screams and stop dead and just stare at the audience, statue still. And the longer he did that, the more the girls would scream. D.J. Fontana used to say that strippers knew the same tricks.

'Play with them, amuse them, tease them,' he would encourage.

Soon older people would start saying that what Elvis was doing was dirty. But Elvis never thought so. To him it was all a tongue-in-cheek game. He never saw himself as a threat. The kids got the joke even if some of their parents didn't.

'I bet I could burp and make them squeal,' he would laugh.

But how did he know how to do all that stuff? He never said. Probably, he never knew. Movement came instinctively to him when he sang, as it had done to Gladys when she'd been a girl and to some of the people he'd seen in church when he'd been little. So, after that first time in Memphis, his act turned into a sort of conversation with the fans. He would do something with his leg, and the fans would scream in reply. So he'd do it again, maybe a little more, and there'd be more screams. And so on. He loved the fans. He liked the same music that they did, and felt that he was one of them. He would always be nervous before a show, but as soon as he was out on stage he would put away the nerves and feel completely at ease. He was young and the fans were young, mostly even younger than he was. He'd call them *friends*. 'Thank you, Friends,' he'd say, like a preacher or a politician, because they seemed like friends to him and their reaction was as much a part of the show as he was. They were the judges. If the music that he and the band did wasn't good, if they weren't putting on a good show, with him singing songs the kids liked, in a way that they enjoyed, with a rhythm that would get their hearts and feet moving, no amount of hip shaking would have got them screaming. He knew that. The music did it. He just happened to sing it the way the fans wanted to hear it. But he never stopped working and figuring what to do, how to look and what to sing, and making sure he got it all right.

And it wasn't long before other bands started noticing, and began doing it themselves. It was at a date in Lubbock, Texas, just after New Year 1955, that he met an unknown Buddy Holly for the first time. A couple of years later, their records were fighting it out in the record stores at the top of the Hot Hundred.

8

'That Colonel . . . he's the Devil himself.'

Gladys Presley

The first time he met the man who called himself Colonel Tom Parker was a day or two after his twentieth birthday, when he and the band were in Shreveport for the *Louisiana Hayride*. At first he thought Parker, who was a big plain man in his mid-forties, was just doing Bob Neal a favour by helping the new manager get them some bookings. Parker had been around for a while and had a lot of contacts. But, after getting to know him just a little, it became quickly clear that Parker always had more on his mind than doing favours.

The gossip around the *Hayride* at the time – and every Saturday night the place was thigh high in rumour – was that Parker had just been fired by singer Eddy Arnold, whom he'd managed for nearly ten years. There had been a falling out over money, it was said, and now Parker had gone into partnership with another country singer, Hank Snow, in a company called Jamboree Attractions. Whatever the reasons for Parker's sacking, within a week, Elvis, Scotty and Bill were out on a Hank Snow tour playing bigger venues than either Scotty or Bob Neal had ever been able to fix for them. That wasn't all. Before the tour had even begun Parker had sent Elvis a cheque for $425 as an advance. Elvis had never had an advance before; never, in fact, seen such a big figure on a piece of paper with his name on it. So, he was impressed. And when another big cheque from Parker arrived a couple of weeks later he was even more impressed.

Although their pay went up, too, Scotty and Bill never liked Parker. He was a blunt, awkward fellow, and whether or not people took to him wasn't the sort of thing he ever considered. With a cigar semi-permanently between his lips, he was, first and last, a money man.

'That guy wouldn't know a song from a barrel of beer,' it was said around the *Hayride*, which Elvis couldn't deny. But what mostly riled the two musicians was that Parker had approached some of Hank Snow's band and enquired if they would like to replace them in backing Elvis. Nothing came of it, but it was clear the way Parker's mind was working. Why pay for two bands, when one band could back both singers? He didn't understand that Scotty and Bill were helping Elvis make the sound the kids wanted to hear. Indeed he would never understand music other than as a balance sheet on a piece of paper. Elvis knew this, and in the beginning kept Parker away from any musical involvement. Later it would become a real and damaging problem.

Bill could always see the funny side of everything, and would laugh a lot over the story that Parker had once had a job as the official Tampa Bay Dog Catcher in Florida. But there were other tales, too, the veracity of which no one knew. According to Parker he'd been an orphan, and had grown up working on his uncle's Great Parker Pony Circus, before moving on to fairgrounds, where he would paint sparrows yellow and sell them as canaries. Elvis had no idea whether that episode was true, and it probably wasn't, but it struck him as funny, anyway. When Parker was in a good mood he could amuse people. But when he wasn't, he came across like a retired military man, telling people what to do, ordering them around and snapping demands.

In a sense that was funny, too, because everyone knew that Parker's army-sounding title was just a vanity thing given to him by Louisiana governor Jimmie Davis. The story was that Parker had done Davis a favour in an election, and, as a reward, Davis had bestowed on him the honorary title of 'Colonel'. State governors could do that in Louisiana. In fact, another governor of Louisiana, Earl K. Long, would make Elvis an honorary colonel, as well, in 1956. Such commissions were ten a penny, and most recipients would thank the governor and stick the title in a drawer and forget about it. That was what Elvis did with his title, and Scotty, too, when he was given one. But not Tom Parker. He began using it on letters, wires, contracts . . . everywhere he could. He must have thought it gave the impression that he had once been a high-class military man, and conferred on him more authority than plain Tom Parker. It probably did.

But it annoyed drummer D.J. Fontana. He said it was phony, and he would never call Parker 'Colonel'. 'It just ain't right,' he would say, and Parker simply had to put up with D.J. calling him 'Mr Parker'. Sam Phillips felt the same. He never called him anything but Tom Parker. Sam didn't like the Colonel either. But then not many people did like him. He was a control freak.

None of this bothered Elvis. He saw the money he was earning increasing all the time and he was grateful to the Colonel, as *he* always called him. What did get to him, though, and to all who came into contact with Parker, was that it was impossible to argue with him. Parker would fix whoever he was talking to with unblinking blue eyes until the subject of his stare would look away in embarrassment. He did it to Elvis when they first became acquainted. Sometimes the stare would end with a smile when things were going well. When they weren't it would make whoever Parker was talking to feel very uncomfortable. That, Elvis thought, was why Parker was such a good negotiator. He would rather have him negotiating for him than against him.

Nor did Parker mince words. Right from the beginning he told Elvis that if he ever did anything to disgrace him, he would be out. The way it was put, Elvis was a lucky boy to get Parker to manage him and without him he would soon be back in obscurity. Elvis believed him, never, apparently, wondering if it wasn't in fact Parker who had got very lucky. When Parker had been managing Eddy Arnold there had been a story that Arnold got so exhausted by his manager's continual interference he said to him one day: 'Don't you have a hobby or anything else to do?' To which Parker is said to have replied: 'You're my hobby.' Elvis would become the most lucrative hobby Parker could ever have imagined.

Until Parker became involved, Elvis, Scotty and Bill had made up a little three-man band who shared everything. But as Parker began to book them into new parts of the South, the relationship within the band changed, until soon Bill and Scotty were put on salary rather than their initially agreed 25 per cent each of the group's earnings. Parker only ever talked about Elvis; 'getting *Elvis* on television as quickly as possible', and 'getting *Elvis* out to Hollywood'. Elvis knew

Scotty and Bill weren't happy with the way things were going, but, even on salary, they were earning more than they'd ever earned before, so, if they complained about the new arrangement, he never heard it or, at least, never admitted to hearing it. Did he let them down? They would have thought so. But, as Parker told Elvis, they could all see what happened when they were on tour: he was the one the girls screamed for.

Not that they screamed quite everywhere yet. In March 1955, Parker flew them to New York to audition for the *Arthur Godfrey's Talent Scouts* television show. This was Elvis's first time on a plane. It was exciting – and, as it turned out, the most exciting part of the trip, because they didn't even get past the audition to get on to the show. A while later Buddy Holly failed, too, although Pat Boone was selected. Obviously Elvis and Buddy weren't what the judges were looking for. Or perhaps it was that the judges didn't like what they were looking *at* when they saw Elvis. Quite apart from his hair and sideburns and clothes, Elvis's hormones had decided to go into fast spin that week and acne was erupting with a vengeance all over his cheeks and forehead. No amount of make-up could disguise the craters and what looked like imminent explosions on his skin.

The rejection was disappointing, although not completely surprising. All the same, after that, Elvis always felt that New York would never be a natural home for him, and that 'sophisticated East Coast folk' were sniffy about him and his music. There may have been some truth in that.

So it was back down South and on the road again for dates in Mississippi, Alabama and Texas in the brand-new Lincoln Elvis had bought himself – though it didn't stay new for long when Scotty drove it into a hay truck. The next car he got, an almost new 1954 pink and black Cadillac, soon burst into flames and burned out. Those were the hazards of touring. Musicians got used to them, and, one way or another, got themselves to their next date. But when Elvis and the boys were late for a gig, Parker would withhold some of their pay. Did he have a legal right to do that? The question was most likely never asked.

Florida was Parker's favourite territory and in May 1955 they played several dates at the Gator Bowl baseball park in Jacksonville, coming on stage just before Hank Snow, who was closing the show. One night as they were finishing Elvis called out, jokingly, 'Okay, girls, I'll see y'all backstage,' the result being that hundreds of kids got up from their seats and ran to try to get to his dressing room. Hank Snow wasn't too pleased. He had to play to a half-empty stadium.

It was that week that Elvis met a woman called Mae Axton. She was a publicist for the tour, and, after a show in Daytona Beach, she found Elvis sitting by himself on a balcony at the hotel looking out at the sea.

'You know, Mae,' he said, 'I'd give anything in the world if I had enough money to bring my parents down here to see the ocean.' Mae would soon help him make that possible.

Although technically Bob Neal was still Elvis's manager, the Colonel was already pulling nearly all the strings, and Neal wasn't happy with the way things were going. He was, however, no match for the Machiavellian Parker. It would only get worse.

Elvis was having problems, too. Going home to Memphis to do some recording that spring, he found Gladys waiting for him with some bad news. Dixie had been over to see her a few days earlier and asked her to give Elvis a message. She wanted Gladys to tell him that she was going out with another boy. She'd been scared to tell Elvis herself, because she'd known he would talk her out of it.

He should have seen it coming. While he was away getting famous, she was at home sitting and waiting. So in a rational sense he understood. But emotionally he was shattered. He never took any kind of rejection well, and never would. Considering the way he'd been behaving on the road, he knew he probably didn't deserve Dixie, but he'd been brought up in a super macho world, where there were girls you married, and girls . . . who were, well, just for fun. He had to accept that Dixie didn't want him. All the same, he mentioned her in interviews for the next two years as the girl in Memphis with whom he'd been in love.

He got over it. He was twenty and there were girls everywhere he looked. The Colonel would lecture him about how one little slip could ruin his entire career, but sometimes it wasn't always easy for him to remember, especially as he didn't have to feel guilty any more.

There were still problems, though. On one of the first occasions he took a girl back to his hotel room, the condom burst. 'What do I do?'

he asked Scotty and Bill, who were waiting when he went back down to the hotel lobby.

'Well, you'll either have to marry the girl or leave the damned town real quick,' Bill laughed.

In the end Elvis took her to the emergency department at a hospital where she was given a douche. But the experience frightened him. He was working full out on the job of being Elvis Presley, listening to records every day, trying to discover the little piece of magic that Ray Charles or Clyde McPhatter put into their singing, planning his stage shows, choosing his clothes and the way he looked, talking to any small-town disc jockey who asked him. Then there was driving thousands of miles a month all over the Mid-South – the band reckoned they did over a hundred thousand miles on the road that year alone, playing nearly two hundred and fifty dates. Elvis couldn't afford to make any mistakes. It wasn't only about his career, either. He would, he knew, be letting his family down, too. And financially his parents now depended on him for the new little bungalow in Memphis he had begun renting for them.

Not that his sex life was the only thing that Parker lectured him on. No matter what Elvis did physically when he was singing, and increasingly his performance was being described as lewd, any kind of smutty talk or innuendo on stage was forbidden; and that ruined one routine. Because he put so much energy into his singing, moving all over the stage, Bill and he had devised a little patter so that he might catch his breath between songs. Bill would say: 'Roses are red, violets are pink.'

And, probably still panting, Elvis would stop him and say: 'No, Bill. Roses are red, violets are blue.'

Bill would shake his head: 'No, Elvis. Roses are red, violets are pink.'

So Elvis would say again: 'Bill, violets are *blue* . . . !'

At which point Bill would say: 'No, they're not. Violet's are pink. See, I got them right here.' And he'd pull a pair of pink panties out of his jacket pocket.

It seemed pretty harmless to Elvis, and the audiences always liked it. But the Colonel didn't, so out it went.

Soon the Colonel was making all the non-musical decisions, and, sometime between the summer and autumn of 1955, he gradually went from being merely the band's booking agent to becoming a special adviser to Bob Neal. Elvis wasn't aware of half of what was going on, because, as Parker kept saying: 'This is business, Elvis. You just sing.' So he turned his eyes away and did just that.

Having dealt with Scotty and Bill, the next hurdle for Parker was Sun Records. For months he'd grumbled that Sun was too small a label for Elvis to make any real headway in his career. And, as Sam Phillips hadn't yet got a good national distribution deal for Sun, Parker had a point. So, now, Parker began openly suggesting that Elvis leave Phillips.

Elvis didn't want to go. He'd just recorded the song Sam Phillips thought was his 'masterpiece', 'Mystery Train', as well as 'I Forgot to Remember to Forget You', his strongest coupling so far, and 'Baby, Let's Play House' was still on the *Billboard* national country music chart. It seemed to him that Sam knew how to get the best out of him in a recording studio.

But, instigated by Parker, offers were now coming in to Phillips from other record companies wanting to buy Elvis's contract. MGM approached him, as did Columbia in New York. Ahmet Ertegun and Jerry Wexler at Atlantic were also keen, and then there was RCA, with whom Parker had dealt for years over Eddy Arnold and Hank Snow. At first Sam sent them away by demanding $40,000 for his star, a price so high he knew they wouldn't pay it. Ertegun and Wexler at Atlantic could only find $20,000, and gave up. But Parker had connections and made sure that one of the suitors never went away completely. So, while Elvis was out on the road singing, his future was being plotted and argued over.

Finally, and because Elvis was still under age, in October 1955 Parker wrote to his parents asking them to sign a document giving him the right to negotiate a new record deal on their son's behalf. Bob Neal, who knew nothing about this, was furious when he found out about Parker's duplicity. Parker had gone behind his back, and there was friction now whenever he and Parker worked together, with Parker blaming Neal if things went wrong – and even when they didn't.

Elvis watched all this with mixed feelings. He could see that what Parker was doing was in his best interests – as well as Parker's own.

But he didn't care for some of the man's bullying tactics. Perhaps deep down he knew he should have spoken up more, but with things going so well he didn't want to rock the boat. He was ambitious.

He knew Daddy was calling in at Sun every other week wondering where the royalties were for the hundred thousand records he had now apparently sold. But he believed Sam when he said he was waiting for the distributors to pay him. This was the music business where nothing is ever straightforward, and Daddy really didn't know much about any kind of business, let alone music. At first Vernon had been cautious about the Colonel, but the more Parker talked, and the more Elvis's pay per show went up, the more he came to like him.

Gladys felt differently. She didn't trust Parker and she never liked or felt easy with him. And although he always made sure he sweet-talked her, she would often say to Elvis, 'that Colonel . . . he's the Devil himself'. Knowing how she felt, Parker even got Hank Snow, whose voice she loved, to call her from time to time, to tell her what a great guy the Colonel was. But, following her instincts, she was never convinced. People like Gladys didn't talk about Faustian pacts, but, regardless of how much fame and money Parker was pushing Elvis's way, it seemed to her that her boy was selling his soul and talent to an earthly Satan.

Elvis had thought she would be happier when he moved her and Vernon to the bungalow where there was more space for Grandma. But all the time Gladys was feeling worse with her 'nerves'. Her son's career had now taken over all their lives.

The bargaining went on for weeks. Sam was worried that Elvis was racing his new motorcycle around Memphis, always afraid that he'd end up in hospital and maybe lose his voice or his looks, or even his life. James Dean had been killed in a car crash at the end of September, and that had shaken everyone, including Elvis. Elvis hadn't yet seen *Rebel Without a Cause*, but, like almost everybody else of his age, he'd been mesmerised by Dean when he and Dixie had seen him in *East of Eden*.

Whatever pressures were put on him, Phillips kept on holding out. In his heart he didn't want to let Elvis go. He was fond of the boy and proud of what they'd done together. But one night at the end of October, while they were in the studio recording 'When It Rains It Really Pours', a blues song Elvis liked, as a flip side for 'Trying to

Get to You', Sam got a phone call. Scotty, Bill and Elvis waited in the studio while Sam took the call in his office.

When it was finished, he came through to the studio and took Elvis aside. 'I didn't want to do it, Elvis,' he said. 'But I've agreed in principle with Tom Parker to sell your record contract to RCA. I can't say I'm happy, but I believe it will probably be the best for you and your career. And your Daddy will be pleased.'

The figure he'd asked for was astronomical in those days, and Elvis was flattered that Sam had achieved it. But he was worried, too. 'If I go to RCA, will they record me as well as you do, Mr Phillips?' he asked.

Sam just looked at him kindly. 'Look, you know how to do it now,' he said. 'You go over there to RCA in Nashville and don't let anybody tell you what to do. They believe in you enough that they've laid down some solid cash, so you let them know how you feel and what you want to do.'

Elvis's days at Sun Records were finished. The following week, as 'I Forgot to Remember to Forget You' went to number three on the *Billboard* national country chart, the deal was signed in Sam's office. RCA, which was then one of the biggest record companies in the world, paid Sam $35,000 for Elvis's recordings, including those not yet released, plus $5000 for the outstanding royalties yet to be paid, which was the highest deal ever for a singer. Elvis got a 5 per cent royalty on his records, where Sam had only been paying 3 per cent, a sweetener cash advance of $5000, and a further $1000 in cash from Hill and Range music publishers Julian and Jean Aberbach, who were backing the Colonel.

Their plan was to set up a publishing company in Elvis's name, Elvis Presley Music, owned jointly by Hill and Range and the singer. If Elvis recorded any of the songs the company published he would get, usually, between a third and a half of the songwriting royalty, as well as a share of those for publishing – all on top of his singing royalty. As publishing royalties for the sales and radio plays of records are usually split 50–50 between the publishers and the song's writers, this meant that Elvis's, and therefore the Colonel's, slice of the royalty pie per record was huge. The Aberbachs wouldn't be doing too badly either, able to make publishing deals on any songs brought to Elvis by other publishers.

Naturally, Elvis was thrilled, so thrilled he probably didn't think to ask what the songwriters thought about having to give up a large share of their income in order to get him to sing their songs. Having his own music publishing company must have seemed ideal, in that instead of having to search through old records for material, new songs would now be tailor-made and offered to him. It would be a while before he would realise that there was one major flaw in this money-grabbing side deal, namely that he would eventually find himself under pressure to record songs which he co-published, rather than songs for which he didn't own any of the publishing. And they might not be as good. Many weren't.

Naturally, Parker did well out of the deal, too, taking a 25 per cent commission from it and a share in the music publishing, in addition to all his expenses, which were never inconsiderable. Until this moment he'd been in a partnership with Hank Snow, but Snow was now promptly dropped – although the country singer didn't realise it until he discovered that his name wasn't on the Elvis contract. He'd been conned.

What Elvis hadn't known until it was agreed was that Phillips had insisted on a non-returnable $5000 option while negotiations were going on and that the Colonel had paid that out of his own pocket – or, most likely, with help from the Aberbach brothers at Hill and Range. Whichever way it was, it was something Parker never let Elvis forget when the singer got difficult.

Quite why Sam let him go, Elvis never really knew. As with most things, there was probably no single reason, but money played the biggest part. Phillips was stretched financially because of late payments from distributors, and he'd just set up the first all-women radio station in America in Memphis, WHER, on which Marion Keisker was a presenter. On top of that, he had new talent coming along. Carl Perkins, Jerry Lee Lewis and Johnny Cash had all been drawn to Sun because of the success he'd had with Elvis.

But there may have been something else. Phillips could see that Elvis's ambition was to be more than just a record star. He really did want the best for the boy, whom he described as 'one of the most introspective people I ever met'. He knew he wouldn't be able to fulfil Elvis's ambition at Sun. Sam was Memphis. He loved it. It wouldn't have been for him to be going out to Hollywood. So he sold. Nor did he do so badly out of the sale, clearing his debts, and investing some of the money he'd been paid for Elvis in a new company that was starting in Memphis at the time. It was a hotel chain called Holiday Inn.

And, as he assured Elvis, he would still be there at 706 Union Avenue whenever the boy needed to talk.

For Elvis the future must have seemed to offer nothing but excitement. What he wouldn't have realised was that from then on nearly all decisions about his career would be governed solely on their moneymaking potential.

9

'If I can't move, I can't sing'

Elvis didn't know it then, but that December of 1955 was the last time he would be able to go Christmas shopping like anybody else. People recognised him in the stores in downtown Memphis, of course, because he'd been in the local newspapers quite a bit lately and the sideburns gave him away, anyway. But he didn't mind. He liked it. There were no riots and there was no hysteria. Mainly, people just smiled, were pleased to see him and let him get on with spending his money. And he spent a lot. This was the first Christmas he'd ever had any money to spend worth mentioning.

Vernon and Gladys had always done their best at Christmas, and in Tupelo they'd had big family affairs with the Presleys and the Smiths, though there hadn't been any extravagant presents. Now, with his advance from RCA, and a year spent touring, Elvis's wallet was stuffed. He'd earned $25,240 over the year, which was about ten times what Crown Electric would have paid him had he stayed on there. So he was enjoying himself. Lanskys meant yet more clothes and the record stores, which he visited whenever he went home, must have been very pleased to see him. He bought a lot of equipment at Ed's Camera Shop, too, including a projector to show cartoons and a movie camera to make his own little films, and he festooned his parents with gifts. It would have been good to have had a girlfriend at Christmas, a proper, nice girl that Gladys would have wanted to see him with, but that wasn't the way things were going.

So, he shared Christmas with the fans by doing an especially long set on the *Hayride*. The Colonel half-spoiled this by sending a note to Bob Neal, who was just about still involved, telling him to make sure that Elvis didn't make any vulgar gestures or come out with any provocative ad-libs. This interference with what Elvis did on stage irritated the singer, and he should have complained, but Parker was making him more money than he'd ever seen before. So, again, instead of protesting, he enjoyed himself by singing the Platters' 'Only You'. The Platters would remain his favourite group for years.

Christmas came less than a month after he'd signed for RCA, and he hadn't yet recorded for the company, but every day was now a race. When they were touring, Red West, his football team friend from high school, was now frequently accompanying him as an unpaid driver and bodyguard. With Scotty, Bill and D.J. looking after their instruments and travelling in a separate car, he needed someone to make sure the fans, and maybe some of their boyfriends, didn't get carried away. And it was good to have someone from outside the band to talk to when things got tetchy. There's never been a band who, after a week or two on the road, don't start bitching at each other. And the increasing amount of attention that was now coming his way, rather than towards Scotty and Bill, must have been aggravating for them. He understood that.

Red was with him when RCA flew him to Nashville to introduce him to disc jockeys at the Country Music Disc Jockey Convention. He was still awkward at these events, so it was a relief when he spotted a friendly face – Mae Axton, the publicist he'd met earlier in the year in Florida.

'Elvis, I want you to hear something,' Mae said immediately, in the kind of voice that wouldn't take 'no' for answer. 'This is going to be your first hit on RCA.'

And she insisted he go to her room and listen to a demo record she had with her, telling him she'd written the lyrics after reading in a newspaper about a guy who'd left a note saying 'I walk a lonely street', before committing suicide.

Suicide didn't sound to him like the subject for a hit record, and he really didn't want to hear it. But when he did, he immediately saw its potential. 'Hot dog, Mae, play it again,' he said. And she did. Again and again. 'Heartbreak Hotel . . . ' where 'the bell hop's tears keep flowing, and the desk clerk's dressed in black . . .' It was so unusual he couldn't get it out of his mind and he began singing it on the road immediately.

So, by the time he and the band arrived in Nashville for his first RCA session on 10 January 1956, two days after his twenty-first birthday, they all knew how they were going to play the song. Elvis was still worrying that without Sam Phillips at the controls he wouldn't sound the same, and the big, high-ceilinged former Methodist church hall that RCA then used for sessions had a quite different acoustic from Sun's little studio. What he didn't realise was that there were people at RCA who were just as apprehensive as he was, mainly Steve Sholes, the producer. He was the man who had talked his company into paying so much for Elvis's contract, and, as a kind of insurance, he'd invited Ben and Brock Speer, two gospel singers, along as well as Chet Atkins on guitar and Floyd Cramer on piano as back-up musicians. And, since Scotty had based his career on doing what Chet did with a guitar, he was probably a little overawed, too.

The first track they recorded was Ray Charles's 'I Got a Woman', which they must already have done two hundred times on tour. Their familiarity with the song should have relaxed them, but it didn't, and Elvis kept going off mike when he moved around as he sang. The engineers insisted that he stand still in front of the microphone, but, when he did, all the energy went out of him.

'If I can't move, I can't sing,' he told Steve Sholes, who was worrying behind the glass in the control box.

'Just try, Elvis,' Sholes said at first. Finally, though, he understood, and the problem was fixed when extra microphones were set up on either side of the singer, so that he could move and sing at the same time.

Meanwhile Chet Atkins was so astonished, not to say amused, by the way Elvis performed and moved when he recorded, he called his wife during a break and told her to come down to the studio immediately, because she would 'never see anything like this again' during a recording session.

They did 'Heartbreak Hotel' next. A doom-laden, spooky blues, it practically pleaded for what Sam Phillips used to call the 'slapback' echo he got at Sun through his two connected Ampex tape recorder system. The RCA engineers, however, just couldn't get the same effect. In the end the record came out sounding as though Elvis was hollering down a well. But, with the Floyd Cramer piano break in the middle, Elvis knew what they had. He also knew that, as agreed in his new contract with Hill and Range, he would have a share in the songwriting and publishing as well.

Altogether he recorded five songs over the next couple of days, which was about half of what he and the band had released over eighteen months at Sun. RCA didn't believe in spending a whole night or maybe two or three nights on one song the way Sam had done. The Drifters' r and b hit 'Money Honey' was always fun on tour, so they did that, and then there were a couple of new ballads, too. Elvis had wanted to record 'I Was the One' at Sun, but Sam wouldn't let him, so he did it now, accompanied by the two backing singers. It was the first time other singers had been on one of his sessions, and, to loosen everybody up, he sat down at the piano and sang a couple of gospel hymns with them before they began recording. He didn't know what the RCA people thought about that, as they watched the clock, but it made him feel better, and it would become something he did at many sessions from then on. Sportsmen limber up by jogging around the field before they play. Elvis got ready by singing hymns.

To his way of thinking, the sessions went well, and he was feeling pleased with himself when, home in Memphis a few days later, he returned to Humes High School and sang a couple of songs at a Father's Day night.

Back in Nashville, however, Steve Sholes wasn't so sure. He'd sent tapes of the sessions to the RCA top brass in New York, and they didn't like what they heard, not at all . . . and particularly not 'Heartbreak Hotel'. They weren't alone. Sam Phillips didn't like it either. When it comes to music, Memphis is a small town where everyone talks, and the gossip was that when Sam first heard 'Heartbreak Hotel' on the radio his response was that it was a 'morbid, melodramatic mess'. Elvis didn't often disagree with Sam, but this time he knew Sam was wrong. They all were. He never had any doubts.

There must have been a moment at RCA when they considered not putting the song out at all. But they must have liked everything else from the Nashville session even less, because they did release it, on the day before Elvis was to make his national television debut on CBS's *Stage Show*.

Jackie Gleason, who was a big TV star then, co-produced the show with the bandleaders Tommy and Jimmy Dorsey, and Elvis was looking forward to meeting the Dorseys. They were, he would say, a couple of 'nice old guys from the swing era'. But when he first got to the TV studio in New York he could see them looking at him as though he'd just emerged from the backwoods.

The show went out live on a cold, wet New York Saturday night from CBS Studio 50 on Broadway. With top star Perry Como over on NBC at the same time, it hadn't been the most popular show for some time, and, with CBS having trouble giving away free tickets that night, the theatre wasn't even full. Sarah Vaughan was also on the show, but at that point Elvis was completely unknown in New York, and no kind of draw at all.

He was wearing a long drape jacket with light flecks on it, and the kind of loose pleated trousers he liked. His shirt was black and his tie was light. In the days of black and white television everything was grey, so colour was less important than contrast. Miraculously his acne had cleared up quite a bit since his last visit to New York, and the CBS make-up girls did a job around his eyes the way he liked them.

This was his first appearance on coast-to-coast television, and with Scotty, Bill and D.J. already waiting on the set, he paced up and down in the wings, as Bill Randle, a Cleveland disc jockey he knew, introduced him.

'We think tonight he's going to make television history for you. Ladies and gentlemen . . . Elvis Presley.'

And with that Elvis raced out on to the set as though he was late for work. 'Well, get out of that kitchen and rattle those pots and pans . . .' he sang, the opening line of 'Shake, Rattle and Roll', and all his nerves went. He knew what to do and how to do it. He'd been warned by the producers, 'this is prime time TV, so don't do too much of that moving around'. So he didn't.

By his standards he was restrained and at first the audience was subdued. But by the time of Scotty's guitar break midway through the song, when he began to move a little, prompting at first laughs and applause and then a few amused screams, he could sense a surprised excitement. No one there would have known what to expect that night. Now they didn't know what to think.

Before the show he'd assumed, naturally, that he'd be singing 'Heartbreak Hotel'. That was what usually happened when an artist had a new record out. But at rehearsals he'd been told the producers didn't want it. Seemingly, they didn't like 'Heartbreak Hotel' either. The irony was, if they'd listened to the lyrics of 'Shake, Rattle and Roll' there's no way they would have let him sing those words; nor would the no-smut Colonel. The song, which is about sex, had been a bowdlerised hit for Bill Haley a couple of years earlier. Elvis's version, however, was based on the original Big Joe Turner record, and included a couple of lines from 'Flip, Flop and Fly', another of Turner's hits. He would sing it for months before even he realised how earthy the lyrics were.

'I'm like a one-eyed cat peeping in a seafood store, I can look at you and tell you aint no child no more,' he sang.

But, if CBS wanted 'Shake, Rattle and Roll', who was he to argue?

He'd only been booked for one song, but, during rehearsals, Jackie Gleason had surprised him. He liked what he was hearing. 'Get him to do "I Got a Woman" as well,' he'd suggested to the Dorsey brothers. So that was what Elvis did.

The following day Colonel Parker said that the phones never stopped ringing at CBS that night, so many people had complained about Elvis. But, around the corner at the Warwick Hotel, Elvis had gone to sleep happy. Millions of Americans had watched him, more than would have seen him in ten years of touring. He'd been paid $1250 for the appearance, which was $1232 more than he'd earned exactly a year earlier for appearing at the *Louisiana Hayride*. And he was due back on the show the next Saturday. Maybe they would let him sing 'Heartbreak Hotel' then.

First, though, Steve Sholes wanted him back recording as quickly as possible to remedy what his bosses still saw as the Nashville disaster, and, first thing Monday morning, Elvis, Scotty, Bill and D.J. set up in RCA's New York studios on East 24th St. No backing singers had been booked for them, so there was no hymn singing this time. But they did have a Broadway show pianist by the name of Shorty Long helping out. By this time Carl Perkins's 'Blue Suede Shoes' was just showing on the *Billboard* Hot Hundred, Sam Phillips having arranged a better distribution deal for it than he'd ever managed for any of Elvis's records, so Elvis chose to cover that first. He didn't think he did it as well as Carl Perkins, just faster and without the bar break between the stops, but, as it was intended as an album track, it didn't matter. He wasn't competing with Carl. As a matter of fact, as Perkins had written the song and Phillips owned some of the publishing, he was doing them both a favour by putting it on his album, although Sam wanted a promise from Steve Sholes that RCA wouldn't be releasing Elvis's version as a rival single.

RCA kept their promise as far as a single for the US was concerned, but they did release it as the lead number on a four-song extended play a few weeks later and it became a single in the UK and Canada, selling enough copies to warrant a gold record. By that time, however, the Carl Perkins version had sold a million copies across the US so he didn't complain, and his songwriter's royalties from Elvis's record over the decades must have been substantial. What he might have felt aggrieved about was that the song became identified with Elvis more than him, although he'd had the bigger US hit.

Altogether Elvis recorded eight tracks over two New York sessions that January week, all the others being covers of rhythm and blues standards which would be enough to put alongside some unreleased Sun tracks to make up his first album – *Elvis Presley.* The photograph for the album sleeve had already been selected. It showed him in black and white having what looked like some kind of singing paroxysm while on stage, with his name in pink and green down the left hand side and across the bottom of the cover. For its time the design was a statement in itself. It was incendiary, and by far the best cover RCA ever produced for an Elvis Presley album. It was also provocative for those who didn't like him, and naturally some critics in the music world chose to review the cover rather than the songs. But, as the Colonel said, 'Don't worry about what they say, Elvis. It's all publicity, and it's free.'

He was only in New York for a week that winter, but it turned out to be the longest he ever stayed in the city. When he called home every night, Gladys would ask about sightseeing and the skyscrapers. Memphis only had one tall building then, and it wasn't a quarter as high as the Empire State Building. Really, though, Gladys just wanted to know that her son was safe and happy. He assured her he was, as the RCA and CBS staff were going out of their way to be helpful and make him feel at home. Except that with all their fast talk and smart ways they still sometimes made him feel left out.

With its twenty-four-hour noise and brash confidence and different kinds of people, New York City was about as far from his home as any place on earth that he could imagine.

Julian and Jean Aberbach, the Hill and Range publishers who had backed Colonel Parker in the RCA deal, were based in New York, and took it on themselves to show Elvis around a little on his days off. They were a couple of Austrians who'd gone to the US in the thirties, become involved in the country music business and done very well. Music publishing certainly was the business to be in, Elvis must have thought to himself one evening when Julian invited him to dinner at his swanky home to meet some people in the business. It was all very friendly, and Julian's wife was a nice lady, but when dinner was served the star of the party nearly gagged when he saw some pink, rare lamb on his plate.

'But it's still bleeding,' Elvis said in horror.

Mrs Aberbach looked surprised, then quickly took the plate away.

There followed one of those moments when Elvis wished he'd just kept his mouth shut. Everything was smoothed over quickly, but he'd never been served underdone lamb before. That wasn't how they ate it in Memphis. Years later he would joke that he liked his food 'Well done. Cooked. I ain't orderin' a pet', but on that evening in New York he'd embarrassed himself.

After his nervousness before the first *Stage Show*, he was more confident for his second appearance, when he went back to CBS the following Saturday. There was, however, bad news. 'Heartbreak Hotel' wasn't selling yet, so, once again, the producers wouldn't let him sing it. He was disappointed. But as 'Baby, Let's Play House' had just been re-released by RCA and was on the country chart, he sang that instead and followed it up with 'Tutti Frutti'.

Everyone liked Little Richard songs, maybe even the Dorsey brothers, because after the show they took the band out to the Roseland dance club on Broadway, where, they told him, they'd played a generation ago. This place had been one of those ten-cents-a-dance places back in the thirties when they began playing, Tommy Dorsey explained, as they all sat at a big round table and looked around the floor.

A few couples were jiving and an older, attractive woman from

CBS turned to Elvis, and indicated the floor. Did he want to dance? A small crowd had now noticed him and were watching. All week he'd been getting second glances and stares, and a few kids had followed him, asking for autographs – although nothing on the scale he encountered in the South. Now, after this second TV show, he was receiving more attention, so he really didn't want to make a fool of himself on the dance floor.

'Well, I would if I could, ma'am. But I'm sorry, I never did learn how to bop,' he said, as he always would when asked to dance.

The CBS woman looked surprised. Was he serious?

'I meant to say, I can't dance *with* anyone,' he stuttered, embarrassed.

The Dorsey brothers must have been amused. He didn't drink, he didn't smoke, and now he was saying he didn't dance either.

Jackie Gleason, meanwhile, had something important to tell him. 'Elvis,' he said, 'you're going to be a very big star. Here's some advice. Don't hide. Walk the streets, go to restaurants, but don't hide. Because, if you do, you're going to be the loneliest guy in the world.'

Was Elvis listening, or was he too enthralled by the machinations of his manager? In a telegram to the Colonel that week, he wrote: 'You are the best, most wonderful person I could ever hope to work with. Believe me when I say I will stick with you through thick and thin . . . I love you like a father.'

10

'Why should music contribute to juvenile delinquency? If people are going to be juvenile delinquents they'll be juvenile delinquents if they listen to Mother Goose rhymes.'

Television did it. After every appearance on *Stage Show*, and he'd now been re-booked for four more, there was a rush to buy tickets not just for the show, but for the dates he played between TV appearances, too. And it wasn't only the white teenagers who were coming now. Obviously there was no segregation in the studio audiences in New York, but as he'd performed almost exclusively in the Southern states so far, the black fans had usually been allowed only in the balconies. At the time that hadn't struck him as particularly strange. He'd grown up with segregation. He was used to it. But with many of the songs he was singing having been written by black songwriters and musicians, and with his records now being played on race stations and appearing on the rhythm and blues charts as well as the pop and country lists, separating his fans didn't make any sense.

Perhaps, like Bill Haley, he should have refused to play to segregated audiences, but he didn't. Did he think about it? Possibly. But, as Colonel Parker always told him, it wasn't his job to get involved in politics. So he did what he was told, abided by the rules and kept on singing; and not a moment in the day was wasted in the schedule of one night stand appearances that Parker was now setting. So, by two o'clock on the Sunday afternoon following his second CBS appearance in New York, he was in Richmond, Virginia, beginning a three-week tour right along the East Coast through the Carolinas and on down to Florida.

With just Saturdays off to fly back to New York for the TV

appearances, he and the band never stopped moving. When he'd been a boy, Saturday night had been for church and gospel singing, followed by more church on Sundays. But he wasn't getting to church so much any more. Saturday night was a big night for entertainment and on almost every Sunday he and the band were booked for a matinee performance as well. Although they only did six songs a show, sometimes they did four shows a day, with the other acts on the tour standing in the wings to watch him, as he whipped up the audience. For a deferential, quiet, well-mannered boy, his on-stage behaviour was a revelation to himself as much as to anyone else.

'My whole body gets goosed up,' he would explain. 'It's like a surge of electricity going through me . . . I feel my heart is going to explode.'

He was undoubtedly enjoying the excitement he was provoking, but sometimes in more reflective moments he would also wonder if all the hysteria might be counter-productive.

'I'll never make it,' he worried one night after a show. 'It will never happen. They're never gonna hear me, because they're screaming all the time.'

He would get used to it, and, at last, 'Heartbreak Hotel' was on the charts. So on his third show the CBS producers let him sing it – even though they then ruined it by having the Dorsey band add their own brassy accompaniment. He thought the arrangement was awful, but just grinned ruefully and got through it, as he always got through all the set-backs. The Dorseys had got it wrong, though. If 'Heartbreak Hotel' was about anything it was about romantic despair. Everyone experiences it, especially the kids who would be buying the record. But here was the Tommy Dorsey Band laughing at the song, and laughing at Elvis for singing it, by putting a phony, tongue-in-cheek musical slurch to it. As Scotty said later, if they'd put that Dorsey arrangement on the record, RCA wouldn't have sold a single copy. Tommy and Jimmy Dorsey were pleasant enough guys, but they were from another era and just didn't get it. Elvis was too young and inexperienced to take on CBS, but he made sure that Steve Sholes at RCA knew how he felt. His protest must have worked, because the big band arrangement wouldn't be used when he did the show the following week.

As it happened, he didn't have much time to fret about it, anyway, because at 7.30 the following morning he and the band were back in the air heading for Norfolk, Virginia, for three shows that Sunday.

Because of all the travelling, Elvis's cousin Gene Smith was now assisting Red on the road, while Vernon had helped build a little white and pink trailer to carry the guitars, Bill's double bass and Elvis's suits. The way Elvis figured it, the fans wanted to see a show as well as hear one and by then he reckoned he had twenty different outfits, all as flashy as he could find. It was all part of the experience. He'd learned that from watching Liberace on TV. There was no one flashier than Liberace, but the guy could play the piano, too. People who didn't like Liberace forgot that, when they were dazzled by the glitter. The same would happen to Elvis. Those who disparaged him forgot he could sing: or deliberately didn't listen when he did.

Vernon was proud of the trailer he'd built, which Scotty and Bill would tow behind their car, though Red said he thought it looked like an ice-cream van. By this time Vernon had given up work in order to take care of his son's personal business. When the newspapers found out, they mocked him and reported that he'd retired at thirty-nine, hinting at rumours that he'd always been work shy. That wasn't how Elvis saw it. It didn't make sense to him, he would say, to know that he could earn in a day what his father earned in a year. Daddy was much more important helping him than if he'd still had a job. There was more and more fan mail now, and all kinds of things were piling up, stuff the Colonel just didn't do. So Vernon found himself with a second career.

So far Elvis was enjoying everything there was to enjoy about fame, but during the first months of 1956 something cropped up that began to worry him. He had already realised that the Colonel wasn't the one to go to for sympathetic advice, and, not feeling able to talk about his problem to his parents, he paid a visit to the only other adult he knew in whom he could confide – Sam Phillips.

'Mr Phillips, can I ask you something in complete privacy?' he asked.

Of course, he could. Sam had told him to come back any time he needed to talk. 'What's the problem?' Sam asked.

'Well, Mr Phillips, I believe I might have syphilis.'

Sam Phillips wasn't a man to show surprise easily, but on this occasion he couldn't hide it. 'Syphilis?'

'Or something of that nature,' Elvis went on. 'I have the symptoms.'

'You know what the symptoms are?'

'I read about them in a magazine.'

'Well, shouldn't you see a doctor?'

'I'm scared to, in case it got out and was in the papers and everything.'

Sam shook his head. 'Elvis, there's a thing called the Hippocratic Oath that forbids doctors from talking about their patients' illnesses. Besides which, I'd be very surprised if you have syphilis. It's very uncommon.'

'But I have a lump.'

'What kind of lump?'

'On my, you know . . .' And Elvis indicated his groin.

'Well, to the best of my knowledge, that don't sound like syphilis to me,' Sam came back. 'But . . .'

Both men were embarrassed, but after a little more talk it was decided that Elvis should lower his trousers to show Phillips the lump, which was in his pubic hairs.

On seeing it, Sam smiled. 'Well, I ain't no doctor but I'm sure as daylight that that ain't syphilis. What you've got there is a carbuncle, probably caused by an ingrowing hair or some such thing. Why don't I call a doctor I know down at St Joseph's Hospital and have him lance it for you? We can go in there by a back entrance. No one will know.'

Which was what happened. Sam had been more than a record producer to Elvis, and his good counsel was missed in that first year of fame. There had been talk that RCA had put feelers out to him suggesting he work for them as an independent producer with Elvis, but Sam would never be a company man. Besides which, the Colonel was now in control of Elvis's career. He would never have allowed Phillips back in.

A house of her own had always been his mother's dream, and Elvis had always promised that as soon as he could afford it he would buy her one. So the very first thing he did when he had any amount of money was to buy a ranch-style, seven-room home in Audubon Drive, which was a quiet address in a Memphis suburb. He paid $22,500 for it in cash, which was a lot of money then, and he was proud to say that the Presleys' house was the only one in the road that didn't have a mortgage. People would sometimes ask why he didn't just buy his folks a house and go and live somewhere else by himself, as he could have afforded to. But it never occurred to him to live anywhere other than with his family. To Elvis his parents were home and what was his was theirs. That would always be his attitude.

He'd been on tour when his parents had moved into Audubon Drive, and he would rarely be at home during 1956. But the first time he lived there he became uncomfortably aware that the furniture his parents had brought from their old home didn't fit. It looked shabby. They needed some better furniture. So he took them downtown and bought everything new until the house was stuffed with furniture. Too much, actually. That would always be a side of him. He overdid everything, especially when he wanted to please.

He could see that his mother was grateful and proud of the new home, but she seemed even more timid now, and she fretted about the neighbours when fans began congregating outside in the road. He could sense that she felt that she didn't belong there.

'It's like a palace, Elvis,' she kept saying uncertainly. 'Like a palace.'

'You'll get used to it, Mama,' he told her.

And then there was her health. It wasn't good. She was still taking slimming pills, but she was drinking a little more, too – quite a bit more. When he had to leave she was sad and worried again, so he was grateful that Daddy could be with her at home all the time. He didn't want her being lonely in their new house.

After weeks of non-stop touring, he did his fifth and final *Stage Show* in New York at the end of March. It was only two months since his first appearance, but it seemed that half the country was now talking about him. 'Heartbreak Hotel' was high in the pop, country and rhythm and blues charts, his first album was in the shops and his first extended play record was alongside it. As 'Blue Suede Shoes' was on the album as well as on a bestselling EP, both RCA and CBS wanted him to sing it on the last show. But he couldn't do that.

For months he'd been in a friendly rivalry with Carl Perkins, having known him at Sun when they would sit together in Taylor's café and talk about music. But a couple of days before the CBS show, as their records raced each other up the Top Forty, Carl and his band had been involved in a car crash. On their way to appear in *The Perry Como Show* on NBC, their driver had fallen asleep at the wheel and been killed, and Carl's brother, who played with him, had a broken neck. Carl would be in hospital for months.

Gladys had been right to worry. Constant touring could be dangerous. There was no way now that Elvis could sing 'Blue Suede Shoes' that night, no matter how much CBS and RCA tried to persuade him. Instead he did 'Money Honey'.

Scotty, D.J. and Bill drove back to Memphis after the show and, on their way, called in at the hospital in Delaware to see Carl. Elvis would have gone too, if he could, and he sent a get-well telegram. But by then he was on a plane, on his way to Los Angeles. The Colonel and the William Morris Agency had been pitching him hard in Hollywood and the chance of a screen test with Hal Wallis at Paramount was an important step.

Before he'd even started his career, Elvis had harboured dreams of one day becoming a movie star. Seeing James Stewart in *Broken Arrow* and *Winchester 73* when he was a boy, and then watching all the big movies, from *The Wizard of Oz* right up to *The Wild One*, *From Here to Eternity* and *On the Waterfront*, had created a parallel dream alongside his singing. He simply wanted to be in the movies. He knew that many young people harboured the same dream; that's the vanity of being young. But he probably wanted it more than most, although at school he'd hardly done any acting, except perhaps in Christmas concerts when he'd lived in Tupelo. He hadn't even put himself forward for the plays they did in high school. But now that girls were screaming at him, his little reverie didn't seem quite so silly. Perhaps James Dean had made a difference for him. Whenever *Rebel Without a Cause* had been playing in any town they'd stopped in, he would go and see it.

From the first time Hollywood was mentioned, he had told Parker he wanted to be a serious actor, that he didn't just want to sing in movies. It seemed to him that singers would come and go, but movie stars could be around for a long time. Parker said he would pass the message on. Whether he did or not, or whether anybody listened if he did, Elvis never knew. But it didn't work out that way.

Everything was happening so quickly that he wasn't lying when he told a reporter it really did scare him. Fame had come from nowhere, it seemed, and he worried that it could 'one day go out like a light . . . just like it came on'. He was trying to keep a level head, because half of the time he didn't know where he was going from one day to the next. He had so much on his mind and he didn't want to let anyone down.

'I know right from wrong,' he would say, 'but it's so easy to get into trouble. You can get trapped into something maybe you didn't think to do. But my parents don't worry about that. The worst kind of trouble I've ever been in was stealing eggs when I was real little.'

He was, however, permanently tired, sometimes getting no more than three or four hours' sleep a night and probably taking too many NoDoz pills or Benzedrine to stay awake. He'd hoped to catch up on his sleep while flying to Los Angeles that first time, but it was impossible. He was too excited, and kept going through the screenplay that Paramount had sent him to read. The scenes he had been told to learn were from a film soon to be made called *The Rainmaker*, which was to star Katharine Hepburn and Burt Lancaster. Just the thought of those two scared him.

Tom Parker's right-hand man, Tom Diskin, was waiting when he arrived in Los Angeles, and he was driven by limousine up to Beverly Hills. He wasn't tired but he didn't go out and see the town. He called home instead. As Chuck Berry would write and Elvis would later sing, '. . . This is the Promised Land calling and the poor boy is on the line.' That was Elvis in March 1956. Only he suddenly wasn't so poor any more.

Compared with the excitement he was used to whipping up in the South, his arrival in California was a quiet affair in that his records were only just beginning to take off there. But when he got to Paramount Studios the following day he began to feel more at home, as secretaries called each other around the lot, and left their offices to come and take a look at him. He didn't know anything about movie people . . . but girls, he knew how to handle them. And although the secretaries might have been used to seeing film stars, he was the first rock star they'd encountered.

The plan was that he would do a couple of scenes with an actor for a screen test and see how it went. He was worried about his stammer, but Hal Wallis told him it wouldn't be a problem because it would just make him appear more natural. So he just tried to put himself in the place of the character he was playing and to act as naturally as he could.

He thought he did okay. But, despite what he'd told the Colonel about not wanting to sing in movies, Hal Wallis wanted to see how he looked on celluloid when he was singing. So they played him a recording of 'Blue Suede Shoes', gave him a little fake guitar and asked him to mime. He should have realised at that point that it was his singing they were really interested in, but, as always, he was just doing everything he was asked to do.

A few days later a newspaper reporter enquired how the screen test had gone and he told her that he was going to be appearing in *The Rainmaker*, believing that he was. So it was embarrassing when the Colonel told him that he wasn't, and that although he'd signed a contract with Hal Wallis, he'd immediately been loaned out to Twentieth Century Fox for another movie. He was puzzled by that. While he could see that it was flattering that two studios wanted him, he also felt a little like a rental car being casually passed from Paramount to Fox. And the Colonel hadn't been very happy that he'd talked to the reporter.

'It's best you don't talk to newspapers, Elvis,' Parker told him. 'They'll only twist what you say.'

But it wasn't always easy to avoid them after shows, especially when there were articles on him in *Time*, *Newsweek* and *Life*, and people, whom he thought should have known better, accusing him of being vulgar, suggesting he was encouraging drug taking and juvenile delinquency with his singing.

'Why should music contribute to juvenile delinquency?' he retorted to one journalist. 'If people are going to be juvenile delinquents they'll be juvenile delinquents if they listen to Mother Goose rhymes.' It seemed to him that what he was doing was healthy and fun, that no one had to be drugged-up to either do it or enjoy it. 'I don't think I do anything obscene on stage, or anything that would embarrass my Mama,' he said. 'I really don't.'

And he hated it when, a little while later, someone invented the phrase 'Elvis the Pelvis'.

'That,' he snapped, 'seems to me the most stupid thing an adult person can say.'

11

'The coloured folks have been singing and playing it just like I do now, man, for more years than I know. They played it like that in their shanties and juke joints and nobody paid it no mind until I goosed it up.'

In the music business in those days it didn't matter how successful you were, as soon as your latest record reached the top of the charts everyone was chasing you to make a follow-up. So after a couple of shows in San Diego, an appearance on television's *Milton Berle Show* in Los Angeles and a short tour, Elvis, Scotty, Bill and D.J. were heading back to RCA's Nashville studios.

The day started badly when the pilot of the little chartered plane they'd hired in Wichita Falls, Texas, realised he was lost and didn't have enough fuel. 'I think we'd better all look around on the ground to see if there's somewhere we can land,' he told them. Naturally enough, they were all scared, but eventually one of them spotted a landing strip. The plane got down safely and they all went for something to eat while an attendant refilled the plane's tanks.

When they set off again, Scotty was sitting up front in the co-pilot's seat, when the pilot suddenly said to him, 'Here, you take it, while I look under the seat for a map so I can find out where we're going.'

Scotty froze: 'I don't know how to fly a plane.'

Behind him, sitting with Elvis and D.J. was Bill, who was just about making his last will and testament.

'Just hold it steady,' the pilot said. But, just as Scotty took over, both engines spluttered and stopped.

They all looked at each other. They were six thousand feet up in the air and the engines had cut out. This was it. But then the pilot flicked a knob and the engines started again. They reckoned later that he'd probably just forgotten to switch back to the main tank before they'd taken off again, but they were all shaken. When they eventually got to Nashville, Elvis said: 'We're done with this guy. We'll take an ordinary commercial flight when we go back.'

They were still tense when they arrived at the studio, but so was everybody else. Chet Atkins may have been a great guitarist, but Elvis didn't get the feeling that the older man considered him as anything more than a flash in the pan. He'd asked that the Jordanaires, a male vocal quartet he had much admired after meeting them on the *Louisiana Hayride*, should accompany him, but instead RCA had only booked one Jordanaire, Gordon Stoker, to join the two other singers, Ben and Brock Speer, who had been with him on 'I Was the One' at the last Nashville session. They were good, but Elvis needed that extra voice in the middle of a quartet for the harmony to be the way he wanted it. So he was angry. He had the top-selling single, EP and album in the country, yet RCA were cutting corners to save a few dollars on the session.

The other problem was the material. Neither Steve Sholes nor Elvis's publishers, Hill and Range, had come up with anything outstanding for him to sing. 'I Want You, I Need You, I Love You' was the best they had, but it sounded to him more like an album track. They did the best they could in the three-hour slot RCA gave them, but Elvis knew it could have been a better record with more time. It was released as soon as 'Heartbreak Hotel' and 'Blue Suede Shoes' began going down the charts and it got to number one, with 'My Baby Left Me', another Big Boy Crudup number they'd recorded in New York, as the flip side, doing well, too. But, although he sang it on tour for a couple of months, he only ever did it twice on television. The fans probably liked it more than he did, although that could be said for a large number of his hits, which, once recorded, he never sang again. Despite everything, however, the session turned out to be a useful experience. From that moment, he made sure he took all the decisions in the recording studio, and he didn't record in Nashville again for two years.

One of his happier, quieter memories from around that time was when they'd finished a show in Houston and they went across town to a little club drummer D.J. knew, where Lowell Fulson was playing. Elvis was a fan and had bought Fulson's record of 'Reconsider Baby', so he was thrilled when the blues singer invited them up on stage to jam with him. Watching Scotty and Fulson playing together as he sang was a rare treat. Four years later he returned the compliment and recorded his own version of 'Reconsider Baby'.

When Elvis and the band had begun touring they'd mainly been appearing with hillbilly acts, but, not wanting any other music taking the spotlight off his client, the Colonel now began sending them out with a comedian to keep the audience happy until Elvis came on. It was also a lot cheaper than having to book other musicians.

Whatever faults Parker had, he was meticulous in his details, getting up at 5.30 every morning at his home in Madison, Tennessee, or wherever Elvis was on tour, to plan everything – and usually getting a lot of it right in those early days. Not always, however. He didn't understand the fans who bought the records, so when he booked Elvis into the New Frontier Hotel in Las Vegas for a two-week season, Bill Black wasn't the only one who had his doubts. 'Hell, we'll give them heartburn over their steaks when we come on,' he laughed.

He was right. For the first time in his short career Elvis died every night. They all dressed up for the occasion, the band in bow ties and Elvis in a sports jacket and loafers, but they just couldn't get through to the audience, who were middle-aged to elderly, hardly anyone under thirty-five, anyway, and all sitting at tables. It was a new experience for Elvis to find the bald comedian Phil Silvers, then universally known as Sgt Bilko, in the audience instead of screaming girls. After the shows Elvis would go out into the street to try to puzzle out what they were doing wrong. But it wasn't them, and it wasn't the audience. They just didn't match. Unfortunately, when an audience didn't react he would get nervous and try to get them onside by joking.

'Get out of the stable, Grandma, you're too old to be horsing around,' he would gag. Or, 'Friends, never milk a cow on a rainy day. If lightning strikes you might be left holding the bag.'

The Colonel wasn't there to hear some of this, but when he was told through the William Morris Agency, Elvis got a lecture on not upsetting an audience with barnyard jokes. They were, Parker said, off-colour. Elvis didn't know about that. The audience laughed at the jokes. It was the singing and the songs they didn't go for. So, as they only had to do two shows a night of about twelve minutes each, and there was no travelling involved, he treated Las Vegas like a vacation. Unlike the Colonel, he never gambled, so the slot machines and tables weren't for him. Flirting with the show girls was more fun. And then there was riding the dodgems at the fair all night. He loved Vegas for play, but he didn't work there again for thirteen years, by which time he was getting towards the age of the audience, and thirty-five didn't seem that old after all.

Probably the best thing professionally that came out of those two weeks was that he saw Freddie and the Bellboys a couple of times at the Sands Hotel singing the Big Mama Thornton hit 'Hound Dog'. It's really a woman's song, telling a no-good guy to stop snoopin' around her door, wasting her time and eating her food. But Freddie had changed it around a little by singing, 'you ain't never caught a rabbit and you ain't no friend of mine'.

The lyrics didn't make any sense, but the song sounded to Elvis like the perfect showstopper. So, as soon as he began touring again, which was pretty much the following week, he ended the show with 'Hound Dog' everywhere they went, night after night, right across the Midwest, and then all the way down through California, and it never failed. All the time the screaming was getting louder, so loud now that Scotty said he couldn't hear himself playing any more. And, every day, the accusations by the newspapers were getting sharper.

A second appearance in Los Angeles on *The Milton Berle Show* at the beginning of June seemed to uncork a wave of anger about Elvis that had been building for months. He did 'Hound Dog' without a guitar this time and just let his legs and arms do what they wanted . . . waking up the next day to read newspaper columnists describing him as 'morally degenerate', 'primitive', 'lewd', 'obscene', 'suggestive' and 'vulgar', with one even saying that he looked as though he'd been doing a striptease with his clothes on. They also said, once again, that he couldn't sing, and that he was leading kids, by way of rock and roll, into juvenile delinquency and drug taking. The newspaper barrage went on for weeks, wherever he played. As much as the fans would scream with excitement, newspaper pundits, teachers and preachers would howl with rage. When he called home, Gladys would be unhappy, and NBC were talking about cancelling an appearance he was due to make on *The Steve Allen Show* in New York at the beginning of July. The Colonel kept telling him not to worry, that all publicity was good publicity, but Elvis, still only twenty-one, couldn't not be perturbed by the avalanche of abuse.

Finally, when a reporter followed him into a restaurant, he snapped. They were in Charlotte, North Carolina, and the local newspaper there had just reprinted something really unpleasant about him from the *New York Herald Tribune*. That had really got to him. Debra Paget had been on *The Milton Berle Show*, too, he said, and she'd been a whole lot sexier than he was.

'She'd had feathers on her behind where they wiggle most and she'd bumped and pushed all over the place. I never saw anything like it. I was like Little Boy Blue in comparison. But who did the newspapers say was obscene? Me!'

He then told the reporter straight out that all the newspaper people who were writing bad things about him just didn't understand the music.

'The coloured folks have been singing and playing it just like I do now, man, for more years than I know. They played it like that in their shanties and juke joints and nobody paid it no mind until I goosed it up. I got it from them. Down in Tupelo, Mississippi, I used to hear old Arthur Crudup banging his box the way I do now, and I said if I ever get to the place where I could feel all that old Arthur felt, I'd be a music man like nobody ever saw.'

The reporter was a little surprised, but Elvis hadn't finished.

'When I sing hymns with my parents back home I stand still and look like you feel when you sing hymns. But when I sing this rock and roll, my eyes won't stay open and my legs won't stay still. But I don't care what they say, it ain't nasty.'

Of course that interview got syndicated to a lot more newspapers, too. Elvis had ignored the Colonel's advice not to talk to reporters, and he was glad. He had got a lot off his chest. As Gladys told him: 'No matter what people say, you know who you are. That's all that matters.'

Naturally, NBC didn't cancel his appearance on *The Steve Allen Show*. It had been an idle, publicity-seeking threat. But they made him wear a tuxedo with tails and sing 'Hound Dog' to a basset hound that was tied down. That would soon be against the law as cruelty to animals. At the time it was just cruelty to Elvis. He felt stupid. There was something unpleasant about television in those days. The producers may have thought the dog was just good, family fun. But it was no fun for him. What the snobby writers and some TV people never understood was that this was a serious business for Elvis and his band, that they were doing what they did to the very best of their abilities, trying to get more emotion into a song and more entertainment into a show. It may have sounded like cheap music to the producers, but emotions aren't cheap. It was his intensity that sold his records. It seemed to Elvis that the people who mocked it, and who called the fans who enjoyed it 'idiots', were mocking the kids, too, often their own children. And that was a shame.

'Rock and roll is a healthy thing. You don't have to be doped up to do it,' he would insist, overlooking, perhaps, the odd amphetamine that was helping him along.

Not that it mattered what he said. The pundits weren't listening. He would have to wait a generation before rock and roll would be taken seriously, by which time he wouldn't be singing it so much.

Judging by the reactions he got when he performed 'Hound Dog' on the road, he knew it was a hit when they went into the New York RCA studio the afternoon after *The Steve Allen Show* to record it. Once again he and the band knew it so well it should have been easy, but it took thirty-one takes to get it right. Elvis was in charge in the studio now, so, as he listened to the playback, he kept insisting on one take after another as they tweaked first this and then that, and had the engineer open up the microphone on D.J.'s drums until they sounded like a machine gun.

The Aberbach brothers at Hill and Range had brought along another couple of songs for him to listen to. One was 'Don't Be Cruel', which he did next, almost a cappella, along with the Jordanaires, who were now working with him all the time – so he'd won that battle, too. Normally he tried to put the more obvious hits out separately to double the sales, but 'Hound Dog' and 'Don't Be Cruel' were released on the two sides of the same disc, which made two monster hits on one record, both going to number one. They were both good tracks, and became hits, the size of which neither he, nor anyone else, had ever had before, selling five million copies in the US alone. That wasn't bad for an afternoon's work. It didn't matter now what the newspapers said: the fans adored him.

With every day having been packed for the last six months, he decided to go home from New York to Memphis by train, along with a photographer called Alfred Wertheimer who had been taking pictures of him in the studio for RCA. By this time he'd become so used to being photographed, with flashbulbs popping wherever he went, he hardly noticed him, but it was unfortunate that Wertheimer wasn't with him when he ran into Gene Vincent at Pennsylvania Station as he hurried for the train.

Gene had his first big hit on the charts at the time with 'Be-Bop-A-Lula' and was quickly anxious to tell Elvis that he hadn't been copying him, although he clearly had. Elvis went along with it, and didn't tell him that Gladys, as well as Scotty, Bill and D.J., had all thought it was Elvis singing when they'd first happened to hear 'Be-Bop-A-Lula' on the radio. He didn't mind that Gene had copied him. So far as he was concerned it was a pretty good record whoever was singing it.

After sleeping through the night, they changed trains at Chattanooga and caught the local one. But, keen to get home without too much hoopla, when they halted at a signal stop just outside Memphis, he picked up his bags, climbed down from the train and set off across the fields on foot.

From the day he'd started singing there had always been girls. Some had been serious and some not so serious; some of them even had well-known or semi-famous names, and the newspapers and magazines had hooked on to them hoping to discover some secrets. For the most part, however, the girls he dated weren't well known: whether or not she was famous, a pretty girl was still a pretty girl. Over the years some of the girls kissed and told, and that would disappoint him.

He never talked, though. He tried to stay friends with all his ex-girlfriends, and still kept in touch with Dixie who would write to him now and again. So when he had his home break that summer he called at her house and took her for a ride on his motorbike – making sure they got back early in case her new boyfriend called. Then there was her school friend, Barbara Hearn, and a girl he'd met in Biloxi, June Juanico, whose parents told the newspapers the two were engaged after they'd spent a few days together in New Orleans. They weren't engaged, but Colonel Parker got mad, saying it would ruin Elvis's career if the fans believed the story, reminding him that he'd made him a promise not to get married for three years – something Elvis had no intention of doing, anyway.

A few nights after he got back to Memphis, Parker was complaining again. Elvis had been to a Blackwood Brothers all-night gospel meeting, just like he used to, and had gone up on stage and joined in with them.

'How many times do I have to tell you, you don't sing without a signed contract through me and unless you get paid,' Parker drummed on. 'Do you understand? You don't sing in public for nothing.'

Elvis wasn't surprised. Parker had been unhappy when he'd heard about the Lowell Fulson night out in Houston, too. But after the Blackwoods night he never went up on stage again to join in with anyone. It had been fun, and he'd enjoyed it, but it caused too much aggravation. So he spent most of his month off doing a little water skiing at nearby McKellar Lake, some horse riding at a dude ranch, visiting relatives in Tupelo and taking his parents down to Biloxi, Mississippi for a few days' vacation.

Vernon was loving the new life he was having, with three Cadillacs and a Lincoln parked outside the house in Audubon Drive, so that, he would say, it looked like a 'Presley Used Car Lot'. Sometimes Elvis would be sitting at home when Daddy would suddenly giggle and say: 'What happened, son? The last thing I knew you was driving a little truck. And now . . .'

But Gladys would just sit there, gazing into space, saying over and over: 'I can't believe it. I really can't.'

Elvis couldn't either, but, almost before he knew it, the month was up, and he was back on the road in Florida, where a judge put police deputies on either side of the stage with instructions to arrest him if he moved any part of his body other than his little finger when he sang. So he just moved his little finger, and that drove the girls wild, too.

After which he set off to Hollywood to become a movie star.

12

'Imagine! A Memphis boy with Natalie Wood sitting behind me on my motorbike.'

If Elvis Presley had never existed, the film *Love Me Tender* would still have been made. But it would have been called *The Reno Brothers* and wouldn't have had any songs in it. The story going around Hollywood in the summer of 1956 was that *The Reno Brothers* was a cheap, black and white, quickie B-picture that was on the brink of shooting, when Elvis was suddenly parachuted in to play a younger brother, Clint Reno. That called for a quick rewrite of the screenplay, four new songs and a new title. The melodies of the four songs were all in the public domain, with the tune to 'Love Me Tender' going right back to the Civil War, when it was called 'Aura Lee'. It had also been used as recently as a couple of years earlier when it had been the background theme in another Western.

So, when Ken Darby, the Twentieth Century Fox musical director on *Love Me Tender*, put lyrics to the tune (under his wife's name of Vera Matson) and made it into a hit, he was utilising an already proven melody. The other name on the song credits was that of Elvis himself, when Julian and Jean Aberbach insisted that Elvis should be listed as a co-writer, as they had on 'Don't Be Cruel'. Elvis would candidly admit he hadn't written a word or a note of either song. But, then, neither had Vera Matson. The attribution of songwriting credits to Elvis occurred several times early in his career, until, embarrassed by it, he asked that it be stopped. It seemed deceitful to take credit for anything he hadn't done.

'I've never written a song in my life,' he would say. 'It's all a big hoax.'

Nevertheless his songwriting company still took a half share of the songwriters' royalties, from which he, the Colonel and the Aberbachs all benefited. That was the way the music business worked; the way it often still does.

The songs were recorded at Twentieth Century Fox before shooting began, with Scotty, Bill and D.J. flying out to Los Angeles to accompany Elvis. They needn't have bothered. The movie's producers thought they weren't hillbilly enough, which was news to Scotty and Bill who'd been in a hillbilly band when Elvis had met them. Instead Fox provided some local Los Angeles session musicians and Elvis did the best he could. He always liked one song, 'We're Gonna Move', as it was an old spiritual tune, but only 'Love Me Tender' sounded anything like a hit.

In fact the lyrics and tune to 'Love Me Tender' were so simple he knew, when he was recording it, that it couldn't fail. But when, after just two takes, the producer was satisfied, he wasn't. Listening to the playback, he thought he might occasionally have sounded a little flat and wanted to do it again. But nobody else thought that, and, as he didn't have the muscle at Twentieth Century Fox that he now had at RCA, he was overruled. He didn't make a fuss about it. That was that. A little flat or not, he had one of his most enduring hits with a tune that was a hundred years old.

'Until then a lot of people thought all I could do was belt,' he would say, when the record got to number one.

One of those who had probably thought that was actor Dennis Hopper. An up-and-coming Hollywood hopeful, he'd wheedled his way into the session and had stood, he said, 'about ten yards behind Elvis in the studio to see how he worked'. When he suddenly heard the playback coming over the speakers, however, he was astonished. He might have been close to Elvis, but he hadn't even heard him singing. 'Love Me Tender' is a quiet song. Elvis had sung into the microphone at just about the level he would if he'd been saying those words to a girl. That was why it worked, and that was why Hopper hadn't heard.

Shooting his part in the movie took less than three weeks, and Elvis had read the script so often and was so keen to impress that he'd memorised all the other actors' parts, too. Debra Paget, whom he'd met on *The Steve Allen Show* a few weeks earlier, was playing the female lead, and, although he hung around her throughout the entire shoot, she obviously wasn't interested in him. Later he read that she'd assumed he was 'a moron' before they'd worked together, and that she had then been 'pleasantly surprised' when she discovered he wasn't. Obviously she hadn't been pleasantly surprised enough.

Just five years earlier he'd been a cinema usher after school, and now here he was appearing in a movie himself. He was, he would say later, 'totally green' about movie production, but it got better when he discovered that the producer, David Weisbart, had produced the James Dean film *Rebel Without a Cause* the year before. Weisbart was patient as he questioned him about Dean, and then introduced him to Nick Adams, who, along with Dennis Hopper, had played one of the high school gang in *Rebel*. After that, in the way these things go, Adams took Natalie Wood, the female lead in *Rebel*, to the singer's suite in the Beverly Wilshire hotel. Rock and roll was a small world, and now, Elvis began to realise, so was Hollywood. One connection just led to another. Looking back he didn't suppose 'Mad Nat', as he would privately come to call her, was that impressed when he quoted Dean's dialogue to her, but it was his turn to be a fan.

Although his name and image would be all over the poster, his part in *Love Me Tender* was actually fairly small, so he had time to make a new album in the evenings at Radio Recorders studio on Sunset Boulevard while in Hollywood. The RCA strategy was simply to flood the market with Elvis records before the fans bored of him, so this was his second album of the year. And with all his Sun singles now available on his new label, seven more singles were released in one day while he was filming. The result was that he simultaneously had nine records in the Hot Hundred. Nothing like this had ever happened to anyone before.

Putting out so many records, however, meant he was always short of new material and the best track for the new album, a Jerry Leiber and Mike Stoller song called 'Love Me', was rushed out on an EP as soon as it was recorded, meaning it was soon fighting it out in the charts with 'Love Me Tender'. More time to find new songs and decide how to record them was needed, but time was something he didn't have, and in the end the second album was filled out with three Little Richard covers. Little Richard songs always went down well on tour, but they were his hits, not Elvis's.

One hit he did miss, because he hadn't had time to listen to the demo the publisher had sent him, was 'Don't Forbid Me', which became a big seller for his rival Pat Boone instead. He liked Boone's version, and loved Boone's voice, but wished he'd heard the song first, suspecting it had been written with him in mind.

If it was overkill in the recording studio it was pretty much the same on television. Ed Sullivan had always said he wouldn't have Elvis on his show at any price, but when Sullivan was injured in a car accident, CBS hired the actor Charles Laughton as a stand-in presenter.

'Music hath charms to soothe a savage breast . . .' Laughton quoted in his big theatrical voice before Elvis sang 'Love Me Tender' for the first time on TV. Without Sullivan, but with Elvis, Sullivan's show got the most viewers of any show in television history.

Elvis had been back to Tupelo many times since he'd left with his family when he was thirteen, but he'd never performed there. So when an invitation came for him to appear at the Mississippi-Alabama Fair and Dairy Show – the venue where he'd first sung 'Old Shep' – there was no way he was going to miss it. The show was on 26 September 1956, the mayor named it 'Elvis Presley Day' and the town was dizzy with excitement. With a parade going through the streets and reporters arriving from all over the world, Movietone filmed the entire afternoon performance.

Knowing that almost everyone he knew from junior school would be there trying to fathom out how he'd gone from being that shy, skinny little kid to this famous star who was being condemned by the newspapers (except, obviously, the *Tupelo Daily Journal*), was a special thrill for Tupelo's most famous son. And, of course, Gladys and Vernon were there as well as several Mississippi relations.

Altogether it was quite a homecoming, with old friends popping up all day – including Vernon's former boss at L.P. McCarty, the grocery wholesaler, who, by firing him eight years earlier, had prompted the move to Memphis and Elvis's eventual success. Vernon wasn't one to hold a grudge. He was pleased to see the guy again, to show him how well they'd done.

Gladys didn't see it in quite the same way. 'It makes me feel bad coming back here like this to remember how poor we was,' she said.

Elvis put on a special show that day, although he could hardly hear himself. It was staged outside in the Fairgrounds in front of a large marquee, and, as he sang in the afternoon show, he could see, over in the background, a long freight train rolling past. No one minded, least of all him. He was wearing white buck shoes, and a dark blue velvet shirt that Natalie Wood had given him, but which Gladys had had to alter to make it fit.

The Mississippi National Guard surrounded the stage for the evening show, but, as he was finishing 'Hound Dog', the girls rushed forward. Fearing a riot, Elvis and the band had to drop through a trap door at the back of the stage and were in a police car before the fans had realised. Encores were now never possible after his shows. One day an announcer would tell the fans over a loudspeaker, 'Elvis has left the building', so that they would know that the show was over, and it was time for them to go home. But not yet.

Gladys hadn't been to many of her son's recent appearances and was shocked by how hysterical the fans had become, and was now becoming increasingly scared that one day Elvis would get hurt. She just couldn't become accustomed to the way life had changed for them.

'Elvis, the Colonel is going to work you to your death. It ain't right,' she would say repeatedly.

It wasn't right and it never would be, but Elvis wasn't complaining. As he would tell reporters when they asked him how he felt about suddenly becoming a millionaire: 'The Lord giveth and the Lord taketh away. I might be herding sheep next year.' They would laugh, but he meant it, if not quite the herding sheep part. He would never be able to believe the success he'd had, so he never turned down work, and Parker made sure the offers kept coming. Never taking a vacation from work, the Colonel didn't see why anyone else should either.

As soon as the Tupelo show was over, Elvis was off hopping around the country again, pausing only to visit Los Angeles and have his teeth capped for the second time. His parents hadn't had money to spend on dentists and braces when he'd been a boy, but the big screen demanded a brilliant smile, so more work had to be done. It was important that Elvis Presley, now a movie star, had perfectly even teeth, which he would brush obsessively several times a day for the rest of his life.

It was back to the studio next to record another verse to the 'Love Me Tender' title song. Twentieth Century Fox had given a sneak preview of the movie and some audiences had been upset when his character had died at the end. So, the plan now was that his ghost would show over the end titles, singing a few more lines of the song to reassure fans that he was all right, really. After which it was a short tour of Texas, and then up to New York for the second *Ed Sullivan Show*. This time, Sullivan was there himself, eating his words, shaking Elvis's hand and being friendly and complimentary. It was amazing, Elvis must have thought, how quickly TV people changed their minds about him when they saw their ratings go up when he was on their shows.

Equally amazing was the number of American children whose parents took them to be given the Salk polio vaccine after Elvis was photographed being vaccinated the day following the Sullivan show; a total of 84 per cent of the US child population would receive the jab within six months.

Then it was back down to Memphis to meet Natalie Wood off the plane from Los Angeles. He was used to girls following him around, but Natalie was a movie star, and he was flattered that she'd come all the way from California. So, he took the chance to show her off, taking her to Guthrie Park to watch him playing football with Red West and friends, then riding her around town on the back of his Harley-Davidson, hoping people would see them together. 'Imagine!' he would joke to his friends. 'A Memphis boy with Natalie Wood sitting behind me on my motorbike.' And when he took her in to see Dewey Phillips, the usually ultra-verbose disc jockey could hardly speak for surprise.

So, yes, he was star struck. To him, and a whole generation of young people, Natalie was the girl who had stood between the revving cars and brought her arms down to start the chicken run in *Rebel Without a Cause*. Some movie scenes you never forget, and Elvis had dreams that he would be appearing in a movie like that before very long.

What Natalie thought about Elvis and his parents when she met them in Memphis, she never said. They were from different worlds, and Gladys wasn't exactly impressed with Natalie and the way she went around the house in front of Vernon and Elvis and his new pal

Nick Adams wearing just a skimpy nightdress. The builders working on the refurbishments to the house couldn't but notice, either.

Natalie had planned to stay for a week but left after three days, on a made-up excuse. It was a relief to everyone when she went. She was only eighteen and had only just finished high school herself, but she'd been a child actress in Hollywood virtually all her life. While Elvis had been catching dogfish in Mud Creek in Tupelo, she'd been appearing in *Miracle on 34th Street* with Maureen O'Hara at Twentieth Century Fox. So it was normal that she seemed older, and more sophisticated, and, yes, that she was also a lot more sexually experienced than he was. He'd been told that after they'd met in Los Angeles she'd thought he was slow. He probably was with her.

The fans waiting outside the house, and they were always there, morning until night, were glad to see her go, too. They didn't like sharing Elvis, and especially not with anyone so famous. Sharing him with his family was something different.

But even the closest families have their strains and pressures. And just because they weren't all cooped up in a two-room apartment any more didn't mean there wasn't the odd fraught moment. Gladys may have been timid in public, but at home she would go on at Vernon when she got mad, and Daddy would just hang his head. Elvis was sure the fans outside must have heard her sometimes.

Then Vernon would chastise Elvis over some extravagance or other as though he was twelve years old, and Elvis always went out of his way to be extravagant. To his way of thinking, money was for spending and giving.

'Son,' Vernon would say on a regular basis, as he waved some new bill in front of Elvis's eyes, 'you gonna spend us all bankrupt.'

Knowing the poverty his father came from, Elvis understood the fretting, and sometimes it was funny, considering how much he was earning. But Vernon, who was famously tight with money, could become tiresome when he went on about it for too long.

On one occasion when Elvis had just returned from a tour he went out with his cousin Harold Lloyd to buy records in Memphis and came back with a bag of guitar picks, too. You might call them the tools of his trade. They couldn't have cost more than a few dollars, but that wasn't Vernon's point. Why on earth did Elvis want to keep buying guitar picks, when the house was full of them, he wanted to know. He was spending money as though it grew on trees.

So, in front of Harold, Elvis explained that he had bought them because he was always either breaking them or throwing them out to the fans as souvenirs. People stole them, too, but they didn't cost much, so it didn't really matter.

It mattered to Vernon. Elvis was just 'a-wasting money', he said. 'Just a-wasting money.'

Gladys and Grandma, meanwhile, were listening to this exchange with a smile on their faces. They knew Vernon, and they knew Elvis.

Normally Elvis would have just shrugged, but on this occasion Vernon went on and on until he really riled his son.

Finally Elvis said: 'Daddy, you took care of me and Mama when I was little, and you worked hard and I'm grateful that you did. But now it's my turn and I'm taking care of you. But if I want a guitar pick, I'll buy one. If I want a truck full of guitar picks I'll buy it. In fact I might even buy myself a factory of guitar picks if I have a mind. And if I do, it's none of your damned business. It's my money and I'll do whatever I want with it. So don't ever talk to me about guitar picks again.'

Vernon did, of course, but not that night. Living with your parents when you're a fully grown person can have its tensions. But as far as Elvis was concerned, it was worth having a few little angry words now and again, if it meant they would all stay together. That was what he always wanted.

13

'I hate to get started in these jam sessions because I'm always the last one to leave.'

The big event for Elvis in the autumn of 1956 was the rush release of *Love Me Tender*. James Dean's last film, *Giant*, was released a week later, having taken a year to edit since his death: Elvis's film took just a few weeks to cut. Like RCA, Hollywood was cashing in on him while his appeal lasted. But, then, he was cashing in, too, while praying that it would last for ever.

He'd seen the picture before it came out, and he called in at a movie theatre in Memphis a couple more times to sit with the audience and watch it – going in late and leaving early before the fans spotted him.

At first he didn't think he'd done too badly. Because of who he was, he was expecting a scorching from the critics: he was now too big a target for them to miss. But quite a few took careful aim to hurt. And although the Colonel kept telling him that it didn't matter what the critics said, that the movie had made its money back in two weeks, he would have been telling lies if he'd said that some of the barbs didn't hurt. He was used to reading that he couldn't sing and that he was like the Pied Piper leading kids into drugs and sex. He could handle that, because he knew it wasn't true. But reading some of the reviews of *Love Me Tender* was hard. All right, so the movie was a 'horse opera', which he supposed was a way of saying it was a Western. But was he really 'a 172 pound six foot tall sausage' (he was actually only about 160 pounds), 'a goldfish', and did his voice really sound like 'a rusty foghorn'? Had that been printed in a newspaper in Maine or Oregon or the middle of Africa he wouldn't have minded too much, but it was in the *Los Angeles Times*, and he knew that everybody in the film industry would see it and laugh. Rock and roll singers had feelings, too.

Before very long he began to believe he shouldn't have been in the movie at all. The Colonel had just wanted to get him into something, anything, quickly and this had been the one available. It had always seemed to him that all the top actors in movies just played themselves, but in *Love Me Tender* he couldn't do that because the character he was portraying was 'so far from me it wasn't even funny'. He knew his way around a song and a recording studio, but he had a lot to learn about movies.

Thankfully, his breakthrough year of 1956 was finally winding down and after doing a hundred and ninety-one shows in over sixty towns and cities around the country, driving or flying hundreds of thousands of miles, making nine national television appearances, recording thirty-five new songs and making a movie he was given a few weeks off to go home.

When he got there, however, he didn't quite know what to do with himself. He wasn't used to having time on his hands. So it was a relief one afternoon when, cruising down Union Avenue in the new Cadillac he'd just bought, showing a girl he'd met in Las Vegas the place he used to record, he saw three or four other Cadillacs, each one a different colour, parked at an angle to the street outside Sun Records. They looked, as Marion Keisker would say, 'like nothing so much as a row of roosters perched on a fence', and he just had to call in and see what was going on in there. Adding his Cadillac to the line, he went inside.

It was good to be back at Sun. A session with Carl Perkins and his brothers, with new boy Jerry Lee Lewis helping out on piano, had just finished; and there was Sam Phillips welcoming his discovery home and beaming at them all like a proud father as he sent out for some coffee and doughnuts from Taylor's café next door. For Elvis, after months of being the centre of the entire nation's attention, it was like just being a member of the gang again, and it was good to see Carl recovered after the car crash.

Quickly they all got talking, and, as always when musicians get together, it wasn't long before they did their talking through the songs they knew, Elvis mainly at the piano, despite Jerry Lee's presence, as they all sang and played together. They spent hours at it, mainly gospel songs at first, then some Bill Monroe country songs that they all knew from the Grand Ole Opry, before they got to Chuck Berry's 'Brown Eyed Handsome Man', which Elvis would always plan to record and never get round to, and 'Too Much Monkey Business', which he would. He just loved the cleverness of Berry's lyrics.

He'd been to see his favourites Billy Ward and the Dominoes in Las Vegas a couple of weeks earlier, and he now told his friends how he'd gone back four nights in a row because 'there was a coloured guy with them singing "Don't Be Cruel" much better' than he did on his record. So he sang it slower for them the way the Dominoes guy had done it, the way he now wished he'd recorded it. He discovered later that the singer had been Jackie Wilson. He would be a fan ever after.

Sam Phillips was tickled to see all his boys together, so he called Johnny Cash, who had just had 'I Walk the Line' on the charts, and got a photographer over from the *Memphis Press-Scimitar* to take their picture. Johnny then left to do some Christmas shopping.

For Elvis it was like going back in time to a moment before he'd become the famous Elvis Presley, when he'd hang out in the studio for the sheer joy of it.

'I hate to get started in these jam sessions because I'm always the last one to leave,' he said as they had to finish and he got up from the piano.

He meant it. He'd stopped having to play the big star for a few hours and had enjoyed himself. In this studio they were all more or less equal.

Perhaps he thought about that on the way home, and reflected that, as sweet as fame was, it was also a jail, except that he wasn't locked in, he was locked out – cut off from any kind of normal life. He was trapped. It was less than a year since he'd recorded 'Heartbreak Hotel', but people were now saying he was the second most famous man in America after the president. Music and television had catapulted him to an instant, previously unimaginable fame. His life had changed for ever. He'd got what he wanted, he was rich and adored, and hardly ever without a beautiful girl at his side – even on this drive home through Memphis. His music was the sound of the youth of America; his image its totem. He was the young man who every boy with a guitar wanted to be; the boy half the teenage girls wanted for their own. There had never been a fame quite like his for one so young, probably for anyone. It was all too much, so overwhelming, sometimes so hysterical, that it was difficult for him to comprehend. Everything seemed possible. Best of all, he was supporting his parents now, as he'd always promised he would. They even had their own maid – Alberta Holman, who had been a colleague when she and Gladys had worked together at Britling's Cafeteria in Memphis.

But he couldn't be invisible any more. Mixing with the public like anybody else was becoming impossible. 'Don't hide,' Jackie Gleason had told him. It was sometimes hard not to want to. Just a couple of weeks earlier he'd been at a gas station when a bunch of fans had shown up. That had been okay, until the attendant had asked him to move along. Then somehow it had all turned ugly, and the attendant had pulled out a knife. So Elvis had socked him.

'It was either hit or be hit,' he said. 'I can stand slander and ridicule, but if necessary I can take care of myself, too.'

The cops had been there within a couple of minutes and he'd been arrested and made to appear in court. The charges of assault and battery had been dropped, but it had been a lesson to him on how quickly things could get out of hand. It was now getting so that he felt he couldn't go outside his house without causing some kind of fuss. And, as he drove back to Audubon Drive and found the usual carnival of fans waiting outside his new home, he wondered if life would always be like this.

Sam hadn't said much while he'd been at Sun that afternoon, which was unusual for him, but halfway through their carousing he must have quietly asked Jack Clement, his engineer, to slip a seven-inch tape into his Ampex tape recorder. Because, a few days later, a recording of the afternoon's singing was delivered to Audubon Drive as a kind of early Christmas present. The Colonel would have been in a fury if he'd known that his client had been singing at Sun again, and that Sam had recorded him, so Elvis made sure he didn't know.

He probably didn't tell him either how, a couple of nights later, an old high school friend, George Klein, took him to a charity review of what was called 'all Negro talent' that a Memphis radio station was putting on. Rufus Thomas was the disc jockey and B.B. King was on the bill along with 'Mystery Train' writer Little Junior Parker, Ray Charles and the Moonglows, who were a doo-wop group he liked. It was quite a line-up. This being 1956 it was a segregated show, so he stayed in the wings. But when they coaxed him on stage at the end of the night the audience were as pleased to see him as he'd been to see Ray Charles and Little Junior Parker. Those fellows had written two of the songs that had started his career. He would still be singing 'I Got a Woman' twenty years later.

He knew there were some people who were accusing him of stealing black music by recording so many rhythm and blues songs. He didn't understand that at all. R and b was just some of the music he loved. And he knew, too, that there were people who called him a 'white nigger' because of the way he sang and what he sang. He didn't understand that either. At one point, an ugly rumour had begun going around that he'd said to someone in Boston that 'the only thing Negroes can do for me is buy my records and shine my shoes'. He'd been upset by that. Angry. 'People who know me, know I wouldn't have said that,' he told reporters. It just wasn't true. Besides, he'd never even been to Boston.

But then there were a lot of things said and written about him that year that weren't true. It seemed that it was just another part of the price of being Elvis.

14

'I wish we was poor again, I really do.'

Gladys Presley

They had a good Christmas in their first house on Audubon Drive. A pretty dancer Elvis had met in Las Vegas called Dottie Harmony stayed with them, and they put up a big, white nylon Christmas tree with lights, too many lights, and had lots to eat and more than enough presents for everyone. There were gold records, too, some still unpacked, and a house full of teddy bears that had been sent after the Colonel had commented publicly that Elvis must like them, having won so many at fairgrounds.

Every night Elvis sang hymns and carols with Gladys and Vernon as they'd always done in Tupelo – but with him now sitting at a baby organ. He had his own poolroom, too, for when his cousins and friends came round, and the guys played touch football one morning just after Christmas without managing to cause a riot.

But not everything was right. By inviting Dottie to stay, he'd managed to upset two of his other current girlfriends, June and Barbara. This kind of thing was happening all the time as he had girlfriends everywhere he went, and he was falling in love, he said, 'at least once a week'. Many, though not all, of these relationships were no-sex crushes – in those days the girls called it being 'gentlemanly', which he actually rather liked. Maybe a little petting, well, quite a bit of heavy petting with some of them, but, if a girl didn't want to, or was a virgin, he was happy with that. He wanted to marry a virgin, so he put girls who said 'no' on a little pedestal.

But something else was worrying him. Like every other young male American of his age, the draft was hanging over him. And although it was reassuring to be classified '1-A' when he went for a medical assessment at the beginning of January 1957, and perhaps not insulting to be told that he was of 'average intelligence', and therefore not the total dunce some newspaper columnists were suggesting, it also meant he might soon be called up. Actually, it was pretty certain. If the military didn't take him it would have looked as if he was somehow being allowed to dodge the draft. And the Memphis draft board wouldn't want to do that. But when would it be? He didn't know. He said a silent prayer: 'Please God, not yet.'

As far as his career went, television had done its job in getting him to where he was, but already the Colonel was planning a new strategy. He wouldn't be letting the fans see Elvis for free any more, which they did when he was on television. They would have to pay, and that way was through movies. So Elvis took one final trip to New York by train for his last appearance on *The Ed Sullivan Show*.

Travelling with him were his cousins Junior and Gene Smith, and Scotty, Bill and D.J. as well as the Jordanaires. It was like a presidential tour as, looking out of the train window, he could see fans standing at the stations along the line, hoping to get a glimpse of him. When the train stopped at one station some young girls got on and sat near to him, asking him to autograph everything they had for themselves and their school friends. Then they got off at the next stop.

When they got to CBS in New York, policemen on horses had blocked off the streets all around the studio, and Ed Sullivan was now behaving as though he'd discovered Elvis himself. Not only did CBS virtually make the show over to Elvis and let him sing seven songs, including 'Peace in the Valley' from his new EP of hymns, Sullivan even described him as 'a real decent, fine boy' before turning to him and adding, 'We've never had a pleasanter experience with a big name than we've had with you.' Sullivan had certainly changed his tune, but that didn't stop CBS, probably encouraged by the Colonel, grabbing jokey newspaper headlines the next day by shooting Elvis only from the waist up. Elvis didn't care. The fans got the joke and that was all that mattered.

Then it was back to Memphis and Audubon Drive. Now, though, things there were beginning to turn ugly. When they'd first moved into their house, Gladys had welcomed the fans, giving them glasses of lemonade or water when they'd asked, and sometimes letting them use the phone to call home and tell their parents where they were. And when the pool was finished she'd invited some of the neighbours round to cool off on hot days. Theirs was the only house with a pool in the street. But over the following few months, their address had become public property and fans were now turning up in their hundreds, blocking the road with their cars, and preventing the neighbours getting into their drives. At first some of the fans had practically set up camp on their front lawn, which had become churned up with clumps of grass torn out as souvenirs. So Vernon had had a wall built. But then the kids just climbed over the wall to write messages in lipstick on Elvis's cars. There was even an ice-cream van out there in the street at weekends and another man selling hot dogs. By now the neighbours were constantly calling the police, asking them to clear the road and get the kids to turn down the music on their car radios.

When he was home, Elvis was happy to sign autographs until it went dark, because he did actually enjoy the fans' company. And when, after shows, they seemed to be trying to tear the shirt off his back, he would joke, 'well, they paid for it'. But it was now tough on his parents to find themselves virtually marooned inside their home every day, with the shades permanently drawn for privacy.

What really upset him, though, was the reaction of some of the neighbours. At first they'd all been welcoming, excited to have someone famous living alongside them. Most were middle-management, professional families who were proud of their new homes and of how well they were doing in life. And some had invited the Presleys round to their places and been thoroughly neighbourly. But there were others who weren't so nice. He could sympathise with anyone for objecting to all the noise and traffic. They hadn't reckoned on that when they'd bought their homes. But then some of them began to complain about Gladys hanging out her washing, with her underclothes on a clothesline in the garden, and having her relatives from Tupelo to stay.

'It's like she's still living down in Mississippi,' some began to whisper. 'She's dragging the neighbourhood down with her trashy relatives.'

Daddy didn't give a damn what anyone thought, but, when the rumour got around that a couple of neighbours were putting together a petition requesting that the Presleys move out of Audubon Drive, Gladys was upset. And when one day Elvis overheard her on the phone to a friend she'd had in Lauderdale Courts and saying, 'I wish we was poor again, I really do', it broke his heart.

'Our house is the only one paid in full around here,' he repeated, when asked by reporters about the petition. But he'd already made up his mind. If the neighbours didn't want them in Audubon Drive, they wouldn't stay. They would go and live somewhere where they didn't have any neighbours, and where Mama could hang out her washing on the line just like she used to when he was a little boy, and where she could have the chicken run and fresh eggs she'd always wanted. So he told her and Daddy to start looking around for a mansion somewhere where they could live in peace and quiet without upsetting the neighbours, and without the neighbours upsetting Mama.

Then he and the band took the train to Los Angeles on his twenty-second birthday for the start of his second movie. They even had a party on the way, complete with cake and candles. He was travelling by train a great deal now. He'd been scared when the hired plane had nearly run out of fuel that time when flying into Nashville, but, more importantly, Gladys hated him flying. Always the dutiful son, if it meant that she would worry less, and if he could fit it into his schedule, he'd take the train. And, as those long journeys to and from California took a very long time, it gave him both time to think and an opportunity to catch up on sleep, which he didn't often get.

Hal Wallis, who in twenty-five years in Hollywood had created some film classics, was producing the next Elvis Presley movie himself. And, as he wanted the character Elvis was playing to be as much like Elvis as possible, he'd sent the screenwriter, Hal Kanter, who was also the director, to spend some days with the family in Memphis. The songs were stronger this time, with the Aberbachs' cousin, Freddy Bienstock, having asked all the Hill and Range writers to pitch for the slots in the movie. In this way Elvis got another song from Jerry Leiber and Mike Stoller, whose 'Hound Dog' and 'Love Me' he'd turned into hits. This time it was a ballad called 'Loving You', which was so good it became the film's title. Wallis's plan was that Elvis would record all the songs on a soundstage at Paramount, the way they made Hollywood musicals. But a soundstage wasn't where Elvis liked to work. He'd discovered that on 'Love Me Tender'. The sound wasn't right and neither was the feel, as people kept walking in and out, just to take a look at him, breaking into his and the band's concentration when they did.

The way Hal Wallis saw it, notes would be written down in an arrangement, then the musicians would play, Elvis would sing, and that would be that. But Elvis and the boys didn't do it that way. Playing by ear, they all improvised constantly, everything being worked out spontaneously and nothing really rehearsed. So for several days they struggled on the Paramount soundstage until in the end Wallis relented and let them go back to Radio Recorders. He even went to watch them work, as they tried songs one way and then another until they were happy with how they wanted to record them. It was, as with Elvis's experience with the Dorseys, a generational problem, but to give Wallis his due, he admitted that he found it fascinating to see how they put a record together and he didn't interfere again.

One good thing to come out of those sessions was that Elvis got to know the assistant music director at Paramount, a black pianist from Los Angeles called Dudley Brooks who'd worked with Lionel Hampton and Duke Ellington. Showing Elvis a thing or two at the piano, Brooks became Elvis's pianist whenever he recorded in Hollywood, from then right through until 1963. Brooks' background was jazz, but he could play anything, and was good at rock and roll, too. And when they'd finished the songs for the movie he stayed on and played on Elvis's covers of Fats Domino's 'Blueberry Hill' and a rhythm and blues hit, the Smiley Lewis song 'One Night'.

Originally intended as a filler track for the *Loving You* album, when recorded 'One Night' sounded like a possible hit single, until someone mentioned that with those lyrics it would never get played on the Top Forty radio stations.

'One night of sin, is what I'm now paying for, the things I did and I saw', it went, which, although pretty unspecific, sounded dirty.

So, with Baptist ministers and Catholic nuns lining up to take shots at Elvis, it was put to one side until the Aberbachs got permission from the publisher for someone to clean up the words. When Elvis recorded it again later in the year with non-sexy lyrics, it became one of his biggest hits.

His hair, Elvis had always thought, was his crowning glory, but now a Paramount hairdresser had a suggestion to make. On black and white television and in newspaper photographs the pomade he put on it made it look darker than it was. But *Loving You* would be in Technicolor. If he wanted his hair to look dark, why not just dye it black? Yes, why not! So, black it became, after which he never had the confidence to let it go back to its natural colour.

Whether that was good or bad, he didn't know, but he became famous for looking a certain way, and it would become difficult to change. Because he didn't want to disappoint people, his image would become frozen in time until he was almost an impersonation of himself. One aspect of being Elvis Presley meant that he had to look the way Elvis Presley fans expected him to look.

So, with his hair now jet black, and not so greasy any more, shooting on *Loving You*, with its plot about a boy who becomes a rock and roll star, got under way. Lizabeth Scott, who played his manager, and Wendell Corey, who filled the role as her cynical but funny husband, were very helpful, and the love interest was a pretty little girl making her first movie called Dolores Hart. Just eighteen, Dolores was the niece of tenor Mario Lanza, and every time Elvis sang on the set she would go and watch. She breathed innocence, but, all the same, a few years later, it was a surprise when Elvis heard that she'd given up Hollywood and become a nun in an enclosed convent. He was serious about his religion, but Dolores must have been on a whole other level with hers.

Off camera there were other girls, of course. Scotty, Bill and D.J. were older than he was and married, but he was a young, single guy in Hollywood and he wanted to enjoy himself. It might have sounded perfect, but not everything was right, however. He'd already got to know a few young actors in Los Angeles, guys like Dennis Hopper, Sal Mineo, Nick Adams and Russ Tamblyn, but he always felt they were interested in him because of his fame as a singer. He had nothing in common with them. He was acting in movies, but he wasn't being treated like any other actor on or off the set. Sometimes he felt as though he was trespassing by even being in Hollywood. And although, like other actors, he was invited to premieres and other movie functions, he rarely went. It would only have provoked a riot. His enormous fame, once again, was locking him out.

So, instead of joining the Hollywood young scene, he kept to himself, and gradually began to build his own little gang to hang out with, guys he could trust, cousins who'd known him all his life, friends who came from the same Memphis background. Red West had been the first, but now that Red was in the Marines, Junior and Gene Smith, the sons of his mother's brother, Travis, had stepped in as bodyguards and gofers. What Elvis needed was loyalty. He knew that some of his girlfriends didn't like some of the guys. They called them hangers-on and thought some of them were crude and talked dirty, and some of them were and did. Some movie directors didn't like them either, one dismissing them as 'fart catchers'. But Elvis got used to having them around, doing things for him, keeping the world away when he wanted it kept away, and basically being there as paid, or often unpaid, companions. With all their expenses covered, and girls galore, being with Elvis wasn't a bad life for a young man with few career prospects.

Some of them would go with him to the studio when he was recording, but they weren't involved when he was making records. He asked the advice of Scotty, Bill and D.J., or the Jordanaires for that, but didn't give a damn what his cousins thought. They always said they liked everything he recorded, anyway. Vernon never cared for them and thought some were a bad influence, but Vernon had never been Elvis Presley. No one had. No one other than him had any idea what it was like to be the centre of everything the whole time, to have people taking your photograph or shouting and waving at you whenever you went out, and strangers phoning you so much you had to keep changing your number every week. No one could ever meet him now for the first time without just staring, tongue-tied. Neither Daddy nor anyone else had any idea what it was like to be worshipped and adored for just being him. As the words of his song said, 'I was the one'. And he was. There was no one with whom he could share the experience of being Elvis Presley.

Kings and queens must have had that feeling in olden days, he might sometimes have reflected, which was why they surrounded themselves with courtiers and flunkeys, and probably fart catchers, too. And he was a king now. At least that was what *Variety* was saying. 'Elvis Presley, the King of Rock and Roll.' It was, he thought, another dumb title like 'Elvis the Pelvis'. Rock and roll didn't have a king and didn't need one. It was just music, the kids' music. Already people were telling him that he'd changed the world, but, to him, that was foolish talk. All he'd done was sing.

'Just because I managed to do a little something, I don't want people back home to think I've got the big head,' he told a reporter.

Loving You required him to do a lot more acting than he'd done in *Love Me Tender*, but what everyone would remember later were the songs, especially the end sequence of 'Got a Lot of Livin' to Do', when he moved off the stage into the aisle of the theatre as he was singing. All the fans quickly noticed that sitting on the end of the third row were his parents. As he mimed to the playback of the song, he could sense Gladys gazing up at him, but he didn't dare look down and catch her eye because it would have put him off. When she saw herself in the finished film, she told him that she thought she looked fat, but he knew that she and Daddy were thrilled to be in a movie. That was what she'd dreamed about when she was a girl.

After he'd finished shooting for the day, he introduced his parents to everybody; Hal Wallis, Lizabeth Scott and Wendell Corey. They loved Hollywood, and, without embarrassment, he loved showing them around. He was proud of them and sorry to see them go home.

They hadn't been back in Memphis more than a couple of days before they called with some good news. They'd been out driving, Vernon said, and they'd seen a house they thought he might like. It was just outside Memphis, on the road down to Mississippi. It was called Graceland.

15

He was rich, he was flash

As soon as he got home from Hollywood he drove his parents out down Highway 51 to Graceland. It was in Whitehaven, about eight miles south of downtown Memphis, and, in those days, out in the country. Seeing the house from the road, and then going up the long, curving driveway between big, old oak trees he assumed it was an antebellum house, maybe a hundred years old. But it was actually younger than he was. Only built in 1939, by 1957 it was in a pitiful state. On the site of a former cattle ranch, the windows were broken and there were holes in the walls, while the gardens, and the thirteen acres that went with it – some of it pasture – were overgrown. It looked as though teenagers had been breaking in and holding parties and roasting hot dogs in the downstairs rooms, too, and the word was that the YMCA wanted to buy it to turn it into a hostel. There wasn't much call for houses of that size around Memphis.

Then Elvis came along and loved it from the moment he saw it. There was enough space to do anything he wanted, and, with seven bedrooms, he and his parents could invite any relatives and friends to stay. There would be no problem upsetting the neighbours, either, because there weren't any, and the fans could be kept a hundred yards away behind the walls of the estate. He put $1000 down that day and bought it for $102,500 three weeks later, a little less than half of that being on a twenty-five-year mortgage.

Everything needed a lot of work, renovations and redecorating, and he put Vernon in charge while he was away earning the money to pay for it all. He had a pool dug in the garden, although he wasn't fond of swimming, a real soda fountain installed in the basement, and a chicken coop and a hog pen put behind the house.

He rarely stopped making changes from the moment he moved in.

He liked to sleep during the day and come out for work and play at night, so he wanted his bedroom to be in the darkest midnight blue with matching dark curtains in order that the sunlight wouldn't wake him. Then he had a huge nine-foot-square bed specially made. His mother wanted a mail box by the gate at the front of their house, so they had one made and installed, but someone stole it as a souvenir a few days later. The big, iron electronically operated gates with musical notes at the end of the drive were his idea. Some people thought they looked garish, but, after the sneers the family had endured in Audubon Drive, he didn't care what people thought.

Ever since he'd begun singing people had criticised his taste, his hair, his clothes, his cars, the way he spoke and the way he sang. Everything he did or had was, they said, vulgar; the sort of things 'you might expect from a truck driver who got lucky'. Well, he thought, if that's what they still believed that was all right with him. Because, yes, he was rich, he was flash, he was Tupelo, Mississippi flash, and he always would be. That was why he'd greased his hair in the beginning, why he used to chew gum going on stage sometimes, and why he would wear that gold suit when he went on tour in the spring of 1957. Yes, a gold suit.

A girlfriend had given him a gold lamé waistcoat for Christmas, and he'd worn it on *The Ed Sullivan Show*. He liked it. But an entire gold suit? No one had ever seen one of those before and the fans loved it when he wore it in Chicago. It was made of gold leaf spangles and it shimmered in the lights. That was flash, all right, so flash RCA would later put it on an album cover, the second volume of *Elvis' Golden Hits*, which celebrated some of the gold discs he'd been awarded for the millions of dollars' sales of his records. In days gone by kings and queens would dress in gold and glitter so that their people would see them and know how important they were. That's what Elvis did now and would do all his career. Liberace had taught him that. If he wanted to be a star, a really big star, it wasn't enough that people just heard him and saw him. He had to make sure they couldn't forget him. He had to give them a spectacle. A gold suit did that all right, even if it did look a little silly. A gold Cadillac wouldn't be far behind.

Gold was almost a joke with him because of the rapidly increasing number of gold (painted) records he'd earned. But, folded somewhere in the back of his mind, was there the children's story of King Midas and how one day his little daughter had come running and before he could stop her she'd touched him and been turned to gold? At that moment everything Elvis was touching seemed to be being transmuted into gold. Would it end badly for him, too? Gladys, who always had a Bible saying handy, would sometimes remind him of the gospel: 'What doth it profit a man if he gain the whole world, and loses his soul?' He would ponder on that sometimes.

In the meantime, another gold record was coming his way. It was for 'All Shook Up', which had been written by Otis Blackwell, the man who wrote 'Don't Be Cruel', and it went to number one in the US and Britain and all kinds of places around the world the week it was released. It seemed logical to him that he should go to England and tour soon, as he'd already had so many hits there. In fact, he always assumed he would, but, whenever he mentioned it, the Colonel never seemed interested.

In Hollywood the pace never let up. Before *Loving You* was even released, he was at MGM to make *Jailhouse Rock*. For this film he was being paid $250,000 and getting half of the profits, so he guessed it was another 'grab-the-money-while-I'm-still-hot production', and that was why it was in black and white. Movies in colour cost more, but didn't necessarily do better box office or bring bigger profits. All the same, there was a grittiness about the script that he liked and the character he played was a sullen son of a bitch – the sort of guy he'd always identified with when he'd been going to the movies. So he was excited.

As usual in movies they recorded the songs first and once again his way of working collided with the studio's requirements. After he'd spent the morning of the first session loosening up by singing spirituals with the Jordanaires, they all broke for something to eat. But when he returned to the piano immediately after lunch and began another hymn he found he was singing on his own.

'What's going on?' he asked.

Gordon Stoker, one of the Jordanaires, explained. The MGM executive in charge of recording had told them that if Elvis began any more singsongs they weren't to join in, in the belief that it would get him to concentrate on recording the songs for the movie.

The executive couldn't have got it more wrong. Elvis didn't say a word. He just got up from the piano and went back to his hotel, taking his gang with him. None of those people in Hollywood got it. They must have thought he was some kind of singing machine, like a juke box. You just put the dime into the slot, put him in front of a microphone and off he'd go making hits. But he knew himself and his voice. He'd just been on tour in the Midwest, and singing to thousands of screaming kids night after night is a different style from recording. He had to get his voice relaxed again and he knew he could only do his best work when he was ready. And if he was still singing hymns, that meant he wasn't ready. He wasn't being a temperamental star. But the attitude that rock and roll was just dumb, junk music that anybody could do was still there.

Back at the hotel, he threw all kinds of tantrums at his cousins. They always got it in the neck when things went badly. That was partly what they were there for. Two days later he'd cooled off, and going back to work recorded the song 'Jailhouse Rock'. No one at MGM tried to tell him how to do his job again.

Nor was it all fury and frustration, because when he got back to the studio, songwriters Jerry Leiber and Mike Stoller, who'd written four songs for the movie, were waiting for him. Not much older than he was, they were a couple of Jewish boys from the East Coast whose families had moved to Los Angeles, and who had met each other while both were looking through the rhythm and blues records in a record store near Mike Stoller's high school. As far as the charts went, they were on a run with songs like 'Kansas City' and the Coasters' 'Searchin''. In fact they'd had nearly as many hits as he had, they teased, and would later tell reporters how surprised they were to discover that he was as interested in rhythm and blues as they were. How they'd thought he'd come to record 'Money Honey' and 'Good Rockin' Tonight', they didn't explain.

Songwriters weren't usually particularly welcome at recording sessions, but Leiber and Stoller also produced records, so they were more than useful, and it was good to have someone new to talk to about music. His favourite of their new songs was 'Treat Me Nice' and he recorded that several times before he got it right. He thought it would be a bigger hit than 'Jailhouse Rock', but, for once, he was wrong.

'You know, I'd love for you to write me a real pretty love song,' Elvis said to Mike Stoller one day. 'Could you do that?' Of course, they could. At the next session he and Leiber came in with 'Don't'. It was a perfect teenage love song, built around a word that almost every boy heard on a second date.

'Don't, don't, that's what you say . . . Baby, don't say don't'.

What amazed Elvis was how quickly they could write. When, on another occasion, he asked them if they could do him a Christmas blues, they just went off into another room and an hour or so later came back with 'Santa Claus Is Back in Town'. It was raunchy.

'Hang up your pretty stocking . . . Santa Claus he's coming down your chimney tonight . . .' Could he get away with those lyrics, everyone wondered. He did.

Elvis and Leiber and Stoller were obviously a good team, but the Colonel didn't like the way they'd approached him directly with their songs instead of going through music publishers Hill and Range, and therefore him. 'It means,' he explained to Elvis, 'you've come to like a couple of songs and promised to record them before we can do a deal to get a slice of the publishing on them.'

Elvis didn't care, but the Colonel did. By his carelessness Elvis was throwing away money, some of which should have belonged to Parker and the Aberbach brothers. 'I've told you a hundred times,' he insisted. 'If you want to stay at the top and keep on making the money you are, just stick to the singing. Leave the business to me.'

When the Colonel would get into one of those moods it was impossible to argue with him. He'd just stare Elvis out and make him feel ungrateful for everything he was doing for him. So Elvis would just let it go . . .

Watching *Jailhouse Rock*, it may seem as though Elvis and the band were all having a good time, but off camera their relationship was no longer so smooth. Now that Elvis was earning millions and the band, although they appeared in the film, weren't, money was a problem. But frustrations were evident in other ways, too. Bill Black had grown up playing a big stand-up fiddle bass in country bands, but now all the rock groups were buying the new Fender electric bass guitar, which was better for the rock sound, as well as being considerably easier to take from one date to the next.

Unfortunately, Bill couldn't get his fingers around the Fender intro on 'Baby, I Don't Care'. Already Steve Sholes had complained to the Colonel that recording was often being held up because Scotty and Bill weren't as competent as some session musicians, and now Bill couldn't do what he was being paid to do.

'Just give it here,' Elvis said at last, as they were recording.

Without a word Bill slid the Fender across the studio floor.

Picking it up, after a little rehearsal, Elvis played the bass part himself, adding the vocal track a couple of days later. He tried to make light of it. It seemed a funny situation really, but not to Bill. Elvis, usually just a rhythm guitarist, had played lead guitar on 'One Night' a few weeks earlier, but that hadn't been because Scotty wasn't able. Elvis had just wanted to see if he could do it, as he sometimes played piano on his records as well as singing.

Bill, though, was embarrassed at his own failure. And Scotty was none too happy either. While once they had been friends on stage and on the road, playing, driving and sleeping together, now the band even stayed in a different hotel from Elvis in Los Angeles.

There was a problem with the Jordanaires, as well, which was entirely Elvis's own fault. They were paid $200 each a week when they were working and $100 when they weren't needed, during which it was agreed they could do whatever else they wanted. Elvis knew this, but when he learned that earlier in the year they'd sung with Tab Hunter on 'Young Love', the record that had pushed his record 'Too Much' off the top of the charts, he flipped, accusing them of disloyalty. Who sings back-up or plays what on records doesn't mean much to the average fan, but getting on the charts had been so important to him that he momentarily lost his perspective. Often jealous, Elvis was always possessive of those around him.

When he calmed down the following day, he apologised. The Jordanaires told him he didn't have to, but Gladys had always taught him that if he upset anyone, he should always apologise, so he did.

He'd always said that 'fame won't change me none'. But that had been before he'd become famous. He was now realising that once you've tasted fame, real fame, you're never the same person again.

16

'This rancid-smelling aphrodisiac, rock and roll, smells phony and false.'

Frank Sinatra

Playing house in his very own mansion at the age of twenty-two, that's what he was doing as soon as he could get back to Memphis. Vernon and Grace had already moved in while refurbishments were taking place, and now their son bought himself a tractor to drive around the grounds. As soon as word got around that he was home, the fans were at the gates, but he soon put his uncles, Travis Smith and Vester Presley, to work as gatekeepers – which meant employment for two more relatives. By now, including his father, he had five members of his family working for him. There would be more later.

Gladys was glad to have him home, although she was still carping about the Colonel. Things hadn't got any better between those two. She just didn't trust the fellow. Because the size of the house took a lot of getting used to, she was at her happiest when she was sitting at the table in the kitchen with their cook, her friend Alberta. From Alberta on, Graceland, like most other Southern mansions then, would always have a black domestic staff of maids and cooks.

When Elvis was at home, Gladys would chat with his guys, watching all the comings and goings. Vernon didn't like Red West, but she would always have a soft spot for Elvis's old school friend, as well as for George Klein, who, although not an employee, would sometimes go on tour. And, as she knew there was no point in asking Elvis, since it was all a blur to him, she would cross-question George about everything that happened when they were on the road.

As much as she fretted about Elvis, he worried about her. She was still putting on weight and she was getting dark, puffy bags under her eyes. Her legs were getting bigger and she was moving more slowly. He knew she was drinking too much, mainly vodka, which Vernon would buy for her. But, whenever he mentioned her drinking, she would deny it and become angry and upset. She was still taking her slimming pills, too. She'd seen doctors in the hospital, she told him, and had undergone tests but they hadn't found anything too worrying. While he was with her, she was happy, but when he was away he could tell from their daily phone conversations that she was lonely. She often reminisced about sitting on the porch when she'd been a girl, or about when he'd been a baby in Tupelo, and how she used to talk with her family and friends there. She was enjoying having money, obviously, but she didn't spend it and rarely asked for anything. All the money in the world couldn't give her back those days in Tupelo. He'd given her his pink Cadillac, but as she'd never learned to drive and didn't have any inclination to do so, she had to have Vernon or someone to drive her if she wanted to go anywhere. What was mainly on Gladys's mind, though, was the question of Elvis being drafted. She wasn't a worldly woman, had never been very far, and would say she was afraid that if Elvis went into the military President Eisenhower might get the US into a war with the Communists and her boy would be injured or killed. Probably every mother with a son about to be drafted worried about something similar during the Cold War, but that was no consolation to Gladys.

Although he was back living at home, there were still any number of girls in Elvis's life. Just before they'd left Audubon Drive an actress called Yvonne Lime had come to stay and he'd shown her Graceland. But then she'd told *Modern Screen* about her weekend with him and how Gladys made them mashed potatoes and meatloaf for dinner, so she wasn't invited again. One girl who began going to Graceland regularly was a very cute, blonde beauty queen who could sing, called Anita Wood. Elvis had spotted her on Wink ('Deck of Cards') Martindale's Memphis TV show, *Top Ten Dance Party*, and had asked Lamar Fike, a friendly roly-poly guy who used to hang around Sun Records and who had now joined the entourage, to call her and make a date. That was how it usually worked now. If Elvis liked the look of a girl, he nearly always got others to make the first phone call.

Anita wasn't sure about him when their first date turned out to be just driving around Memphis with Lamar and Gene and Junior Smith all eating hamburgers in the car, but things got better after she'd met his parents. Gladys liked her, too. Elvis knew his mother was always hoping he'd settle down soon, maybe open a furniture store or something like that with his money, then marry a nice local girl, like Anita, and have three children. That possibility, if it had ever been remotely likely, was long, long gone. But Anita would soon have her own room at Graceland.

After allowing Elvis a few weeks at home, and knowing that he would soon be out of circulation for two years, Parker and RCA began putting the pressure on again. So, after another short tour in the Pacific Northwest, during which the Mounties in Vancouver threatened to arrest him if he didn't tone down his act, he was back in the studio in Hollywood making a Christmas album. This was something he really didn't want to do. He loved Christmas, but he didn't see where a rock and roll singer fitted into it. The Colonel insisted, however, and, in terms of sales, Parker was right. *Elvis' Christmas Album* would, over the decades, become his biggest-selling long-playing record of all.

The highlight, although he didn't want to do it, was the old country hit 'Blue Christmas', which, he joked, RCA would never release because of the way he sang it. But it was his version of 'White Christmas' that generated most heat, when Irving Berlin wrote to radio stations asking them not to play it. Elvis was miffed. He hadn't heard that Berlin had complained when Clyde McPhatter had released his version of the song a couple of years earlier, and he'd copied McPhatter's arrangement almost note for note. Most likely Berlin hadn't heard the McPhatter version.

The three day recording sessions went smoothly until the very end. For months Scotty and Bill had been unhappy about how little they were being paid – like the Jordanaires, $200 a week when working and just $100 when they weren't – and, not unreasonably, they felt they should now get more. The matter had been raised several times with Vernon, who paid them according to the Colonel's instructions, but nothing had been done. So Scotty and Bill suggested making an instrumental album, with Elvis playing the piano on it, as a way of earning a little extra. And, as Elvis raised no objections, time had been booked in the studio for when the Christmas album was finished.

Then the Colonel found out. There was no way he would let Elvis appear on any record other than his own, and, citing a legal problem, which may or may not have been valid, he instructed his assistant, Tom Diskin, to abandon the session. Elvis was embarrassed. Immediately, Scotty and Bill flew straight back to Memphis, leaving Elvis still in Los Angeles, where, a day later, he was surprised to receive a special delivery from them. It was a letter of resignation.

It was a difficult situation and Elvis was stuck in the middle. Parker, Freddy Bienstock, the Aberbachs' cousin at Hill and Range, who was in charge of finding Elvis new songs, and Steve Sholes at RCA were all telling him that he didn't need the band any more, and that he could hire better musicians who would only need paying when they played. But Scotty and Bill were friends. He'd started out with them. They'd nurtured him. For their part, Scotty and Bill considered Parker a bullying, musically ignorant moneyman who had always wanted to edge them out. They were absolutely right.

Elvis called Scotty when he got back to Memphis and asked him what it would take for them to come to some agreement. Scotty said an extra $50 a week, and $10,000 in a kind of back payment settlement. Elvis told him that he'd think about it, and told Vernon and the Colonel.

Unfortunately, however, by then, Scotty and Bill had already talked to the Memphis newspaper the *Commercial Appeal* about why they'd quit. The Colonel advised Elvis to reply through an open letter to them in the other Memphis newspaper, the *Memphis Press-Scimitar*. In it Elvis wished them good luck and said he was sure they could have worked it out, but, because they'd gone to the papers and tried to make him look bad, it was too late. He would, he said, give them good recommendations. The Colonel, or a lawyer, had almost certainly drafted the letter. Elvis was unhappy about the whole thing. There was a lot about the business he really didn't like. A few days later Vernon sent both Scotty and Bill a cheque each ending their employment. For Elvis, it all seemed like a terrible mistake. They felt he'd been disloyal to them, and he believed they'd been disloyal to him.

He'd already promised to play a benefit for the Elvis Presley Youth

Center in Tupelo, where money was being raised to buy the house in which he'd been born and a few plots around it. But with only his drummer left (D.J. Fontana had always been salaried and hadn't quit with Scotty and Bill) he had to hire a couple of Nashville session players on guitar and bass for the day. The Jordanaires were there, too, and the show went well, but he'd spent three years looking over his shoulder and smiling at Scotty, and he missed the security of his friend's presence. Scotty's replacement, Hank Garland, was good, very good, but Elvis always hated change of any kind. It just didn't seem right.

So, the following week, he asked Tom Diskin to call Scotty and offer him and Bill $250 a show each to come back for some dates in California and Hawaii. He was thrilled when they immediately agreed. They all then drove out from Memphis to California in his limousine and none of them mentioned the fall-out once. It was, more or less, just like the old times. But nothing could really ever be quite the same. Their relationship had changed, he'd changed, and he couldn't change back.

It's a long drive from Memphis to Los Angeles and as the young men drove they listened to the radio. A lot of the stations were playing country music, but when it got to the late afternoon and the kids were getting out of school, they'd find the Top Forty stations along the route. 'Jailhouse Rock' and 'Treat Me Nice' were playing everywhere, of course, but so were records by some new, young guys who wouldn't have been heard on the charts two years earlier. The Everly Brothers had 'Wake Up Little Susie', which was even better than 'Bye Bye Love', then there was 'That'll Be the Day' by Buddy Holly and the Crickets, Paul Anka, who was all of sixteen, with 'Diana', Sam Cooke being almost perfect with 'You Send Me', and a couple of hits from Sam Phillips and Sun Records in the shape of Jerry Lee Lewis doing 'A Whole Lotta Shakin' Goin' On' and Bill Justis with 'Raunchy'. Elvis had never known a time when the charts had been so good. And, as they drove along, he wondered, with so much new talent around, if anyone would miss him after he'd been drafted.

It was a worry born out of insecurity, which would stay with him for the next two years.

But there was something else. Quite apart from fretting about whether he would be forgotten, he was also concerned about what might happen to his voice. He didn't know much about physiology, but he knew enough to be aware that the voice is controlled by muscles and vocal cords, all of which have to be exercised regularly. How was he supposed to exercise his voice when he became a soldier? And afterwards, would he still be able to sing as well if he hadn't kept working those muscles? Would he sound different in two years' time? He just didn't know. Could a footballer or a tennis player take two years off at the height of his career and come back and play as well as he had done? He didn't think so.

So, by the time Elvis and the band got to their show at the Pan Pacific Auditorium in Los Angeles, when he knew that all kinds of Hollywood stars and big shots, and people who wouldn't normally be seen dead at a rock and roll show, would be there, he'd worked himself up into a state. He had become determined that on this night they would see the real Elvis Presley, not 'the lump of lard' that he'd read about. And he really let rip. He'd been rehearsing his moves and now he went shimmying across the stage in his crazy gold jacket, his legs and arms thrashing like scissors, before going down to his knees as though in prayer, and then jumping up on to Nipper, the big stuffed mascot of a dog that RCA insisted on putting on the stage at every show. Some critics said, in thinly disguised words, that he looked as if he was pretending to hump the dog, but that wasn't so, he would insist. He was just showing how he could work a big audience.

From the beginning, Bing Crosby had been fulsome in his praise for Elvis, but every time he met reporters on that tour one or other would tell him what Frank Sinatra thought about rock and roll. Elvis had heard and read Sinatra's wordy and very carefully thought out bitter insult so often he'd almost got it off by heart.

> This rancid-smelling aphrodisiac, rock and roll, smells phony and false. It's sung and played and written for the most part by cretinous goons, . . . the martial music of every side-burned delinquent . . . It's the most brutal, ugly, desperate, vicious form of expression it's been my misfortune to hear.

There was no doubting that he'd been talking about Elvis and his songs. Elvis always tried to stay cool with his answers, but he was steaming inside over this. Sinatra had a right to his opinion, he told reporters, and he admired him as a performer, a singer and an actor. But he thought he was mistaken. Sinatra had been part of a trend in his day, he said. Every generation had its own era of music. What about the cheek-to-cheek dancing and the tight body holds they used to do, he asked. Rock and roll didn't encourage that.

He didn't add that although he admired Sinatra's voice, he didn't like a lot of the songs he sang. But it didn't matter what he said, people would always have their own opinions.

'There are gonna be people who like you, and people who don't like you,' he would say. 'Regardless of what you do, you can't please everybody. Some people hated Jesus and he was the perfect man.'

So, he went back on stage and did his act and the Los Angeles Police Department Vice Squad filmed him and warned the Colonel that Elvis would have to clean up his show or go to jail. But Elvis knew they didn't really mean it. He was Elvis Presley. Who was going to jail Elvis Presley in 1957?

As for the woman reporter who said he made suggestive movements with his body, he had a one-line answer: 'My movements, ma'am, are all leg movements. I don't do nothin' with my body.'

17

'I'm lucky to be in a position to give.
It really is a gift to be able to give.'

A movie which had been planned fell through, so he spent the last weeks of 1957 at home in Graceland, taking care of stuff around the house and going out with his friends. He'd always been a great film fan, but it had become impossible for him to buy a ticket and sit in the cinema, so he'd begun to rent the Memphian theater after the last show had finished, and would invite all his friends to watch movies with him. Sometimes they would see three films back to back and be there nearly all night. At other times he would take over the Fairground and everyone would have free rides. Or they would go to the Rainbow Rollerdrome, the place he'd first talked to Dixie Locke, and play a game where they would make two opposing sides, and, all holding cushions, try to knock each other over. Care would be taken with the girls, like his girlfriend Anita, but some of the guys could get mean when they got into the game, and there would be occasional injuries. He wasn't fool enough to think he escaped getting hurt because he was too quick for the other players. No one wanted to put him in hospital. He was paying the keep of half the guys there. Gladys wouldn't have been very pleased if he'd been injured either.

All the time his entourage was getting bigger. The guys were companions as much as employees, but one night Lamar Fike got into a fight with another fellow while playing badminton and Gladys was so upset that Elvis fired both of them on the spot. He took them back later, as he usually did, but he had made the point. It was fine having parties and playing pool and cards and putting the records on – although never his: that wasn't allowed. But this was his parents' and his Grandma's home as well as his. His friends had to respect it.

Mostly those evenings were fun, though often he would go up to his room and change his outfit – feeling himself to be on display even in his own home when people came round. From the moment he had begun singing, and before that, if you count his high school outfits, he always dressed up, even when just lolling around the house. His shirt or sweater might be casual, but they would always be expensive casual. He didn't ever again want to look poor or nondescript.

His lasting memories of those final few weeks of 1957, he would realise later, were sitting with Gladys in the little dining room off the kitchen when Vernon had gone to Memphis on business or with some other excuse. Although they had staff, Gladys always liked to cook for Elvis herself, and then they would sit and talk. He knew she couldn't begin to understand a fraction of the kind of life he was living or of his ambitions, but she always tried to help.

The previous Easter Sunday he'd gone to church for the first time in over a year, and for some reason, after the service, he'd found himself telling the pastor: 'I'm the most miserable young man you've ever seen. I've got more money than I can ever spend, I have thousands of fans out there, and I have a lot of people who call themselves my friends. But I'm miserable.'

Now here he was in his own mansion and it was nearly Christmas and he was telling his mother the same sort of thing. And she would listen and then say: 'Son, I don't rightly know the answers to your problems, but I do know that if you open up your Bible and read it every day you'll find the answers there somewhere.'

And, to an extent, he would be consoled. He could talk to his mother better than he could talk to anyone else. He knew she liked having him to herself, but he liked having her to himself, too. And he would be grateful ever after that they'd had those moments together at that time. Because, just before Christmas, he received a visit from a member of the Memphis Draft Board to tell him his induction notice had been drawn up.

Both the US Army and the US Navy offered him Special Services status, one plan being that he could entertain the troops for two years. But the Colonel, who now sent out Christmas cards with the message 'from Elvis and the Colonel' on them, and who was making all the decisions, wouldn't hear of it. Elvis, he insisted, had to go and do his duty like any other American soldier. If Elvis didn't, he would never be forgiven.

So Elvis told the reporters he was 'mighty proud to be given the opportunity to serve' his country and that he wanted to be treated just like a regular GI. He could have gone into any of the services, but he chose the army, who agreed to allow him a deferment until late March 1958.

After that, despite the mountains of gifts he gave, it was a bleak Christmas. Gladys wasn't well. Often in her housecoat and slippers all day and close to tears most of the time, she played her son's EP of hymns, *Peace in the Valley*, over and over. She knew that, as likely as not, he would be sent overseas and that frightened her. Elvis's cousin, Junior Smith, who now worked for him, had come home from Korea shell shocked and discharged as being mentally unfit to serve. He now had a drink and pills problem.

For Elvis, the one relief was that he was able to put uncertainty behind him, and an almost reckless need to let off steam began to emerge. Firstly it was seen in a game which he devised called War, which involved buying $2000 of fireworks, and for his gang then to divide into two teams and throw them, lighted, at each other. It was dangerous, but he liked the excitement. A new characteristic was, however, also beginning to emerge. Ignoring Vernon's objections, he withdrew several thousand dollars in cash from his bank account and began to hand out gifts of $100 bills to everyone around him. Even a post boy got a $100 bill for delivering a parcel. Elvis's attitude was that the value of money came with its sharing.

'I'm lucky to be in a position to give,' he would say. 'It really is a gift to be able to give.'

But it was a manic generosity, as though he was embarrassed at accumulating so much by simply doing what he enjoyed most of all.

With the US Army waiting, everything now became a rush. Hal Wallis and Paramount wanted a new movie and RCA were insisting that they get some new recordings to keep releasing while Elvis was out of circulation. So, immediately after his twenty-third birthday, he took the train back to Los Angeles to start recording.

His next movie, his fourth in eighteen months, was based on the Harold Robbins book *A Stone for Danny Fisher*, which he read as preparation. He needn't have bothered. To make it into a vehicle for him, the lead character had been changed from a boxer into a singer, and when Jerry Leiber and Mike Stoller, who were writing some of the songs, turned up with one called 'King Creole', the title of the film was changed, too.

For a week he recorded the new songs for the movie album; this time, though, since the film was set in New Orleans, he had a Dixieland band as well as Scotty and Bill backing him. At first Leiber and Stoller were with them, too, then suddenly they disappeared back to York. They'd fallen out with the Colonel again by telling some Broadway producers they wanted to write a musical based on a book called *A Walk on the Wild Side* and had suggested that Elvis would be great in the main role. The Colonel never let anyone other than him discuss Elvis's projects and there was the inevitable row. With that Leiber and Stoller gave up. Parker was impossible. And when the Colonel later had the effrontery to send them a contract asking for their signature but without a word written on it, just a scribbled note saying 'details to be added later', they didn't bother to reply.

Elvis never saw Leiber and Stoller again. After he got out of the army in 1960, he recorded a few more of their songs, mainly old ones as movie tracks, but their budding friendship had ended. The two went on to have further great success with numerous hits from the Clovers and the Coasters to Peggy Lee and Ben E. King. As for Elvis, he did what the Colonel told him he was being paid to do, and, without arguing, got on with making *King Creole*.

The director was Michael Curtiz, who had made *Casablanca* and *Mildred Pierce*, and it also starred Walter Matthau as well as Dolores Hart again. With location filming in New Orleans and an offbeat little song Elvis sang with jazz singer Kitty White called 'Crawfish', it turned out to be the best movie he would ever make. And on top of that, during a break in shooting, he was even photographed with Sophia Loren sitting on his knee.

Then, suddenly, his life in show business came to a full stop. Back in Memphis he bought himself some new records and spent all night with his pals and girls at the Rollerdrome. And on the morning of Monday 24 March, he went with his parents, his pal Lamar Fike, girlfriend Anita, and the Colonel, down to the draft board on South

Main Street, where he was given a medical and a serial number. No longer Elvis the Pelvis, or the King, or 'the rock and roll matador' as the Germans called him, he was now Private Presley US53310761 and would be earning $78 a month, which he would donate to charity. Outside in the street the Colonel handed out *King Creole* balloons.

Elvis was churning up inside, but was determined not to show it. And mindful that the other recruits who were with him, and their parents and their girlfriends who had turned up to see them off, would have been feeling much the same, he got on the army bus and waved goodbye to the fans and the cameras. Later he would say of his career that 'it had all been like a dream. And now it was finished.'

Or, perhaps, not quite, because, first, there were to be blood tests, the loyalty oath and medical examinations at Kennedy Hospital. Then he was put in charge of his fellow recruits as a hired Greyhound bus carried him and his new comrades across the Mississippi River and out along the road to Fort Chaffee, Arkansas – pursued all the way by a convoy of television and newspaper photographers and reporters, family, friends, many fans, and, of course, his manager. The following day there were vaccinations, and then intelligence tests to see if he was suitable for officer training. He wasn't. 'I never was very good at arithmetic,' he joked. Then, finally, the moment for which Elvis's detractors had been waiting arrived: the symbolic castration of the rock and roll idol, as the army allowed newsreel cameras to film him having his hair cut with the take-no-prisoners electric clippers.

'Hair today, gone tomorrow,' he mused, as first his famous sideburns, then his hair, fell on to the gown at his shoulders.

But for those fans who would watch the scene on television across America and around the world over the next few days there was a surprise. Most young men who are proud of their abundant hair lose their looks when it is cut short. Elvis looked as handsome with his hair cropped as he did with it long. He did look slightly smaller, though, at 5′ 11″. The army didn't allow soldiers in uniform to wear lifts in their boots.

All the time, as he was given his fatigues and boots, the Colonel stood smiling; then, at the end of it all, a press conference was held for the most famous private soldier in the world. Less than four years earlier he had been too frightened to speak to a single Memphis reporter, and Marion Keisker had had to answer for him. Now he handled hundreds of journalists and newsreel cameras with candid aplomb. When asked what he would do now for female company, he simply said: 'I suppose it's a natural thing that when a fellow goes to a strange place, he tries to find a girlfriend.'

Whatever he was thinking, every word he spoke was carefully balanced to present himself diplomatically as an ordinary young American. If he had to go into the army, he was determined that he would work hard to be an exemplary soldier. That was what the Colonel wasn't just advising, he was insisting. So that became Elvis's new ambition. In his eyes Parker had made him famous beyond his wildest dreams, channelling enough money his way to enable him to keep himself and his family in untold luxury for the rest of their lives. How could he not be grateful for that? How could he not be compliant to the Colonel's wishes when he owed him so much?

In theory, Parker was working for Elvis, but in the way their relationship operated, Elvis was employed by the Colonel. It would eventually seem that he trusted Parker's business skills more than he believed in his own talent.

18

'Wake up, Mama. Wake up, Baby, and talk to Elvis.'

Basic training took place over an eight-week period at the sprawling Fort Hood military base in Texas. It was the hardest time of Elvis's life, but he had to hide his feelings. He'd grown up an only child, a somewhat different, other-worldly boy, cocooned inside the little Presley family. After that had come the support of Scotty, Bill and Sam Phillips, followed, as his career exploded, by his ever growing squad of friends, cousins, hangers-on, and, of course, the Colonel. At all times he had been the centre of attention, yet he'd always felt lonely. Now he was lonelier than ever.

'I'll tell you something,' he'd said to a New York reporter in 1957. 'A lot of times I feel miserable. And I don't know which-away to turn. Even though I'm surrounded by people I get lonely and stare at the wall.'

In the army he would still find himself continually watched, and sometimes ribbed by other soldiers. But he also knew that some people who were watching were just waiting for him to make a mistake. As the most famous young man in the world, his experience of recent life was nothing remotely like that of his fellow recruits, and, desperately anxious to fit in, he went out of his way to befriend those who were sleeping with him in their shared hut – buying them all lunch on the first day, and later an additional set of fatigues each. As they worked and trained together he would joke with them, and he waited with them, too, as they stood in line outside call boxes to make phone calls home.

An introduction to military life is taxing for any new soldier, but, with all eyes on him, Elvis had to prove that he was as good as any of the others, even to the point of being grateful for whatever food he was served.

'I've eaten things in the army that I've never eaten before,' he would laugh, 'and I've eaten things I didn't even know what it was. But after a day of basic training you could eat a rattlesnake.'

At the same time, always competitive, he was proud, too, when he completed a fully loaded route march in the hot Texas sun when several others had to drop out. As it happened, the exercise was good for his looks. Within a few weeks he'd dropped twelve pounds in weight. It suited him.

It was the psychological adjustment, however, that was most difficult, and in that, he was fortunate to be helped by a sympathetic recruit sergeant, Bill Norwood. Stipulating only that the distress the sergeant saw in private wasn't displayed in public, Norwood began to allow him to use his own home on base to make phone calls and as a place to meet Anita Wood when she drove down from Memphis. Even more help came from a former disc jockey called Eddie Fadal from nearby Waco, whom he had met when he'd visited a radio station there two years earlier. Realising that Elvis was at Fort Hood, Fadal drove out to the base on a whim and was astonished to be able to talk his way through the barriers to the singer, whom he discovered polishing his boots.

Two weeks later, on his first free weekend, Elvis accepted an invitation and turned up at Fadal's Waco suburban home, from where he immediately called his parents. 'He was very sad, very low, very depressed,' Fadal would say. The call home was tearful.

'It's all over, Eddie,' he would tell Fadal, convinced that he would be forgotten in two years' time. Not even the subsequent visits by his parents and grandmother on later weekends could fully lift his spirits. Most young men saw being drafted as a prelude to, or a break in, their careers. He saw it as the end of his.

What helped was a fourteen-day furlough after ten weeks' basic training. He drove home in his black Cadillac, which had been taken down to the base for him, giving a lift to a couple of other recruits from Memphis on the way back. Then, the very next day he went out and bought himself a new red Lincoln convertible, to add to the seven cars he already owned. There had been eight in his drive, but he'd given his three-wheel Messerschmitt bubble car to one of the Lansky brothers in exchange for whatever clothes he took from their shop. At first he enjoyed nights out with Anita and the guys at the Rollerdrome and some all-night movie sessions. But after taking his parents to a private screening of *King Creole*, he went back to work.

Ever since he'd learned that Elvis was to be drafted, the Colonel had been in dispute with RCA. Believing that scarcity would make Elvis even more attractive to the fans, his plan was that there would be no recording sessions during the entire two years that Elvis was in the army. Instead of making new records, everything recorded so far would be repackaged in album form. In this way he hoped to be able to renegotiate a better deal with RCA and get paid twice for the same records. He also believed that the break in Elvis's career would enable him to appeal to a wider audience when he eventually left the army. It was a monstrous gamble.

RCA, however, who knew more than Parker about the whims of teenage record buyers, were not convinced. They wanted enough recordings to be available to cover the two-year gap, worrying, as much as Elvis, that their chief money earner might never recover from his time away if he didn't keep in touch with his fans musically. So, there were meetings at Graceland, when Parker and his staff, to Gladys's distress, took over the running of the house, Parker even ordering the doors be closed on Vernon while he talked to his client in private. Sometimes Elvis would come out of the meetings red-faced with frustration. But, perhaps, for once, Parker listened to him, because he finally backed down to the extent that he allowed his client a single night's session at RCA's Nashville studio. There could have been more sessions. Elvis could have insisted, and there was nothing in the army rule book that said that he couldn't have recorded in his free time throughout his entire twenty-four months of military service. But Parker had his own rule book and Elvis, as always, didn't insist. So it was just the one night.

But what a night: the most successful session of Elvis's career. Wearing his army uniform throughout, and indeed during his entire leave, because, he said, 'I'm proud of it', he recorded five worldwide hit singles, including 'A Fool Such As I', 'A Big Hunk o' Love', 'I Got Stung' and 'I Need Your Love Tonight'. That had to amount to a combined sale of at least five million record sales over the next year alone from six hours' work.

Unable to get Scotty Moore and Bill Black because they were booked elsewhere, the session musicians who had stood in at the Tupelo concert the previous September, known as the 'Nashville A-Team', together with the Jordanaires, were employed again. And it was true, they did work more quickly than Scotty and Bill. Not only were RCA thrilled with the results, so was Elvis.

Only Parker grumbled. These fellows may have been the best rock musicians in Nashville, he told Elvis, but he didn't like the way their instrumentation was sometimes eclipsing his client's voice. The kids who bought the records wanted to hear Elvis, not a lot of guitars, he argued. He still didn't get it. But Elvis did. He'd always liked his voice to be a part of the band and merged with the backing singers.

On this occasion Parker didn't interfere with the recordings once Elvis had approved the mix. But in years to come he would occasionally send instructions to the RCA engineers in New York, telling them to bring Elvis's voice forward at the expense of the accompaniment before the record was pressed. And when Elvis sometimes first heard his new records on the radio, he would wonder why they didn't sound the way they had when he'd recorded them.

A couple of days after the session Elvis was back at the Fort Hood base for advanced lessons in tank driving. He'd already been assigned to the Third Armored Division, popularly known as 'Hell on Wheels', which was being sent to West Germany in September, but in the meantime he'd discovered that according to army regulations a soldier could live off base if he had dependants living in the area. Vernon, Gladys and Grandma certainly depended on him for financial support, but whether that fulfilled the spirit of the rule might, to some, seem questionable. Nevertheless, by the middle of June he'd rented a house in the nearby town of Killeen, Texas, and he, his parents, his grandmother and friend-cum-employee Lamar Fike had moved in. So when, not only did he receive some good reviews for his part in *King Creole*, but the single from that film, 'Hard Headed Woman', went to number one in the US charts, his spirits began to improve. Away from the base, where he always had to guard his tongue, he could reflect on his career again, and say what he really felt about army life without fear of his comments appearing in the newspapers the next day.

The happiness was short-lived. At the beginning of August, Gladys became ill, and needed hospital treatment for hepatitis. Elvis drove her and Vernon to the train at Killeen. Three days later Gladys's doctor in Memphis, who had warned her that drinking was bad for her, sent an urgent message that Elvis should come to the hospital as soon as possible. Elvis applied for leave. However, because the army didn't want to be seen to be giving him preferential treatment, it was at first turned down. But, the next day, when his mother's condition worsened and he threatened to go AWOL, Gladys's doctor, an ex-army medical, called someone of higher army rank, and leave was granted.

Elvis flew to Memphis and hurried to the Methodist Hospital. Gladys was pleased to see him. 'Oh, my son . . . my son,' she cried as he entered her private room. She looked a little better, too, although none too happy when he told her that he'd come to Memphis by air. She still hated him flying. The following day he stayed with her from morning until midnight, leaving Vernon, who was sleeping in a cot in the room, at her side, and promised to return the following morning.

Vernon called him at 3.30 a.m. Elvis would say later: 'I knew what it was before I even answered the phone.' Gladys was dead.

He raced to the hospital, leaving Lamar Fike to follow in another car. By the time Lamar caught up with him, he could hear Elvis and Vernon sobbing hysterically inside Gladys's hospital room. As a singer Elvis sang with his basic emotions; in grief he couldn't hide his rawest feelings.

The following morning he and Vernon sat crying together, unabashed, outside the front of Graceland as reporters and photographers walked, embarrassed, up the drive.

'She was all we lived for,' he said. 'She was always my best girl. When Mama was feeling bad we used to walk her up and down the driveway here to help her feel better.'

The white shirt with frills down the front that he was wearing, pictures of which would appear in the world's newspapers the following day, might have appeared inappropriate to some. Not to Elvis. Gladys had liked to see him wearing it.

During the days that followed, there were nights when he got little or no sleep and a doctor had to be called to give him some tranquillisers. When Gladys's body, in a pale blue dress that he'd made her buy but which she'd never worn, was laid in the 'best coffin money could buy' and brought home to Graceland, he seemed for a time to revert to a form of infantilism. 'Mama, you never would dress up for me and now here you are dressed up in the most beautiful gown. I never saw you dressed up like this,' he said as he hung over the body.

And when Eddie Fadal arrived from Texas, he invited him to come close, saying, 'Mama, here's Eddie. You know Eddie. You met him in Killeen,' Fadal would recall. And all the time he would be remarking on how pretty his mother looked, and saying, 'Wake up, Mama. Wake up, Baby, and talk to Elvis.' Then, standing over the coffin, he would touch her hands and the little slippers on her feet, and baby-talk her, even pulling out his comb to slightly adjust her hair.

Off stage and in public he had, until then, always maintained complete dignity. But, to the concern of his friends, he now lost control of his emotions completely, hysterically hugging and touching his mother's body, until the funeral director had to put a glass cover over the coffin.

When the Colonel arrived he found what he thought was a hillbilly wake of weeping and pandemonium and ordered in his usual blunt way that Graceland be cleared. In a rare moment of defiance, Elvis refused.

'These people are my friends,' he told his manager. 'Don't you come in my house and tell me to run my friends out of here.'

Parker backed off, but he did convince him and Vernon that with so many people expected, the funeral service couldn't realistically take place there.

The next day, 15 August, Gladys's funeral was held at the Memphis Funeral Home, with the Presleys' favourite gospel quartet, the Blackwood Brothers, singing. It had been intended that they would sing just three hymns, but Elvis wouldn't let them stop, sending up note after note requesting one favourite after another. They sang, they said, about twelve in all. J.D. Sumner, the bass singer with the Blackwoods, would later say: 'I never seen a man suffer as much or grieve as much as Elvis did over the loss of his mother.'

When the cortège arrived at the cemetery, with over four thousand mourners and onlookers present, Elvis's sobbing got worse. Reaching out to the coffin as it was lowered into the ground he cried out, stumbling towards the open grave, prompting Lamar Fike to pull him back hastily. 'People are watching you,' Lamar whispered. Elvis didn't care.

A crowd of people returned to Graceland from the cemetery, but Elvis remained in his room until late in the evening when he got word that Dixie Locke was outside at the gates. He'd been waiting for her, and, coming down the stairs, immediately asked everyone to leave them. Alone, he and Dixie talked for a couple of hours about Gladys, and how she and Dixie had got on so well, and then of the times they'd had together before Elvis had become famous. Seeing the state he was in, and the bedlam that surrounded his career, Dixie wondered aloud whether he shouldn't just give it all up and live a quieter life.

He shook his head. 'There are too many people that depend on me now,' he told her. 'I'm too obligated. I'm in too far to get out.'

When Dixie went to Graceland again the following night the house was full of people and she didn't go in. From this moment on, he would rarely be alone again, forever surrounding himself with friends and employees.

He and Vernon didn't allow an autopsy to be carried out, but it was generally accepted that Gladys Presley had died from a heart attack as a result of cirrhosis of the liver. She was forty-four. For twenty-three years she'd lived her life for her son, pushed him to stay on at school, encouraged his singing and welcomed his fans. She'd asked for nothing for herself; her pleasures had been those of the simple lifestyle of a poor, country-born Mississippi wife and mother. But she'd been shrewd, too. She'd never trusted Colonel Tom Parker, and had worried that her son had sold his talents to a man whose only love was money. Now Elvis wouldn't have her sensible, dissenting voice in his ear as his manager plotted his future.

The inscription chiselled on her gravestone was simple. It read: 'She was the sunshine of our home' – a reference, almost certainly, to when she would have gone around their Mississippi home singing 'You are my sunshine, my only sunshine, . . .' to her little boy, who had then chosen the song for his singing debut at junior school. The chorus of the song ends with the line, 'Please don't take my sunshine away'.

Before he returned to Fort Hood the following week, Elvis left instructions that nothing of Gladys's should be moved from where it had been when she died. Then Vernon, Grandma and Lamar returned to the house in Killeen to be near him. His cousins Junior and Gene were also there, as well as Eddie Fadal and Red West, whose father had just died. Elvis had attended that funeral, too. Off duty in Killeen, with his friends and Anita, it was a subdued Elvis in a chaos of people and emotions, and they would all sing gospel hymns deep into the night.

Five weeks after his mother's death, Elvis and his unit took a troop train to New York from where they were to embark for West Germany as a replacement for the Third Armored Division. A thousand young soldiers were about to leave the US, but only one was given a press conference. At the quayside in Brooklyn the RCA top brass, the Aberbach brothers and the phony Colonel lined up with army officers and newsreel cameramen as over a hundred reporters covered the farewell.

At first Elvis was in the usual jokey, respectful mood he adopted with the press, until towards the end of the conference a reporter asked him if he would be selling Graceland.

'No, sir,' he replied. 'Because that was my mother's home.'

Pressed if he would like to say any more about his mother, he said, without embarrassment:

> I certainly would. I suppose since I was an only child we might have been a little closer than . . . I mean everyone loves his mother, but I was an only child and mother was always right with me all my life. And it wasn't only like losing a mother, it was like losing a friend, a companion, someone to talk to . . . I used to get very angry at her when I was growing up. It's a natural thing . . . a young person wants to go somewhere or do something, and your mother won't let you, and you think, 'Why, what's wrong with you?' But then, later on in years, you find out, you know, that she was right . . . And I'm very happy that she was kind of strict with me, very happy that it worked out the way it did.

And with that, a message for his fans, and several walks up and down the gang plank for the photographers, he waved goodbye, and, stepping on to the USS *General George M. Randall,* set sail for Europe.

19

'The world is more alive at night. It's like God isn't looking.'

His seventeen months in West Germany passed as though he was banned from the only world he knew. It was the height of the Cold War, just two years after the Hungarian uprising, and the role of the US Army, there to protect Western Europe from any surprise Soviet attack, was taken seriously by soldiers and the politicians who sent them. From Elvis's point of view it was Pax Americana. Ten years later young men would flee to Canada to dodge the draft and avoid going to Vietnam, but in 1958 that was rare. And, despite his misgivings over his career, there was a big part of Elvis that was 'proud to do his bit'. He believed in America. It had made his success possible, and over his two years in uniform he would come to believe in the military, too. He liked the uniform, too, and would wear it when it wasn't at all necessary. And he always liked badges.

Yet from the moment he disembarked at Bremerhaven in October 1958, until the day he returned to the US in March 1960, he would alternate mentally between wanting to be considered just like any other private soldier, and, like any other private soldier, being resentful at being drafted.

'I gotta act like one of the guys, but it ain't easy being one of the guys. I ain't never been one of the guys and I never will be one of the guys,' he would complain.

That was certainly true. But though he grumbled privately, never publicly or to his superiors, this interlude away from show business was also a prolonged and much-needed rest. Since 1955 his work load had been crippling. Now he was able to step off the glittering public conveyor belt of opportunity that he, with the help of his relentless manager, had created. His life was now out of his hands and those of the Colonel. He could leave all major decisions to the US Army. In many ways it made things easier, and, although requests that he sing for the troops continued from senior army ranks, his main job would be driving a jeep in a reconnaissance platoon and going on manoeuvres. Throughout everything his attitude was straightforward.

'More than anything else, I just want the folks back home to think right of me,' he would say.

Despite what he and the military might declare, however, he wasn't quite being treated like any ordinary soldier. Because no sooner had he moved into the barracks at Friedberg, a historic town about fifteen miles north of Frankfurt, than, once again, he was given permission to live with his dependants off base when not on duty. Only very rich and hardly 'ordinary' soldiers could possibly do that. But soon a large rented house at 14 Goethestrasse in nearby Bad Nauheim was found for him and those dependants – Daddy and Grandma, who came to cook for him, as well as Lamar Fike and Red West, who had just finished his service with the Marines. Not every soldier took his grandmother and his pals with him when he got drafted. And, despite his generally sombre mood, soon there would be the usual parties, now attended by pretty young German girls, as well as new army friends, such as Rex Mansfield, another Tennessee boy he'd met as they'd both been inducted into the military in Memphis.

Perhaps the two best and ultimately most rewarding friendships he made in the army, however, were Chicago-born Joe Esposito and Charlie Hodge. He'd met Charlie, whom he'd previously seen as lead singer with the Foggy River Boys on television, at Brooklyn as they'd been about to embark, and had been immediately taken by the former gospel singer's simple good humour. And as the ship had crossed the Atlantic, the two had set to work organising a talent competition for the other troops, with Elvis acting as pianist.

Before he'd arrived in Germany he might have imagined that being outside the US would mean some relief from besieging admirers, and that the curiosity about him would be by no means as intense. But German fans quickly discovered where he was and would surround any café where he and his unit stopped for coffee, while knocks on the door of his rented house were so persistent that a sign was put up outside the gate. Autographs, it said, would be signed between seven thirty and eight o'clock every evening – although some of those autograph books left to be signed overnight might not always have been blessed with the signature of the singer. There were only so many hours in the night, and Lamar and Red were already adept at copying their master's handwriting.

Like many soldiers posted to a foreign country, Elvis wasn't interested in sightseeing, bothering to learn much German, or taking advantage of any of the further educational classes that the army offered. In fact he was decidedly uncurious. Instead he saw a couple of Bill Haley concerts and enjoyed the Holiday on Ice spectacular with its dozens of pretty girls skating around in very short dresses.

Before being called up he'd worried for his voice, but now, serendipitously, for the first time in his life he had something approaching a voice coach. Charlie Hodge, who before the army had studied singing and harmonised with Gene Autry and Red Foley, began teaching him breathing tricks and encouraging him to sing out and develop the top of his range. Together they would sing hymns and listen to new records sent over from the States by girlfriend Anita, demos of new songs submitted to Elvis by Hill and Range, and old Ink Spots records.

'I guess I got in more singing in the army than I would if I'd been working on it,' he said later.

It also meant he didn't have to sing the same ten hits over and over every day. Instead, after hiring a piano, and buying a tape recorder, he would try out all kinds of different songs, so that when his eventual release came he would be ready to go straight back into the studio.

His mother had been a fan of the Enrico Caruso recording of 'O Sole Mio', and he now asked the Aberbachs to have some new lyrics written for it. The result would eventually be his biggest hit ever, 'It's Now or Never'.

Although he had to be up at 5.30 a.m. to be taken to the base ('even', he would say, 'if I hadn't got to bed until four' – and frequently he hadn't) his off-duty time was mainly spent at home, as he virtually imported his life at Graceland to Germany. As far as possible, he stayed in his own bubble, as Lamar and Red polished his boots and pressed his dozen handmade uniforms and did whatever was expected of lackeys who were paid only spending money by the ever-thrifty Vernon. The rest of his free time was spent going to the movies on the base, playing touch football, sitting around with his pals and girls and listening to the record shows late at night on the American Forces Network in Germany. And almost every day the Colonel would send him reports of the efforts he was making to keep Elvis's name in the public mind.

He wrote letters, too, at least a couple of which went to Anita in which he asked her to wait for him and more or less promised to marry her, seemingly on the condition that she kept herself 'clean and wholesome', that being the thing that could 'determine our lives and happiness together'.

He also told her that he wasn't dating anyone in Germany, which wasn't actually true, telling a friend in another letter that he was seeing a little German 'chuckaloid' who looked a lot like Brigitte Bardot, and with whom it was 'grind city'. When it came to girls, fidelity was never his strong point, although he always demanded that his girlfriends stay faithful to him.

Dixie and Anita had both discovered that, and now a pretty German girl who had an American stepfather and who spoke excellent English, called Elisabeth Stefaniak, was learning it, too. At first, she and Elvis just kissed, and when she was offered a live-in job with Elvis, Vernon and Grandma as secretary to handle the German fan mail, she accepted. So it came as a surprise when on her first night with the family, Elvis simply climbed into bed with her, as he would do many times for much of the next year. They never had full sex. That, he told her, was something he didn't do with girls he was going to see on a regular basis, because he didn't want to run the risk of her becoming pregnant. But he did enjoy heavy petting.

There was something seigneurial in his attitude towards Elisabeth, as there was to the gang of friends who worked for him. She wasn't allowed to date other men – that would have meant a towering rage and instant dismissal, and he would watch her suspiciously to make sure she wasn't getting too close to his courtiers, Red or Lamar. Expected to be always available for him, she also had to endure watching him spend evenings with other young women, and would often hear them together in his bedroom next to hers. She didn't think he had full sex with them either.

Why did she put up with it? The answer is obvious. She was in love. And, as he knew, Dixie aside, girls didn't leave him. It seems not to have occurred to him that his behaviour was cruel. If he did think about it, he didn't care. As casually generous as he could be, he could also be as casually selfish as the 'spoiled' child he once had been.

Being car-mad, he hadn't been long in Germany before he'd bought himself an expensive BMW sports car, a Cadillac for Vernon and another vehicle for Red and Lamar. Sometimes he would go driving at night, just for the joy of it, or to take girls home, but, although he was no longer quite the prisoner of fame that he had been in the US, his instinct for staying away from trouble, and keeping his nose clean as far as the army was concerned, proved a different kind of jailer.

Vernon, of course, was now in a different position. There had been rumours, never substantiated, that he might have been having an affair in Memphis when Gladys was alive, but now he was a very eligible widower, and very soon began an affair with the wife of an American serviceman. She was Dee Stanley, an attractive, mid-thirties blonde, with three young sons. Elvis suspected that she had originally set her sights on him, but had settled for his father when she realised that would prove impossible. Whether that was the case or not, to him, Vernon's affair, which began less than four months after the death of Gladys, was unforgiveable. To make matters worse, Dee was a noisy lover, and according to Lamar Fike, Elvis would be so embarrassed and upset by the cries of passion coming from his father's bedroom he would sit at the piano and hammer the keys to drown out the noise. Presumably Grandma would have heard the same sounds.

'That woman is just a gold digger, and other things,' she would say pointedly to Elisabeth Stefaniak.

While Elvis's great aunt Christine Roberts Presley would comment: 'I heard about that woman Vernon was with. The Presleys was all bad about such as that.'

Not surprisingly, relations between father and son soured, and for a time Vernon was banished back to Graceland, in the way that Elvis would sometimes fire the boys who worked for him for some misdemeanour or other before rehiring them. And although Dee would marry Vernon in 1960, and Elvis would welcome her sons as his half-brothers, and then employ them when they grew up, he never liked his stepmother.

Most GIs in a foreign country would go to bars or dance halls looking for girls, but Elvis never could. So they were brought to him. And the prettiest of all turned out to be the fourteen-year-old daughter of an army captain called Priscilla Beaulieu. Even before Dixie, Elvis had always liked the innocent charm of younger girls, but, as he would discover, Priscilla wasn't like so many others who would simply be overawed by his presence. As he was shy, too, this was something he would claim to not really understand, saying that he would always try to put others at ease when they met him. With Priscilla, however, this wasn't necessary. She was a confident girl. Having only been in Germany for three weeks, she was, she would later say, sitting in the Eagle Club at the PX, a place where families hung out, at the US Wiesbaden base, when a friendly young soldier called Currie Grant asked her if she would like to meet Elvis Presley. From the distance of over half a century, Grant's motivation in taking a young girl to meet a very famous man whom he knew liked teenage girls appears dubious. But that was the way Elvis met girls.

He was sitting listening to the Brenda Lee record 'Sweet Nothin's', enjoying the playing of the Nashville A-Team musicians who had also backed him, when, wearing a blue and white sailor dress and white socks, Priscilla walked in the door of his rented home. He was smitten, then stunned when she told him that she was still in ninth grade. She was, he would say, and others would agree, extraordinarily beautiful. Like a doll. Soon he was sitting at the piano playing and singing for her, before, a little later, he led her upstairs to his bedroom.

Red had returned to the US by then, tired of being treated like a 'Chinese coolie', one of his favourite expressions, but ever-faithful Lamar watched the burgeoning romance, worried stiff. Just a few months earlier Jerry Lee Lewis had been expelled from the United Kingdom and his career had come to a halt when it had been discovered that he had bigamously married his thirteen-year-old cousin. Priscilla was very young, too.

But for the next seven months she would return to the house in Goethestrasse regularly. At first her parents weren't happy about it, so Elvis drove over to their home and put their minds at rest, making sure to always address her stepfather, a captain in the US Air Force, as 'sir', and promising to take care of her. He did sincerity very well.

To Elvis, Priscilla was perfection. And, as he would tell his friends, she was young enough to be shaped by him. Part of that shaping meant that she was given amphetamines to keep her awake in school after being at his house for half the night. She later said she didn't take them, not then anyway. But he did, all the time.

Amphetamines had become a part of Gladys's life, and were now a regular part of his. While he had despaired of his mother's drinking, he would happily take her Benzedrine pills, and had then begun to arrange his own supply. Once, while giving his army colleague Rex Mansfield a handful, he would explain how truck drivers used them in the States to stay awake at the wheel on long trips. 'Plus, they have no side effects,' he stressed. He was, Rex would later write, already very well acquainted with them and was convinced they were harmless.

Was that why Elvis always had so much energy on stage, night after night?

If he did ever have any doubts about their safety, they would have been expelled when, like many other soldiers, he was handed Dexedrine by his army superiors while on manoeuvres. The theory was that they would help them stay awake while on guard duty overnight.

Being Elvis, though, one pill was never enough. Everything he liked was done to excess, and he would buy bulk supplies by the jar illegally from pharmacies at the base to distribute among his friends. For the weekend, Mansfield would remember, there would be two on a Friday morning, and two more at night, then the same on Saturday and Sunday, with the dosage lowered during the week. Elvis saw no danger in it, not for himself nor for those to whom he gave the pills.

Years later, did he ever wonder why he was always so hepped up, why sometimes he couldn't stop jiggling his foot, or why he had such sudden dramatic mood swings? For someone who would become so savvy about drugs, he must have done.

*

He didn't see much of Europe during his time in Germany, other than occasional nights out to nightclubs in Munich.

'The world is more alive at night,' he would say. 'It's like God isn't looking.'

But he did take two vacations to Paris, where he would visit the Moulin Rouge and the Folies Bergère. After making friends with some of the strippers there, he took a whole chorus line of English Bluebell Girls back to his hotel, where he and Red West played a practical joke on Lamar Fike. Secretly asking a couple of girls to walk around their hotel apartment completely naked as though it was the most natural thing in the world, they watched Lamar's amazed embarrassment. Because of Lamar's size, and he was always a fat boy, he would long be a target for Elvis's jokes, comments and pranks – not all of which were kind.

On a second, ten-day trip to Paris, he went to a karate exhibition, after which karate would play an increasingly large part in his leisure time. And then, with Charlie Hodge, he also went to see a performance by the Golden Gate Quartet, a group of black gospel singers who were on a European tour. After the show, he and Charlie went backstage and spent the rest of the evening singing spirituals and hymns with them. As he said so many times: his first love in music was 'the old coloured spirituals from years back'.

Like all young soldiers, he'd been counting the days until he could go home, and then it was suddenly on him and he was back in front of a press conference of German reporters to say goodbye. In the crowd he spotted a familiar face in a US Army captain's uniform. It was that of Marion Keisker. He hadn't seen her since her affair with Sam Phillips had ended in 1957 and she'd left Sun, before enlisting in the army.

'Marion!' he exclaimed in surprise. 'I don't know whether to kiss you or salute you.'

'Both. In that order,' she told him, beaming.

Young men are often changed during their time in military service, and Elvis was no exception. When he'd been drafted he'd been twenty-three years old, but in some senses, fame had arrested his development, making him still the boy sensation he'd been at twenty, devoted to his mother, and perhaps naïve in many ways.

After two years in the army, his ambition burned as brightly as ever, but now some of the wonder and romance of youth was gone. There was a more brittle, impatient, even arrogant edge to him.

20

'There was a little girl that I was seeing quite often over there . . . but it was no big romance.'

His hair was tawny coloured when he arrived back in the US at McGuire Air Force Base, New Jersey, in a snowstorm on 3 March 1960. Naturally there was a welcome home press conference so that the army could tell the world, without exaggeration, and to the surprise of some top brass, what an excellent soldier he'd turned out to be; and so that Sergeant Elvis could show off the three stripes on his arm.

'Clothes say things about you that *you* can't sometimes say,' he would occasionally remark of his extensive wardrobe.

And his hand-tailored and pressed army uniforms spoke eloquently of the Colonel's plan that he would emerge from military service as a national hero. To match his uniform, he was once again a model of disarming grace in front of the reporters, both in New Jersey and a few days later when he got home to Memphis. What Priscilla Beaulieu, who had gone to Frankfurt Airport to kiss him goodbye, must have thought when she read the newspaper reports, he put from his mind.

'There was a little girl that I was seeing quite often over there . . .' he began, 'but it was no big romance. I mean, the stories came out "The Girl He Left Behind" and all that. But it wasn't like that.' As he knew very well, it had been exactly like that.

Not everyone was left behind. He'd become very fond of secretary and sometime bedfellow Elisabeth Stefaniak, so she was offered a job as his secretary at Graceland, taken to Memphis and given her own car to drive. Before she left Germany he had also prevailed upon her to smuggle a large jar of Dexedrine back into the US in her suitcase. Now, he told her, somewhat magnanimously, that she could date other men. She was torn when she heard that. Did that mean he didn't care for her any more? She drew her own conclusions. But perhaps she also smiled inwardly. Because what Elvis didn't know was that, thanks to the intervention of Grandma, who liked the girl and could see that Elvis was wasting her life, Elisabeth was already seeing another guy. He was Elvis's army friend Rex Mansfield, whom he now wanted as his chief aide. Had Elvis known that, in his eyes, Elisabeth and Rex had been cheating on him with each other, he would have been incensed. There would have been no job offers for either.

For one of the few times in his adult life his personal plans were about to be thwarted. Elisabeth and Rex both knew that because of his jealousy and ego they couldn't work for him and be with each other. Given the choice, they decided that they would rather be together. So, as they would one day write, they secretly left Graceland and were married three months later. When Elvis found out, he considered their behaviour a betrayal. For them it was the right thing to do. Apart from a single Christmas card, they never heard from him again.

Back in Memphis, Elvis visited his mother's grave several times during his first few days at home. 'I don't believe that death is the end,' he would say sadly. 'I just don't.'

Soon, however, old friends began to assemble around him, bringing the usual consignment of new girls. Obviously Anita Wood came, too, his affectionate letters to her from Germany still in her mind. But, although she would live mainly at Graceland for another two years when he was home, there were always other women when he wasn't.

For a couple of weeks it was back to the all-night movies and the Rollerdrome with the gang routine. But, with two years to catch up on, after having his hair dyed black again, he hired a bus and he and the half-dozen guys who now permanently surrounded him were driven the two hundred miles to Nashville.

For RCA and Freddy Bienstock, the Aberbach brothers' cousin at Hill and Range, as much as for Elvis himself, the new recording sessions were crucial. Would the golden boy still have the magic touch when it came to picking and singing hits? Because of the Colonel's insistence on only one night's recording while Elvis had been away, no new single had been released since RCA had run out of suitable recordings nine months earlier; and at a time when a new record every three months was standard for a star, such a long absence from the radio stations was considered dangerous. So when Elvis walked into Studio B at Nashville, careers, other than his own, were resting upon the results of his night's work.

Nominally, Steve Sholes was the producer in charge, along with guitarist Chet Atkins, the guy who, Elvis felt, had first treated him like a one-hit wonder. But now everyone, including Atkins, deferred to him. Elvis chose the songs, including several old favourites, immediately rejected most of the Hill and Range demos that Bienstock had found and brought to the session, and then kept working and improvising around the ones he liked until he was satisfied. Bill Black was now doing well on his own as the leader of Bill Black's Combo and would soon have a big hit with his version of 'Don't Be Cruel', so he wasn't present. But Scotty Moore was, and would stay until 1968, though he'd now been demoted to being just one of several guitarists.

Because Elvis had to be in Miami in a few days' time to guest on *The Frank Sinatra Timex Show* on television – for which he was paid the then astronomical fee of $125,000 to sing two songs – the imperative at the first session was to make a new single. As it turned out, of the six tracks recorded that day the one chosen, 'Stuck on You', was probably one of the least ambitious, being little more than a re-hash of 'All Shook Up'. But it was a familiar sound for the fans, and with a million orders waiting it was on sale and in the charts in less than a week.

He'd returned from Germany by air, courtesy of the Air Force, but back in the US he resumed travelling by train as he journeyed from Nashville to Miami, waving occasionally at the swarms of fans and onlookers who manned every little station platform along the way, hoping to catch a glimpse of him. Perhaps some did, but most would have to wait with the rest of the nation for television to unveil the brand-new Elvis, as, shorn of his sideburns and in a black tuxedo and a cravat of a bow tie, he joked and duetted with Sinatra.

To watch the two harmonising on 'Love Me Tender', no one would have thought that just three years earlier Sinatra had referred obliquely to Elvis as a 'cretinous goon'. The older singer probably regretted his intemperate criticism now, especially as his daughter Nancy had become friendly with Elvis and had been at the airport to meet him on his return from Germany. But they would never become close and settled for a mutually pally politeness. Some years later both would record 'My Way', but, although Sinatra had the first and bigger hit, he never cared much for the song. Elvis, on the other hand, saw it almost as a testament of his own life.

A week after the TV show the Nashville sessions continued at an all-night marathon, with a dozen songs recorded in under twelve hours, including 'It's Now or Never' and 'Are You Lonesome Tonight?' Added to that there were covers of rhythm and blues favourites, 'Such a Night', 'Fever', and 'Like a Baby' by Jesse Stone, the writer of 'Money Honey', pure pop teenage laments like 'Girl of My Best Friend', and a friendly nod to blues guitarist Lowell Fulson with 'Reconsider Baby'. Perhaps to make up for their earlier falling out, Scotty was given a little favour. While Elvis had been in Germany, Scotty had set up his own record label and publishing company and had had a big hit with Thomas Wayne's 'Tragedy'. So Elvis now recorded another of Wayne's songs, 'Girl Next Door Went Walking', which Scotty also published. Finally Charlie Hodge's army friendship was recognised, as he was called on to sing a duet on a Golden Gate Quartet song 'I Will Be Home Again' – a shared memory of a night the two had enjoyed in Paris. Altogether it was a night of hits, r and b classics and favours to friends. Even the Colonel's wife, the rarely seen Marie, was given a treat. 'Are You Lonesome Tonight?' was one of her favourite songs. The result was two massive hits, four smaller ones and probably Elvis's best, and favourite, album, *Elvis Is Back!*

He wouldn't always be recorded well during his career, but, thanks to a new RCA engineer, Bill Porter, the Nashville sessions of the early sixties produced some of his best records. His voice was deeper, pitched slightly lower, and might have lost some of the raw anguish and youthful yearning of his early days. But, thanks to his months of singing with Charlie in Germany, there was a greater elasticity of tone to it, with his range wider now and his falsetto more controlled. As Gordon Stoker of the Jordanaires would say about the recording of 'It's Now or Never': 'We were all surprised. We knew he could sing. But we didn't know he could sing that well.'

Records and television quickly dealt with, it was Hollywood next, and three weeks later he was in Los Angeles recording the tracks for his first post-army film, *G.I. Blues*, for Hal Wallis. He'd looked forward to resuming his movie career, but immediately he found himself facing a problem.

As he would miserably tell Priscilla in long-distance calls to Germany, half the songs for *G.I. Blues* just weren't good enough. For two years he'd talked publicly about making better movies with more dramatic parts and of learning to become a better actor. But the very first film that the Colonel had put him into was a light-hearted romp about the misunderstandings a good-looking GI like him might have with girls while on a tour of duty in Germany. In other words, an exploitation of his army days, with a specially written collection of songs from writers contracted to the Aberbach brothers' Hill and Range company. A couple of numbers submitted by Leiber and Stoller weren't even considered because they refused to give up any part of the songwriting royalties on them. In the end only one song, 'Doin' the Best I Can', from Mort Shuman and Doc Pomus, the writers of 'A Mess of Blues', had any real quality. As the late Mort Shuman said: 'Elvis really got into his Ink Spots routine on that one.'

As for the rest, the songs didn't properly represent him in the way that those on *Elvis Is Back!* did. When Priscilla, with the honest sense of a fifteen-year-old, asked him what the Colonel had said when he'd complained about the songs, he told her: 'Hell, what could he say? I'm locked into this thing.'

Already a clear difference of opinion was opening between him and his manager about what direction his film career should follow. There was Hollywood talk at the time that director Robert Wise had sounded out the William Morris Agency, who fielded all approaches to the Colonel, with the idea that perhaps Elvis might be right for the part of Tony in the movie version of the stage show *West Side Story*, alongside his short-lived flame Natalie Wood. The Colonel, it was then rumoured, turned the idea down with the excuse that he didn't want Elvis appearing in a movie about street gangs and knife fights.

If the story is true, a more honest explanation might have been that there was no way Parker would let Elvis appear in a film featuring Leonard Bernstein–Stephen Sondheim songs which the Aberbachs didn't publish, and in which they, and he, didn't have a publishing share. The downside of the deal that Elvis had agreed when he'd left Sun in 1955 – in which he'd been given an extra $1000 by the Aberbach brothers in exchange for going into a music publishing partnership with them – was now emerging. From then on, when making movie albums, he would increasingly find himself committed to singing almost exclusively songs that the Aberbachs either published or on which they could at least get a share of the publishing royalties. And the songs would usually not be good enough.

In terms of developing Elvis's long-term career, *West Side Story*, which won nine Oscars, would have been the perfect project, a dramatic story with peerless songs such as 'Maria', 'Tonight' and 'Somewhere'. And he now had the voice for them. But, no matter how good or big the film might be, his share of the money would never have been big enough to satisfy his manager. Was he even consulted about the project? Probably not. So, unhappy as he was, he made the best of things. There were two more movies to follow in the next few months. Perhaps the scripts for those would be better.

When he'd left the army a few weeks earlier he'd said: 'The army makes men out of boys.' But when he wasn't working on the set at Paramount, it quickly began to look as though Hollywood was making a boy out of a man, as he and his gang played rumbustious games in the corridors of the staid Beverly Wilshire hotel. He might have complained about the limpness of the script and the songs he had to sing, but in many ways his attitude didn't help. Serious actors didn't, mid-movie, party with legions of girls, and be out in nightclubs way into the early hours, high on amphetamines.

Shooting an Elvis Presley movie never took more than a few weeks, and by the end of June he was back in Graceland for a month's vacation. It was a fraught time. Dee Stanley's divorce had now come through, and she and Vernon were married on 3 July. It was less than two years since Gladys's death, and, rather than go to the ceremony, Elvis went water skiing. He hated the idea that Dee and Vernon would be sleeping together in what had been his mother's house.

Putting on a brave face for the public, he gave Dee a not-very-coded warning. 'She seems pretty nice,' he told the *Memphis Press-Scimitar*. 'But I only had one mother, and that's it. There'll never be another. As long as she understands that, there won't be any trouble.' Asked about his father, he was totally loyal, despite his feelings. 'He's all I've got left in the world,' he said. 'I'll never go against him or stand in his way. He stood by me all those years and sacrificed things he wanted so that I could have clothes and lunch money to go to school.'

He welcomed Dee's young sons at Graceland, too, saying, 'I always wanted a brother, now I've got three stepbrothers,' as he showered them with gifts. Tellingly, though, when he'd bought Graceland, the house had been put in both his name and those of his parents. It was, he always said, their home, too. Now he made sure that legally it was in his name only.

21

'Whatever I become, will be what God has chosen for me.'

Flaming Star was more the kind of movie he'd had in mind. A grown-up Western about race, his part was that of a young man of mixed Native American and European parentage who gets caught up in the hostilities and prejudices between the two worlds. Set mainly on location in California and with a screenplay by Nunnally Johnson, a much valued Hollywood writer who had adapted *The Grapes of Wrath* and *The Three Faces of Eve* and written dozens of other movies, and with Don Siegel, who would later make the Clint Eastwood classic *Dirty Harry*, directing, it should have had great potential.

Inevitably he would have had his mother's stories about his Cherokee great, great, great grandmother, Morning Dove, in the back of his mind when he heard about the role. Even if he was only a little bit Cherokee, he would surely fit the part well, and, after taking riding lessons, with and without a saddle, he even tried brown contact lenses to disguise his lighter eye colouring. Unfortunately, although they revealed to him that he might need new glasses, he didn't like them, so he took them out.

Once again, however, there was trouble with the songs, with, Elvis joked sourly, a couple that were hardly even songs at all. Considering the subject and style of the movie there shouldn't have been any singing at all, but Twentieth Century Fox wanted some musical insurance for their risk in investing in a dramatic Presley film. So, four songs were recorded, only two of which were used, one having to be re-recorded when the film's title was changed from *Black Star* to *Flaming Star*.

All through shooting, 'It's Now or Never' was setting singles records around the world, with over nine million copies eventually sold, making it the biggest Presley hit ever. So he should have been on a high. But the experience of playing a straight acting leading role was proving a disappointment. Don Siegel felt his star's attention was 'removed' from the movie, and he became irritated by the karate chops that the star and his entourage would practise between shots. *Flaming Star* wasn't a bad movie, but Elvis knew it was an opportunity missed. And when it was released, just a month after *G.I. Blues*, to so-so reviews and similar box office returns, it quickly disappeared from cinemas.

Ironically, much as Elvis had disregarded the frothy *G.I. Blues*, his German 'travelogue' was a smash hit, as was the album of songs from it, selling almost three times as many records as *Elvis Is Back!*, of which he was so proud.

Without his mother, Graceland wasn't the same.

'I think of her nearly every single day,' he told a reporter. 'If I never do anything really wrong, it's all because of her. She wouldn't let me do anything wrong.'

And with these thoughts in mind, at the end of October he went back to Nashville to fulfil a promise to her. In the last Christmas of her life, he'd told her that when he got the chance he would record a whole album of gospel songs, and that is what he now did.

To many, it appeared a bizarre thing for the *enfant terrible* of rock and roll to even consider. But musically he saw no conflict, and had no embarrassment about singing church music.

'Rock and roll is basically just gospel music,' he would explain, before further elucidating, 'or gospel music mixed with rhythm and blues.'

And with an attitude quite different from that shown when he'd recently been in Hollywood, he was never more committed as he recorded fourteen tracks in an overnight session. Almost in the style of a preacher he might have seen at Reverend Brewster's church in Memphis, or in the little Assembly of God church in Tupelo, he raced and soared through spirituals and hymns and, best of all, the Children's Bible story of Joshua at the battle of Jericho.

'Gospel music,' he liked to say, 'is the purest thing on this earth,' and, although his religious albums weren't aimed at the charts, their sales over the decades went into millions. For him, the most important thing was that his singing was probably never better.

He took his religion seriously, but his personal behaviour was much changed from the young man who, when he'd gone to the Grand Ole Opry, had left a bar in Nashville because he didn't think it was the kind of place his parents would like to see him in. By now his entire personality was a squall of permanently conflicting currents. Sexually promiscuous, a hopelessly unfaithful lover, frequently jealous, and prone to unpredictable furies, he was also massively generous. If an acquaintance happened to admire some piece of jewellery he was wearing he would often offer it as a gift. He just couldn't stop himself from giving. Friends and relations all got presents, while a maid at Graceland was given a car because he thought it was too far for her to walk from her home to the bus stop every day when she came to work.

On the other hand there were the tantrums, never directed at the Graceland staff but often at the guys, who sometimes seemed to be there specifically as a buffer to soak up his frustrations. His language as a boy had been more restrained than that of his friends, and he'd complained to Red before he'd gone into the army that Red's cousin, Sonny, who now also worked for him, kept saying 'son of a bitch'. Now, as he grew older, he could be as crude as any man, but, in another moment, as a lifelong reader of the Bible, he would pepper his conversations with religious adages like a pastor.

Almost certainly, many of these came from his mother's teaching, and explaining his lavish giving, he would say, 'So, help your brother along, no matter where he starts, because the same God that made you, made him'; of his wealth, his comment was, 'all of this is but for a day'; and on his singing talent, his reply would be, 'whatever I become, will be what God has chosen for me'.

Was there an element of hypocrisy in all this? Sometimes, obviously. But, equally, it illustrates the contradictory mindset of someone brought up, and comfortable, in a narrow spiritual world who didn't understand his own talent and its appeal, and who found himself placed in the impossible position of being globally adored. It would have turned most men's heads, even without the amphetamines that were giving him the confidence and energy he felt he needed to be able to function.

Two movies in six months should have been more than enough, but another was pushed into the hectic schedule before 1960 was out, suggesting perhaps that once again manager Parker and Hollywood wanted to make up for two lost years, and cash in before the Elvis bubble burst. It was called *Wild in the Country* and, once again, the omens were good. With a screenplay by Clifford Odets, who had co-written the classic *Sweet Smell of Success*, and with Philip Dunne, who had recently had a hit with the Carol Lynley teenage hit *Blue Denim*, as director, the cast included Hope Lange and a very sexy teenage temptress played by Tuesday Weld – whose company Elvis had already kept. His role was again that of a poor, sullen, going-nowhere boy, but this time one with a hidden literary talent, a no-hoper whom the Hope Lange character fights, tames and teaches until he eventually goes off to college. Elvis was excited by the part. All of his life it would bother him that he hadn't had more education, and when, just before shooting began, a college fraternity in Arkansas had 'honoured' him on a jokey whim by inducting him as a member, instead of being insulted by the scam, he'd taken it seriously, and been flattered.

Wild in the Country, however, was as big a disappointment as *Flaming Star*. Once again, as last-minute changes to the script were made, songs were added. They weren't bad, but they shifted the mood of the movie completely. And once more Elvis's gang of gofers became a silly distraction around the set.

Something else was wrong though, too. Elvis's temper was foul. He had seen how being cast in *From Here to Eternity* had changed Frank Sinatra's life, and he still hoped that this would happen to him. But a hybrid film like this, neither fully dramatic nor a musical, wasn't the way. And much as he enjoyed working with Tuesday Weld, this wasn't what he had been hoping for. To his pals he would blame the scripts for these movies, but in his heart did he wonder if he just wasn't at ease enough in any character's shoes other than his own? If he did think that, he stifled it, and once again hoped for better things to come.

He was now renting a house on the millionaires' Bel Air estate off Sunset Boulevard, and, as he was driven home along that wide, winding road after filming, did he ever reflect about the character played by William Holden in the movie *Sunset Boulevard*; how Hollywood money had fictionally tempted him to prostitute his talent and how it would eventually kill him?

Possibly he did, because he would certainly have seen the film. But at that moment at the end of 1960 he was, in musical terms, at least, the prince of all he surveyed. With no rivals in terms of popularity, his records were selling in prodigious quantities, to the extent that there were often too many hits to be released. The German folk song 'Muss i denn' from *G.I. Blues* had been given English lyrics as 'Wooden Heart' and put out as a single in Germany where it became a million seller, as well as becoming a perennial favourite in the UK. But with no space for it in the US schedule, a singer called Joe Dowell had the US number one with a cover of the song. Equally, 'The Girl of My Best Friend' from *Elvis Is Back!*, coupled with 'A Mess of Blues', was a number two double-sided UK smash, but a cover hit for Ral Donner in the US.

With so many hits, and so much success, he should have been happy. But nothing was as much fun as it had been before he'd been called up, though the Memphis Mafia, as his entourage had now been nicknamed, did their best to keep him amused.

It was a journalist who had come up with the 'Memphis Mafia' soubriquet for his coterie of pals. The guys, who generally referred to their boss as 'E', mostly loved it, and believing that it gave them an amusing team identity, they began to wear matching black cashmere suits and dark glasses. Elvis hated the name, seeing something seedy in its association with corruption.

His habit of surrounding himself with poorly paid relatives and friends had begun at Sun, but as his appeal had grown, so had his entourage. There was no formal entry to being a member of the gang. If you were liked you became a companion, and if that worked out and you could be trusted you might go on the payroll. None of the guys earned very much, but all living expenses would be found for you while you were with Elvis. It was, however, a twenty-four hour job, seven days a week, and wouldn't necessarily have appealed to young men who had something more ambitious to do.

Some outsiders saw some members of the gang as just a leach of hangers-on, but that would be unfair to Marty Lacker, who had known Elvis as a friend since high school and was the foreman of the entourage for a while. Equally, Joe Esposito from the army had taken Rex Mansfield's proposed job and proved a good and capable captain of the group. Then there was cousin Harold Lloyd, who became a groundsman at Graceland, and another young cousin Billy Smith, whose family had followed the Presleys up from Tupelo. Eight years younger than Elvis, he would become a lifelong confidant. Sonny West was a big, tough fellow who, should the need arise, acted as a bodyguard, and Sonny's cousin Red and Lamar Fike had been loyal enough to follow Elvis to Germany.

But, over the years, there were others at Elvis's beck and call, too. Often without much to do, apart from hang around and joke with their boss, some of them looked like nothing more than a posse of sycophants, joking and nodding on cue. Famously, when a reporter once asked Junior Smith what he actually did, Junior just laughed at the question. 'I don't do nothing,' he said. 'I'm Elvis's cousin.'

Nor was it only in Hollywood that Elvis surrounded himself. Graceland wasn't just his family's home, as Audubon Drive had been. Little by little it started turning into a little fiefdom, where Elvis was the leader of the clan, with relatives moving into trailer homes around the back to keep Grandma company, and army pal Charlie Hodge living in a room in the basement. Then there were his uncles Travis Smith and Vester Presley and their families; they were always there, as were the staff who ran the house and the garden and took care of the estate and the herd of cars. Most of the gang would live nearby in Memphis, but Graceland was their centre of gravity, and, when Elvis was there, that is where they would be, day in, day out.

Always, though, he was the focus of everyone's attention. Everything in Graceland revolved around him, and, like an eighteenth-century English lord of the manor, he made all the house rules down to the tiniest detail. For instance, he couldn't stand the smell of fish in his home, so no one was ever allowed to cook it. Equally no old car was allowed to stand outside the front entrance. He wanted everything neat and clean.

Normally the head of a clan is the patriarch, the daddy of them all, and an older and wiser man. But in 1960 Elvis was only twenty-five, yet responsible for everything. And that was how he wanted it. He loved being Elvis Presley and he loved having his own court and courtiers to attend to his needs and desires, guys who would play boys' games with him when he wanted. He also enjoyed making the rules. It didn't compensate for the loneliness of his life, but it made him feel good, beneficent and powerful. He might not have felt that he was in full control of his own career, and he knew that he was bullied by the Colonel. But he was in control of those who waited on him, and whom he in turn would bully.

If he was already having misgivings about Hollywood, and he was always more of a worrier than he let on in public, there was one certain way to lift his spirits. That was for him to perform on stage again, something he hadn't done since 1958. So, early in 1961, the Colonel arranged a benefit concert, and, summoning the full band with whom Elvis now recorded in Nashville, there was a rehearsal at Graceland and then two concerts in Memphis for twenty-six local charities. He enjoyed being back on stage, but he was flattered, too, when, the following week, he was honoured in Nashville by the Tennessee State Legislature on 'Elvis Presley Day'.

'This is the finest honour I've ever achieved,' he told the assembly as he thanked them. It was a big step for a boy from Lauderdale Courts.

But, perhaps just as telling, was something that happened after the ceremony. While driving his new Rolls-Royce home he stopped off at Tennessee State Prison. He wanted to visit inmate Johnny Bragg, the young African-American with the beautiful voice, who had been the lead doo-wop singer on the Prisonaires' 'Just Walkin' in the Rain'. That had been Sam Phillips' first hit in 1953, one of the records that had helped attract the schoolboy Elvis to Sun. In the eight years since Bragg had made that recording, Elvis's life had changed beyond imagination. For Bragg, it had been eight years in a prison cell, apart from venturing out under armed guard to sing with his fellow inmates, and that was how it would stay until 1969. Was there anything he could do to help, Elvis asked the prisoner. Did he need a lawyer?

A second charity concert a couple of weeks later was staged in Honolulu to raise funds for the USS *Arizona* Memorial Fund, the battleship that had been sunk there by Japanese bombers twenty years earlier. It was one of manager Parker's better ideas, and, with Elvis back in his gold jacket, RCA recorded it as a live album. With any degree of foresight either they or the Colonel would have filmed it, too. Indeed plans had been started to turn it into a television show for NBC, but they'd come to nothing, like many other proposals, when Parker asked for too much money for his client.

As it happened, the technology for live albums was then in its infancy and technical glitches meant the RCA album wouldn't be released for over thirty years, when it could be partly salvaged. That was a pity because by singing 'Reconsider Baby', 'I Need Your Love Tonight', 'Such a Night' and 'Swing Low, Sweet Chariot', Elvis was demonstrating the kind of music he wanted to be singing – and what he did best, before ending with seven minutes of 'Hound Dog', as he had done at every show since 1956.

As he made his escape from the stage in Honolulu that night, he didn't know it, but he would never hear mass teenage screaming again – not for him anyway. He wouldn't sing in public again until 1969, by which time the music world and his part in it would have changed completely.

22

'I didn't have any say-so in it all'

Elvis on Hollywood

The trip to Hawaii in April 1961 wasn't only for him to appear in a benefit concert. His real task there was to star in a Hal Wallis girls, sun and songs movie for Paramount. It was called *Blue Hawaii* and would prove to be his biggest grossing film ever, provide a bestselling album and give him one of his most enduring hits, 'Can't Help Falling in Love'. He no doubt enjoyed the money it earned him, but this hadn't been how he had envisaged his career back in 1957.

Slightly overweight, a matter brought bluntly to his attention by Hal Wallis, he went on a slimming campaign before shooting began, but, from the beginning, he was depressed. The songs, several of which he really hadn't wanted to sing, had already been recorded in Los Angeles at the end of March, when only 'Can't Help Falling in Love' and 'No More' had interested him. Both were based on traditional melodies with new English lyrics especially written for them. The first came from the French love song 'Plaisir d'Amour', and 'No More' began as the Spanish song 'La Paloma'. With new lyrics having been written for 'Love Me Tender', 'It's Now or Never' and 'Surrender', it had become a tried and tested route to an Elvis bestseller. In fact, despite the team of writers attached to Hill and Range, surprisingly few of his biggest hits throughout his career would be new songs, many having been first recorded unsuccessfully by other artists before he got to hear them, or being revivals of older songs he'd always liked. For the *Blue Hawaii* soundtrack, 'Hawaiian Wedding Song' had recently been a hit for Andy Williams, while the title song had been a Bing Crosby standard from the thirties. The other songs were those his publishers had thrust on him, and most were either cute or dull, although that wouldn't have been the word he used to describe them.

But, never wanting to show any ingratitude towards the Colonel who kept telling him how hard he'd had to work to get him such good financial deals, Elvis put aside his reservations and got on with the singing.

'I didn't have any say-so in it all,' he would explain years later, 'so I did it like it was a job'; complaining only to the guys when the day's recording or filming was over.

Quite what he thought when he saw the album sleeve for *Blue Hawaii*, he never said publicly. But, wearing a Hawaiian shirt, with a chain of flowers around his neck and with a little ukulele in his hands, the image was as distant from his first classic album cover, when he'd appeared to be simply howling his rebellion, as any that could be imagined. Even before the needle went down on the first track, the message was unmistakable. At twenty-six the new, plumper Elvis, the guy with the neatly sprayed, patent leather hair, was no longer of the rock and roll world. Between them, Parker, Hollywood and his music publishers had turned the god of youth that had been the boy Elvis into a middle-of-the-road, bland, cash cow of an entertainer.

That, Parker convinced him, was where the money lay. He still wanted to be rich, didn't he?

Well, yes, he did. But, for probably the first time since he'd met Parker, he found himself uncertain about the advice the older man was giving. When he'd returned to the US after his army stint he would have seen how quickly the world was changing. Always a Democrat, he had been for Adlai Stevenson in the presidential primaries ('I'm strictly for Stevenson,' he'd said. 'I don't dig the intellectual bit, but I'm telling you, man, he knows the most'), but a younger man, John F. Kennedy, had won the primaries and then the presidency. And, with the replacement of the elderly President Eisenhower in the White House, a new attitude of youth was flowing through America as baby boomers reached their mid-teens. When he'd started out Elvis had been a one-off, a total self-creation, who had captured the mood of the youth of the nation and far beyond. He'd been the moment. Now, still only in his mid-twenties, he was being pushed to appeal to an older, and musically less critical or currently aware audience, just as the world's record-buying public was growing younger. He was torn. But Parker was dead right about the money. Elvis did want to be rich, and he still felt he owed Parker his loyalty. And, who knows, a good movie script might turn up any day.

So, avoiding confrontation and simply hoping things in Hollywood would get more to his liking, he didn't complain and got on with what he called 'the job'. Though, as if to show what he really felt he should be doing, straight after filming he released his version of an old r and b hit by Chuck Willis, 'Feel So Bad', as his next single, putting the *Wild in the Country* film theme song on the B-side. Then, back in Nashville, he recorded two songs by New York songwriters Doc Pomus and Mort Shuman, 'His Latest Flame' and the rocker 'Little Sister', which he listened to with pride over and over until 7.30 in the morning. His rock judgement was still spot on. Together those recordings made his best double-sided hit since 1956.

An income from record sales couldn't, however, compete with movie money and already his recording career was being pushed to the margins, so that one film might follow another regularly every four months, each with an album of its own to be promoted.

'Not all the films were bad,' Elvis would later reflect, slightly defensively. 'Some were quite funny . . . entertaining.'

That was true of his next movie *Follow That Dream*, in which he played a singing, good-hearted, simple hillbilly boy for laughs. With a pleasant enough script, it gave him the opportunity to demonstrate an easy ability for comedy. But, as soon as it was completed he was back in front of the cameras again, this time playing a singing boxer in *Kid Galahad* – his sixth film in eighteen months. It was movie overkill.

The formula for the rest of the sixties was dazzlingly clear to Tom Parker and the Aberbachs. Elvis would have to put aside his dreams of playing serious roles, or even comedy parts. With *Loving You*, *G.I. Blues* and especially *Blue Hawaii*, Hal Wallis had made three big hit Elvis movies with simple plots, lots of pretty girls and even more songs. That was the way to go, and between 1962 and 1967 he would appear in a further fifteen, each with a break in the story every few minutes for a song to be inserted into the action.

The enormous success of *Blue Hawaii* had changed everything. It was a peak, all right, but it was also the top of a slippery slope as far as movies were concerned. For Elvis it would be a long slide down. When, a decade later, he would be asked about the treadmill he'd found himself on, he would loyally say, 'It's nobody's fault except my own,' and then explain how difficult it had been for his music publishers to find twelve new songs for every film.

Well, maybe. But did his publishers not make it a great deal harder for themselves than it need have been by demanding a third of the income the songs earned for the writers as a kick-back? Of the fourteen songs recorded for *Blue Hawaii*, only two weren't fully published by one of Elvis's two publishing companies with Hill and Range. To Julian and Jean Aberbach, who jointly owned Elvis Presley Music and his other company Gladys Music with him, and to their cousin Freddy Bienstock, who was now their working link with Elvis, it all made good business sense. It made good sense to the Colonel, too, who also had a share in the companies, and whose 25 per cent plus commission on whatever Elvis earned was always further increased by the side deals he made with the film studios – from having rent-free offices to a fee for what Parker called 'technical assistance'.

It must have made a kind of sense for Elvis, too, if he didn't think about it for too long. Running the estate that was Graceland, renting an expensive home in Bel Air, and keeping so many staff in board, lodging and salary in both Memphis and California, not to mention his often out-of-control spending and carefree generosity, called for an endless river of money.

With the best will in the world, however, the Hill and Range songwriters would never be able to provide over thirty good new film songs a year for three movies.

'What am I supposed to do with this piece of shit?' Elvis would grumble to Gordon Stoker of the Jordanaires, when faced with a truly terrible number to record . . . before obediently getting on and singing it. He could, of course, have gone to the Aberbachs and demanded better material. But then he knew that would have meant getting songs from writers other than those with whom Freddy Bienstock could negotiate a shared publishing deal. And that would have lost them all money. Did he ever think it was greedy of his publishers and management to insist on such kick-backs? Probably. But he wasn't a businessman, and would have been told that it was standard practice in the music business.

He wasn't stupid. He fully realised that bad songs and poor movies were damaging his career. Better to earn less and have bigger hits and a greater sense of satisfaction from his singing, one would have thought. But did he have the guts to say that to his manager? It would appear not. He hated and avoided confrontation almost as much as Parker loved money and control.

He was never told, nor probably ever asked, about all the intricacies of negotiation, but when Hal Wallis baulked at some further financial demands Parker put on him, the Colonel simply turned to other movie studios for instant money. Thus in a four picture deal in 1961, MGM agreed to pay Elvis half a million dollars a movie, plus 25 per cent of the net profits, and the usual bit more on the side for the Colonel on top of his commission. The Aberbachs would again control the songs. Put all that together and one wonders how there was enough money left to make a movie, or at least a film of any quality – which would have meant employing a good screenwriter and an imaginative director.

Parker never made a secret of the fact that he didn't read scripts. 'Why would I?' he would say. 'They aren't going to pay Elvis a million dollars and then give him a lousy script, are they?' But they were. At what point did Elvis realise how absurd the situation had become, when, arguably the biggest draw in the world, he was agreeing to appear in movies before he or his manager had seen the scripts? What other star in the world would have done that? Can we imagine Paul Newman or Steve McQueen allowing their careers to be run in that way? Parker's attitude sometimes belies comprehension.

'I felt obligated to do things I didn't believe in,' Elvis would eventually admit. 'I was locked in.' But, did he ever ask himself who had turned the key in the lock when he'd signed those movie contracts? Had his need for money to finance his lavish lifestyle, homes and hangers-on meant that he'd helped turn that key himself?

So, what did the young man worth the unprecedented sum of a million dollars for three weeks' work do when he wasn't filming? Basically he played with his pals in Bel Air, or scooted off to Las Vegas whenever he could, where he would go to see acts he liked, such as Fats Domino, Della Reese and Jackie Wilson.

Mainly, though, his free time was spent in California, being amused by the behaviour of Scatter, a chimpanzee he'd bought, which had been taught by a previous owner to entertain by picking up the hems of young women's skirts in order to see their panties. The guys thought this was hilarious: the girls less so. The guys also thought the fitting of a two-way mirror in a changing room by the pool was fun, too. Asked why he needed it, as most girls would undress for him anyway, Elvis is said to have replied, 'It's more fun this way.'

Then there were the touch football games at De Neve Park, just off Sunset Boulevard, against other teams of Hollywood friends, like Ty Hardin, who was starring in the *Bronco* cowboy TV series, Rick (formerly Ricky) Nelson and Johnny Rivers. He could have gone to movie previews almost any night, like other Hollywood luminaries. That way he might have met screenwriters, producers and directors who could have suggested his career went in a different direction, but he never did. Would he have felt uncomfortable in such a situation, being treated more as an equal? Possibly. But the Colonel would have raged at him if he'd ever looked beyond him for advice. So he stayed at home every night with the guys and the girls.

Often, while a party was going on downstairs, he would lock his bedroom door and call Priscilla, still at school in Germany and often in his thoughts, or Anita, mainly back in Memphis, and waiting for him; before, late in the evening, he would change his clothes. Then, checking that not a lacquered hair was out of place, he would make his way down the stairs to join the gang and meet the girls – sitting like pretty maids all in a row, hoping to be the chosen one.

For once he didn't go home for Christmas in 1961. Without his mother to see, and with Vernon now with Dee, and therefore no family to enfold him, there was nothing for him there. Besides he was furious that Dee had changed the curtains at Graceland while he'd been away.

'If she thinks she's going to just take over Graceland, she has another think coming,' was his message that got back to Vernon.

Soon Vernon and Dee and her three sons would have to move out to a separate home of their own in a nearby road.

Instead of Memphis, Elvis's festive season was celebrated in Las Vegas with the guys and their wives and girlfriends and with whoever he hooked up with. *Blue Hawaii* was a hit in the cinemas and the

Eighteen-year-old actress Dolores Hart was the romantic interest in Elvis's second film *Loving You.* A niece of tenor Mario Lanza, she personified innocence and would later appear in *King Creole*. Then at the age of twenty-four she left Hollywood and entered a Catholic convent as a nun, where she stayed for the rest of her life.

Elvis's drafting into the army in March 1958 broke the hearts of millions of fans, but none more so than that of his mother, Gladys. Also waving him off was his father and his girlfriend, Anita Wood, as well as friends who had been out with him all the previous night.

Elvis sits crying with his father, Vernon, on the steps of Graceland as reporters and photographers walk up the drive after the death of Gladys in August 1958. He wore the white shirt with frills because Gladys had liked to see him wearing it.

Suddenly he's just a number. Elvis reflects dolefully on his change of status as he becomes Private Presley US53310761, earning $78 a month.

The girl he left behind. Fifteen-year-old Priscilla Beaulieu braves the weather to say goodbye to Elvis as he leaves Frankfurt Airport to return to the US at the end of his army service in 1960. They would marry when she was nineteen.

Frank Sinatra had obliquely referred to Elvis in 1957 as a 'side-burned delinquent' and 'a cretinous goon'. By 1960, however, he welcomed him on his TV show where they sang 'Witchcraft' and 'Love Me Tender' together, but they would never be best friends.

'The only thing worse than watching a bad movie, is being in one,' Elvis liked to say. This poster shot for *Blue Hawaii* in 1960, one of many beach movies he starred in, sums up in a single image the wrong turn his career took in Hollywood.

Elvis is honoured in Nashville by the Tennessee State Legislature on 'Elvis Presley Day' in 1961. On the way back to Memphis he visits Johnny Bragg, a young African-American inmate in Tennessee State Prison who had been the lead singer on the Prisonaires' record *Just Walkin' in the Rain* – Sam Phillips's first hit.

Elvis and Ann-Margret, whom he nicknamed Thumper after the rabbit character in *Bambi*, during a break in shooting *Viva Las Vegas* in 1963. She was unattached, and, when he was in Hollywood and Priscilla was back in Memphis, he believed he was, too.

Elvis liked to be mothered – maybe even on the day of his wedding to Priscilla in 1967.

He may not have been a favourite of her father, but Nancy Sinatra welcomed him home from Germany in 1960 and was his co-star in *Speedway* in 1968. By then Elvis was a married man, so Nancy insisted that there was no off-camera romance.

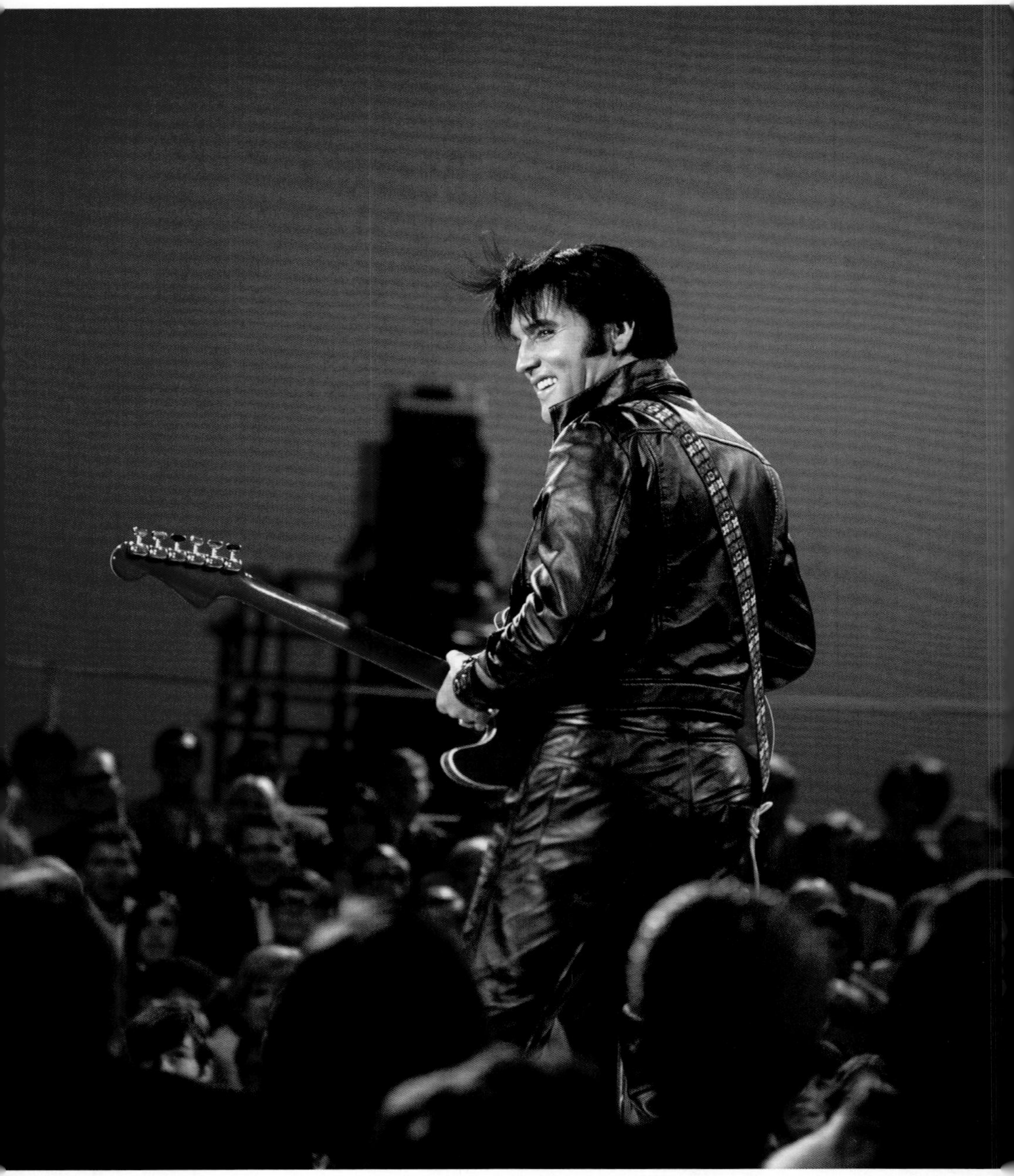

By 1968 Elvis's movie career was almost finished as the fans bored of what he called the 'travelogues' he'd been starring in since his army days. Back to television, the 1968 NBC special, in which he wore this black leather suit, reinvigorated his entire career.

album charts, two more films were waiting to be released, and 'Can't Help Falling in Love' was a number one record in the US, UK, across Europe and down to Australia, and on its way to becoming one of his all-time classics. But was he happy? Not in the way he had been.

His mother still ghosted through his life. She always would. One day he suggested to his friend Red, who dabbled in songwriting, that 'Someone You Never Forget' might make a good title for a song. Red picked up the message and together they wrote: 'The way she held your hand, the little things you planned, You know she'll wait for you, that's someone you never forget.'

He never doubted that his mother would be waiting for him; that he would see her again.

23

The schoolgirl who carried a derringer in her bra

Despite the various relationships he'd had in the two years since he'd left the army, some of which may have lasted as long as location work on a movie, others that didn't make it through a night, and while Anita was still his steady girlfriend whenever he was in Memphis, it was Priscilla Beaulieu at school in Germany who continued to command his greatest fascination. When he'd returned to the US he and she would, in their more realistic moments, have probably imagined that months apart would dull his fascination with her. But it hadn't happened. He was unpredictable about keeping in touch on any regular basis, and he didn't write her letters, as, with nothing much else to do, he'd written to Anita while he'd been in Germany. But he called her, usually when he was at home at Graceland, and, when he did, the conversations would go on for hours. So what was it that made her so special to him? Youth, beauty and virginity all no doubt played a part, but there was something else.

He'd been lonely when he'd met her in Bad Nauheim in the year after the death of his mother, and he'd been worried about his career. He could always talk to girls and women more easily than he could to men, with whom he would assume a more confident, cavalier persona, and he was always more comfortable with young, sexually inexperienced girls than those been-around-a-bit film actresses he'd met in Hollywood. He'd needed to talk, and Priscilla had been a good listener. In some undefined way, she reminded him, he would say, of the way his mother had been when he'd been a little boy. So, as thoughts of her still lingered, and he sent her records he liked or the new ones he'd made himself, he began to suggest, first to her, and then to her parents, that she should visit him in Los Angeles – where, of course, he promised, he would take care of her and she would be chaperoned at all times.

It took a while to convince her parents – months, actually – but he could wait. He had another movie to make in Hawaii, *Girls, Girls, Girls* – in which he played a singing charter boat pilot this time, after another warning from Hal Wallis about his weight. And, in the meantime, he had yet another number one hit record in the spring of 1962 with 'Good Luck Charm'. It was a well-produced pop song that he'd recorded in Nashville, but he would never sing it again after the session.

Nor, more surprisingly, did he ever return to the flip side. That was 'Anything That's Part of You'. On the surface, the song's lyric is about a deserted lover who is trying to hold on to memories of a woman who has left him. Elvis, though, would see it in another context. On returning from Germany, he'd looked sadly at his mother's belongings, all left, as he had ordered, as they had been on the day she died, before having them put in boxes and stored in the Graceland attic. He kept everything.

The lyrics of 'Anything That's Part of You' spoke directly to him. 'I kept a ribbon from your hair,' he sang, 'a breath of perfume lingers there . . .' And then comes the final agonised lament: 'I'd give all of someone new for anything that's part of you.'

His emotions dictated the way he sang. When given good material he was known to underline specific words on the song sheet in order to wring the maximum feeling from them, showing more dramatic conviction in a recording session than ever he did in front of a film camera. Like most great interpreters, in order to get the best from a song he had to believe the words he was singing. His performance suggests that he believed the words to 'Anything That's Part of You' perfectly.

At last, in June 1962, Priscilla, her hair in a teenage pony tail, arrived in Los Angeles, to be met at the airport, not by Elvis, but by Joe Esposito, whom she'd known from Germany. Quickly she was driven to the Bel Air house where she found Elvis surrounded by his guys at a pool table. He was obviously pleased to see her, but he didn't show it too much in front of his pals. That wouldn't have looked cool.

She was now seventeen, almost grown up, but her presence still worried some of the guys, the legal age of consent in California being eighteen. That, however, troubled Elvis not at all. And despite the agreement he'd made with her parents, Priscilla spent only that first night in the whole two weeks she was in the US not sleeping with him, although, once again, as with so many other girls, full sex did not take place.

'I was ready,' Priscilla would later write. 'He wasn't.'

When they'd been in Germany together she'd never taken the amphetamines he'd given her to keep her awake after a late night. But in the States, now two years older, she did, as well as the sleeping pills he routinely handed out to her and members of his gang. Did he consider for a moment that he might be breaking the trust her parents had put in him? If he did, it didn't bother him. He was Elvis, and he and everyone around him was having a good time on uppers, so he wanted her to join in, too. Where was the harm in that?

For Priscilla, or Cilla, as he called her, the pills were her introduction to the upside-down, night-for-day life he lived, and were followed by nearly two weeks in the Sahara Hotel in Las Vegas. He loved her youth and innocence, but in a direct contradiction, he also wanted her to look more glamorous than she was. So there followed a shopping spree when thousands of dollars' worth of fashionable, and sometimes gaudy, clothes and shoes were bought. Then came a session with a beauty artist, who added double-decker lashes to her eyes, and finally some hours with a hair stylist, who dyed her brown hair black, like his, and on his instruction, then teased and waved it until it appeared to have twice its volume. In short, he threw money at her pretty, schoolgirl look and turned her into an over made-up, tartily dressed, mascara-eyed party doll. It may have been his idea of what the perfect girlfriend in Vegas looked like at the time, but by grooming and moulding her into what he imagined was his perfect woman, he was destroying the freshness that he had found so compelling when they'd first met.

For a schoolgirl, the opulence in which he lived, the coterie of courtiers who hung on his every word and fulfilled his every request, and the sheer power of the extreme fame that he enjoyed, was astonishing and exciting. But Priscilla was quickly to see a side of him that he'd never shown in Germany. One day, while playing her some unreleased demos he'd recently recorded he asked her for an opinion. She answered honestly. She said she liked them, but she preferred his rock and roll numbers.

Immediately he erupted, something those close to him would see frequently. He hadn't asked her what style she thought he should be singing, he told her. 'Don't tell me how to do my job,' he ranted. He'd just wanted to know what she thought of the songs.

Priscilla put the sudden mood swing down to the uppers he was taking on a daily basis, and they almost certainly contributed. But it's equally likely that, in her innocence, she seemed to be questioning his taste. The guys knew never to do that.

Just as quickly as he'd lost his temper, the anger subsided, and soon he was laughing and charming again. But for Priscilla it was a valuable lesson for her life to come with him. It wasn't, and never would be, her place to criticise him. Only the Colonel was allowed to do that.

As soon as she returned to Germany and school, he went home to Memphis, where, as always, Anita was waiting. There were the usual nights out at the Fairgrounds and the private screenings at the Memphian, where they watched *West Side Story* together, a film he might just have been appearing in under different circumstances. But he now found himself torn between the two girls, and one day, while discussing his dilemma with Lamar Fike and another member of his staff, Anita happened to overhear. That was the end for her. She made the decision for him. Though he pleaded for her to stay, she called her brother to pick her up, left Graceland and never went back. Like Dixie before her, while she might be in love with him, her time with Elvis was finished.

He didn't take it well. He never did when abandoned.

As always, though, another movie was soon there to distract him and a few weeks later he was off to Seattle filming *It Happened at the World's Fair.* Whatever he privately thought of the script in which he was now a singing crop duster, or the songs – and the fans would have their say the following year by boycotting both film and album in hundreds of thousands – he continued in public to be loyal to his manager's decisions.

'If I can entertain people with the things I'm doing,' he told a sceptical reporter, 'I'd be a fool to tamper with it.' He *was* a fool. And he wasn't even kidding himself.

A new venture, however, was in the offing that really did excite him. 'Return to Sender', from *Girls, Girls, Girls,* had recently put him back at the top of the charts, so the Colonel began negotiating with RCA for a forty-three-city US tour for 1963. It was what Elvis enjoyed doing most. But it never happened. Parker had become hooked on the 'million' figure, boasting about it all the time, and he demanded a guaranteed million-dollar advance from RCA. They turned him down. That was too much for them, they said, and suggested a more limited tour for less upfront money. For Parker to have backed down would have been a loss of face. He refused, and an opportunity was lost. His greed and ego had once again priced Elvis out of the market.

With Anita now gone from Graceland, Elvis could invite Priscilla over from Germany to spend Christmas with him. Again promises about her being chaperoned and taken care of were made to her parents, and again they weren't kept. When Priscilla arrived and complained that she couldn't sleep because of jet lag, he promptly gave her a couple of Placidyls to relax her. They did that all right. She slept for nearly two days and missed Christmas. The guys were worried stiff, and Vernon and Grandma wanted to call an ambulance. Elvis didn't, and he made the rules. Instead, he walked Priscilla round and round his bedroom.

In the end, she woke of her own accord when she was ready. But it had been a foolhardy thing to do, and downright dangerous not to have listened to Vernon and sought medical assistance. Though he never touched street drugs (at least, not then), Elvis would throughout his entire life have a naïve faith in prescription medicine. He once told a reporter he might have wanted to be a doctor had it ever been possible, but a well-studied *Physicians' Desk Reference*, with its details of every legal drug available, was as far as that ambition got. Though he continually read up about prescription drugs and their possible side effects, he was always careless with them.

For Priscilla it was a steep learning curve, going from bobby socks to a beehive and mascara, from history and algebra to uppers and downers, in a house just filled with people day after day. The only place she could talk to Elvis alone was in his bedroom. But it gave her a chance to see what would soon be her home. Would she like to live here, he asked her before she went back to Germany.

She said she would, and, although her parents refused point blank when she mentioned it, not many people said 'no' to Elvis for long. And, little by little, in long phone calls from Hollywood, where he was filming *Fun in Acapulco* (in which he played a singing lifeguard and sang 'Bossa Nova Baby' to Ursula Andress), he set about charming Captain Paul and Ann Beaulieu. His mind was made up. He wanted Priscilla with him, and even before the movie was finished, Captain Beaulieu was in Los Angeles delivering his stepdaughter to him. She would, it was agreed, live in Memphis with Vernon and Dee and complete her senior year at the Catholic Immaculate Conception High School.

It was all a big risk. Colonel Parker must, at the very least, have been worried. Technically, Priscilla was still a child. What if it leaked out that Elvis had moved his schoolgirl girlfriend into his home, which he did almost immediately? What if the staff at Graceland talked? It could ruin his career. But it didn't leak out. The staff didn't talk. They never did.

For Priscilla, it meant the beginning of being a living secret. Chauffeured daily to and from school by Vernon, until Elvis bought her a red Corsair of her own, and taken to Mass on Sundays by a couple of Dee's Catholic friends, she was unable to make any proper friends at her new school, to hang out with them, or to ask them back to her home. There was so much she couldn't tell anyone, like, for instance, the fact that she sometimes carried a pearl-handled derringer, a gift from Elvis, in her bra – although probably not under her school uniform. It was a lonely time for her, and she must have wondered if she and her parents had made the right decision. Had her parents been aware of what was going on in Memphis they would have known that they hadn't.

Living a lie, afraid to chat to the guys in case Elvis thought she was flirting – and he was ever suspicious, vigilant and jealous – she, not surprisingly, lost her bearings. What was her role exactly at Graceland? At the same time, although she may have spent a lot of time in Elvis's bedroom when he was home, he still refused to have full sex with her, although she wanted to. Instead he would, she later wrote, get her to dress up in her school uniform and then take sexy

Polaroid photos of her. That turned him on. The rest of the time they watched TV in bed.

Quite why the local press were so dilatory in covering what could have become a major scandal can only be explained by the relationship they had with Elvis. He was the hometown boy who had, so to speak, put Memphis on the world map and who gave lavishly to local charities. Everyone loved him, and he was easy to love. It would have been a more than brave Memphis newspaper editor who questioned too closely the goings-on at Graceland. Elvis knew that. He guessed, rightly, that, in those less prurient times, blind eyes would be turned. And they were.

And when a friendly local journalist spotted him and Priscilla out together one day, and Elvis stopped to chat with him, the conversation was of movies, not the dazzlingly pretty young girl ('she's just a friend') the singer had at his side. Yes, Elvis said, he'd seen *Lawrence of Arabia*, but he'd been more impressed with *To Kill a Mockingbird*. 'That's a wonderful movie,' he said. Was he also thinking that that was the kind of movie that he ought to be making, a story about racial discrimination in the South, something he knew a lot about? Or had he been simply relieved that the reporter hadn't questioned him about Priscilla?

Almost before he'd settled Priscilla in at Graceland, he was off to Hollywood again. Naturally he expected her to sit at home; she had to go to school, anyway. And, since she didn't know anyone outside his circle, that was what she did. But it probably never crossed his mind to be faithful to her. He wasn't.

His next movie was *Viva Las Vegas* for MGM, in which he was now a singing racing car driver, with Swedish-born Ann-Margret, fresh from her first big success in *Bye Bye Birdie*, a satire based on Elvis's own army call-up, as his co-star. He'd had flings with some of the actresses in earlier movies, but this turned out to be different. Within days he and Ann-Margret, whom he called Thumper, after the rabbit character in *Bambi*, had hit it off. She was unattached, and when he was in Hollywood, he believed he was, too.

Nor was he the only one captivated. Thumper charmed his entire gang, who were astonished when Elvis would ride off with her, each on a Harley-Davidson, and not tell anyone where he was going. He'd never behaved like this before with any other woman. But he hadn't met anyone like Ann-Margret before. She was more than a girlfriend. She was a pal, and he treated her as an equal. He'd never done that before, either.

Back in Memphis, Priscilla, who was absolutely not being treated as an equal, began reading, with growing unease, about the blossoming Hollywood romance in the showbusiness columns in the newspapers. As always when confronted, Elvis lied about his co-star. 'She comes round here on weekends on her motorcycle,' he told her on the phone. 'She hangs out and jokes with the guys. That's it.' Priscilla didn't believe him.

As a film, *Viva Las Vegas* was one of the better Elvis movies, a proper musical directed by George Sidney, a real Hollywood pro who had previously made *Annie Get Your Gun*, *Pal Joey* and *Show Boat*, all of which Elvis had seen. And, whatever Priscilla felt, Ann-Margret and Elvis worked well together on screen. Once again, though, the songs were the problem. The best new numbers were the jazzy blues 'I Need Someone to Lean On' and the wordy, spirited title track, 'Viva Las Vegas', both by Doc Pomus and Mort Shuman. But both belonged more in a Broadway musical than a movie. And although 'Viva Las Vegas' would end up as a classic decades later, when initially released it was Elvis's first flop in the charts. Interestingly, although he would later appear hundreds of times on stage in Las Vegas, he never sang it again.

Perhaps, and to no one's surprise, the only one in the team not to fall for Ann-Margret was the Colonel. The movie's production costs had gone over budget – meaning the profits would be smaller, which he blamed on too much time being spent on promoting Ann-Margret. So he complained to MGM that she had too many close-ups, and he made sure that the duets she and Elvis recorded were dropped from the film. This was, he reminded the producers, 'an Elvis Presley film', not an 'Elvis Presley and Ann-Margret film'.

Naturally, Elvis was embarrassed by his manager's interference. He could and should have said something, but, ungallantly, he didn't insist that Ann-Margret's close-ups and their songs together stayed in the movie. The duets weren't even included on the EP when the film came out.

That might have broken up many relationships, but, though he hurried back to Memphis as soon as shooting was over, he called Ann-Margret every day. He was in a quandary. He'd committed himself to Priscilla, but now he wasn't sure. Had he made a terrible mistake? Was it possible to be in love with two women at the same time? Or had Thumper just been a location romance? Naturally Priscilla was noticing, and on his next trip to Los Angeles to shoot *Kissin' Cousins* she insisted on being there, too.

Kissin' Cousins was a new low – a seventeen-day epic for the fabled 'King of the Quickies' Sam Katzman, in which Elvis played two roles, a singing soldier and a singing hillbilly. Not only was it totally risible, it also set a bargain basement template for Elvis's next four years in Hollywood. He hated it. So when, on returning from shooting one day, Priscilla confronted him about a newspaper article that said that Ann-Margret had told a London journalist that she was engaged to the singer (a quote she later denied), he was in no mood for soft talk.

'Look, goddamnit!' he told her. 'I didn't know this was going to get out of hand. I want a woman who is going to understand that things like this might happen. Are you going to be her, or not?'

He had turned the tables on her with an ultimatum. At his urging Priscilla returned to Memphis, and, although he promised not to see Ann-Margret again, he did. When a few weeks later, on 22 November, President Kennedy was assassinated in Texas, they spent the day together in his house in Bel Air watching the TV footage from Dallas all afternoon and into the evening.

Then suddenly it was Christmas and he was back at Graceland with Priscilla. Although he would continue to see Thumper, and the two would stay friends for the rest of his life, the romance was drawing to its inevitable conclusion. He wanted a woman in the old-fashioned sense, someone who would always be waiting at home for his return. That wasn't Ann-Margret.

Whether Priscilla had fully comprehended that side of the offer when she'd consented to live at Graceland is unlikely. But she was the one he'd chosen for that role.

24

'If we can control sex, then we can control all other desires.'

Elvis to Priscilla

He'd seen the Beatles coming. At first only dimly aware of their presence in the British record charts, gradually, as 1963 had worn on and they'd had number one after number one in the UK, he'd become increasingly intrigued. But only when they hit the US at the beginning of 1964 did he fully recognise that something completely new was happening. With Priscilla at Graceland, he was enjoying a break in Las Vegas with the guys when he watched the group's first appearance on *The Ed Sullivan Show* on 9 February. With the excitement in the New York TV theatre and the hysteria building across America it all seemed so familiar. But this time it wasn't for him. It was only seven years since his last appearance on *The Ed Sullivan Show*, but it felt like decades. Just twenty-nine years old, he was only six years older than John Lennon, but as the Beatles dominated conversation and newspapers, he suddenly felt out of touch.

The biggest market after the US for his records had always been the UK, and, through RCA and Freddy Bienstock of Hill and Range, he'd kept a casual, if flattered, eye on the charts there. The volume of records bought in Britain might not nearly have matched that in the US, but he'd had more number one hits there, several of which hadn't even been singles in America. Now the Beatles were totally dominating the British charts.

Like many Americans, when he'd first seen newsreel of the Beatles he'd been amused. They looked like nothing he'd ever seen before outside a Marx Brothers movie, and disc jockeys had ignored them when their records had first been released in the US on a variety of small labels. But then, just after Christmas 1963, backed by a huge

Capitol Records publicity campaign, 'I Want to Hold Your Hand' had catapulted past everything in the US charts to number one in less than three weeks. And now every radio station he turned to was playing them – virtually all the time. When he'd been on the first *Ed Sullivan Show*, he'd pulled in the biggest TV audience ever. Now an even bigger audience had turned on to watch the Beatles.

At the Colonel's suggestion an open telegram had been sent to the group welcoming them to the US.

'Congratulations on your appearance on The Ed Sullivan Show and your visit to America,' it read. 'We hope your engagement will be successful and your visit pleasant.' Signed: 'Elvis and the Colonel.'

It had been a gracious, if hardly enthusiastic, gesture of recognition from the man the press still called the King of Rock and Roll to a new band of young pretenders – easy to do, but pretty meaningless and hardly sincere. Elvis didn't wish the Beatles success. How could he? They'd become serious rivals. He was jealous of them. Some of his guys tried to reassure him, laughing them off, and describing them as a flash in the pan. But he'd heard that said before, when the detractors had been talking about him, and it had turned out that they couldn't have been more wrong.

But there was something else. While he had managed to antagonise parents and teachers, and seemingly the entire US population over the age of twenty-five, the Beatles were being welcomed by everyone, from children to high school kids, college students, parents and newspaper pundits; even by *The New York Times*. Overnight it felt as though the entire country had fallen into a state of collective love with them. They brought smiles of amusement with the way they would all shake their freshly shampooed girls' length hair, and then, all together, hit a kind of falsetto squeal, and with their cheeky, funny ripostes in their strange Liverpool accents. He'd never heard anyone talk like that before.

As he watched their endlessly repeated televised press conferences, he reflected on all the times he'd spoken to reporters and television interviewers, and thought of how careful to be respectful he'd been. The Colonel had insisted on that, and a quiet deference had come so very naturally to him. But these guys didn't care about respect. They were impudent jokers, and a part of him envied that there were four of them to share the load of fame. When he'd first heard their records, and when he'd watched them perform, he'd wondered at first which was the lead singer, and where the power in the group lay. But then, after deciding that there were two leaders and that the other two sometimes sang as well, he wondered how it must feel to share stardom equally. Right from the beginning of his career, the spotlight had never found Scotty, Bill or D.J. And it had never occurred to any of them that it should. The Beatles were doing it all in a different way. All four were stars.

Musically he was puzzled by them. As a band they weren't as skilled as the Nashville A-Team who now backed him, but were they more innovative? Yes, they probably were. They brought to mind the Everly Brothers, and though on their first few records their harmonies seemed more ragged than the Everlys', they had a shared, boyish drive that seemed to suggest they were having a terrific time together. He couldn't not like their first records; his favourite was 'I Saw Her Standing There'.

'She was just seventeen, you know what I mean . . .' Yes, he knew exactly what they meant. But then he learned that they'd covered Little Richard and Chuck Berry songs as he had done, and he recognised the graft and expertise that went into their playing and singing. They might look like a cute band of long-haired English boys, but they were experienced musicians, who not only played and sang, but who also wrote their own hits. So, no matter what his gang told him, he knew they were formidable.

It didn't occur to him immediately, but, as he watched, he could see that a musical sea-change was taking place, that the rhythm of the Lennon and McCartney compositions was slower, the heavy beat more pronounced. He'd usually raced through his twelve-bar rock songs that kids could jive to before the twist craze had come and gone. But dancing was different now, it was individual, not in pairs. The Beatles' records were good to dance to, the kids said. Were his records good to dance to these days? 'Devil in Disguise', which had been his last big hit the previous summer, changed rhythm several times. Could you dance to it, the way they were dancing now, the way they danced to Motown hits, with that steady uniform 4/4 beat of 'four on the floor'? He'd always been a worrier, unsure of himself. Did he now have something to really worry about? The Colonel didn't think so. At least that was what he said. But the Colonel didn't know anything about music.

A month before the Beatles had arrived in the US, Elvis had been to Nashville to record the Chuck Berry song 'Memphis, Tennessee'. It seemed a natural for him and he was sure, after an earlier failed attempt, he'd done the song justice. A song that little bands all around the country did, it was, he thought, his best rock and roll recording since 'Little Sister'. He would put it out soon. But not quite yet.

Why not yet? Was he worried that it would get overlooked by disc jockeys in the maelstrom around the Beatles? Possibly. So he hesitated some more and, while he did, he played a demo of it to friends, including Johnny Rivers, who, like many other performers, already sang it in his own act. Rivers liked what he heard, and, very quickly, as Elvis delayed, put out his own single of the song which went quickly to number one. He who hesitates is lost. Suddenly Elvis saw that there were rivals all around him. He could easily have rush-released his own version, but he didn't.

'I don't want to see Rivers' ass around here anymore,' he fumed, and put his own prized recording aside to be hidden on a later album.

It was just a slip-up in timing. When Carl Perkins had been in hospital instead of on TV promoting 'Blue Suede Shoes', Elvis had been making the song his own. Now Johnny Rivers had beaten him to the draw with 'Memphis, Tennessee'. That was the music business. He knew that. But, symbolically, by his refusal to even put up a fight against Rivers and Beatlemania with a rock record, he was already conceding defeat.

Meanwhile there was yet another movie. It was called *Roustabout* – a story about a singing fairground worker. As he read the script, did he comfort himself with the thought that he was a film star, and that the Beatles were just a British pop group; that he had moved on and that his personal income from films was now nearly three times that from music and recordings? Or did he look at the pages of arch dialogue and remember that he was already contracted to two further dumb movies that year?

And, what was he thinking when he opened *Billboard* magazine on 4 April and saw that the Beatles had the top five singles in the US charts and the top two albums? No wonder he lost his temper in the studio, where he was usually so polite.

Ready to record a *Roustabout* song, he asked The Jordanaires to help him out on the chorus, only to find the director hurrying up to him, saying: 'Elvis, I don't think you understand where this song is going to be in the picture. You're riding down the highway on a motorbike singing. If The Jordanaires are singing, too, where are they supposed to be?'

Elvis just looked at him. 'The same damn place the band is,' he snapped.

Even had he wanted to, it was no longer possible for him to go to church any more, but the religion and sense of the spiritual that his parents had given him had never gone away. At home, he loved to vividly recount stories from the Bible to Priscilla and the guys like an energised Southern preacher – which, to his annoyance, they all found amusing. But his first astonishing bloom of fame had been so sudden he'd never had the time, or the youthful inclination, to analyse his extraordinary situation, assuming, as did everybody else, that it wouldn't last.

But it had lasted, and it had spread and grown. And, when he now thought about it in those lonely hours when the sleeping pills didn't kick in, he would ask himself over and over: Why? Why had he become one of the most famous men on earth? Why had he been given this particular voice that could communicate to so many millions of people? Why him? Had he been chosen? His mother used to think he had. But, if so, was it for some particular reason? Why had his twin, Jesse, died at birth and not him? His religion had taught him that nothing happened for which God didn't have a purpose. And he believed that. So, did that mean that God had given him that voice and those looks for a special purpose? If so, what was that purpose?

One side of him would perhaps have argued that it had all been a matter of luck that he'd inherited his looks and musical genes from his parents and forefathers, even from Morning Dove, that Jesse's death might well have been the result of his mother's lack of antenatal care, that it was twentieth-century recording techniques and communications that had made the dissemination of his appeal possible, and that, as he had often said: 'I just happened to come along in the music business when there was no trend.' Furthermore, the fact that he was an American, who spoke the English language, might have explained better his universal appeal than any divine plan; to which, a musicologist, had one been consulted, might have added that being born and musically nurtured where he was at that particular crossroads in racial and cultural history could have played a pretty important part, too.

He would have understood all that. But then another voice would have been asking him why God had designed it so that he would be the beneficiary of those genes and all those influences. So, what was his part in God's great design?

If his mother had been still alive he might have talked to her about all this, and she would have tried to help and direct him back to his Bible, where, she had told him, all the answers lay. But she wasn't there to help any more.

Someone else was, though. It was a hairdresser called Larry Geller, who worked for Jay Sebring, the top Hollywood men's hair stylist of the day – the same unlucky Jay Sebring, incidentally, who would be murdered along with Sharon Tate and others by the Charles Manson gang in 1969.

Geller, like many others, was into the New Age alternative religions that were popping up in California in the sixties, and then, by chance one day, Elvis's regular hairdresser wasn't available, and Geller was asked to go up to Bel Air to take his place. Somehow, as the scissors snipped, Elvis began to talk about his mother and religion and soon found that Geller had a more spiritual side to him than anyone he'd met since he'd been a boy. But Geller wasn't preaching what they preached down in Mississippi. And, as he listened to Geller's theory that life was a journey to find the very purpose of life, Elvis realised it fitted exactly into all the self-absorbed questions he had been asking himself.

Sensing a disciple, the following day Geller turned up at Paramount with a collection of books for Elvis to read, mainly volumes on Eastern religions but including one called *Autobiography of a Yogi*. Others followed: there was Krishnamurti's *First and Last Freedom* and Kahlil Gibran's *The Prophet*, as well as books on cosmology, numerology and metaphysics. Elvis had never been academically inclined at school, but now he uncritically read everything he was given, scribbling notes in the margins of books, spending hours talking with Geller.

Being Elvis, and subject to sudden crazes, he could never get enough of his new interest, so he enticed Geller away from the Jay Sebring salon into becoming his personal hairdresser, and, therefore, spiritual adviser. Not surprisingly the guys weren't happy. Some thought Geller was brainwashing their boss, others that he was a joke, a Rasputin figure, and they called him the 'Guru'. And all of them were jealous at the closeness he had quickly assumed with Elvis. Like the court of any French monarch, there were factions and rivalries, and Larry Geller bothered everyone.

For her part, Priscilla had conflicting attitudes towards the hairdresser and his influence. While on the one hand she liked him and his wife, she also became frustrated and angry that Elvis became so wrapped up in cosmic theories that he lost all other interests, including having any kind of sex with her.

'We have to control our desires so they don't control us,' he told her. 'If we can control sex, then we can control all other desires.'

Worse than that, he expected her to read the books, too, and should she fall asleep, exhausted by the way he preached on and on about the metaphysical, he would wake her up in order to read some particularly 'insightful passage' to her.

Whatever the reason, whether he was just deeply depressed by his career, or whether his senses were being confused by the daily cocktails of amphetamines and barbiturates he was taking, he'd become an early convert to a new fashion, and wanted to share it with her. Priscilla, more grounded in reality, was unable to do that, which he resented.

As might be expected, the Colonel was furious with what he called Geller's 'bullshit' and 'mind control' when he saw how it was unsettling his client, and was especially worried when Elvis began talking about forming a commune or going into a monastery 'to gain emotional balance'.

'You missed your calling,' Parker said to Geller, hinting that the hairdresser should have been a stage hypnotist, which to the guys had more than a ring of irony. Some of them suspected that there was something of the hypnotist in the Colonel.

With his periods of spiritual intensity fluctuating with less obsessive times, Elvis's adventures with metaphysics, the cosmic and Eastern mystics lasted a full two years in the mid-sixties, and when in Los Angeles he would drive off by himself down Sunset Boulevard to visit the Self-Realization Fellowship Lake Shrine at nearby Pacific Palisades. At the time it wasn't uncommon for rock stars to become involved in mysticism, or to become curious about LSD, as Elvis did through Timothy Leary's book about the mind-altering drug, *The Psychedelic Experience*. In fact Priscilla and he, together with some of the guys, even tried LSD. What was surprising was that it was Elvis – who by then had come to be considered so straight he could hardly get a mention in any self-respecting rock magazine – who was secretly in the vanguard of the counterculture, 'drop out, turn on, tune in' lifestyle.

Geller would say that the new self-realisation made Elvis more generous than ever, which brought despair to Vernon, who spent his days desperately in the counting house trying to keep a check on what he saw as his son's wilful extravagance. But then it can't have been easy for any of the family or the entourage to be around a depressed man who, while driving through the desert, saw a vision in the sky that turned from being the face of Joseph Stalin into that of Jesus. And that was what Elvis said he saw.

So Priscilla, the Colonel, Vernon and the guys were relieved when on visiting a leader called Sri Daya Mata (real name Faye Wright from Salt Lake City) who lived in the Self-Realization Fellowship spa, Elvis would be gently dissuaded from his plan to give up his singing career in order to spread the word.

That, Mata diplomatically put it, wasn't what God had intended him for.

25

'The only thing worse than watching a bad movie, is being in one.'

Throughout the mid-sixties Elvis was asleep so far as his musical career was concerned. With movie following movie, musically speaking he didn't know what to do. Off stage for too long and out of touch with the fans, his confidence was shaken. At his last Nashville session before the British invasion he'd recorded a new song called 'It Hurts Me' which had been written by Charles E. Daniels, later of the Charlie Daniels Band, together with the man who would soon produce Bob Dylan and Simon and Garfunkel albums, Bob Johnston (writing under his wife's name of Joy Byers). It was another of his heart-ripped anguished ballads, but, when released on the flip side of the lightweight, formulaic hit 'Kissin' Cousins', it slipped by unnoticed in the slurry of poor film songs.

So, here he was; the musical revolutionary who less than a decade earlier had stunned with 'Don't Be Cruel' and 'Lawdy Miss Clawdy' was now reduced to sawing his way through 'Fort Lauderdale Chamber of Commerce' for the film *Girl Happy*. Then there was 'Go East, Young Man' when he played a singing sheik in *Harum Scarum*, or what about 'Petunia, the Gardener's Daughter' for *Frankie and Johnny* and 'A Dog's Life' for *Paradise, Hawaiian Style*? The best that could be said of any of these, and dozens more like them, was that they weren't 'Song of the Shrimp' from *Girls, Girls, Girls*. No wonder he felt frustrated.

As he would later admit: 'When the script arrived for the next film I would just read a few pages and know that it was pretty well the same plot as the last time, with the names changed.'

On the sidelines at every movie recording session, Scotty Moore, demoted now to playing rhythm guitar for a session fee, kept his sad opinions to himself. As far as he was concerned, neither Colonel Parker nor Freddy Bienstock at Hill and Range had Elvis's best interests at heart. He was right. But nor was it any less frustrating for the executives at RCA in New York and Nashville as they struggled to get their most important, and erstwhile profitable, star to record anything other than soundtrack albums, which were selling fewer and fewer copies as the years passed. Having long ago ceded control to the Colonel of what went into Elvis's albums, there was little they could do. And Parker saw records simply as another part of movie promotion. That was where the big money was, wasn't it? Well, maybe.

Parker couldn't see it, but the music business was changing rapidly in the sixties as songwriters increasingly wanted to be recording artists themselves, and they, as well as those who were happy to just write the songs, weren't so willing to give up some of their royalties to have Elvis record their work. Why should they? That policy might have worked in the fifties when getting Elvis to sing your song was like winning the lottery, so great were his sales figures. But that was no longer the case. For the Aberbachs and Parker to have continued with a kind of music industry blackmail ('give us a slice of your song, or Elvis doesn't record it!') for as long as they did wasn't only greedy: it was short-sighted.

Did it ever occur to them that, instead of trying to squeeze one more limp movie number out of the exhausted team of writers at Hill and Range, they might, for instance, have given John Lennon and Paul McCartney a call and asked them if they'd like to write Elvis a song? The two would have leapt at the opportunity, so long as there was none of that funny business about giving Hill and Range a third of the royalties that would be due to them as writers. But, of course, Lennon and McCartney were never asked, nor were any other top writers of the time.

When Elvis chose to sing Chuck Berry's 'Memphis, Tennessee' it was because for once he'd made up his mind to do exactly that and there was nothing Parker or the Aberbachs could do to stop him. But why didn't he make up his mind more often? Why did he wait until 1969 before recording a Burt Bacharach song? Why didn't he stand up to Parker and insist that the word be put out to the best songwriters in the business that he was looking for new material – no royalty-slicing strings attached? Why didn't he assert himself? What possible reason could he have had for being so compliant?

The answer has to be *fear*. Under the Parker and Aberbachs Hill and Range deal he'd become rich, and he was grateful to Parker for lifting him and his family out of the poverty of what he called 'the common working man', which was how he had expected his life to unfold. Now, though, he was afraid, as was his father, that if he argued too much and simply refused to do the things which Parker would insist were for his own good, he might be cut loose by the Colonel. Then what? The spectre of the poverty of his childhood, and the ever repeated moves from one home to another that his parents had endured, never left him. Graceland was now his home, and his castle, and he would do whatever it took to keep it – including mortgaging his talent.

Neither he, nor Vernon, was sophisticated as far as money went. If they had been Parker wouldn't have been allowed to take so much of a percentage for himself or have so many side deals. Nor did Elvis have grand, long-term pension plans, investments in stocks or complicated tax-friendly financial schemes.

'I have no involvement in Elvis's financial affairs,' Parker would tell this author grandly in 1969. 'Mr Vernon Presley takes care of that.'

Which, for the most part, Vernon did in a very straightforward way. The money came in, and went into the bank in Memphis to be spent as and when it was needed. And it certainly was spent. As late as 1962, by which time Elvis must have earned many tens of millions of dollars, he was forced to take out a mortgage of $134,000 to buy the lot of land facing Graceland across Highway 51, to prevent anyone else (a gas station or supermarket for instance) buying it and having a direct view of his home.

To everyone around him, and to the world at large, he was fabulously wealthy, the unique, archetypal, powerful rock star, who was in a position to do anything he wanted, and go anywhere he wanted. But that wasn't how he saw it. He said on numerous occasions that he wanted to tour Britain, but he never did. But, then, it wasn't what he wanted, it was what Tom Parker wanted – or, in this case, didn't want.

Constantly some of the other guys wondered to each other how

Parker could so easily reduce the singer who was so commanding with them to a state of virtual subservience. But it wasn't difficult. All Parker had to do was to point out that not only had many of the movie contracts already been signed, but that the money Elvis was earning from music didn't compare with the amount Hollywood was paying him. Elvis only had to look at the figures his own accountants were providing for the Internal Revenue Service to see that. In 1964 they reported that his personal income was $1,508,000 from movies, and only $506,000 from music, of which total he paid $784,000 in income tax. Every year throughout the sixties he earned at least three times as much from films as he did from music. Movies, Parker would say, were quickly made, extremely profitable, and would provide a stream of income for years to come.

Even if Elvis had been prepared to risk a cut in income if it meant better songs to sing, the Colonel certainly wouldn't have been happy, and neither would the Aberbachs and Freddy Bienstock at Hill and Range. So, trapped by his own lavish lifestyle and the avarice of his manager and publishers, Elvis turned up on time on the movie sets having learned his lines in the car on the way to the studio, relieved his frustrations by karate-chopping planks of wood between scenes with his pals, and hurried back to Bel Air as soon as shooting was finished for the day and prepared himself for playtime.

The recording studio had once been his control room, where he would do take after take on songs he liked searching for that little bit of magic needed to make it special. But, increasingly, from 1963 onwards, he began to allow the band to record backing tracks without him for the movie albums, and then dub his voice on later, thus forfeiting the opportunity to shape the songs and their arrangements. Gordon Stoker of the Jordanaires remembered how as Elvis despaired more and more he unconsciously backed further and further away from the microphone as he sang.

In the end, Stoker said, 'the studio engineer would put the mike as close to the wall as possible and Elvis would lean against the wall . . . Then they put a soundboard around him to pick him up. The material was so bad that he felt he couldn't sing it.'

That was how it was to be Elvis Presley in the mid-sixties, an increasingly pathetic figure, even mocking his own performances as he screened his movies with his gang.

'Who's that guy up there from Memphis talking so quickly?' he would joke bitterly.

Then he would mention again a newspaper piece he'd read about Hal Wallis. Talking about his latest film, *Becket*, which starred Richard Burton, Peter O'Toole and John Gielgud, and which would win six Oscars, the producer was quoted as saying: 'In order to do the artistic pictures it is necessary to make the commercial Presley pictures.' That had hurt. As had the Colonel's quoted comment in the *Los Angeles Times* that 'Elvis Presley movies won't win any Academy Awards. All they're good for is making money.'

It's quite possible, even probable, that Elvis would never have had a successful career as a serious actor, and that Parker would never have been able to get him a dramatic, non-singing starring role. His great fame for simply being Elvis might always have made that impossible. But as the years passed he began to realise that both Wallis and Parker had, from the beginning, been less than candid with him. He'd put his trust in them, and they had abused it. As he would ruefully say: 'The only thing worse than watching a bad movie, is being in one.'

But if he wasn't making records and he wasn't touring, and none of the movies took as much as a month of his time, including costume fittings and album sessions, that meant he was only working at most for four months a year. For many movie stars, and indeed rock stars, that would be about right. But ever since his school days he'd always had a huge appetite for work. He was a restless person, awake all night, needing to fill his time. So when he was in Memphis, and not on his cosmic kick, or when the lure of the Fairgrounds had eventually palled, as Priscilla became increasingly less interested in them, he would go to the movies. Regularly renting out the Memphian from midnight until dawn, night after night, he would order new and old movies, *Dr Strangelove* being a particular favourite that he watched five times, with Peter Sellers his favourite comic actor. Then in a long list there was *The Robe, Tom Jones, Miracle on 34th Street, Wuthering Heights, It's a Wonderful Life, The Great Escape, King of Kings* and even the Beatles' *A Hard Day's Night*. Since his teenage days as a cinema usher he'd made a point of seeing as many of the popular movies as he could, and would sometimes surprise actors in his own films by reminding them of parts they'd played years earlier.

That being said, he never liked Hollywood or indeed most Hollywood people. As Priscilla would say: 'He saw Hollywood as the home of phonies.' But, a real movie buff, he loved the films they made there.

So what else did he do with his time? Well, he read a lot, watched hundreds of football games on TV and enjoyed long-running series like *The Fugitive*. And then, of course, there were the parties in Los Angeles and Memphis, and the journeys, mainly along Route 66, to and from Los Angeles several times a year. Remembering Gladys's worries, he still didn't like to fly, but gone were the days of taking the train. Now, as his retinue followed in a convoy of cars, he would often drive a motorhome himself, giving one hitch-hiker a story to last a lifetime when the guy realised the identity of the driver who had stopped to give him a ride. It gave Elvis a buzz to see the hitch-hiker's expression, in the same way that he liked to please the fans by driving down to the gates at Graceland occasionally to talk to those who would congregate there when he was home. Many stars found the constant attention of their fans onerous, and went to lengths to avoid them. Elvis actually enjoyed it, as he always enjoyed being recognised.

In no way could it be said that his relationship with Priscilla during those mid-sixties years was normal. How could it be when her very presence was a denial? But, though it took a while, gradually she began to fit into the regime that he demanded and to make friends with some of the wives of the guys as well as with Patsy, another Elvis cousin, who worked in Vernon's office.

When Priscilla had graduated (and, realising his presence would cause excitement and spoil the moment for her, Elvis hadn't attended the ceremony), her classmates at Immaculate Conception High School in Memphis had been making plans to go to college. That was never an option for her. Lacking further education himself, the last thing Elvis wanted was a college-educated girlfriend – even Ann-Margret, the great exception to most of his romances, had dropped out of Northwestern University in her first year.

What he did want was a beautiful, glamorous partner, so Priscilla took dance classes and a modelling course. As she later said: 'He wanted my skirts shorter, my eyeliner darker, my make-up thicker, my hair dyed jet black . . . I was his doll whom he loved to dress.' She was being groomed to be the perfect, unquestioning consort.

And so 1964 moved into 1965 and all the time the franchise in vapid Elvis movies continued with *Tickle Me, Harum Scarum* and *Paradise, Hawaiian Style.* In his office in Madison, Tennessee, or at MGM in Los Angeles, the Colonel seemed interested only in renegotiating Elvis's contracts upwards, but at RCA in New York they had begun searching in desperation through their backlog of tracks for anything that might make a new single. 'Such a Night' from 1960 did well enough, but one leftover recording stood out. Always a big fan of the Sonny Til and the Orioles doo-wop group, Elvis had covered their hit 'Crying in the Chapel' for his gospel album *His Hand in Mine,* five years earlier, only to leave it off the album when he decided he hadn't done the song as well as they had.

By 1965, however, the quality bar had dropped a long way. By the standards of everything else he was now doing, RCA thought it perfect, and, getting Elvis's permission, they put it out as a single. To everyone's surprise, including the singer's, it turned out to be his biggest and most unlikely hit in years. Going neck and neck with the Rolling Stones' 'Satisfaction', the Beach Boys' 'Help Me, Rhonda' and the Beatles' 'Ticket to Ride' it went to number three on the US charts, and number one in the UK.

But there was an even bigger surprise to come. The Beatles, his usurpers in the affections of so many fans around the world, were about to pay him a visit.

26

'If you guys are just going to sit and stare at me,
I'm going to bed.'

– Elvis to the Beatles

They might have been curious to meet him, but he didn't want to meet them. It was, he guessed, a stunt dreamed up by their people, and the Colonel, sensing some good publicity, had gone along with it. What the Colonel hadn't considered, however, was how Elvis might feel about having to entertain the Beatles in his home and pretend that he was happy at their phenomenal success.

They arrived in a couple of cars at the house at 525 Perugia Way, Bel Air, at about 10.30 on a Friday night in August 1965, during a Los Angeles break while on their second tour of the US. All day some of the guys, and especially their wives and girlfriends, had been excited about the Beatles' visit, and although she'd tried to hide it, he could see that Priscilla was thrilled, too. But, then, she was more their age.

He and Priscilla, along with Joe Esposito, Larry Geller and Marty Lacker and their wives and some other members of the gang, were all watching television in the den with the sound turned off when they heard the cars arriving. Everyone was overdressed for the occasion, Priscilla in a sequined minidress and high heels, her bouffant hair piled high on her head, and Elvis wearing a red shirt and black jerkin and plucking nervously at the strings of a Fender bass guitar. He wouldn't have wanted to show it, but he was probably unsure of how he should behave.

For some reason he didn't go to the front door to greet his guests, as he knew he really should, because he'd always made a point about being polite. But then, suddenly, they were overflowing into the room, bright and cheeky. The Colonel was there, too, along with the Beatles' manager Brian Epstein, a couple of their publicity fellows and road managers, and a young English journalist called Chris Hutchins, who had hustled the Colonel into agreeing to the meeting. Normally Elvis was good at putting strangers at ease, but the atmosphere in the room was starched, as all four Beatles just gazed at him, with what looked like puzzled embarrassment.

Finally he found something to say. 'Well, if you guys are just going to sit and stare at me, I'm going to bed,' he joked.

That broke at least some of the ice, and, when he went on to mention that he'd seen on the TV news how an engine on their plane had caught fire while they'd been flying into Portland, an exchange ensued about the perils of being on tour. 'Beatles and children first,' John Lennon had quipped at the time, which one of them repeated to some amusement. So he then told them how a little plane he'd once hired ran out of fuel on the way to a recording session in Nashville in 1956, and how the fans in Vancouver had once charged the stage at the end of his show and he and the band had all had to run as it had been turned over.

It was all stiff, inconsequential stuff, with John Lennon putting on a funny accent as though he was Peter Sellers, but somehow without being funny. So, when the conversation lagged, Elvis edgily returned to picking out the bass line on his Fender to Charlie Rich's 'Mohair Sam', which was playing on the juke box. The fact that he was playing a bass interested Paul McCartney, the Beatles' bass player, so the two compared notes on Fenders.

'You're coming along quite well, Elvis. Keep up the rehearsals and Mr Epstein and I will make you a star,' Paul tried to joke.

As music seemed a better language of communication than English, at this point Elvis suggested that guitars be given to the guests. Only Ringo was left out. 'Sorry, there's no drum kit for you,' he called to the drummer. 'We left that back in Memphis.'

'That's okay. I'd rather play pool,' Ringo shrugged, and, along with Elvis's young cousin Billy Smith, he headed for the pool table in an adjacent room.

So, as the Colonel set up a roulette session in a corner for Brian Epstein and himself, the Beatles' road managers chatted with Elvis's guys, and the women just watched in almost silence, the other three

Beatles and Elvis went into a jam session of 'Memphis, Tennessee', 'Johnny B. Goode' and 'See See Rider'.

Usually Elvis enjoyed jam sessions, and this was by far the most successful part of the evening, but, though the guests remained until nearly two in the morning, the people who got on best were Elvis's gang and the Beatles' road manager, Mal Evans, who, as it turned out, was a huge Elvis fan.

The problem was the sheer phoniness of the meeting. Elvis was ill at ease, feeling that everyone was watching him to see how he would react towards those who had eclipsed him – and was determined not to betray any inner feelings. But, he must have realised, he looked wrong. His hair that had once fallen across his forehead in mid-song to teenage delight was now uniform Hollywood short and firmly cemented into place like a helmet, while the Beatles' long hair looked natural and boyish.

George Harrison was, it was clear to everyone, very stoned, and after a while he wandered outside to look at the garden. In a year's time he would become interested in mysticism, as Elvis already was, and would have had much in common with his host. But on this night he just looked out of it, and, in front of the Colonel, Elvis was hardly going to start talking about his cosmic philosophies. In some ways it was as though Elvis and the Beatles were two sets of children being forced together by their parents in the shape of the Colonel and Epstein, so all were on their best behaviour. Paul McCartney did his diplomatic best to keep the chat and the songs going, while John Lennon, drink in hand, was living up to his reputation for being jokily abrasive. At one point the conversation got around to rock and roll and both he and Paul admitted how much they'd loved Elvis's early rock records. To which Elvis replied, as he often did, that he was thinking of doing some more like that.

'Oh, good,' flipped back John Lennon. 'We'll buy them when you do.'

It probably sounded ruder than it was meant. John Lennon was known for being brusque and to the point. He said what he thought. But Elvis would have flinched at the implied criticism of his current output. It was a long time since those around him had voiced any real reservations about his records. They left that for him to do. These guys from England, who were effortlessly writing hit after hit for themselves, and who had complete control over what they recorded, had no idea of the publishing and recording arrangements he was locked into.

Priscilla's memory of the evening was that she felt it went well, although she did notice that Elvis didn't ask the Beatles a single question about themselves. For Elvis it probably felt as though the Beatles and their friends were all in on a private joke to which he wasn't party. Did he wonder if he was the joke? As the party broke up, John Lennon, more than a little drunk by now, said in his unfunny European accent, 'Thank you for zee music, Elvis. Long live zee King.' Once again it probably came out like a snap of sarcasm. But Lennon actually meant it.

At the door, Brian Epstein invited Elvis and Priscilla to a return evening at the Beatles' rented house in Benedict Canyon the following night, but Elvis made an instant excuse.

'We'll see,' he said. 'I don't know whether I'll be able to make it.'

Priscilla knew immediately, that meant they wouldn't be going. Elvis was used to being the absolute centre of attention in any gathering, and that would not have been the case had he met the Beatles on their territory.

Some of his guys went, though, reporting back that John Lennon went out of his way to tell them that he wanted Elvis to know that 'if it hadn't been for Elvis, I would have been nothing'.

He never met any of them ever again.

During his conversation with Paul McCartney about bass playing, the name of Bill Black had naturally come up, as, when the Beatles had made their first US tour a year earlier, Bill Black's Combo had opened for them. By 1965, however, Bill's health was fading after surgery for a terminal brain tumour. He was only thirty-nine. When Elvis had heard about his illness he'd gone to visit him, taking Bill's wife Evelyn to one side to tell her that if they ever needed anything she only had to ask.

Vernon and Dee went to the funeral, and Scotty and D.J. Fontana were pallbearers, but Elvis didn't attend. He'd told Evelyn beforehand that he didn't want his presence there to turn it into a circus, as it certainly would have done, but after the ceremony Evelyn and her children drove out to Graceland to talk to him. Despite Bill's differences with Elvis over money, she and Bill had always liked him, still seeing him as the boy they'd first met in 1954.

Elvis had many reasons to be grateful to the bass player with whom he used to joke on stage between songs. Those had been the happiest and most exciting days of his career. And he often liked to reminisce about the sheer fun of it as the three of them had toured small towns in the Southern states playing anywhere that anyone wanted them. The journey, he now knew, was often so much better than the destination.

'Bill was a very great man,' he told a Memphis newspaper the day before the funeral. 'This comes as such a very great shock to me that I can hardly explain how much I loved him.'

27

'I know that I'm a joke in this town.'

Elvis on Hollywood

Back at Sun Records, Sam Phillips used to say that there was no place Elvis would rather be than in the recording studio, an observation later repeated by Mike Stoller. That was where Elvis did his most committed work. So, when he eventually returned to Nashville in May 1966 for the first time in three years, it was, following the success of 'Crying in the Chapel', not surprising that he was there to make another religious album.

The change from the bored and sometimes downright angry attitude he'd shown at so many Hollywood sessions was, at first, pronounced. After planning the songs carefully, he wanted a big church sound, and was cheered when bass singer Jake Hess, whom he'd admired as a boy, was booked for the session along with Hess's new gospel group the Imperials. With a soprano and two contraltos added to the Jordanaires, that would make eleven backing singers in total – a full church choir. With them came a fourteen-piece band of Nashville's finest musicians.

Encouraged by new producer Felton Jarvis (replacing Chet Atkins, who didn't enjoy keeping 'Elvis hours' – in other words, working through the night), everything seemed set for a memorable Nashville restart.

The album, which would be called *How Great Thou Art*, was, once again, a mixture of traditional spirituals and hymns, and would become Elvis's only album to be awarded a Grammy – 'the best sacred album of 1967'.

From the very first track, the traditional spiritual 'Run On', there was a new vitality and personality in song as Elvis became the fiery, playful preacher, entertaining from the altar.

'I been down on my bended knee, talking to the man from Galilee,' he sang. 'My God spoke and He spoke so sweet, I thought I heard the shuffle of angel feet.'

This was Elvis at his very best, and it was followed by 'How Great Thou Art' itself, a hymn suggested by Charlie Hodge, which would later become an emotional highlight of his stage shows. Full marks for the album.

But what RCA also wanted were a couple of single hits, too, and after neglecting that side of his career for so long, Elvis's judgement on commercial material was no longer assured. For two years the music he had been enjoying at home had borne no resemblance to the movie albums he'd been making – indeed, like so many of his now disappointed fans, he hadn't even bothered to keep some of his movie albums. Why would he? He'd never liked them.

But what should he record now? Throughout his career, whenever he was at a loss to know what to do next he would sift through his old r and b collection. So, now, between hymns, he revived 'Down in the Alley', a largely forgotten r and b Clovers hit from 1957.

Priscilla, meanwhile, had been enjoying Peter, Paul and Mary albums, and everyone would sing along to '500 Miles' and Bob Dylan's 'Blowin' in the Wind'. He didn't care for Dylan as a singer, but he liked some of the songs he wrote. So, on another night, he recorded Dylan's 'Tomorrow Is a Long Time' which he had heard on an album by folk singer and Civil Rights activist Odetta. This was the direction he should have been going in had he wanted to regain the respect of rock commentators. But it was just a token. When 'Tomorrow Is a Long Time' was released, it and 'Down in the Alley' were chucked carelessly into yet another movie soundtrack album, as a couple of 'bonus' tracks, and completely overlooked.

The first of three singles from the session was a revival of the wartime Victor Young song 'Love Letters', from the film of the same name, which although it went high in the UK charts, where the fans were more loyal, peaked at number 19 in the US. In the summer of the Mamas and the Papas' 'Monday, Monday', Percy Sledge's 'When a Man Loves a Woman' and the Troggs' 'Wild Thing', it wasn't in with a chance. Besides, Ketty Lester had had a hit with the same song and an almost identical arrangement in 1962.

With every year that passed he was drifting further away from the popular taste of the time. A year earlier Red West had suggested he record 'Green, Green Grass of Home' after they'd both heard a Jerry Lee Lewis version of the song, but Elvis had dismissed it as 'too country' for him. Then he heard, and fell in love with, the Tom Jones recording, and realised his mistake.

The euphoria about having made a good sacred album evaporated before the sessions ended, and he suddenly left the studio. But three tracks short of the minimum stipulated by RCA, he returned a couple of weeks later. His mood was worse now, and, complaining of a cold, although a surfeit of the wrong pills might have been a more honest diagnosis, he stayed in his motel room, and sent Red to the studio to lay down guide tracks with the expensively assembled musicians and singers. Standing in for his boss, and singing one of the songs he'd written himself, Red did well; so well that the following day Elvis, having quickly recovered, went to the studio and copied Red's interpretations syllable for syllable and then quickly returned to Memphis. The difference was that while Red's voice would have graced many an amateur choir, Elvis's gift was in his tonality and intensity.

Not that that helped the new singles. When the next two were released they died in the charts, while the best song of the sessions, 'I'll Remember You', a Hawaiian favourite which Elvis had heard while filming, disappeared into the same black hole of a soundtrack album as the Dylan song.

He was depressed, but that was hardly surprising. Due back in Los Angeles for another two more movies – *Double Trouble*, which would have him singing 'Old MacDonald Had a Farm', and *Easy Come, Easy Go*, where one lyric went '. . . how I can take this yoga serious, When all it ever gives me is a pain in my posterious' – he'd travelled a long way backwards since 'Don't Be Cruel'.

'I know that I'm a joke in this town,' he said to at least one co-star over the next few months. He was being laughed at, he added, knowing that *Easy Come, Easy Go* would be his last movie for Hal Wallis. The old producer, exhausted by the Colonel's demands ('I'd rather try and close a deal with the Devil,' Wallis would say of Parker's negotiating tactics), and cognisant of the falling revenues from the

Elvis franchise, had had enough. Once upon a time Wallis had liked to say: 'A Presley movie is the only one sure thing in show business.' It wasn't any more.

Elvis pretended to be glad to say goodbye to Wallis, but he couldn't escape the fact that the producer and Paramount were dumping him when he was of no more use to them. His options were narrowing. His career was in freefall, and, embarrassed to be seen as a failure in Hollywood, he rented a house in Palm Springs.

To Priscilla and the guys he would blame the conveyor of beach movies.

'Hollywood has lost sight of the basics. They are a lot of fancy talkers who like to pigeon-hole you,' he would say.

But he'd gone along with the pigeon-holing. He still never publicly criticised the Colonel who had guided him, and, when presented with a new contract which gave Parker 50 per cent of some of his earnings, he didn't argue. Was he afraid to?

By the end of 1966, mired in depression, he might still have been seeking occasional spiritual guidance from Sri Daya Mata at the Self-Realization Fellowship, but he was no closer to discovering the point about being Elvis Presley. Then, back at Graceland, as he donated his usual hundred thousand dollars plus to Memphis charities, he gave a rare newspaper interview to Jim Kingsley of the Memphis *Commercial Appeal*. It was Christmas, and an incident that had happened in 1954 came to mind. He, Scotty and Bill had just been paid for a gig, he reminisced to the reporter, and were on their way home to Memphis when they were stopped by the police for speeding. 'There goes my Christmas money for a traffic ticket,' he'd thought. But, luckily, the cop let them off with a warning.

'After the officer left,' he continued, 'the three of us got out of the car and counted out our money by the car headlights. The money was mostly in dollar bills. Man, that was the most money I'd ever had in my pockets at any one time. I blew the whole bundle the next day for Christmas presents.'

Then, as he talked, he became pensive: 'There's a lot of difference in Christmases today from when I was growing up in East Tupelo. But honestly I can't say these are any better. We are just in a better position to spend. But that's not the important thing. It's the friendships and the devotion that really count. Everything is so dreamy when you are young. After you grow up it kind of becomes . . . just real.'

Now life was about to become real for him in another grown-up way. After living with Priscilla for over four years, and following increasing encouragement from her stepfather to make good on the promises he'd made when she'd been a schoolgirl, he finally proposed.

But, did he really want to get married?

28

'Some of you maybe think that Elvis is Jesus Christ who should wear robes and walk down the street helping people. But that's not who he is.'

Colonel Parker

He'd always loved Westerns. From Roy Rogers movies on Saturday mornings to *The Magnificent Seven*, those films had offered him and his generation a romantic view of the West. Like all boys, he'd always seen himself playing the hero, and when television had taken up the storytelling with *Rawhide* and *Cheyenne* in the late fifties, his role models had seemed even closer to him.

Graceland was more *Gone with the Wind* than *Bonanza*, but there were several acres of pasture behind the house, and it was for there, at the end of 1966, that he bought palominos for both Priscilla and himself. It was, however, hardly Wyoming either. In the years since he'd bought his home, Memphis had grown, spreading one of its tentacles out along the now increasingly busy Highway 51. What he needed was somewhere more private for his new hobby, and he spotted the solution one day while out driving: a small ranch in the north Mississippi hills.

It was, Priscilla would write, 'picture postcard perfect: a lake, a barn, a beautiful house. A hundred and sixty acres of paradise.' There was also a herd of cattle to go with it. Elvis had to have it, and the owner of the ranch, Jack Adams, who had made his fortune selling used aircraft, saw him coming. They made the deal on a handshake.

When Vernon heard that Elvis had agreed to pay $450,000 for the ranch, he was livid, shouting that their finances had been destroyed. But Elvis wanted it, so a mortgage was arranged. He called it Circle G Ranch, the 'G' being for Graceland. He wanted more horses, too, for the guys, and when word got out that he was buying, the price of horses in that area soared. The vet who looked after them, Dr E.O. Franklin, could only watch with astonishment at the spending spree.

'We would go out and look at a three hundred dollar horse,' he said. 'But when the people found that it was maybe for Elvis it became a three thousand dollar horse.'

Elvis didn't care: three hundred dollars or three thousand dollars, it made no difference to him if he wanted it.

Naturally all the horses had to have saddles and bridles, and he and Priscilla and the entourage and their wives and girlfriends needed the right clothes to wear, the boots and the belts, the hats and the chaps, just like the drovers wore in *Rawhide*. It was every boy's Western fantasy. Then another thought emerged: if they were all going to be living the country life, there had to be a pick-up buying spree, too.

'One day he bought eight pick-up trucks for all the guys in his entourage,' Franklin remembers. 'Then he bought house trailers so the guys could have someplace to stay. The money he must have gone through!' Even Grandma got a trailer home on the ranch.

It was spending on a massive scale, a further $98,000 in total, Vernon reckoned, which might not have been simply the result of simple generosity and over-enthusiasm for a new hobby. Elvis already had a dentist in Los Angeles who was prepared to write him prescriptions for whatever pills he told himself he needed. Now a pharmacist in Memphis got a knock on his door one evening from the star himself. Obligingly, the surprised pharmacist managed to rustle up something special for him. There were always ways to get what you wanted when your name was Elvis Presley – and if the drugs came from a pharmacist, where could be the harm in that?

There were still ways to make money, too, and *Clambake*, his twentieth movie in less than seven years ('same story, different location', he would snap when asked about it), helped cover the ever-rising expenses and partly pacify Vernon. Once again Elvis didn't want to make the movie, and managed to have shooting delayed while he tried to slim, claiming he was saddle sore from too much horse riding – and even getting a new Memphis doctor, George Nichopoulos, to prescribe some ointment. It would be the first of many, many prescriptions written by the man who became known as Dr Nick.

When he finally got to Los Angeles – 'fat as a pig', he would admit

– he was so overweight that shooting had to be delayed. Then one night he slipped and fell at his Bel Air home, hit his head on the bathtub and suffered concussion.

The Colonel was called, and, bringing along a medical team, visited Elvis in his bedroom. He hadn't come to sympathise. Once it had been ascertained that Elvis hadn't fractured his skull, and strongly suspecting that the accident had been the result of a cocktail of pills, some to sleep, some to help his client lose weight, and some for whatever else the singer liked, Parker had some home truths to impart. Unless Elvis quickly began to mend his ways, he was told, he would soon ruin his career, and would, with financial disaster beckoning, be likely to lose Graceland.

That frightened Elvis. Graceland defined him. It showed him how far he had come, and he loved the house and estate as only a person born in the deepest poverty can love a house. It was the home he had promised his mother, and he was enormously proud of it. By threatening him with the possibility that he might lose it, Parker was taking aim at his most vulnerable spot.

Having achieved his first goal, Parker then turned his ire on the guys. What was wrong with them all? What did they think their job was? How could they have let Elvis get this way?

'Some of you maybe think that Elvis is Jesus Christ who should wear robes and walk down the street helping people,' he said. 'But that's not who he is.'

From that moment on someone was going to have to be with him twenty-four hours a day – even when he had to go to the bathroom.

Then, looking at Larry Geller, he said what he had been longing to say for two years. All of Elvis's religious books had to be removed immediately. 'Right now! Do you understand me? And don't you dare bring him another one.' Henceforth, he concluded, Larry's job would be as a hairdresser only. Considering Larry and the guys worked for Elvis, not him, Parker was speaking out of turn, but he hadn't finished. And when, a couple of days later, Vernon and Priscilla arrived from Memphis, he continued his tirade with Elvis, now recovered, standing meekly at his side. From now on, Parker said, things were going to be different, expenses would be cut back, and, without naming names, he hinted that some people there should start looking for other jobs.

Elvis couldn't meet anyone's eyes. He was being humiliated by the Colonel in his own home in front of his own wife and staff, knowing, too, that Daddy was silently rejoicing at seeing the guys brought to heel. At the beginning of the year, Parker had adjusted his business relationship with Elvis into that of a partnership. Now the Colonel was behaving like the senior partner.

Chief aide Marty Lacker, who never made any secret of the fact that he didn't like or trust Parker, and who had developed a problem with amphetamines himself, resigned a few months later, although he remained a close friend. Larry Geller went sooner. In her autobiography Priscilla, who secretly agreed with much of what the Colonel said, would recall that Elvis accepted that the religious books had confused him, so he and she burned them in a bonfire in an old disused well at Graceland. Geller would dispute that, saying that Elvis later told him that only a few of the books had been burned. Certainly some were kept: a copy of Kahlil Gibran's *The Prophet*, with annotations by the singer – and from which he would quote for the rest of his life – would be on display at Graceland over forty years later. All in all, however, it seemed that the Colonel had pulled off a power coup, and there was nothing Elvis could do about it.

He'd put it off for as long as he could, and on the morning of 1 May 1967, in a short, private ceremony in a not very large suite at the Aladdin Hotel in Las Vegas, Elvis and Priscilla became man and wife. It was what her parents had been pressing for, and Vernon was delighted, too. His son was thirty-two, it was time he stopped fooling around. But just as happy was the Colonel, who stage-managed the entire event. For years he'd urged that Elvis stay single – which was a state that had suited his client perfectly. As Elvis had once joked to a journalist to Parker's distaste: 'Why buy a cow when you can just reach through the fence and take the milk?' But after the way Elvis had been behaving recently, Parker's view was that marriage and a settled-down life couldn't come quickly enough.

Elvis saw it differently. In romantic moments he entertained the notion of being converted overnight into a faithful family man. He loved sentimental movies that showed happy families. But he knew what he was like, and what he enjoyed most – the thrill of the chase. And he knew, too, how women behaved when they were around him. Then there was the matter of love. Yes, he loved Priscilla, he was pretty sure of that, but it wasn't that he was mesmerised by her the way he had been in 1960. How could he be after all this time? Did she feel the same way about him? Probably not, not all the time, anyway, not from the way she would sometimes go on at him. But, yes, he was sure she loved him and she certainly wanted to be married. It had been a long wait.

So, he was getting married, keeping at least one promise he'd made to Priscilla's parents. He was nervous on the day. 'Ed Sullivan didn't scare me like this,' he joked, as he and Priscilla made their vows to 'love, honour, cherish and comfort' before a Nevada Supreme Court judge.

The two senior members of the entourage, Joe Esposito and Marty Lacker, were the best men, and it wasn't until after the ceremony, as a little band played the theme of *Love Me Tender* at the wedding breakfast for a hundred guests, that Elvis began to realise that not everybody was celebrating. In fact, not everyone he expected to be there was present. Red, for instance. Where was Red?

Red had known Elvis since school, he'd been his bodyguard since Sun, he'd sung harmony with him and even written songs for him, and had, quite naturally, assumed that he would be invited to the wedding. But going to Joe Esposito's room just before the ceremony to enquire where he and the guys and their wives should be, he was told that the suite Parker had chosen wasn't big enough to hold everyone. And that meant that most of the guys, including Red and his wife, Pat, weren't invited.

Red was devastated. He considered Elvis more than a best friend. He was his rock. He had even asked him to be his best man. Red might not have suited everyone as a pal, but, 100 per cent loyal, he would do anything for Elvis. Now Elvis had left him out on the biggest day of his life. Red couldn't have been more hurt. The other guys who didn't get invitations blamed the Colonel. But Red blamed Elvis, too.

Elvis was mortified when he realised what he'd done, and was sorry that it had been handled so badly. They should have had a bigger venue, he and Priscilla agreed. They should have organised more of it themselves. The Colonel hadn't thought about how feelings might be hurt. But then, he never did. It was left unsaid, but was Elvis also fretting about his own weakness? He knew he should have insisted that all the guys were at the ceremony. It was *his* wedding. Once again, though, he'd stood by and let it happen. As for Priscilla's idea of organising more of the day themselves – that was just whimsy. Outside a recording studio, Elvis had never organised anything in his entire life. Everything had always been done for him.

This being a Colonel Parker event, there was a small press conference and a time for photographs and newsreel cameramen before the wedding breakfast, to which some of the guys were invited, Red and Pat among them. They didn't go. Staying in their hotel room, they watched the TV news of the wedding they'd missed. Red's mind was made up. He wouldn't work for Elvis again.

With Elvis's fear of flying now overcome, and no Gladys to worry, the newlyweds borrowed Frank Sinatra's Learjet to fly to Palm Springs after the wedding. Then they went on to the Circle G Ranch a few days later, where they slept in one of the trailer homes. It was a honeymoon adventure with picnics and horse riding, almost like camping out. With no staff to take care of them, Priscilla behaved like the new little housewife, and, although the rest of the gang, minus Red, soon arrived, they tended to keep their distance. For once she had Elvis more or less to herself. And it must have pleased her that, as if to put a permanent full stop to any lingering romantic rivalries, Ann-Margret married Roger Smith, the star of television's *77 Sunset Strip*, just over a week later, on 8 May 1967.

For a couple of weeks life on the ranch, with its barbecues and their friends, was about as close to normality as Elvis and Priscilla as a couple would ever enjoy together. And before the honeymoon was over Priscilla was pregnant.

29

'What am I going to do if they don't like me?
What if they laugh at me?'

The Colonel may have talked about the need for change, but it hadn't come yet in the area it was most needed, and hardly was Elvis back from his honeymoon than he was making yet another movie. Now a singing stock car driver in *Speedway*, not even the attraction of chasing his affectionate, but non-obliging, co-star Nancy Sinatra around her location trailer could compensate for his sense of self-debasement with some of the songs. And, yes, as he'd feared, father-to-be though he was, he still couldn't resist pursuing other women.

With his status in the rock world now reduced to that of ridicule – while he'd been recording a *Speedway* song called 'He's Your Uncle Not Your Dad' the Beatles had been making their *Sgt. Pepper's Lonely Hearts Club Band* album – he knew he desperately needed a strong hit single. Then he heard Jerry Reed's 'Guitar Man' on the radio. It hadn't been a hit, but it had something that appealed.

Unfortunately, when he got to Nashville to record it, neither Scotty nor either of the two other session guitarists there could match the verve of the Jerry Reed original. The only solution was to get Reed into the studio to play it himself, so Reed was quickly located and brought back from a few days' fishing on the nearby Cumberland River.

'Lord have mercy! What is *that*?' joked Elvis when Reed arrived unshaven, wearing his fishing clothes.

'The Alabama Wild Man,' said producer Felton Jarvis.

Wild man or not, the session was like a flip back in time to when Elvis had been recording for the fun of it. And, individualist that he was, Reed wasn't diffident about telling everyone how it should be done. Quickly 'Guitar Man' (basically a copy of Reed's own record) turned into a duet between Elvis's voice and Jerry Reed's guitar, becoming the best-produced Presley single in years. In fact, so happy was everyone with the recording, he and Reed immediately went into the classic Jimmy Reed (no relation) r and b hit 'Big Boss Man'.

For some reason Freddy Bienstock hadn't yet done the usual Hill and Range deal that would have given Elvis Presley Music a third of the publishing rights on 'Guitar Man'. And when it was finally put to him, Jerry Reed, who was its writer, singer, guitarist and publisher all rolled into one, refused.

'Why didn't you tell me this before I come here?' he said to Bienstock. 'I could have saved you a lot of effort. You done wasted Elvis's time. You done wasted all these musicians' time, and RCA's time. I'm not going to give you my soul.'

Reminded by Bienstock that the likelihood was that the record wouldn't be released unless he agreed to do a deal, Reed called his bluff.

'I'll put it to you this way,' he said. 'You don't need the money, and Elvis don't need the money, and I'm making more money than I can spend right now – so why don't we forget we ever recorded the damn song.'

He had them over a barrel. Whatever Bienstock said, Elvis had already recorded the song and loved it: he would insist that it was released. As usual, though, he stayed away from business, not getting involved in the argument, while Scotty watched in admiration at Reed's ornery pluck. It was a turning point. The Alabama Wild Man had brought a breath of fresh air and common sense that would blow a gale through the wall of blinkered self-interest that had been wrecking Elvis's records for so long.

Reed wasn't there the following night as the row lingered on until a settlement was reached. But excited by his input, a jam session on 'Hi-Heel Sneakers' became another r and b flip side, something that would have been unthinkable in a movie soundtrack session.

As it happened Elvis's next film, *Live a Little, Love a Little*, did produce a hit – but not until forty years later when a digital remix of 'A Little Less Conversation' turned it into a million-selling number one around the world.

At last, though, with Hollywood doors closing on him one after the other, Parker began to see the error of his ways. As far as movies were concerned it was too late. Despite Elvis being one of the most famous people on the planet, and having now made twenty-five films, neither the Colonel nor Elvis knew any of the hot producers, directors or screenwriters. So, in desperation, Parker turned to the medium that had made Elvis an overnight star – television – and he pitched NBC with a plan for an hour-long Christmas special.

Elvis liked the idea of television but he wasn't happy about a Christmas show. He wanted to show the people 'what I can *really* do', he told the NBC executive in charge when a meeting was arranged. It was a rare act of defiance against Parker, but one that would change the rest of his career.

As the TV negotiations were beginning, things back at the Circle G Ranch were ending. Whether it was due to the expense of running another home, or taking care of all those cows and horses, Elvis's fantasy of living the cowboy life had run its course in less than a year. He'd got over his latest craze. And to Vernon's great delight an auction was held to dispose of whatever could be sold in the way of all those pick-ups and trailer homes. The few horses that his son wanted to keep would, in future, be stabled back at Graceland, and eventually the ranch was sold for $440,000 eighteen months later. So the loss wasn't too great.

Elvis would still own a second home, though. Priscilla had already found a house in Beverly Hills. Now that she was Mrs Presley, she'd had enough of being left behind; if Elvis was going to be working in California, that was where she wanted to be, too. And buying a small house for just the two of them, with a room each for only a couple of the guys, had to be cheaper than renting one of the Bel Air mansions that Elvis had been living in since 1960.

Then on 1 February 1968, the family got a new member when Lisa Marie Presley was born at the Baptist Memorial Hospital in Memphis. Like almost every other man who becomes a father, Elvis surprised himself at how thrilled he was.

Mistakes had been made and remade during his movie career, but on television it had never gone wrong, and what became known as the ''68 Comeback Special' got it right, too. Most directors of his movies had hardly been in the first flush of youth; Norman Taurog, who made nine of them, had been born in 1899. But NBC's choice of Steve Binder, who had won awards for filming a concert that had featured Chuck Berry and the Rolling Stones, was absolutely right.

Elvis liked the basic storyline of a rock and roll odyssey built around the song 'Guitar Man'. And with interludes planned to demonstrate his different styles of singing, from gospel to rock and roll, blues and ballads, he was asked to participate in the show's creation, something that the clichéd movie makers had never even considered.

As taping approached, however, he was still unsure about doing a whole show on his own, admitting that he was 'scared to death'. So when Binder suggested he send for his original musicians, Scotty and drummer D.J. Fontana, he agreed immediately. Having overheard Elvis and Charlie Hodge singing and playing together in a dressing room, it seemed to Binder that the best way to get the 'raw' Elvis might be to go back to basics and film him, *cinéma-vérité* style, jamming with his old friends.

All the same, Elvis had a panic attack just before taping began. Sitting in his dressing room at NBC's Burbank Studios he was sweating profusely.

'I haven't been in front of an audience in eight years,' he said. (A slight exaggeration. It was seven years since his last appearance on stage in Hawaii in 1961.) 'What am I going to do if they don't like me? What if they laugh at me?'

The exact reverse happened. The improvised jamming session, with Elvis roaming through a dozen or more of his favourite old songs, from 'Lawdy Miss Clawdy' and 'Trying to Get to You' to 'Love Me', became the most memorable part of the show, even though he would say he was 'just about boiled alive' in his leather suit under the hot TV lights. Nearly four hours of songs were taped, and then edited down to a twenty-five-minute slot. About as primitive a set-up as could be imagined, it was a forerunner of what would become known in TV as an 'unplugged' session over twenty years later.

Not surprisingly, as the show progressed and Elvis listened more to Binder than to Parker, the Colonel became increasingly irate that his idea for a Christmas show was being sabotaged. At the very least, he was still demanding that Elvis sing a carol or maybe 'I'll Be Home for Christmas' at the very end of the programme, when news came that Robert Kennedy had been assassinated in San Francisco.

It was just two months since the murder of Martin Luther King in Memphis. Elvis had been in despair over that, ashamed that it should have happened in his home town. Now with the murder of a second Kennedy, he could talk of nothing else. He'd bought and read the Warren Commission Report on the death of JFK, and talked over and over about how the murder of Martin Luther King would just confirm the widespread view of racism in the South. Altogether it was an emotional time, which suddenly prompted Binder to ask the show's music arranger, W. Earl Brown, if he could write something that would reflect how Elvis had reacted to the Kennedy and Martin Luther King killings.

The result was 'If I Can Dream', a song about peace, hope and brotherhood that was based directly upon King's 'I Have a Dream' speech made on the steps of Washington's Lincoln Memorial in August 1963. When Brown played and sang his song to Binder and the producer of the show they were excited. The Colonel's response, however, was predictably dismissive: 'That ain't an Elvis kind of song,' he growled, which showed how unfamiliar he was with the gospel side of his client. Brown's hopes were dashed. Mentally he had already decided that if Elvis didn't record it, he would send it to Aretha Franklin.

But then, from behind him, Brown heard another voice: 'Play it again.' It was Elvis. Brown hadn't known he'd been there, listening. So he played it again, and then again. 'We're doing it,' said Elvis at last. It didn't matter now what Parker said.

As usual with any song he thought important, Elvis studied the lyrics carefully, then, satisfied, he wrote in a corner of the lyric sheet, 'My boy, my boy, this could be the one.' He recorded it a few days later, with a forty-piece orchestra of horns and strings, which was a first on an Elvis record. He'd hardly ever sung in front of anything bigger than a little rock band before. As they sang, the black backing vocalists the Blossoms, whom Elvis had insisted accompany him, had tears running down their cheeks, watching as he closed his eyes and dropped down to his knees as though in revivalist supplication. Afterwards one of them, the now famous backing singer Darlene Love, told Brown: 'He just loves it. He means every word.' It would be the only hit song Brown would ever write.

'Steve,' Elvis said to Binder after the recording, 'I'm never going to sing another song I don't believe in. And I'm never going to make another picture I don't believe in.'

As it happened, he did record quite a few more songs that he didn't much care about, but nowhere near as many as he had done for Hollywood. As for the movies, there were only three more to go, anyway.

The Colonel had been overruled completely in his plans for the Christmas special, but his scorn for 'If I Can Dream' didn't prevent him from ensuring that Hill and Range got the rights to the publishing. He still whinged, of course, until a couple of verses of 'Blue Christmas' which had been cut from the jam session were put back in to appease him. He just had to have his little victories. Most of all, though, it had been a victory for Elvis over him.

Elvis was on a high. Months earlier he'd asked Scotty, who owned a little studio in Nashville, if he could copy some old 78s for him. Naturally Scotty agreed, and Elvis sent him a little attaché case with all the treasures of his teenage years carefully wrapped in newspapers so that they wouldn't break. Twenty-six records in all, mainly r and b, they included songs by, among others, Ivory Joe Hunter, Big Joe Turner, the Dominoes, Ray Charles and Brownie McGee, which were all copied to reel-to-reel tape for him.

So, when, at the Burbank sessions, Elvis suggested that maybe he and Scotty should get together at the guitarist's studio and play together for a week just to see what came out of it, Scotty agreed. It sounded to him like a great idea. It was. But, not only was it never mentioned again, he and Elvis would never play together again either.

Taping the *Elvis* show was completed by the end of June, and a five-month wait followed as editing took place before it would be transmitted. So after a week in Palm Springs it was off to Arizona to make a quickie Western called *Charro!* At last Elvis had a straight acting part. It didn't work. Nor did the next film, *The Trouble with Girls*, which was shot immediately afterwards. That was no good either. It almost seemed that the deck was being cleared of all his Hollywood obligations before the new, comeback Elvis could be revealed.

The question was, would anybody be watching?

30

'I heard the rumour that Elvis slept with all his co-stars except one. Well . . . I know who the one was! And what was I thinking?'

Mary Tyler Moore

He watched the screening of the NBC show on 3 December 1968, sitting in his new Beverly Hills home with Priscilla. It wasn't the first time he'd seen it, but seeing it now, knowing that millions of other people had tuned in to it, was a quite different feeling. It was as if he was doing a public audition, as his first TV appearance with the Dorsey brothers in 1956 had seemed; a night when, as then, the rest of his career was at stake. The Hollywood B-movies he'd made, and he knew that was what most of them were, had turned him into an anachronism. Now, as he saw himself in his white suit singing 'If I Can Dream' at the end of the show, he could see, for the first time in years, a future for himself. And he was still only thirty-three.

He was very quiet during the transmission, hardly speaking to Priscilla, only for the phones to start ringing and never stop from the moment the end titles appeared. Friends never call to say 'you screwed up', but he enjoyed their excited flattery just the same. And although not all the newspaper reviews the following day were complimentary – some critics still didn't get it – several of the classier ones were. The *New York Times* rock critic, John Landau marvelled: 'There's something magical about watching a man who has lost himself, find his way home.'

Even better news came when the ratings for the show were released. They were the biggest of the year for NBC, with 42 per cent of the American viewing public having watched. That was astonishing, almost back to Ed Sullivan-type figures. The single 'If I Can Dream' had been issued a month earlier to lukewarm reaction, but now it raced up the charts, as did the album of the show. One hour on television had turned Elvis's life around.

So, what next? He had told Steve Binder he wanted to go back to live performances, but, while the Colonel was chewing on that, a follow-up album and single couldn't be delayed. So in January 1969 some of the guys met at Graceland for dinner to consider his future. A return to the RCA studio at Nashville was the most likely scenario, until his friend, but no longer employee, Marty Lacker said: 'Why not record here in Memphis? Why not use the American Sound Studio? I just wish you'd try Chips Moman and his rhythm section. They're great.' The house band at American Sound with its emphasis on bass and piano gospel chords was indeed highly regarded; Jerry Wexler had recently hired it and the studio to record Dusty Springfield's 'Son of a Preacher Man', while Otis Redding, Joe Tex and Aretha Franklin had all worked there.

Intrigued, Elvis took Lacker into another room and played him a song by Mac Davis (the writer of 'A Little Less Conversation') which he'd been given. It was 'In the Ghetto', which, to their eternal regret, had been turned down by the Righteous Brothers. Elvis would record it in Memphis.

Recording began at the run-down American Sound Studio in a poor part of Memphis on the night of 13 January 1969. It was the first time Elvis had recorded in the city since 1955 when he'd been with Sun, and the building had a reputation for being infested with rats. 'What a funky place,' he joked as he looked around.

But it was the house band, all of whose members were new to Elvis, that was funky, and, of course, the producer, Chips Moman. Technically RCA's Felton Jarvis was still the man in charge, but it was Chips, a master technician and engineer, who took over, and straight away Elvis was singing a song that would, in less than a decade, become oddly prophetic. Called 'Long Black Limousine' it was about a girl who leaves a small town and goes to the big city, vowing that one day she'll return 'With a fancy car for the whole town to see'. Now she had come back and finally got her dream. She's 'riding in a long black limousine' – on her way to the town cemetery, a victim of ambition and life in the fast lane. Elvis must have known that one day that would be him. He just didn't know when.

The sessions went well. There was a song from one of his favourite writers, Mort Shuman, 'You'll Think of Me', a cover of Glen Campbell's hit 'Gentle on My Mind' and another Mac Davis song, 'Don't Cry Daddy', which, as a father now, appealed to his sentimental side. Interestingly the first two described the feelings of a man who couldn't settle down with one woman, while 'Don't Cry Daddy' was about the break-up of a marriage. Then there was 'Wearing That Loved On Look', which was about infidelity, and soon would come 'Suspicious Minds', another hint at adultery. It was the first time he'd sung so many songs with adult themes. Had Priscilla listened closely to the lyrics, they might have given her food for thought.

He even did a couple of songs sent to him by Hill and Range, but most of their submissions ended up in the air as, getting back from the studio, he would listen to the new demos at home and then send them skimming across his den in rejection.

'From now on,' he told the guys, 'I want to hear every song I can get my hands on. If I've got a piece of the publishing, that's fine. But if I don't and I want to do the song, I'm going to do it.' Then he insisted that they should all go and look for good songs.

Naturally, Freddy Bienstock still pushed, but Jerry Reed had set a precedent with 'Guitar Man', and when Chips Moman was put under pressure for a share of the publishing of 'Suspicious Minds', a song he partly owned, his response was straight to the point. As far as he was concerned, RCA could take the $25,000 they were paying for the entire session and 'stick it up their ass and consider this the most expensive demo session in history'. The row was only settled when an RCA executive who had been overseeing the session spoke up for Moman: 'This boy's right. We're gonna stay here and we're gonna do the sessions his way.'

Again Elvis kept out of it. He just wanted to make good records. However, when Moman complained about the interference he was still getting from the music publishers and some of the guys, Elvis told them all to leave.

'It would be almost like he thought he had to perform for them,' Moman would remember of Elvis's behaviour in front of his guys. 'He'd say something cute or do something funny to make 'em laugh.

When it was just him and me, one-on-one, he was just one of the easiest people to work with.'

Tom Diskin, standing in for the Colonel at the session, immediately called his boss in Palm Springs to tell him of Elvis's mutiny. Parker's response was dry. He told Diskin to get back to Los Angeles, and 'let him fall on his ass'.

But Elvis didn't. The grip that the Colonel and Hill and Range had had was seriously buckled, though not yet completely broken. Of the thirty-three tracks recorded over two separate Memphis sessions in the winter of 1969, Hill and Range only got a share of thirteen of them. Instead Elvis recorded songs published by many other companies and from writers such as Burt Bacharach, Neil Diamond, Percy Mayfield, Bobby Darin, and even Lennon and McCartney. (Although, in the latter's case, not very well since, not knowing the lyrics, he only did a guide track to 'Hey Jude', which should never have been released.)

Altogether it was the most productive time in a recording studio he would ever have, and one of the most enjoyable, particularly when he discovered that singer Roy Hamilton was using the same studio during the day. Turning up early one evening before Hamilton had finished recording, he told the classically trained singer how much he'd been influenced by him when he'd been growing up. Then, on an impulse, he gave Hamilton a song he'd intended to record himself, a Barry Mann–Cynthia Weil composition, 'Angelica'. It would, he thought, suit Hamilton perfectly. It did. They never met again. Sadly Hamilton would die suddenly, a few months later.

'In the Ghetto' was an obvious hit, but there were worries among the guys that Elvis was taking a risk with some of his fans by recording it. The Colonel wasn't happy either. He'd been careful never to let Elvis voice a political opinion, and he now advised against releasing 'In the Ghetto' as a single, believing it identified Elvis too closely with black America. Even Chips Moman worried about 'what people might think about a white guy singing about life in the ghetto'. But as Elvis said: 'When I heard the song, I couldn't ignore it.' It became one of his biggest ever hits.

He'd always liked Mary Tyler Moore when she'd been in her TV show with Dick Van Dyke. Who didn't? But her appearance with him in

Change of Habit, in what would be his last dramatic movie role, did nothing for either of their film careers, nor, for once, his love life. Years later Mary would joke about the untrue rumour that Elvis had slept with every one of his co-stars in his movies except one by saying, 'Well . . . I know who the one was! And what was I thinking?'

What Elvis was probably thinking was that this was at last a semi-serious role, but that, all the same, it was just another quickie movie. He was playing a doctor, and Mary Tyler Moore was a nun in disguise, that is, not wearing her religious habit, which rather militated against there being a romantic ending. It probably seemed a good idea at the time.

Perhaps the most memorable moment for him came during a break in shooting when actress Barbara McNair, who was playing another nun, introduced him to gospel singer Mahalia Jackson who was visiting the set. He was a fan, but when she asked him to lend his name to a fundraiser she was organising, he fobbed her off.

'Mrs Jackson, I'm so happy to meet you,' he told her. 'I'd love to do it. But I have to ask the Colonel.'

After Mahalia left, he turned to Barbara McNair and admitted sadly, 'I'll never do it. The Colonel won't let me.' Despite his victory in the recording studio, the Colonel still made the other decisions. Elvis would never be completely his own man.

To no one's surprise *Change of Habit* hardly caused a ripple when it was released in 1970. It was, the critics generally agreed, neither good nor bad nor anything. But, by then, its star was the hottest ticket in America again.

31

'I want musicians who can play every kind of music.'

Even before the NBC special had been transmitted the Colonel had begun negotiating with the management of the new International Hotel in Las Vegas. It had a barn of a supper-showroom on top of its vast ground-floor twenty-four-hour casino, and Elvis was booked to sing for an hour twice a night for four weeks for $100,000 a week. As the bait to lure the punters to the casino, this would be the hardest labour his voice had ever undertaken.

First, though, he needed a band and a gospel quartet to play and sing around him and naturally Scotty, D.J. and the Jordanaires were approached. Scotty had been hurt at not being invited to play on the Memphis sessions, and, having talked with Elvis about doing a European tour in 1969, he was surprised to be told the plans had changed and the engagement would now only be for a month and only in Vegas. Unfortunately he, the Jordanaires and D.J. had session work booked for the month of August. If they took the money they were being offered by the Colonel it would mean not only letting other people down, but taking a salary cut as well. After meeting in Nashville to discuss the offer, the six of them turned it down. Had they known that there would be touring afterwards, it might have led to a different outcome, Scotty would say later. But none of them knew that.

Gordon Stoker of the Jordanaires always regretted their decision. It seemed to him that Elvis was never the same again . . . 'as though he'd lost his family'. Elvis felt let down by Scotty and the others. But it has to be said, and not for the first time, Scotty felt let down by Elvis. It was the same carelessness from which Red had suffered.

But, if it wasn't going to be Scotty, Elvis had to find a new lead guitarist around whom he could build his band.

'I asked around everywhere and two names kept coming up,' he said, 'Glen Campbell and James Burton. Glen Campbell was doing his own thing . . . so I called James.'

Burton was a busy Los Angeles session musician, but had become well known among rock fans as the seventeen-year-old virtuoso who in 1958 had played lead guitar on Dale Hawkins' 'Susie Q', and would later play on Ricky Nelson's hits. Quickly he and Elvis began auditioning.

'I want musicians who can play every kind of music,' Elvis said.

He was no longer going to be just a rock and roll singer. He wanted music that would demonstrate all his styles, and which would be able to convey the wide array of American music he liked. From now on he would sing country, gospel, blues, rock and big ballads, and there would be a thirty-five-piece orchestra of strings and brass with two groups of back-up singers to accompany him.

'All the musicians around me were handpicked,' he said later, explaining his new direction. 'We auditioned for days and days.'

Choosing the drummer was the most difficult decision until they tried Ronnie Tutt, who tried to keep his eye on Elvis as he played, because all the moves Elvis made on stage 'made it like playing for a glorified stripper'. The Jordanaires were to be replaced by the Imperials, who had sung on 'How Great Thou Art', while the three-woman soul group the Sweet Inspirations were chosen because Elvis liked the way they'd backed Aretha Franklin. All former church singers, they included Cissy Houston, the sister of Dionne Warwick and mother of Whitney Houston.

All through the planning there were battles with the Colonel. Parker thought Elvis was being extravagant with the number of musicians and singers he wanted, who Elvis would be paying – around fifty in total – to which Elvis replied that it was a big stage for him to cover.

'We rehearsed about fifty songs,' he would say, 'of which I have to choose about twenty a night. If it isn't working after the first four or five numbers I change it around and do other songs.'

A few weeks before his Vegas opening, he took Priscilla to see Tom Jones on stage at the Flamingo Hotel. Having met him in Hollywood, Elvis liked Jones as a friend and loved his voice, although when he saw him on stage he suspected he had a sock pushed down the front of his trousers. He thought his stage act was 'vulgar', too. 'I was never vulgar,' he insisted, to wry amusement from some of his entourage. But, if Tom Jones had anything to teach him about playing a two-thousand-seat dining room twice a night, he was eager to learn. Could he do what Tom Jones did to an audience of adults?

He found out on 31 July, in a Las Vegas liberally plastered with his name and image. Once again he was sweating with nerves before the show. But then, wearing what looked like a tailored black karate suit, he slipped almost sheepishly on stage as the band played a rock and roll riff. Then, handed his guitar by Charlie Hodge, he went straight into 'Blue Suede Shoes', before, without a word to the audience, racing through 'I Got a Woman' and 'That's All Right'. Musically, he was taking everything too fast, and later 'Don't Be Cruel' and 'All Shook Up', delivered on full acceleration, weren't sung nearly as well as on the records; but the excitement in the supper lounge was uncritical. Even the unnecessary karate chops with which he ended some of the songs were applauded.

Eventually, taking a break, he began telling a potted version of his life story – although almost the whole audience must have known it very well. But that was Elvis. Frequently, on greeting strangers who looked awkward in his presence, he would introduce himself by saying, 'Hello, I'm Elvis Presley,' as though they might not know.

Because of the lights he couldn't see very far into the showroom, but he knew that down there at the tables Priscilla was in a white minidress, alongside Vernon and Dee, and the Colonel and his rarely seen wife, Marie. Then there was Felton Jarvis on his honeymoon with his new wife, various show business acquaintances who had made the short flight from Los Angeles, music journalists from New York, Los Angeles and London, and two plane loads of friends, family and staff from Memphis whose tickets he'd paid for himself.

Ann-Margret and her husband were there, too, and would go backstage to see him after the show, and then there was Fats Domino, whom he'd been to see many times in Vegas and who was now returning the compliment. Pat Boone, once a rival, was also present, as were Paul Anka, Shirley Bassey and TV disc jockey producer Dick

Clark. Then there was Burt Bacharach with his wife Angie Dickinson, George Hamilton, Henry Mancini and Liberace. Most of his guys were watching in the wings, but he knew that Sam Phillips was there somewhere, because he'd invited him himself, explaining that he wanted the support of some of his friends from Memphis. Phillips had, as always, given him a lecture, telling him he'd be 'just fine as long as you get yourself the best little rhythm section you can find', which was exactly what he'd done.

What he didn't know was how many of the people in movies who had written him off had turned up to see him. They'd had a wrong image of him all along, and it bothered him. Were they all now realising how wrong they'd been? For the rest of his life the way he had been encouraged to lose his direction in Hollywood upset him. 'I sure got into a rut with those films,' he would say, pretending to joke and shaking his head ruefully. But it wasn't a joke to him.

That first show flew by. In the old days he had invariably finished his set with a long version of 'Hound Dog'. But he had a new ending now in 'Can't Help Falling in Love'. And with that, the curtain came down and the new live-on-stage Elvis was launched. Overnight, the movies were forgotten. It had been, he would say, 'one of the most exciting nights of my life'.

Three days later he talked to a couple of English journalists, including the author of this book. Sitting on a red Spanish sofa in the sitting room of his backstage suite with four of the Memphis Mafia, he was sipping from a bottle of 7 Up, and worrying that the dry Las Vegas air was getting to his throat. He'd slimmed down to appear in the NBC special the previous year, and now he was even slimmer – the result, he said, of a strict diet and sweating off several pounds during every show. He didn't mention the slimming pills he'd been taking. As he chatted, quiet and friendly, saying how he wanted to make another r and b album, he played some air-guitar and sang a little of his favourite Beatles song 'I Saw Her Standing There', and then promised that he would soon play on stage in Britain.

'I know I keep saying I'll come to England one day, but I will.'

The Colonel, meanwhile, in a short-sleeved shirt and shapeless trousers, sat separately, watching like a gamekeeper to ensure that nothing amiss was uttered.

The chat was good-humoured, Elvis laughing at himself when, asked which his favourite current group was, he replied without thinking 'the Platters', who were hardly current. The Beatles had sent a telegram wishing him well for his opening, which he'd had taped to the door; while some of the guys were amused by the girl who had thrown a pair of panties at him on stage the previous night, which he'd caught and with which he'd wiped his brow.

Only when asked about his films did he glance anxiously towards the Colonel. 'I wouldn't be being honest with you,' he admitted, 'if I said I wasn't ashamed of some of the movies I've been in and some of the songs I had to sing in them. I'd like to say they were good, but I can't. I had to do them. I signed contracts when I came out of the army.

'I knew a lot of the songs in them were bad and it used to bother the heck out of me. But they fitted the situation.' But there would not, he insisted, be any more bad movies.

'I've been wanting to perform on stage again for the last nine [sic] years, and it's been building up inside me since about 1965, until the strain became intolerable. I got all het about it. I don't think I could have left it much longer. The time is right.'

As for money, he laughed. 'I've no idea about the money. I don't want to know. You can stuff it.'

At which point the Colonel quickly explained his own situation. 'Can we just say this,' he interrupted. 'The Colonel has nothing to do with Mr Presley's finances. That's all done by his father, Mr Vernon Presley, and his accountant. He can flush all his money away, if he wants to. I won't care.'

Elvis must have registered the little dig. He'd been hearing it for fourteen years. What he might not have realised in that week of triumph was that with the International Hotel already picking up the option for him to appear there summer and winter for another five years – without an inflation clause – it was also ensuring that the Colonel would be there for a month twice a year, too. For a gambling man like Parker that would be very convenient.

Certainly it would be more convenient than going on a European tour, and later that week Parker would contradict his client over breakfast with this author. Elvis, he said, wouldn't be going to

Britain any time soon. The Colonel's wife, 'Mrs Parker', had some medical problems and wouldn't be fit to travel, and it wouldn't be right for him to leave her behind, he explained.

There would always be an excuse for Tom Parker never to have to leave the United States.

32

'I don't want some sonofabitch crazy bastard pictured sneering in the newspapers about having killed Elvis Presley.'

The way he saw it, nobody was at fault. It was just a situation that they'd found themselves in through decisions made years earlier when they'd both been a lot younger. Now, apart from Lisa Marie, he and Priscilla didn't have a great deal in common. He'd tried to mould her into his perfect woman, and she was certainly very beautiful. But her being at home all the time, where he wanted her to be, somehow made her less exciting than the girls he met who were out there in the world, and forever flirting and teasing with him. Obviously he didn't want a flirty woman like that as his wife, but . . .

She'd been brought up a Catholic and he in the Pentecostal First Assembly of God, but they believed in the same basics and religion had never been an issue between them, not until he became involved with the Self-Realization Fellowship, anyway. That had been something else. Priscilla was as dubious about it as the Colonel and most of the guys. It bored her, and that really got to him, because it was important to him.

But there were other things. Priscilla enjoyed music, but she wasn't a musician or a singer, and he could never talk to her about music in the way he used to with Scotty or how he did now with James Burton, Charlie, and the Sweet Inspirations. Often between shows he would drop in at the Inspirations' dressing room just to chat. There had been an incident early on in Vegas when he'd got into a fit of giggling while singing 'Are You Lonesome Tonight?', and Cissy Houston, who was the soprano, had just carried on doing her coloratura behind him as he'd tried and failed to get through the recitation, laughing all the time. No matter how much he'd struggled, with tears running down his cheeks, hysterical at the notion of getting a fit of giggles in front of all these people, Cissy had just kept on trilling away, which had made the situation all the funnier.

He loved to laugh. 'It's pure freedom,' he would say, 'like being a kid again.'

And he and the Inspirations would laugh together recalling that night, and then talk about music they liked and hymns they all knew. It was good to relax with them sometimes. Unpressured. He'd always loved being with women, talking to girls, telling them about his mother, asking them about their lives. There were always new girls to meet, new adventures to enjoy, and he didn't see why he shouldn't enjoy them since he'd soon realised that his marriage had been a mistake.

Nor did all his friendships with women include sex. Many didn't. Unhappily his relationship with Priscilla wasn't about sex either since the birth of Lisa Marie. He'd once told her he could never make love to a woman who'd had a baby and she wondered whether that was the problem. She would never know for sure because he didn't want to discuss it further. All she did know was that shortly after his nightly sleeping pill had kicked in, he would be asleep, and she would increasingly feel rejected. Her role was to wait on him, and wait *for* him. When challenged about other women he would always deny his philandering, but they both knew that she didn't believe him. A denial simply averted, or at least postponed, a row. When he was at home she babied him, doing everything for him, even sometimes cutting his meat. Was that how his mother had pampered him? He behaved as though he expected it. But Priscilla wasn't his mother and much of the time they were apart. Now that he was working in Las Vegas, while she was at home in Los Angeles with their little girl, he would, she knew, be partying with his pals and the girls he attracted. So, at his suggestion, she took some more dance classes and then some acting lessons and hoped things would improve between them. Like him, she took karate classes, too. He encouraged that. It was good that she was doing something that he liked.

For Elvis, as long as he was singing he was happy. Sitting at home in Memphis at the piano he would sing to himself, or call Nancy, one of the maids, to join him so that they could sing a hymn together. He came alive when he was performing. Even in band rehearsals or recordings he would give a full act, complete with moves, when the only audience were the musicians. All he ever really wanted was to entertain people. So when the season in Vegas finished at the end of August 1969, with 'Suspicious Minds' heading to the top of record charts all around the world, he was at a loss to know what to do with himself. Much as he'd despised the movies, they'd given him a routine. But there was no film location to go off to this year, no pretty new actresses to meet, and no soundtrack album to make and then complain about.

So, in need of a break, he took Priscilla to Hawaii. They weren't alone, of course; they never went anywhere alone. Vernon and his second wife Dee were invited, along with Joe and Joanie Esposito and another member of his gang, Jerry Schilling and his wife. For a few days while they were there they considered going to Europe next, until the Colonel found out and gave Elvis a lecture about how if he turned up in London on vacation while not having toured there yet, he would upset British fans who had been so loyal for so long.

It sounded like the nonsense it was. But, unquestioning, Elvis meekly obeyed, as if he'd still been the twenty-year-old whom Parker had latched on to in 1955, the insecure youth who couldn't answer back when bullied by an overbearing father figure. So instead of going to London and Paris, they went to the Bahamas, where he was befriended by an astonished Irish show band called the Witnesses, who were playing in the same hotel. He even queued to go and see them. There wasn't much else to do there in the evenings and he always liked music, whatever it was. The only Irish song he knew, he told them, was 'Danny Boy'. His mother used to like that one. He would record it one day.

It rained for much of the rest of the time, and Elvis and Priscilla fell out again, as unhappy couples often do when they go on holiday together.

When they got back he was restless for the remainder of 1969 and into 1970, and, calling himself Colonel Jon Burrows, and accompanied by a couple of the guys, he would make discreet little trips down to Dallas to see an air stewardess he knew there. Meanwhile the hits from the Memphis sessions kept coming regularly every three months, just like they used to – 'In the Ghetto', 'Suspicious Minds', 'Don't Cry Daddy', 'Kentucky Rain'.

Back in high school he'd had a need to be noticed – hence the pink and green outfits and sideburns. Later there'd been the gold suit in 1957, followed by leather for the NBC special. The black karate outfit for the International launch had been stylish, but the design with which Bill Belew, who had created his gold suit in the fifties and the leather outfit for the '68 Comeback Special, fitted him out in February 1970 for his next Vegas season would stay with him for the rest of his life. Basically a white jump suit ('so that his shirt didn't come out of his trousers', Belew said), it would, with increasing rhinestone embellishments and eventually a matching Superman-type cape, evolve over the following few years into a look that simply screamed *ELVIS*. Parker had complained during the first Vegas season that with so many people on stage, Elvis sometimes got lost. Well, not any more. Not in one of those suits.

Priscilla, increasingly reduced to watching from the sidelines, saw something sad in the ostentation. With his voice, looks, talent and charisma, she thought her husband didn't need to dress up like that. It all looked to her like a cry for help. But if Elvis was crying for help, he didn't know it. He never would. He was the centre of his own world. He never ever asked anyone for any kind of help. He was Elvis, he was the one who gave the help.

The second Las Vegas season was just as successful as the first, as he replaced some old songs by going to the piano to do 'Old Shep' and 'Blueberry Hill'. An old favourite he'd never sung before was 'The Wonder of You', which was recorded live on stage as part of an album and released later to become a hit single. He did that several times with other songs, which pleased the Colonel no end. As the band and backing singers were already being paid for the show, it made a cheap and quick way to get a big hit.

It was nearly three in the morning when the midnight show at the International finished that February as Elvis kept adding song after song as though he couldn't bear to leave the spotlight. Then, quickly, he was on his way to Texas for the Houston Livestock Show and Rodeo at the Astrodome.

He'd always liked Texas, the signal from the *Louisiana Hayride* radio show having been clearest there, giving him his first real following outside Memphis. But before he even arrived a rumour got around that one of the Houston promoters had said that he could 'leave the black girls behind' for this gig. The quote may not even have been true, but his answer, Myrna Smith, one of the Sweet Inspirations, said, was that if the girls didn't come, there wouldn't be any show.

As it happened there wasn't much of a show for any of them at first. With echoes bouncing off all sides of the arena, it was clear that the sound system hadn't been designed with a rock and roll concert in mind. But it got better. And, over three days more than 200,000 fans turned out to see him, more than the number who had seen him in a month in Las Vegas. Elvis and the Colonel were back in the money. Big time. Touring would follow. Personal appearances had been a way to sell records in the fifties. In the seventies stadium rock was where the money was to be found.

Musically, the next logical move would have been to return to American Sound in Memphis for the next album. But too many noses had been put out of joint there for logic to stand a chance. Both the Colonel and Freddy Bienstock had resented being beaten in the publishing row over 'Suspicious Minds', and producer Felton Jarvis, who had now left RCA to concentrate solely on Elvis's recordings, was miffed about the way Chips Moman had elbowed him to one side. So, it was back to Nashville in June, with a new studio band. Both Scotty and D.J. were in town, as were the Jordanaires, but they weren't invited back.

In terms of quantity the new Nashville sessions couldn't be faulted. Thirty-five songs recorded in five days. That was a lot of singing. But the quality slipped as Elvis raced from one song to the next. Material for three albums and several singles was recorded, but the only lasting hit was a cover of Dusty Springfield's classic 'You Don't Have to Say You Love Me'. And the session was only saved from being disappointingly run of the mill when, halfway through recording, the idea arose that twelve of the songs should be put together to make the *Elvis Country* album, with a photo of Elvis, aged two, on the cover. Furthermore, Felton Jarvis just wasn't as good a producer as Chips Moman. It was a step backwards. Hill and Range were happy, though. They either published or had a taste in the publishing of two thirds of the songs.

All the same, Elvis was hot again and the cashing in began once more. Just as in 1956, the market was flooded with Elvis material, several albums being released in 1970 alone, mainly repackages on RCA's budget label. The Memphis sessions had substantially raised his artistic profile, but now the shine on it quickly began to lose its lustre as the lure of quick money was chosen over long-term career respectability. That Colonel Parker, who organised the reissues, was now taking a 50 per cent share of Elvis's earnings from reissued material might have raised questions in another client's mind. But if his manager's extraordinarily large slice bothered Elvis, he didn't complain. Besides, there was already something bigger on the horizon.

In May 1970, a documentary movie was released of the Woodstock rock festival that had taken place in the mud in upstate New York the previous summer. And whatever Woodstock could do, so could Elvis, if not for the same audience. Not all his fans could get to Las Vegas or one of the cities on his new touring schedule, so the Elvis show would go to them at their local cinemas, and plans were made to film him in rehearsal and on stage at the summer Vegas season. The movie would be called *Elvis: That's the Way It Is*, and, like the *Woodstock* movie, it would have an album in tow.

With its limited ambitions it couldn't go wrong. And, still a regular feature on late-night television, forty-five years after it was made, Elvis, in his white suit, tassels flying, singing 'Polk Salad Annie' is how most people in the world now remember him.

It was, however, his clothes and accoutrements off stage that increasingly began to show a quite different side of him. He'd always liked uniforms, from briefly wearing one as a cadet in the Junior Reserve Officer Training Corps at high school to his service in the army. But his craze for collecting badges from various police forces, which emerged in 1970, was almost spooky. Its roots may have been in his teens when he'd briefly considered a career as a cop; but then had come fame followed by gratitude to police forces across the country for protecting him from over-excited fans.

Gradually, however, as the sixties had, in his eyes, turned dark and threatening, the idea of an attack by unknown, insane, drugged-up Charles Manson-like characters was edging him ever closer to identifying with the police and authority in general. He didn't understand or like the hippy ethos. Intensely patriotic, he hated to see the country he loved criticised and mocked by what he saw as long-haired, druggy decadents. And when he read the anti-war – and, he believed, anti-American – diatribes by younger musicians in *Rolling Stone* he was incensed. He couldn't comprehend how young people could burn the Stars and Stripes in protest at the Vietnam War, or how they could routinely refer to the police as 'pigs'. He had friends who were cops, and he would often invite them to his regular all-night movie screenings in Memphis, leaving the company of his own party of friends in order to ask an officer how his day had been. To Elvis, a cop's working day seemed often so much more eventful than his own. It frequently may have been.

So, when in Houston the chief of police awarded him a gold deputy sheriff's badge after his appearance there, it was as if a dam in his mind had been breached. Some guys become obsessed with model trains; others with stamps; Elvis decided he liked badges. Priscilla would say he collected 'millions' of police badges that were given to him as he crossed the country on tour. Well, perhaps not millions, but certainly more than a few.

And then there were the guns. He might have been given a guitar rather than a gun for his eleventh birthday, but he'd always had guns since he'd been an adult. It was, however, only when anonymous phone calls to both the Colonel and his chief of staff Joe Esposito threatened him with kidnap, that he went gun crazy. Naturally, the Las Vegas police and the FBI were notified about the calls and nothing came of the threats. But, as the target, he was fuming. He was confident enough that his karate skills could take care of any physical attack, but if guns were used he had to be ready to fight fire with fire. From then onwards he would go on stage with a handgun in each boot, while all the guys round him got licences to carry firearms. He didn't want to be dead, he would say, with 'some sonofabitch crazy bastard pictured sneering in the newspapers about having killed Elvis Presley'.

The awarding of a second deputy sheriff's badge in October 1970, this time by Shelby County, Tennessee, which was where he lived, gave him the legal right to carry a gun in Memphis, and two weeks later in Los Angeles he would order gold handles for his new Colt and Beretta pistols. Then came an honorary badge from the Denver police, followed by a gold commissioner's badge from the Los Angeles Police Department as a reward for a $7000 donation to their community relations programme. It was all turning into another expensive craze and twenty thousand dollars was spent over three evenings in a Beverly Hills sporting goods shop on guns and ammunition, then more money a week later in November in a Las Vegas gun shop, after which the guys would have to practise shooting against a wall at Graceland.

There were, said Nancy, the Graceland maid, guns all over the house, with a visitor once sitting on one by accident when it was under a cushion in the sitting room. Then there was the day Elvis turned a Tommy gun on a toilet in his bathroom. 'I never did like that toilet,' he said, as, hearing the rattle of explosions and the commotion, Nancy raced upstairs and peered nervously around the bathroom door to find the shattered porcelain all over the floor. She didn't like to ask what the toilet had done to offend him.

Money was pouring in again and he was pouring it out again just as quickly. There was a new, bigger house in the Holmby Hills area of Los Angeles, and a new Mercedes limousine for himself. Then there was a car as a present for the youngest member of the entourage, Jerry Schilling, who as a twelve-year-old had played football with him and Red in Memphis in 1955. And a new car for his father and three snowmobiles for Graceland, although Memphis rarely saw much in the way of snow.

Then there was the jewellery – firstly in the shape of a ten-thousand-dollar gold and jewelled belt. A couple of years earlier he and Priscilla had designed a motif in the shape of a lightning bolt for what can best be described as a sort of exclusive fraternity for him, his family and the guys called Taking Care of Business – TCB, for short. So now he wanted sixteen gold bracelets for his enlarged touring gang, each one with a nickname engraved on it, followed by silver TCB pendants for everyone, too . . . and a new Cadillac for an ex-police weapons training inspector who was getting married.

For whatever reason, his buying spree was out of control, when in December, with the Christmas tree dressed and the trees along the drive at Graceland twinkling with fairy lights, Vernon brought out a ledger of his son's spending.

'He's gonna bankrupt us all,' he moaned to Priscilla, who would inevitably find herself sucked into financial discussions on Daddy's side.

Elvis had been hearing this for years, but this time, fuelled by whatever it was that kept prompting the spending, he exploded. Unable to believe that his father and his wife, who owed everything they had to him, were telling him how he could spend his money, he raged back. He'd only given Vernon the job of managing his private spending so that his father would have something to do.

To which Vernon told him he'd been on the phone to the Colonel, and that Parker was worried, too.

That made it even worse. 'Fuck the Colonel!' Elvis responded – a word he would never have used to his manager's face.

Priscilla then tried reasoning with him, but, stoked up on his prescription of magic pills, as he had been for weeks, Elvis didn't want to reason; he wanted to be allowed to do exactly what he wanted to do and for everyone to step aside and let him. Leaving the room in a rage, he stumped upstairs to his bedroom, only to come down a short time later, get into his car and drive away.

He'd show them.

33

'Mr President, you got your show to run and I got mine.'

Quite what he intended to do, as the Graceland gates swung open to let him through and he accelerated away down Highway 51, he didn't know. He'd done this before, driven off after a row, before going home a few hours later when he'd cooled down. But this time, fuelled by uppers, frustrated at his disintegrating marriage and furious at the sense that he was no longer in control of his own home and money, he just wanted to get away.

In all his life he'd never travelled any distance by himself, apart perhaps from the occasional drive down to Tupelo years ago. But now he found himself heading for the airport at Memphis, parking and then going inside to buy a ticket for a flight to Washington. He'd never bought his own ticket before. There had always been someone with him, someone to do the everyday things.

There was a girl he'd met in Las Vegas called Joyce Bova. She was twenty-five and she'd told him she worked for the federal government in Washington DC. He'd liked her. She was a twin like him, and he'd liked her twin, too. He could talk to her. He would, he decided, look her up.

Sitting on the plane alone must have been strangely exciting. He knew people were watching him, but they were smiling, unlike Daddy and Priscilla at home who would now be wondering where he'd gone and when he would be back. They wouldn't be too worried yet. But what would they do when he didn't come home? Would they call the police and report him missing? Would a message go out for a runaway thirty-five-year-old man?

'Missing: Looks and sounds a lot like Elvis Presley.'

The thought of that would have amused him. As he told the guys afterwards, he was beginning to enjoy himself. This was turning into an adventure.

Arriving at Dulles Airport in Washington, he found a limo company and was driven to the Hotel Washington, where he checked in. The trouble was he'd lost Joyce Bova's phone number and didn't remember which office of the government she worked in, so looking through the Washington telephone directories didn't help. Checking out of the hotel again, he returned to the airport and got on a flight to Dallas, where he was told that the plane wouldn't take off while he was in possession of a firearm. Not prepared to hand over his gun, he got off the plane, only for the pilot to smooth things over and let him back on board – with his gun. He was Elvis. People did things like that for him.

If he couldn't see Joyce he was hoping that when he arrived in Dallas, he might meet up with the American Airlines stewardess he'd been seeing. But he had no luck there, either. She was out of town on a flight, he was told. Gradually, though, a plan of action was forming in his mind. Booking an onward flight to Los Angeles, before boarding he went to a payphone and called Jerry Schilling. Jerry, who had lived in the Graceland basement for a time while he'd been in the entourage, was now working at Paramount in a cutting room. Telling Jerry that he'd be arriving in LA at around two in the morning, he asked him to telephone the usual limo driver he used in Hollywood, an Englishman he called Sir Gerald, and for the two of them to meet him at the airport. It was, he said, important that Jerry should tell no one where he was. The adventure was evolving into a mystery story.

Jerry, Sir Gerald and the limo were waiting as the plane landed in Los Angeles. By this time, however, Elvis had developed a rash on his neck as a reaction to some antibiotics he'd been taking, so he needed Jerry to find him a doctor. And, as he'd been chatting to a couple of stewardesses during the flight, he insisted they then drive them home. It was nearly dawn by the time he got to his house in Beverly Hills and a waiting doctor.

The next afternoon, after a few hours' sleep, and a little something to prompt his usual late start to the day, the plan was becoming clearer in his mind. He was going back to Washington and Jerry was going with him. Bodyguard Sonny West, who was at Graceland, was called and told to tell Vernon and Priscilla where he was, and ordered to fly to Washington and meet him there.

Then, dressing in a purple velvet coat and cape, over a black suede suit and a big collared white silk shirt, wearing amber tinted glasses, a massive gold belt and gold chains around his neck and carrying a bejewelled lion's head walking cane in his hand, he was driven to the Beverly Hills Hotel where he cashed a cheque for $500. After which he and Jerry were driven back to the airport where they boarded the overnight red-eye to Washington. Only when they were in the air did he divulge to Jerry the purpose of the flight: he wanted a Bureau of Narcotics and Dangerous Drugs badge to add to his collection. He had, he said, meaningfully, contacts at the Bureau.

Whatever Jerry was thinking, he didn't say because soon Elvis fell into conversation with a GI who was going home on leave from Vietnam. The two didn't talk for long, just long enough for Elvis to decide that the soldier and his comrades needed the $500 cash that he'd just picked up at the Beverly Hills Hotel more than he did. It would help them buy Christmas presents, and he insisted Jerry hand the money over.

Still working on his plan, they were halfway across America when he came up with his masterstroke. He would call in on the president of the United States at the White House while he was in Washington and elicit his support in his plan to get a Bureau of Narcotics and Dangerous Drugs badge. That would obviously be the most direct way. And, asking the stewardess for some stationery, he wrote a letter to President Nixon.

> Dear Mr. President,
>
> First, I would like to introduce myself. I am Elvis Presley and admire you and have great respect for your office . . . The drug culture, the hippie elements, the SDS, Black Panthers, etc. do not consider me as their enemy or as they call it the establishment. I call it America and I love it . . . So I wish not to be given a title or an appointed position. I can and will do more good if I were made a Federal Agent at Large and I will help out by doing it my way through my communications with people of all ages . . . I have done an in-depth study of drug abuse and Communist brainwashing techniques and I am

> right in the middle of the whole thing where I can and will do the most good.
>
> I am Glad to help just so long as it is kept very private . . . I would love to meet you just to say hello if you're not too busy.
>
> Respectfully,
>
> Elvis Presley
>
> P. S. I have a personal gift for you which I would like to present to you and you can accept it or I will keep it for you until you can take it.

Then, adding all his phone numbers, he asked Jerry to read the letter, then put it into an envelope, and addressed and sealed it, just as if he had been writing to a local schoolteacher or small-town mayor.

The plane landed in Washington at around 6.30 in the morning and he and Jerry took a limo to the White House where he presented his letter to an astonished guard at the gate and asked that it be shown to the president as soon as possible. Then getting back into the limousine, he returned to the Washington Hotel, washed and shaved, and, leaving Jerry to wait for the president's office to call him, went over to the Bureau of Narcotics and Dangerous Drugs building to try to persuade their deputy director to give him a badge.

He didn't get one. But what an amazed Jerry got while Elvis was out . . . was a phone call from the White House. The president would be pleased to see Mr Presley in thirty minutes' time. The letter had worked.

At 12.30 that day, after leaving Jerry with Sonny West, who had only just arrived from Memphis, in an outer West Wing room with the guards from the president's Secret Service, Elvis was led into the Oval Office.

Trying to put him at ease, President Nixon smiled, and, looking at his outfit and diamond-encrusted fingers, said: 'You dress kind of wild, don't you.' A White House official, Egil 'Bud' Krogh, looked on and made notes.

Unfazed by his surroundings, Elvis responded easily: 'Mr President, you got your show to run and I got mine.' Years of handling press conferences and chatting on stage between songs, not to mention a pill or two that he'd taken to give him a little extra pep, ensured his usual folksy charm when he needed it.

Quickly he explained his mission. The American Dream had given him the chance to go from being a poor boy in Mississippi to becoming a world famous star, and he was now worried that the minds of the youth of America were being poisoned by the 'filthy, unkempt appearance and suggestive music of the Beatles' and people like the Smothers Brothers and Jane Fonda. What he wanted to do was to spend his free time meeting and advising young people, using his status to help them change their ways and solve their problems. All it took to achieve this was for him to be allowed to carry the badge of a fully-fledged federal narcotics agent. And, taking out some of his collection of police badges, he spread them across the president's Oval Office desk.

In his eyes, it seemed a perfectly reasonable request, and he must have assumed it appeared a good idea to Richard Nixon, too, because, after a swift conversation with an aide, the president ordered that 'Mr Presley' be given a BNDD badge.

Elvis was overjoyed, and, with tears in his eyes, he put his arm around the president. He was going to be a federal agent. But he hadn't finished. He had a couple of assistants outside, he remembered. Had the president a minute or so to meet them, he wondered. The president said he had, and Jerry and Sonny, both in a state of awe, were ushered into the Oval Office. And as Nixon gave Elvis and each of the smiling minders cufflinks bearing the presidential seal, the unlikely summit was quickly preserved on film by a White House photographer.

Elvis had one further request. 'Sir, they have wives, too,' he said, indicating his guys; whereupon Nixon obediently rummaged in his desk drawer and produced a couple of presidential pins for the guys' spouses.

It had been a totally unlikely, crazy, absurd, but triumphant encounter, and to cap it all that evening Elvis finally got together with Joyce Bova, the Washington girl he'd been hoping to see two days earlier. When he got home to Memphis he could talk of nothing but his White House escapade all through Christmas, the row with Vernon and Priscilla that had sparked the adventure quite forgotten.

Exactly what Richard Nixon thought of the encounter has never been divulged. He must have been aware that the crazily dressed guy with the bizarre fixation on collecting police badges whom he'd made a federal narcotics agent was sky high on some drug or other. But he never commented publicly on the meeting, and the photographs of the two of them smiling together in front of an array of White House flags wouldn't have done his popularity any harm. Later he politely wrote to Elvis thanking him for the gifts of the pearl-handled gun and the pictures of his family that Elvis had been made to leave with the Secret Service guards. Not even Elvis had been permitted to take a gun into the Oval Office.

34

'When I was a child, I was a dreamer. I read comic books, and I was a hero of the comic books. I saw movies, and I was a hero in the movie . . . Every dream I ever had has come true a hundred times.'

By Christmas 1970 he'd reached a new peak of ambition. Not quite thirty-six, the president of the United States had honoured him at the White House and his concerts were sell-outs wherever he played. Then in December he received word that the Junior Chamber of Commerce of America (more commonly known as the Jaycees, a non-profit organisation for the development of business and community service skills) had selected him as one of the nation's Ten Outstanding Young Men of the Year. His new single, 'I Really Don't Want to Know', might not have been quite as good a record or gone as high in the charts as he'd been hoping – although it would earn him yet another gold disc – but, otherwise, everything was going right for him, thus proving Priscilla, Daddy and the Colonel, and all those who doubted him, wrong again. And he celebrated by driving down to Tupelo to get another sheriff's badge for his collection, before indulging his hobby by buying more guns and handcuffs, having a police radio and a blue police light fitted to his car and calling in at the headquarters in the early hours of Christmas Day to wish the officers who were on duty a 'Happy Christmas'.

And when Sonny West got married just before New Year, it seemed to Elvis, in his weird new fantasy as a lawman, to be the perfect place to show off his sheriff's star, the two guns in his gold belt, another in his boot, and a heavy, new police flashlight. Some guests looked at him, exchanged quiet comments and wondered what he was on. But people always looked at him. His wedding present to Sonny was a Mercedes.

The Jaycee awards were to take place in January 1971 in Memphis, and, although he would later say that he ad-libbed his acceptance speech, that the words 'just came to me at the time', Priscilla would remember that he spent several hours in his study the previous night working on ideas. No matter how he came by it, what he said surprised many at the ceremony at the Ellis Auditorium, including Senator George Bush, who was standing in for Vice President Spiro Agnew.

'When I was a child, ladies and gentlemen,' he began as he addressed the assembly, his voice high with nerves in such company, 'I was a dreamer. I read comic books, and I was a hero of the comic books. I saw movies, and I was a hero in the movie. So, every dream I ever had has come true a hundred times.'

Then he turned and gestured towards his fellow award winners, who included a Boston Civil Rights activist, and a Harvard medical researcher.

'These gentlemen over here, these are the type of people who care, they are dedicated, and they realise it's possible that they might be building the Kingdom of Heaven . . .'

Then he ended with a quotation from a hit song by the late Roy Hamilton.

'I'd like to say that I learned very early in life that, "Without a song the day would never end, Without a song a man ain't got a friend . . ." So I just keep singing a song. Good night. Thank you.'

It was a dignified performance, a happy day almost out of another person's story, which included a reception at Graceland for the award winners, with the host very proudly leading a grand tour around the home he loved. It was a day, too, that was made perfect when he spotted Marion Keisker at the reception. He hadn't seen her since that last day in the army in Germany and there she was sitting in the audience seeing how far he'd come in life.

'She's the one I told you about, who made it all possible,' he gushed to Priscilla as he introduced the two. 'Without her, I wouldn't even be here.'

*

The pride and high spirits didn't last long. By the end of the month he was back in Las Vegas doing his contracted month at the International Hotel, but, always quickly bored, he was already beginning to tire of the twice-nightly schedule, which he was now realising was not good for his voice. He was relieved when it was over.

The intention had been to devote the second half of March to recording in Nashville, and he began the sessions with 'Amazing Grace' and then two covers of Gordon Lightfoot songs he'd heard on a Peter, Paul and Mary album. When he was in the mood he was always more than good and 'Early Morning Rain' would be one of his best tracks of the seventies. Songwriter Gordon Lightfoot reckoned it the best version of any song he ever wrote.

But three hours into the session Elvis found his eyes were stinging so much he had to stop and return to his motel. And when, the following day, he was diagnosed with secondary glaucoma at a Nashville hospital, he was frightened. He knew that Ray Charles had gone blind in childhood from glaucoma. Was that about to happen to him? At the best of times he was self-absorbed, now he had something to be absorbed about. Automatically, as always, he decided he needed female comfort, and, worried though he was, he was still able to juggle his women. First, twenty-five-year-old Barbara Leigh, an occasional companion who was a model and TV actress, arrived from Los Angeles to minister to him; then, when she left, Joyce Bova took time off from her federal government duties and came running from Washington DC. Priscilla, who was in California, wasn't summoned to her husband's bedside. His wife's company wasn't the kind he needed.

Further tests quickly showed that he wasn't going blind, it being possible that the stinging might have merely been caused by the dye on his eyebrows running into his eyes when he sweated. But the treatment did involve a shot of cortisone without an anaesthetic directly into his eyeballs, and from then on he would rarely be seen in public without his tinted glasses.

After a break in Palm Springs he was fit to resume recording in May, but he was restless and just couldn't get interested in most of the songs. Once a perfectionist in the studio, now he settled for the first or second take, as he had done in his Hollywood days. Only when he sang unscheduled songs off the cuff, which just happened to spring to mind but to which he rarely knew all the words, did he become committed. A jam of Bob Dylan's 'Don't Think Twice, It's All Right', with the two verses he knew repeated for over seven minutes, was the best track of one night; while the 1947 blues classic 'Merry Christmas, Baby', which he would have known since his teens, was the best on another. A song his mother had always liked, 'I'll Take You Home Again, Kathleen', which he would have heard Bing Crosby singing on the radio, found him accompanying himself sadly at the piano, when it seemed everyone else had gone home.

He would manage to make another Christmas album in that week, which would sell well that coming December, with fans enjoying his version of 'The First Noel' and 'Oh Come, All Ye Faithful', but his hopes for a big hit single were dashed when the outstanding new song of the session, 'I'm Leavin'', didn't even make the US Top Thirty.

Kris Kristofferson had been excited to know that his hero was recording his song 'Help Me Make It Through the Night', but when a demo of the session was secretly slipped to him and his friend Billy Swan, his response on hearing it was a disappointed shrug: 'Well, at least it's Elvis.'

It wasn't the Elvis he remembered, not the revolutionary force that he'd once idolised, not the comeback king of the NBC special of 1968, nor even the Las Vegas champion of 1969. Too much singing in the dry, desert air of Nevada, where Elvis often complained of laryngitis, was deepening and coarsening his voice. The emotion might still have been there for the right song, but the elasticity of his tone, and the delicacy of the falsetto that he'd been so proud of a decade earlier, was now rarely heard. Worst of all, though, his approach to songs had changed, too. His show was more middle-American bombast than rock and roll, as demonstrated by the adoption of 'Also Sprach Zarathustra', better known as the theme from the movie *2001: A Space Odyssey*, for his entry on stage. He'd always been vain, never passing a mirror without a quick check to make sure everything was as it should be, but now he was opting for grandeur over shy, boyish charm.

When he'd appeared in Vegas two years earlier he'd mocked himself in a semi-comic stream of consciousness between songs, imagining what some of the audience might have been thinking.

'Is that him?' he'd joked about himself. 'He's got his name on his guitar. I thought he was bigger than that. Hair flying everywhere, he's got to be a weirdo. Stone cold natural freak. That's why he ain't been seen in public for nine years . . . Get him outta here. Oh, Lord have mercy.'

But by 1971, as he played Lake Tahoe as well as Vegas and then made a twelve-city tour that took him from Boston to Salt Lake City, the jokes had been replaced by self-aggrandising theatricality. There would be wonderful moments that no other performer could match, and who else would have dared to sing the hymn 'How Great Thou Art' like a revivalist in a set that included 'Heartbreak Hotel' and a speeded-up 'Hound Dog'? But as concert followed concert it must have begun to occur to him that many in the audiences weren't coming to hear him, so much as to witness a national institution. Sometimes, he would reflect to his friends, he never knew if a woman was with him because she really loved him or because he was Elvis Presley. But he knew, too, that could have been said about everyone around him. Like the Statue of Liberty he was something to see.

So the months passed as he moved restlessly back and forth across the US between his homes and his girlfriends in Washington, Dallas and California. In Palm Springs he and the guys would entertain without their wives, in Memphis, where Priscilla was rarely seen, he would still go to the movies most nights, while back in Los Angeles he changed homes yet again. The house on Hillcrest had been small by his standards, a family home, deliberately chosen by Priscilla. Now he bought a mansion on Monovale Drive, just above Sunset Boulevard, a place big enough to have at least a few members of his court around him. It seemed that whatever Priscilla thought of their presence didn't really matter. The two had been living virtually separate lives for over a year. The pretence of a marriage was gone.

The end to the marriage came when they were both back at Graceland for Christmas, when, just before New Year, Priscilla told him that she was leaving him. She didn't love him any more, she said, and, taking Lisa Marie, then not quite four, with her, she flew back to their home in Los Angeles.

35

'The human being is one thing. The image is another. It's very hard to live up to an image.'

A poet will distil the pain of loss into a few lines: a composer finds a way of describing it in music. Elvis sang about it. After Priscilla left he would be drawn to songs of loss and self-recrimination for the rest of his life. 'Always on My Mind', from the writers of 'Suspicious Minds', was, in effect, an apology for taking a partner for granted, and would eventually become the most famous of his regretful songs. But there were others. In recording sessions the band would try, usually without success, to get him to lighten up by playing some Chuck Berry rock and roll riffs or the one that his guitarist James Burton had come up with for Dale Hawkins' 'Susie Q'. They and he knew that was what the fans wanted to hear. But rock and roll wasn't what he wanted to sing. He preferred: 'If I made you feel second best, I'm so sorry, I was blind . . .' That was a lyric he now knew something about.

It wasn't that he was still madly in love with Priscilla. He hadn't felt that way about her for a long time. But he'd always treasured the idea of family, the *feeling* of family, like the one he'd grown up in. He'd been raised believing that marriage was a lifelong commitment, and had, as a younger man, always shunned approaches from divorced women.

He'd wondered sometimes what Priscilla did when he was away from her, and he was away from her a great deal, not always for work and often with other women. But he didn't know that she was having an affair, and that the guys were covering for her when she went missing. They'd always known, of course. The servants always know everything first.

Did he sometimes half suspect that there might be someone else, and purposely not ask in case she should question him about his own behaviour? Possibly. Or did vanity blind him when it came to his wife? Could any woman choose another man over him? He found that difficult to believe. For the past year they'd rarely been much of a family, though, and Priscilla, not unexpectedly, hadn't taken it well when he'd been served with a paternity order. She'd taken it even more amiss when, while high, he'd dismissed the accusation by telling a Las Vegas audience that he always used a condom, as his wife would testify. The blood tests would eventually prove that the charge wasn't true, but, played out in public, the entire episode had been humiliating for his wife.

They'd parted with promises that they would keep the news from the press for now, that Priscilla would come to his opening night in Vegas in February as usual, and that they would try to protect Lisa Marie from the effects of their split. Then Priscilla had set off to begin a new life without him. He was the one whose emotions were most fragile after the break-up, and, as the lyrics of his songs told him, he only had himself to blame.

By the time Priscilla returned to Vegas for the last night of his season, he'd decided to tell her he would change if she came back. She stopped him before he got all the words out. She was, she told him, having an affair with her karate teacher, champion Mike Stone, and she wanted a divorce. He was staggered. He and Priscilla had met Stone at an international karate championship in Hawaii in 1968. Now he saw her leaving him as a double betrayal. The secret of their separation would still be kept, but the wound would fester over the coming months.

Ironically, his personal life might have been collapsing, but his record sales were improving again, although his judgement of what made a hit was still slipping. He'd been convinced that 'American Trilogy', the Mickey Newbury song which tied together 'The Battle Hymn of the Republic' with 'I Wish I Was in Dixie' and 'All My Trials', and which Priscilla had heard while driving down Sunset Boulevard and suggested he record, would repeat in the charts the wild success it had when sung at concerts. But he was proved wrong, at least in the US – although, once again, it would become one of his classics in years to come. On the other hand 'Burning Love', which he'd only sung as a favour to producer Felton Jarvis, would be his biggest US hit of the seventies; while 'Always on My Mind', which he had relegated to the B-side of a single in the US, was an international bestseller.

As a manager, Tom Parker only ever had one real idea, which was to get maximum publicity, see what worked and made the most money, and then repeat it until it stopped working. So as the documentary *Elvis: That's the Way It Is* had been a low cost, but profitable, success in 1970, why not repeat the trick with another documentary, *Elvis On Tour*, in 1972?

The intention this time was for Elvis to provide a conversational commentary which could be dropped into the film wherever necessary, so he spent time with its two directors agreeably running through his life story. In the end, however, little of his narration appeared in the final film. Did his implied criticism of Hollywood and the Colonel's decisions go too far? No names were mentioned, and he even diluted his attack by saying he had no one to blame for his career mistakes but himself. But the anger, resentment and self-disgust at what he'd allowed the movie world to do to him was all over the recording.

'I'd thought that they would give me a chance to show some kind of acting or do a very interesting story,' he said. 'But it didn't change. It did not change. And so I became very discouraged.'

Then lapsing into his country, double negative vernacular, which he very rarely did when speaking publicly any more, he continued: Hollywood 'couldn't have paid me no amount of money in the world to make me feel self-satisfaction inside'.

Yes, he was still angry, but something else was inadvertently revealed in the interview. He hadn't given up hope, and still believed that one day he would be given a better part in a movie. It was as though he was shouting out to Hollywood, 'I'm here, come and get me', and hoping to be heard. He still loved movies – just not the ones he'd appeared in. It was almost pitiful, but locked in his bubble he didn't yet fully realise that he'd had his chance and wasted it.

Hollywood may have dumped him, but, in a sense, New York had still to discover him. Apart from television appearances in the fifties he'd never appeared there, feeling, right from the beginning, that East Coast city folk looked down their noses at him and his music. Some certainly did, when they'd thought he was just a hillbilly singer from Mississippi, which he'd resented.

'Those people in New York ain't gonna change me none,' he'd said on returning home to Memphis after a TV show.

Now, as an appearance in the Big Apple approached he was nervous, admitting to Tom Jones that he was afraid that New Yorkers wouldn't come to see him. He was wrong. He was now something to behold, and he packed Madison Square Garden for four shows at the beginning of a new summer tour in 1972. Right from the press conference, when dressed in an azure suit with black trim and a massive collar over a floral shirt, his hair as fashionably long as he would ever wear it, and with that big gold jewelled belt around his waist, his long-practised, self-effacing charm worked a treat.

When asked about his image as 'a shy, humble country boy', he stood up to demonstrate his outfit and joked: 'I don't know what makes them say that . . .' And when questioned about his act in the fifties, he grinned: 'Man, I was tame compared to what they do now. I didn't do anything but jiggle.' *Jiggle!* It was a strange, almost, but not quite, sexual word to use.

New York may be renowned for its tough reporters, but most of the questions were easy for him to bat back with a shrug and a joke. One query sounded as though it was about to relate to a paternity suit that was ongoing, but he saw it coming, interrupted, then gagged his way out of it.

'Honey, I'm not really aware of this particular suit that you're talking about, so I can't answer you accurately. I don't even know the details about it. I went to Hawaii to get a tan . . . for New York, so I'm not aware of it.' And he turned to another reporter.

Only one question caused pause for thought. Was he satisfied with his image? 'Well, the human being is one thing,' he came back. 'The image is another. It's very hard to live up to an image.' So far in his career, protected by the obedient silence of his staff at Graceland and the complicity of the guys, he had protected his image. But, did he live up to it? He knew he didn't.

But that was show business, it was the image that counted, and New York fans and critics were at one in their praise. They, and the three million who bought the live album of the show, liked his version of Three Dog Night's 'Never Been to Spain', written by Hoyt Axton, the son of the woman who had co-written 'Heartbreak Hotel' in what seemed like another century. They even liked his cover of the Righteous Brothers' 'You've Lost That Lovin' Feeling', although it wasn't anywhere near as good as the original. It didn't matter. It was Elvis. His image and voice as familiar to everyone as those of a close relative, he had moved beyond being merely a world famous rock star. In flesh and blood on the stage he became, for a brief moment, a dazzling wonder of the modern celebrity world.

Which was fine for as long as he was on stage, and doing what he did best. Only when the lights had gone out did the spell break. The audience could go home and get on with their normal everyday lives and smile when they remembered the magic they believed they'd witnessed. He couldn't do that. He would still be Elvis. And the next day he would be singing in another city, and in another on the day after that when the veneration would be repeated as he worked his spell as only he could. He was Elvis. But in the midst of adoration he was alone, as he always had been. And by 1972 the strain was beginning to tell.

Whatever his failings, no one could ever accuse Tom Parker of not putting every effort into promoting his client. Since the fifties, when he'd helped fill bargain stores with toy guitars, calendars, belts, posters, T-shirts, bubble gum cards, scarves, bracelets, purses and all manner of teeny souvenirs upon which someone could stamp the Elvis name and image, he had never let up on the heavy Elvis sell. Every city on a tour and every concert hall, radio station and newspaper was now blasted with Elvis reminders before the caravan of trucks carrying lights, stage suits, instruments, staff, make-up, food and whatever it took to create the magic, reached it.

But, as Elvis was becoming increasingly aware, something was changing. The Colonel had only ever had one interest in all the years he'd known him, and that had been him and all the ways in which he might be promoted most profitably. And, although he might be a 'lardass, bad tempered son of a bitch', as Elvis would describe his manager to the guys, living relatively modestly with his wife, Marie, with whom he had no children, and working with just his secretary and a small loyal staff, he'd never appeared to have any of the usual show business vices. He didn't chase women, so far as anyone knew, he never did drugs, and, like his client, he didn't even drink. 'I get mean when I drink,' Parker would warn. And, with his cheap baggy shirts, baseball cap and flannels, and his reluctance to pick up any tab he didn't have to, he was renowned for never spending a penny more than necessary.

So Elvis had been surprised when a new financial dimension had entered the Colonel's life. The more time they spent in Las Vegas, the more hours the Colonel spent at the tables. He'd always been something of a poker player as far as contract negotiations were concerned, and, from *The Ed Sullivan Show* onwards, he'd won many more times than he'd lost. But now that Elvis was touring again, and an avalanche of money was coming both their ways, gambling was turning into more than a casual, occasional recreation. As quickly as Elvis sucked in the money to then throw away on his cars, guns, hobbies and pals, Parker was laying it down no less carelessly on the tables.

'Tom Parker,' said Alex Shoofy, the boss of the International Hotel, 'was good for a million dollars a year' for the casino.

Whether he was playing four machines at a time, or off at a private roulette table, Parker gambled and gambled, and lost and lost. Year after year. Elvis had to sing a lot of songs for his manager to be able to waste so much money. And he did. Tour after tour, show after show, he sang and sang and sang. The Colonel's growing habit astonished the guys, too, whose own failings Parker was never slow to point out. But, just as Elvis would tell his father that what he earned was his money to do with whatever he wanted, so replied the Colonel to those who questioned his profligacy. He and his wife were both getting on. They had no children to leave their money to. Why not gamble if that was what he enjoyed? It was the rationalisation of the addict.

With Elvis back on stage routinely, big offers were arriving regularly from London, Berlin, Japan and Australia for Elvis to appear in their cities, but, still, Parker always rejected them. Elvis still keenly wanted to tour abroad; but the Colonel was always adamant. The time wasn't right. Besides, there was still a mountain of money to be made in the US.

There was. But Elvis wasn't twenty-one any more, when everything had been new and exciting. The big venues such as Madison Square Garden, when he'd had to stretch himself, had been exciting. But the thrill had gone out of the Vegas gigs. Already they, and the flying around America from city to city, had become just as much a treadmill as the movies had been. And treadmills need regular oiling if they are to keep working. Elvis needed a new challenge.

Although an acceptance that Priscilla had left him for ever didn't finally come until a divorce settlement was drawn up in August 1972, Elvis was never without a woman for more than a few days, usually running two or three at the same time in different parts of the country. Keeping them, however, was becoming more difficult. Not long after Priscilla flew away, Joyce in Washington also decided that life in Elvis's topsy-turvy, night-for-day, mood-changing, eccentric, prescription druggy world wasn't for her either. And while there was still the airline stewardess in Dallas, and a dancer in Los Angeles, the pretty Barbara Leigh in Hollywood had a regular boyfriend now.

Naturally the guys would still assess the girls in the queues outside the concerts, discreetly asking the unattached and prettiest whether they would like to meet Elvis backstage after the show. So there was always the chance of meeting someone new to party with, as the euphemism went. But what their boss needed to put some kind of stability back into his life was a new girlfriend.

For a few weeks it looked as though that might be the very beautiful Cybill Shepherd, once a Memphis beauty queen and now the star of *The Last Picture Show* movie. He took her to his home in Palm Springs and tried to impress her with his wealth and fame, but she, like Natalie Wood a generation earlier, was already too sophisticated for him, in spite of being a full fourteen years younger than he was. Nor was she enamoured of his habit of offering her sleeping pills every night. He might have convinced himself that he couldn't cope without them, explaining to her his lifelong trouble with falling asleep, but she didn't need them. As it turned out, she didn't need him either. And yet another beautiful woman walked away.

By this time he'd already met Linda Thompson, a blonde, twenty-two-year-old Miss Tennessee, when she and a friend, Miss Rhode Island, were spotted and invited to one of his all-night movie screenings in Memphis. Immediately smitten, and there was nothing he liked as much as a beauty queen, he moved seats so that he could be close to her during the film. At the time she thought he was still married, so he quickly explained that he and Priscilla had separated. Her reply amused him: 'You should have married a Memphis girl.'

Normally he didn't go for any woman more educated than he was, and Linda had had four years at Memphis State University. Wary of people he classed as intellectuals, he believed they brought 'dissent and envy and jealousy'. But Linda, definitely more of a sparky girl than a bluestocking, wore her college education lightly. In fact she'd dropped out to follow her beauty career.

The two had much in common, and simply got on well together. She'd been raised a Southern Baptist, and when he took her to his bedroom on their second date, so that they could 'get away from the guys', she later told friends that they just read the Bible together.

Their third date was in Las Vegas after he had called asking her to join him there. He expected that they would sleep together, and they did, but, she would later say, it was months before they had full sex. Linda was a virgin, which pleased him greatly. As both Anita Wood and Priscilla had known he liked his special girls to be 'pure'; and his relationship with Linda progressed in a way very similar to his courting of Priscilla. Linda liked to describe his behaviour as being that of a 'gentleman'. He was in no hurry, he would tell her, and was happy to wait for full sex until she was 'ready'. There was never any pressure, he was just happy that she was with him, and proud to have such a beautiful, glamorous woman at his side, and, as with Priscilla, he immediately sent her shopping to buy the most expensive, fashionable clothes. That was important, too. Her beauty had to complement his.

Like other women to whom he was close, it wasn't long before he'd christened her with a nickname.

'Nicknames are really powerful,' he would say. 'They can hurt or they can tie you to people in an affectionate way.'

His mother had been *Satnin*, Anita Wood was called *Little*, Priscilla became *Nungen*, and Ann-Margret had been *Thumper*. Linda, in her turn, became *Mommy*, and she called him *Buntin'*, as in the nursery rhyme *Bye Baby Bunting*. Their nicknames for each other described their relationship. She mothered him and he liked it.

The guys took to her, too. While some of them had never really gone for Priscilla, whom they'd considered an outsider, local girl Linda was one of them. They liked her, and not just for herself. They could see how capable she was. On one occasion when a doped-up Elvis dozed off while eating an apple, she promptly turned him on his side and slapped his back to prevent him from choking. Mommies did things like that with sleepy babies. There would be several similar incidents.

She cared for him, worried about him and put up with his occasional infidelities when she found out, although he usually lied about them. Nor did she complain when he talked endless religion and spiritual matters with Larry Geller, his hairdresser guru, or obsessively played the same record again and again (often, weirdly, Charles Boyer's recitation of the lyrics to 'What Now My Love?'), or sat at the piano to accompany himself over and over on 'The First Time Ever I Saw Your Face'. Even an Elvis lover might get tired of the same song after a while, but he loved that one, although he never got it right in the studio. Roberta Flack showed him how it should have been sung, and he was disappointed when she had the hit, and not him. But he was losing his touch for the simplicity that had so marked 'Love Me Tender'. He needed a better, stronger producer. But it was a brave man who would tell Elvis Presley he was wrong about anything, especially how he should sing a song.

In the main, though, Linda was a breath of fresh air when she moved in with him, and everyone hoped he would be happy now: because, as with any dictator, his mood affected all those around him.

36

'I'm sorry, ladies and gentlemen . . . Sorry that I didn't break his goddamned neck, is what I'm sorry about.'

An audience of 1.4 *billion*? Even he was stunned. It didn't seem possible: nearly one and a half billion viewers around the world watching him singing live via satellite television.

'It's very hard to comprehend,' was all he could murmur when asked by reporters for his reaction, 'but it's my favourite part of the business, a live concert.'

He was talking about *Elvis: Aloha from Hawaii*, as RCA, NBC and the Colonel made the announcement and drummed up sales for the world's first ever satellite TV music concert. He'd seen Muhammad Ali and Joe Frazier boxing in the Philippines by satellite in the contest that was called the Thriller in Manila, but the notion of entertaining so many millions all at once, a plan that RCA, not the Colonel, had dreamed up, was stupefying. If he was nervous and wired up before any show, and, as he admitted, he always was and always had been, how would he feel going out on stage to face over a billion people?

'Terrified,' he would tell the guys.

But fear always energised him. And, after he'd spoken to the director of the concert, Marty Pasetta, the man who regularly did the Academy Awards show, he just loved the idea. It couldn't fail to appeal to his vanity.

Firstly, though, Pasetta had a message for him: 'I want you to go on a diet. I want you to lose some weight,' he told him.

There was a moment, then Elvis just took off his dark glasses and laughed. 'You know, it's one of the first times anyone has been honest with me. I'll go on a diet for you.'

Recommending a diet wasn't something that those close to him would have dared suggest. If he even mentioned his weight, they would immediately seek words to allay his self-doubts. Flattery, if only by being economical with obvious truths, was part of everyone's job. Told the straight fact by Pasetta, however, he immediately set out on a diet. If he was going to be seen by so many people he wanted to look his best.

He would also need a new stage outfit, and Bill Belew, whose job was to vary the costumes for each fresh Vegas season or tour – from the gold Inca, the peacock, the mad tiger, and the Mexican sundial to the Jack of Spades – was taxed with coming up with something special. Elvis liked the idea of the American eagle as a motif, and so it was emblazoned with glass jewels and embroidery on the suit's sleeves and trousers, as well as the cape. This show was going to be seen in countries all around the world, so he wanted to emphasise that it was an American show. He was proud to be an American. And just in case anyone still hadn't got the message, he was going to sing 'American Trilogy', too.

His depression after Priscilla had left and the eccentric, sometimes morbid way he had begun behaving had been a growing worry for his entourage. How could anyone explain his strange compulsion to visit funeral homes at night, chat to the overnight undertaker about any new bodies that had been brought in, and take a look at them? It was, they all agreed, spooky.

But with a new girlfriend and a new challenge, he quickly began to clean up his body. Twenty pounds quickly fell off him, the pasty, puffy face and double chin were replaced by a leaner handsome tan. He eased up on the pills, too – except those pills which helped make him slimmer. The message he was telling himself was that he could do it when he tried.

Garlanded with flowers when he landed in Honolulu for rehearsals a few days before the show, he was met with a city and an island high on excitement, as the local tourist industry spotted an opportunity. As always, anyone who could see a way of generating money out of some aspect of him had been very busy. He'd always understood that and never minded. It was part of being Elvis. And when Honolulu declared the day of the show 'Elvis Presley Day', he took that in his stride, too. After so many years of adulation, nothing surprised him any more, or even flattered him. It was normal.

The concert was actually two shows, in that a full-scale rehearsal with an audience of six thousand was filmed and recorded two days earlier, in case there was a problem with the transmission on the big night; and his usual band, backing singers and orchestra were with him for both. Inevitably, he sang some of his early hits, but increasingly, more varied songs had been slipping into his set for months. He didn't want to be anchored by his past. So, along with the Beatles' 'Something', there was 'My Way', and the old Peggy Lee arrangement of 'Fever', as well as 'I'll Remember You', the Hawaiian song he'd recorded years earlier. In all he performed twenty-two songs, with five more recorded for the US market when the audience (who'd got in free, but were expected to make a contribution to a cancer charity) had gone home.

Not every fan saw the show live. Time differences made that impossible. In Europe it was shown a night later, while the US had to wait a few weeks for it and then got a longer version. But where it was live, it was an astonishing celebration of the global appeal of one man, not least in Australia and New Zealand and all over the Far East – with an estimated 98 per cent of the potential viewing public watching it in Japan. Within days an album of the concert would be high in the bestsellers in many countries, his biggest album hit since *Blue Hawaii* in 1961; while a single of James Taylor's 'Steamroller Blues', taken from the show, also made the world charts.

The big night was Saturday, 13 January 1973, and he had just turned thirty-eight years of age. He knew that rock fans would criticise the way he raced through his rock and roll hits in favour of the big ballads he now preferred. But he knew, too, what his main audience now liked, a leavened mixture of country, blues, rock, patriotism and love songs. The only thing missing from his usual repertoire was religion and 'How Great Thou Art'. But a hymn might not have gone down so well in non-Christian parts of the Far East.

By almost any measure, the show was the biggest milestone in his career. Ever since 1954 he had, despite the lean Hollywood period, been facing challenges and overcoming them. This was the peak. But it was also one he could never hope to equal. As usual he'd taken his father and Dee and all the guys and their wives and girlfriends to Hawaii for the show, and a celebratory picnic on one of the islands was planned for the following day.

It never happened. Before the concert he took a vitamin injection laced with amphetamines. And when the show was over, he returned exhausted to his hotel suite, and, as a reward, treated himself to extra doses of some of the medication that he'd weaned himself off during the previous three months. When Linda went to collect him for the picnic the following day, it wasn't possible. He was on the balcony of his hotel suite, zonked out of his mind, sweating profusely and virtually unable to speak.

The picnic was cancelled.

After the energies and stress expended in Honolulu, he really should have had several months off to recover and recharge. But just two weeks later he was back on stage with a twice-nightly month's engagement at what had been the International and was now renamed the Las Vegas Hilton. Only the sight of his old lover Ann-Margret in the audience on the opening night ('keep the spotlight on her, man, she's beautiful, I want to look at her') eased the toil of having to go back to work so quickly.

After that, it would become his most difficult season so far. In his entire career he'd very rarely been too sick to appear, but now three shows were missed and he had to leave the stage one night, when he lost his voice. In fact, he struggled right through the month, seeing several Las Vegas doctors for his various ailments, some real, some imagined, one of whom gave him a stimulant injection before every show and another shot containing a sedative after he'd finished, in order to bring him down again and help him sleep. Red West, who, despite his anger when Elvis had left him out of his marriage ceremony, had eventually rejoined the entourage, told him, as did some of the other guys, that he didn't need stimulants, that his medical problems were all in his mind. But it was easy for them to talk: they didn't have to get out there night after night, worried that their voice might crack at any moment. Without the injections, he didn't know if he could do it. It has to be possible that, right through his career, the pills had been giving him a confidence he didn't naturally have.

Then, midway through the season, his anxiety about his own security seemed about to come true when four young men jumped on the stage in the middle of his act. He had no idea what they wanted, but he feared the worst, and as one came to embrace him he stepped forward to hold him off. Immediately Red and a couple of Hilton security guards joined him on stage in a melee. Then Vernon arrived, and he, Elvis and Red pushed the first intruder back into the audience.

The interruption was quickly controlled, and the possible assailants bundled away. But Elvis was in a fury, lashing out with karate kicks and swearing as members of his band tried to compose him. Eventually, calming a little, he managed to return his attention to the show.

'I'm sorry, ladies and gentlemen . . . Sorry that I didn't break his goddamned neck, is what I'm sorry about,' he said to the surprised audience.

It was a telling, ugly thing for him to say, an exploding of the facade of the good-natured calm which he always assumed on stage. The first time he'd ever lost control in public, it revealed a potentially violent side to his nature. The guys had lived with his sudden furies for years, as well as his obsession with karate demonstrations, which were always choreographed to make him look good. But the violent temper had been kept from the fans until now.

For those present in the audience the moment would be quickly forgotten, or accepted almost as part of the show, and no police charges were brought against the intruders, who were believed to be simply over-excited, drunken young South Americans enjoying Vegas. But, over the next few days, as a sick Elvis, drugged-up on a diet of various pills, continued to reflect on the night, the incident conflated in his mind with Mike Stone, Priscilla's lover – the man he now saw as having stolen his wife.

He still rang Priscilla regularly, often during the night when he couldn't sleep, but now, lying in his pyjamas in his Hilton bedroom, he brooded and brooded, as Linda watched and worried. Finally the side effects of the drugs he was taking told him what to do. The only solution for the pain that Mike Stone was causing him was that the guy should be killed and that his bodyguards should do it for him. Getting out an M16 rifle, he pushed it into Sonny West's hands. Sonny was having none of it. He left the room.

So Elvis tried Red, who had been so loyal for so long. 'The man has to go,' Elvis insisted. 'He's destroyed everything and hurt me so much and nobody cares. Find someone who can wipe the sonofabitch out. He has no right to live.'

Linda was crying, frightened. To Red, it seemed that if he wasn't actually being asked to kill Mike Stone himself, he was being ordered to be an accessory to murder. He froze. Being with Elvis wasn't playing football or the silly adolescent games he and the guys had enjoyed in the Hollywood years any more. His boss, whom he always considered his friend first and foremost, was talking about murder. His initial thought was to try to talk Elvis round. But it was impossible. The drugs weren't listening.

In the end, Red decided to play for time, and agreed that he would try to find a hitman. Meanwhile Linda called a doctor to give Elvis a sedative. For reasons of loyalty which he would later never understand, Red did, in fact, a few days later, come up with the phone number of a hitman. But he never made the call. Mercifully, by then, the insanity had passed.

'Maybe that's a little heavy,' Elvis said. 'Just leave it for now.'

The entire entourage breathed a sigh of relief. If they hadn't realised it before, they knew it now. When Elvis was out of control, it wasn't just extraordinary acts of generosity of which he was capable. He could be dangerous, too. He was already a danger to himself.

To the world at large he was, however, still the handsome, worshipped man with the golden voice, and most nights between shows he would greet other stars in his suite and smile as they told him how great he was. Only when Muhammad Ali, then the most famous and admired sportsman in the world, turned up did he meet his superstar match. Although they jocularly exchanged gifts, Ali, shrewd as ever, put his finger on the real problem in Elvis's life.

'I felt sorry for him,' he would say of their meeting. 'He didn't enjoy life. He stayed indoors all the time. I told him that he should get out and see people. He said he couldn't because everywhere he went, they mobbed him.'

Elvis, who had always wanted and enjoyed fame, was no stranger to being its prisoner. He could handle that in Memphis, and even in California. But in Las Vegas and on tour it was different. He couldn't go anywhere. Out in public he was always stalked. Crowds quickly assembled around him, so he would go back to his room. Red put it this way: 'I would sit there with him in Vegas and I was going nuts, too.'

Going nuts and taking more and more prescription drugs, that was Elvis. Quaaludes, Demerol, Valium, Tuinal, Seconal, Percodan, Nembutal and Placidyl, he'd study them all in his *Physicians' Desk Reference* and charm or bribe tame doctors to write prescriptions for him. Linda attempted to stop him, and sometimes he would try, he really would, but it was to no avail. He wasn't hooked, he would insist. The pills he took, the injections he had, weren't dirty street drugs. They were legitimate treatments for his ailments that came to him via doctors' prescriptions. Once again he was fooling himself.

Vernon and Parker were worried, and asked Elvis's lawyer in Los Angeles, Ed Hookstratten, to find out which doctors were prescribing the drugs. Aided by a couple of ex-narcotics agents, Hookstratten got the names of the suppliers, and Elvis was told in no uncertain terms how he was endangering his health. But nothing further was done. No one knew what to do. It was up to Elvis to stop, and he didn't want to. Perhaps the Colonel should have tried harder. But he wasn't a nurse, he would say. The guys, whom Parker didn't like or wish to be associated with, were there to protect Elvis from himself. His job was as a manager. Money was what mattered most to him, and it mattered now more than ever.

Ever since Parker had come into his life, Elvis had never had to worry about money. And as, year by year, the deals and contracts had become ever more complicated, more and more money had flowed his way. He may have raged when he suspected that Parker had asked RCA to remix his recordings, and regretted his film career. But when it came to the money he'd been paid, he had no complaints. It seemed to him that the Colonel did what was best for Elvis, and what was best for Elvis was obviously best for the Colonel. That was how he and Vernon looked at it, and Daddy still had a voice in his son's money matters.

So when, in the spring of 1973, the Colonel asked Elvis how he would feel about selling the potential future royalties on all his earlier records to RCA for a one-off down payment of $5.4 million he assumed it was yet another brilliant Parker plan. All his hits had now been released many times on singles, EPs, albums and cassettes.

Surely there couldn't be much value left in them. If RCA wanted them for their Record Club or some other kind of repackaging, that was fine with him. Happily he signed the contract put before him, and forfeited any further rights to every record from 'That's All Right' in 1954 right up to the end of the previous year. That was over six hundred and fifty recordings, his lifetime's work. He had accountants to advise him, but they simply took care of his tax problems. If Daddy thought it was a good deal, and Vernon certainly did, and the Colonel was bragging about how he had once again put one over on RCA, that was good enough for Elvis.

It *wasn't* good for Elvis. Had he sought external advice from someone who wasn't about to benefit hugely from the deal, as Parker was, he would almost certainly have received different counsel. What he was doing was the equivalent of cashing in his pension for a lump sum, half of which would go immediately to his manager, and 50 per cent of what was left to the US Internal Revenue Service. He would end up with only a quarter of that $5.4 million RCA were offering. Had he been sixty-five, like the Colonel, with big gambling debts to repay – and in Vegas it was pretty important to pay your casino debts – it might, just about, have made financial sense. But for a man of thirty-eight, who during the previous year had earned, after expenses and Parker's take, six million dollars and paid nearly two million in income tax, it was nonsensical. The only parties it benefited were cash-strapped Parker, RCA Records, and presumably those to whom Parker was indebted. But Elvis agreed, and RCA immediately set about sophisticatedly packaging a series of *Elvis: A Legendary Performer* albums of out-takes and forgotten tracks, the first of which immediately sold better than the poor, shoddily packaged albums he was currently making. Although Elvis was given another gold record for its sales, RCA kept the royalties.

In truth, Elvis hadn't really liked his manager for years. They rarely went to each other's homes, although they both had houses in Palm Springs, and the Colonel never visited his client's suite while in Vegas or on tour. But he trusted Parker.

He shouldn't have done. Perhaps if Gladys had been alive, as a sounding board, he wouldn't have done. 'Elvis, that Colonel is just workin' you to death,' she would worry back in 1957. She could have had no idea how true those words would prove to be.

How carefully did Elvis read the contracts he signed? How much did Daddy, who was always in awe of Parker and dazzled by big figures, and who had had very little formal schooling, understand of the details in those contracts? Were they both too embarrassed to raise any doubts before Parker? Did they think that would look like ingratitude? Did they ever question Parker on details and figures and the way the income was divided – which, including the Colonel's little side deals, meant that the manager was, on some contracts, now getting more than his client?

Since Elvis willingly signed all contracts put in front of him, it would appear unlikely. But, then, as the Colonel had told him from the beginning, it was his job to do the business. All Elvis had to do was sing, and so, just a few weeks after his Las Vegas stint, he was back touring through Arizona, California, Oregon, Washington and Colorado, from where he flew directly to the High Sierra Theater in Lake Tahoe, Nevada, for a seventeen-day engagement. That took care of much of May, while June was devoted to a further two weeks' tour from Pittsburgh to Georgia. The pace was relentless, leaving just the end of July for recording. Then suddenly it was August again and he was back in Las Vegas twice nightly for the month.

Packhorses had it easier.

37

'If you want me to leave, you're going to have to pay me what you owe me.'

'Colonel' Tom Parker

Part of the new deal with RCA looked forward as well as back, with a guarantee of half a million dollars a year in royalties to be split 50–50 with the Colonel. But Elvis was surprised when a new, strict attitude by the record company became apparent in July 1973. A letter from a senior vice president virtually ordered him back to the studio to make two new albums and four new singles, as he had agreed. He might have been the company's biggest star, but between the lines in the letter, in which his records were simply referred to as 'merchandise', there lurked a schoolmasterly growing impatience with him and his erratic behaviour. So, although he'd already spent the first six months of the year singing on stage, contractually he had no option but to obey. RCA offered him the choice of studios in either Nashville or Los Angeles, but he chose to stay at home in Graceland and record once again in Memphis.

Unfortunately the American Sound Studio, where he'd made 'In the Ghetto' and 'Suspicious Minds' four years earlier, was now no more than a parking lot, so Stax, on McLemore Avenue, where his old friend Marty Lacker now worked, was chosen.

It was not a happy session. Feeling sick and fat, Elvis didn't bother to turn up on the first night, so the musicians recorded backing tracks, hoping he might add his voice later. The next night, armed with guns, and showing little interest in music, he arrived accompanied by Linda, Lisa Marie, now aged five, who was staying with him at Graceland for a month that summer, and his karate teacher, Kang Rhee. He was always primarily a singles performer, but of the ten tracks eventually recorded that week in between his frequent karate demonstrations, only one, 'I've Got a Thing About You, Baby', a Tony Joe White song, sounded anything like a hit. But at only two and a half minutes long it was too short. Then, when his favourite microphone went missing, he just gave up and went back to Los Angeles to rehearse for his summer show in Las Vegas.

RCA were not pleased. They couldn't control their star, and he, seemingly, couldn't control himself. He had all the talent in the world and was wasting it, a view shared by many critics when Elvis opened at the Hilton in Vegas.

'It is tragic, disheartening and absolutely depressing to see Elvis in such diminishing stature,' said the *Hollywood Reporter* critic of the opening night.

It would get worse on the closing night when, amused by a joke only he could see, he appeared on stage with a toy monkey attached to his neck. After singing an X-rated version of 'Love Me Tender', he ended his set by telling the owners of the hotel that they ought not to fire an Italian waiter whose job was in jeopardy and with whom he had become friendly. He was enjoying himself, letting his hair down, and as high as a kite. The Colonel was furious. Who the Hilton hired or fired had nothing to do with him, Parker raged at him after the show.

In Elvis's heightened state this was too much. His spirit reinforced by drugs, his decades-long supine attitude towards his manager was finally infused with some backbone. He'd been hearing about the Colonel's gambling debts, and he wondered if maybe Parker owed the Hilton Casino money; and then there was always the mystery about how he would never leave the US or let Elvis sing abroad. He'd had enough of 'the old man' telling him what he could and couldn't do. The Colonel was past it.

Words were exchanged. Soon accusations, and then profanities he'd never ever dared say to Parker before, were spat out. Parker threatened to quit, then finally Elvis shouted: 'You're fired.'

'You can't fire me. I've already resigned,' Parker hurled back. 'But if you want me to leave, you're going to have to pay me what you owe me.'

And, with both threatening to call a press conference the next day, the row abruptly ended as the Colonel went back to his suite to tot up exactly how much Elvis did owe him.

As Elvis retired to bed with Linda, the Colonel worked on his figures, and by the following morning he had his grand total – over two million dollars.

Exactly how accurate that was no one knew. He and Elvis had been together for so long, and neither Elvis nor his father had ever kept a tally of Parker's financial dealings with them. Vernon was distraught when he saw the figure. Two million! If Elvis hadn't bankrupted them already, it looked as though the Colonel would now do the job.

For a singer who had generated, by that stage in his career, hundreds of millions of dollars, it seems puzzling that a bill for two million should have caused such consternation. But Elvis did not have two million dollars, or anything like that amount. At best Graceland was then worth half a million, and he was continually bleeding his bank account so dry that he often had to ask Lowell Hays – a Memphis jeweller who often travelled with him with a little case full of diamond rings, brooches and bracelets, in case he was in the mood for giving – for time to pay.

For days he and Daddy worried over the figures. The Colonel did nothing. He didn't have to. He was a poker player and he was calling their bluff. Had Vernon, who had left school at thirteen, been more financially sophisticated, he would have insisted that they show Parker's bill to a firm of independent outside accountants and ask them to study the numbers to see if they were anything like plausible, never mind accurate. They didn't do that. Elvis's lawyer Ed Hookstratten was kept informed, and Jerry Weintraub, whose company Management III had managed several of the tours and who personally managed John Denver, was considered as a replacement for Parker, but neither was seriously approached.

As Vernon fretted and the Colonel kept his distance in the stalemate, Elvis found something else to district him – a group of gospel singers called Voice, whom he'd brought to Vegas as a present for Tom Jones. Discovering that Jones had already booked the Blossoms for his season, Elvis decided to hire Voice himself. Making out a contract on a piece of toilet paper, he showed it to the lead tenor singer Shaun (then known as Sherrill) Nielsen. It was for $100,000, for Voice to be available for him twenty-four hours a day, to sing on stage and on records and write songs, too, and also to join in privately with him around the piano if he felt like having their harmony at home or in his hotel suite. They would be his private minstrels and all expenses would be covered.

They agreed on the spot, whereupon, pleased with himself, Elvis picked up the phone and called his father. 'Daddy,' he said, 'I just want you to know I've finally got my own group.'

Vernon's despair deepened. Not only did Elvis no longer have a manager, he was also out of control again and going on another spending spree. As the week wore on, all the guys were worried. Elvis's future would affect them, too, and their wives and children. Meanwhile the Colonel waited. Neither man held a press conference.

Elvis blinked first, as Parker had guessed he would. Neither Elvis nor Vernon had a clue as to how to move forward or find the two million dollars. They were both afraid of the unknown. Swallowing his pride, Elvis called the Colonel. Things would go back to the way they'd been, he told the guys.

It was an opportunity missed. At that point Elvis needed someone strong and forward-thinking. Tom Parker was stuck in the past and was in hock to the casinos. He had no conception of current popular music or an album as an art form. The modern groups of the mid-seventies, bands like Fleetwood Mac and the Bee Gees, would spend months getting the songs and sounds of their records just right. Parker still thought pretty much that Elvis's voice, loud and clear, on any ten scrabbled-together songs was enough for an album, especially if Hill and Range had most of the publishing. Parker had always been at sea musically, but, having finally been junked by Hollywood, Elvis's innate talent had managed to disguise his manager's blustering, know-all shortcomings.

Now, that talent, impaired by drugs and depression, was beginning to wilt. A new manager might, at least, have made some serious attempt to help Elvis overcome his addiction, and given him challenges to conquer, such as the many offered dates in London or Tokyo. And, having got him into better physical shape, Hollywood might again have been interested in giving him one more chance. A younger, more switched-on, relevant manager could have opened his client's eyes to a world of new possibilities, found him new songwriters and a better producer for his records, insisted upon more time being spent in the studio and demanded that his subsequent albums were made and marketed with the commercial reverence his stature deserved. And a new manager would, no doubt, have laughed at the worry that Elvis owed Parker two million dollars. If that was a true figure, and it just might have been, the money could very quickly have been borrowed from a bank and repaid from a single, small European tour.

But a new manager wasn't sought or hired. The Colonel had won. He knew Elvis and he knew the timid Vernon, too. The future literally *was* back to the way things had been.

Relieved that the problem was over, Elvis bade farewell to Linda for a few days and flew to his house in Palm Springs with some of the guys, soon to be followed by an RCA mobile recording unit. The plan was that he would put his voice on to some of the backing tracks recorded at Stax a few weeks earlier, but first he wanted his new group Voice to record a couple of songs. Then, becoming interested in Shaun Nielsen's receding hairline, he suddenly decided the fellow needed a hair transplant. And, while guitarist James Burton and the engineers, all of whom had been flown there to record, waited, he watched as the operation was performed in his living room.

Finally, with Nielsen, his head covered in bubbles of blood and bandages, standing alongside him, he did sing something, although none of the songs to which there were backing tracks. He chose instead to cover 'Are You Sincere', an old Andy Williams hit which he remembered from just before he'd gone into the army. Complete with a mid-song recitation right out of the fifties, it was another dive back into the comfort of the past.

'Are You Sincere' would eventually become a country music hit, but for now Elvis went back to partying with the guys and a few girls who'd been rounded up for the weekend. The moment for change, and the possibility of career and perhaps personal salvation, had come and been missed. Or had it been too late by then anyway?

Making up with the Colonel wasn't the only argument he had to settle that summer. After Priscilla had left him, she had accepted, without engaging her own lawyer, a modest settlement of $100,000 and $1500 a month for alimony and child support. There had been other ad hoc payments, of course, like a new Jaguar and $50,000 to furnish her new apartment in Los Angeles, but now she wanted a new separation agreement. This time, with lawyers involved, she was given $725,000 in cash, with Elvis making a commitment to give her a further $1,250,000 in monthly payments of $6000. Alimony came to $1200 a month for five years, and child support for Lisa Marie was put up to $4000 a month. On top of that Priscilla got half the proceeds of the sale of their smaller Beverly Hills house and 5 per cent of the stock of two of her former husband's music publishing companies.

The money didn't bother Elvis. But he hated the settlement being dragged out in public, and a few days after leaving the divorce court in Santa Monica he flew to Memphis, where, after having had to be carried off the plane, he was admitted to the Baptist Memorial Hospital for tests. The story given to the press was that he was suffering from breathing difficulties. That was true. What the press weren't told, however, was that the difficulties were a result of having become addicted to the painkiller Demerol, which he had been receiving in daily injections from a doctor in Los Angeles. He also had a bleeding ulcer owing to cortisone he had been taking, the pain of which was being disguised by the Demerol. He stayed in hospital for two weeks while he was detoxified, replacing the Demerol with Methadone. Linda slept in a bed at his side as he dried out.

When he recovered, he apologised to everyone and promised not to do it again, and for a while his spirits rose. Then, after a period of convalescence at Graceland, he returned to the Stax studios. It was a Monday night and the first thing he did when he arrived was to send a couple of guys out to buy the biggest television set they could find, so that they could all watch the Monday night football.

Only after the football had finished did he turn his mind to music. It turned out to be his best session in eighteen months, recording material for two new albums and three new singles in a week. 'Promised Land', one of his Chuck Berry favourites, became a big international hit, as did 'My Boy', the melodramatic French song about a divorced man and his child that actor Richard Harris had first recorded. And then there was 'If You Talk in Your Sleep', which had been written by a very proud Red West. The best track of all, though, was a cover of the Tom Jans song 'Loving Arms'. When he sang as well as that, he was back to being the Elvis of 1960:

> If you could see me now, the one who said that he would rather roam . . . if you could only see me now.

38

'I'd rather be unconscious than miserable.'

The renewed good spirits didn't last long. In January 1974, he turned thirty-nine, and while the city of Memphis declared his birthday Elvis Presley Day, and held a parade down the section of Highway 51 past Graceland that had been renamed Elvis Presley Boulevard, the health problems that had begun to plague him the previous year soon returned. At first, they were niggly – a persistent ingrowing toenail, then toothache, which is never good, and he saw his dentist regularly. And, when he was away from home, other dentists were useful for writing prescriptions for other drugs he believed he needed.

For the past four years he'd played twice nightly in Las Vegas for the entire month of February. But on the advice of Dr Nichopoulos, who was now taking full-time care of him when he was in Memphis, the engagement had been cut to just two weeks. Almost immediately after that, though, came three weeks on the road from Texas to North Carolina during March. That still added up to forty-five performances in five weeks, the last show being back home at the Mid-South Coliseum in Memphis. The work load never slackened, and, after a short break, he was back touring in California, before a week's twice-nightly engagement at Lake Tahoe in Nevada; while June meant twenty-five more shows throughout cities in the Mid-west. Not surprisingly, the reviews were not good, his performances described as 'listless'.

The money, though, was substantial, so he went on another buying bonanza, forking out in one day for nine Lincolns for his retinue, which he then took back and changed for Cadillacs the following day. The drugs were acting as if they were paying for everything.

Linda got a car, as well as expensive clothes and hundreds of thousands of dollars' worth of jewellery. Then another girl received a brand-new Corvair shortly after her first night with him, while a Cadillac went to an elderly lady he didn't know, but whom he'd spotted looking longingly through a salesroom window. He'd always thought that the ability to 'share money is what gives it value', and he loved to see the expressions on the faces of the recipients when he handed them the keys to a brand-new, shining car. All his life he'd loved cars, that most potent symbol of Americana, and it seemed to him there was no better gift. That some of his entourage would later sell the vehicle he'd bought them for cash never bothered him. It was the moment of giving he enjoyed.

At an increasing speed he was losing touch with reality, and would sometimes stop while driving if he spotted an accident, produce his police badge and offer to assist any injured. Being Elvis meant living in a fantasy world when he chose to.

But, as bountiful as was his generosity, there was also a thoughtlessly cruel side to him. While always declaring his total love for Linda, he quite casually shuffled her to one side, regardless of her feelings, when a new woman took his fancy. Though some of the now much younger women with whom he slept would indiscreetly report that he seemed more interested in cuddling and petting than in full sex, the possibility of a new conquest was hard to ignore. It flattered his vanity to have a new, beautiful woman at his side, at his shows and in his bed. None of them lasted for very long, after which the long-suffering Linda would return.

He'd always insisted that the guys he employed were loyal to him, but the reverse wasn't necessarily the case. Close as he was to the now divorced again Jerry Schilling, who was as much a friend as an occasional employee, that didn't stop him having a one-night stand with Jerry's new girlfriend. It wasn't quite *droit de seigneur*, but it seemed to be heading in that direction.

By July 1974 he had lost any real interest in his concerts, at which he sang more or less the same songs night after night like a juke box, with only a few variations. The shows were simply a means to an end: money. What did still interest him, though, other than numerology and spiritual books, was karate, and he fantasised about making a karate movie, with himself as the star, like an American Bruce Lee. That came to nothing, because he wasn't fit enough to even pretend to play the part. But then a better idea was floated for a documentary about 'the purpose of karate and how it had traditionally been used to help the weak, helpless and oppressed of all classes, creed or religion' for which he would read the narration.

But, although he would occasionally attend classes at the Tennessee Karate Institute, and Jerry Schilling was made executive producer of the project with an office in Hollywood, no film was ever completed. As with everything he planned, Elvis had neither the organisational capacity to launch such a venture, nor the courage to do it without the Colonel's help. And the Colonel's interest in karate, or in any of the people involved, with the exception of Elvis, was nil.

The only place where Elvis was completely his own master was at Graceland. Vernon, who had now separated from his wife Dee and set up home with a nurse and her family he'd met in Denver, came round one day giggling about some strange, 'ugly' Polynesian furniture he'd just seen in Donald's Furniture Store in Memphis. Intrigued, Elvis went to take a look and loved it.

'That's the weirdest furniture I ever saw,' he said. 'I want it in my living room.'

And immediately he bought every piece of the display and set about having his den at the back of the house turned into what later became known as the 'jungle room'. Complete with waterfall, it wasn't to everyone's taste. Some people considered it tacky. Elvis didn't care. It amused him. Years earlier when he'd first moved into Graceland he'd been asked why there were no expensive antiques in it, since he was so rich. It was a snobby implied criticism of the lack of taste of this get-rich-quick young man and his hillbilly family. But he had a ready answer.

'I saw enough old stuff when I was growing up in Tupelo to last me a lifetime,' he would say.

That was Elvis. He always wanted everything *new*, spotless and tidy . . . he really liked tidy, and polished cars. The jungle room might look weird to some. But it was new. It was fun. And it was different.

His outburst on stage in Vegas the previous February had almost led to his breaking up with the Colonel, but that was just a foretaste of what was to come during his two-week August season there. Night after night he took to addressing the audience in long, rambling monologues between songs. Sometimes the audiences were amused as he would start by mocking Johnny Cash (who always opened his shows with the line 'My name is Johnny Cash'), saying 'Good evening, ladies and gentlemen, my name is Johnny Cash . . .' or 'Pat Boone' or 'Bill Cosby' or 'Little Richard'. And then he would tell them how he and his guys had sneaked into the Showroom in the wee small hours and painted one of the small statues that stood in recesses in the walls black – for the fun of it. Almost every night he would go off on a stream of consciousness, like a stand-up comedian but without the jokes. For twenty years he'd done virtually no proper press interviews, but now he just couldn't stop talking to his audience as if he knew every one of them personally, making confidants of the amorphous mass whom he couldn't see because of the spotlights. No subject was out of bounds. One night he talked about his divorce and Mike Stone, while on another the subject was a girlfriend from the fifties who was in the audience. Then there was a liver biopsy he'd had the previous week, a book written by a friend who'd been a narcotics agent, his paunch, his broken finger and the real meaning of the word 'nigger'. He got that wrong, but he wasn't being offensive. Finally, at another show, he talked about his drug problem which had been alleged in a movie magazine, and at this point he got angry. He didn't like being described as 'strung out'.

'Well, by God, I'll tell you something,' he told the audience. 'I have never been strung out in my life, except on music . . . If I find or hear of the individual that has said that about me, "I'm gonna break your goddamn neck, you son-of-a-bitch". That's dangerous. "I will pull your goddamn tongue out by the roots".' Then, remembering his audience, he said, 'Thank you very much,' and sang another song.

It was a bizarre spectacle that appalled Priscilla, who was in the audience with Lisa Marie that night. Elvis, however, felt better after his rants, no matter how much Parker still scolded him.

On the subject of drugs, he was in a state of denial. He may not have been 'strung out' by his understanding of the term, inasmuch as that implied an addiction to heroin. But he was certainly high, and his outburst only increased the rumours around Vegas that he couldn't control himself.

Almost as if to prove that was true, as soon as he got back to Memphis he went on another buying spree, with new cars for friends and family, one for a new maid so that she could get to school, and another for her mother, and a house for his cook, Mary Jenkins, which he went out and chose for her. Charlie Hodge got a boat, while cousin Billy Smith, to whom he was very close, was given a trailer house parked at the side of Graceland.

RCA had been pestering for a recording session towards the end of the year, but, after another short tour of smaller towns in the Midwest in October, he retreated to his bed at a clinic in the home of his new Las Vegas medical adviser, Dr Elias Ghanem, for what was described as a medically 'induced sleep diet'. Whatever that was, it appealed. He craved sleep, no matter how it was achieved.

'I'd rather be unconscious than miserable,' he would say.

Depression was smothering him, and 1974 was the first year since 1959 (when he'd been in Germany) that he hadn't set foot inside a recording studio. But now his voice, as well as his weight and general fatigue, was troubling him, too. He knew it wasn't what it had been. Age had made his tone deeper, while the wear and tear of constant touring had stolen the plaintive, yearning tones he'd once had, and the top of his range was narrowing.

Then, back home in Memphis, on 8 January 1975, he turned forty. He had always seen himself as the boy who had broken the mould. He was now older than his father had been when 'Heartbreak Hotel' had been released. Daddy had retired at thirty-nine, and he'd thought of him then as a middle-aged man. Was that how he was now seen? The newspapers congratulated him with the snide comment that he was 'fat and forty'. He hated it. He'd become, for reasons he would never comprehend, a living legend and he didn't like being laughed at. To outsiders it might have seemed that his fame had made him impervious to criticism. But in his bedroom at Graceland he would look out at Elvis Presley Boulevard, the road running behind the trees and past his house, and say: 'I'm not that road, you know. I'm human. I bleed when I'm cut.' He was bleeding now, as he reflected on what the future might hold. He wasn't old, but he'd been famous for so long he felt old. What next? Would the fans still love him as he got older still?

Some of his staff and friends assembled for a small birthday party at Graceland. There were cards and presents, with Liberace sending him his cookbook. But Elvis didn't leave his bedroom all day, staying in hiding behind its gold-painted door.

Then two weeks later he was back in the Baptist Memorial Hospital undergoing more tests after Linda found him struggling to breathe. He stayed there for two weeks as another attempt was made to get him to dry out, a regime sometimes hampered by the secret little presents some of the staff, and, it was alleged, members of his extended family, would occasionally sneak to him.

His family had always been his bedrock, and he was proud of his role as head of it, but it could be a cause of pain, too. And when Vernon had a heart attack and was hospitalised, it was arranged that they should be in adjacent hospital rooms. That may not have been the best idea for either man. In conversation one day, while Billy Smith was visiting them both, Vernon turned on Elvis. 'I have you to blame for this,' he said, indicating his heart. Then he went on: 'And you worried your Mama right into her grave.'

Elvis wept.

For the press, Elvis was diagnosed with an impacted colon, hypertension and an eye condition. He also looked bloated, 'like Mama Cass', he would joke dryly. But morbid self-absorption and his addiction to Demerol were his biggest problems.

Only when it was suggested that he do a benefit concert to help victims of a tornado in McComb, Mississippi, did his mood begin to lift. As Vernon would often say, his son 'always did have a generous heart', and here was a chance for Elvis to do something worthwhile. The charity concert wouldn't take place until May, but it gave him something to aim at, and his condition began to improve. By March he was fit enough to return to Los Angeles and the recording session he owed RCA. It was the first work he'd done in four months, his longest rest in his entire career.

It wasn't a classic session, but for the only time in nearly twenty years, he wasn't expected to record songs published by his own companies. Freddy Bienstock, who now ran Hill and Range after the retirement of the Aberbach brothers, had given up. Instead Elvis went mainly for good songs he liked, just as he'd done at Sun. Then, when it had been just him, Scotty and Bill on bass, they'd created a musical revolution. Now there were ten other musicians backing him, and three singers, while later all the recordings would be finessed by seven further musicians, four different singers and both string and horn sections. That would make around thirty people in all. The recordings weren't bad, but mainly they were covers of other singers' hits and anything but revolutionary. Only one stood out. It was called 'Pieces of My Life' by a writer called Troy Seals, and he'd first heard it on a Charlie Rich album.

It was the last song of the three-day session, and he stayed and played his recording over and over into the early hours of a Los Angeles dawn long after the musicians had gone home. It could have been written for the place he was in his life.

> I'm lookin' back on my life . . . But I guess, I threw the best parts away . . .

By this time, no one sang about regret as well as Elvis Presley.

39

'I'm self-destructive, I know, but there's not a lot I can do about it.'

When Elvis heard that Barbra Streisand was at the midnight show in Las Vegas in March 1975, and that she wanted to see him afterwards, he was mildly flattered. But he was astonished when, after expecting just another round of mutual compliments, Streisand, then the world's most popular woman singer, had an offer for him. Sitting in his dressing room with her then boyfriend, Jon Peters, a Beverly Hills hairdresser, she came straight to the point. She wanted to do another remake of the film *A Star is Born*. She would star alongside Elvis, and she and Peters would produce. Peters would also direct it. Warner Brothers were backing her.

He knew the James Mason–Judy Garland version of the story. It was a remake of the classic Fredric Marsh/Janet Gaynor film of 1937, about how an ageing star helps a younger one as his career is destroyed by drink. And when Streisand explained that the film she was planning would be moved from the Hollywood world to that of rock music, he was more than interested. This was what he had been waiting years for: a strong straight movie role. For the next few days he was babbling with excitement.

The Colonel, who Streisand had deliberately not invited to the dressing-room meeting, wasn't so sure. Irritated that she had gone directly to Elvis, rather than through the William Morris Agency and himself, behaviour he deemed unprofessional – though it also showed how little he knew of how Hollywood players met and talked movies to each other all the time – he immediately began to find fault with the project. Did Elvis think his fans wanted to see him playing the role of a drunken, or maybe druggy, loser who was going to die at the end of the movie, leaving the younger Streisand character triumphant? With Streisand and Peters as producers would they be looking after Elvis's interests or hers? Besides, Jon Peters was a hairdresser not a film director. Would he even be competent?

It all looked risky to him, he said, and when he received the producers' suggested contract he was scornful. The offer of half a million dollars up front, and 10 per cent of the gross receipts after the film had broken even, was nowhere near enough. No matter how keen Elvis was to play the part, and he still was, Parker insisted that he had to protect his client. So he sent Streisand his demands: a million dollars up front for Elvis, with $100,000 expenses, plus 50 per cent of the gross, and Elvis to have top billing over Streisand.

That finished it. Warners weren't going to pay so much. The deal was off. Streisand got Kris Kristofferson to play the part instead – ironically a songwriter much admired by Elvis. When it was released the following year, the movie had cost six million dollars to make and grossed over a hundred and fifty million dollars worldwide, while the soundtrack album sold fifteen million copies. Jon Peters hadn't directed. Warners insisted upon having someone with a track record behind the camera in the shape of Frank Pierson, so Peters had settled for the role of producer, and the beginning of a career as a Hollywood titan.

Considering how keen Elvis had been to be in the film he should have been furious with his manager for ruining his opportunity. But, by the time he realised he was no longer being considered, even he seemed to have cooled on the idea. Some of the guys were disappointed, however, seeing it as a last chance for their boss to get his body and mind back into shape. They blamed the Colonel's greed again.

But, was there something else preying on Parker's mind? Apart from wondering whether the self-destructive addictions of the character in the film were too close to the drug problems of Elvis, was he also worried whether Elvis would ever be fit enough to play the part? Could he be trusted to get clean of drugs? And, despite everything Elvis said about abhorring street drugs, it was believed by Red West that liquid cocaine had sometimes become another element in his dope diet. Did Parker, and perhaps, secretly, Elvis, reckon that it was better to get out of the movie now with dignity, rather than risk a meltdown just before, or even during, shooting?

Had the offer come three years earlier Elvis would, almost certainly, have grabbed it, no matter what the Colonel said. But it was too late. Though the fans still uncritically packed his shows, grateful simply for the chance to be in his presence, he must have known his health and his career were in freefall. As he would admit, he was self-destructive, 'but there's not a lot I can do about it'.

There was actually a great deal he could have done, had he been willing to admit the depth of his problem. The guys hinted at it; Vernon talked about it; his lawyer had two former investigators ask him about it; and two Denver police officers whom he had befriended would soon suggest a private clinic. But to seek serious help, rather than a quick detox, would have involved facing the truth, giving up his little black leather bag of pharmaceuticals that he took wherever he went, and confronting the fear of going on stage without an injection or pill to get him out there. And that was something he told Tom Jones he could never do. He liked to say, 'No medicine in the world is as strong as healing from within', but he never listened to his own advice. He was addicted to Demerol and Dilaudid, a painkiller usually only given to cancer patients, and there was never any shortage of doctors prepared to write out the prescriptions.

Everyone around him, from the Colonel to his maids at Graceland and the Memphis police, who saw so much of him, had to have been aware of his condition. But they covered for him and kept a conspiracy of silence, excusing away his erratic and often peculiar behaviour and frightening mood swings. The shooting up of chandeliers in his Vegas suite, and a television set because he didn't like Robert Goulet who was appearing on a show, was put down to high jinx. But the Vegas staff must have known it wasn't. Everyone connected with him knew.

But instead of getting on to a drug rehab programme, after the Colonel had walked him away from *A Star is Born*, Elvis gave himself the present of an aeroplane which cost a quarter of a million dollars. Then he spent another half a million on having it fitted out like a glitzy flying Vegas en suite bedroom, complete with a queen-sized bath and gold taps, and named it *Lisa Marie*. After which he bought Linda a house of her own near Graceland and rented her an apartment in Los Angeles, and then set off on a thirty-two-concert tour of towns in the Southern states, for which he was paid over half a million dollars.

Then, after some cosmetic surgery on his eyelids, which the surgeons themselves said he didn't need, he was off again on a twenty-one-concert tour down the East Coast after which he bought another plane for half a million dollars and spent $140,000 in one day on fourteen Cadillacs as gifts for friends. By which time he was due in Las Vegas for his summer season, which is where, after four days, exhaustion caught up with him and he had to cancel, returning to Memphis and hospital, from where he bought yet another plane for half a million dollars.

The more millions he earned, the more he spent. All year the purchases and gifts, jewellery for some, a $200,000 interest-free loan to Dr Nick, went recklessly on and on, until in November, realising he was short of money, he was forced to borrow $350,000 from a Memphis bank. It was hardly surprising that Vernon had heart problems.

Despite his lavish generosity, increasingly his behaviour was antagonising those around him. A girl called Sheila Ryan, whose relationship with him, she would later say, had begun when he'd asked her to inject him with Demerol, had moved on and she was now with actor James Caan. Linda's loyalty was wearing thin, and one night one of his backing singers, soprano Kathy Westmoreland, with whom he'd had an earlier affair, walked off stage after he'd made a crude comment about her.

'She'll take affection from anybody, any place any time. In fact she gets it from the whole band,' he said.

Why he would say that, no one knew, because he was very fond of Kathy. He thought of it as teasing, and told her he thought it was funny, but it wasn't. Nor was his comment on stage to the Sweet Inspirations that he smelled onions and green peppers and believed they'd been eating catfish. That could have been construed as a racist comment, but the backing singers said they didn't see it that way. It just seemed hostile, so two of the Sweet Inspirations left the stage, too. They all came back after an apology, but there was little joy on the tours any more.

He'd always felt that he was alone, but now that he usually flew separately from the band and singers, and often stayed in a different hotel, he was erecting a barrier around himself, blocking others out. He even blew up in public at his Aunt Delta. She'd been living at Graceland since 1967, partly as company for Grandma, and she wasn't always the sweetest woman. But when, during a Christmas Day party in mid-air aboard *Lisa Marie*, she accused the other guests of only being there because 'all you sons of bitches . . . just want his damn money', Elvis lost control.

'Get this drunken bitch off my plane,' he hollered, and much more, before hours later, back at Graceland, Billy Smith managed to calm him down. Sometimes the greater the truth, the greater the embarrassment: she'd touched a nerve.

For years he'd held a New Year's Eve party at a Memphis club, where Memphis soul singers and bands would entertain him and his guests. But in 1975 *he* became the New Year's entertainment for an audience of 64,000 when, accompanied by Linda and Lisa Marie, he flew up to Pontiac, Michigan, to appear before a sold-out Silverdome. It was freezing cold, and he split his pants while on stage, but the Colonel was pleased. It was a massive pay day.

As an athletic young man he'd enjoyed water skiing at a lake near Memphis, but when he and Linda, together with Red and Patsy, Joe and Joan Esposito and Jerry Schilling with singer Myrna Smith, flew to Vail in Colorado for his first winter sports vacation just after New Year, the only skiing he did was sitting on a snowmobile . . . late at night. It was a happy enough time for six friends on vacation, but, before a week was through, Jerry, exhausted by the constant demands made on him, left. After that, there seemed nothing more for Elvis to do than to buy Cadillacs for his friends among the Denver cops, who had accompanied him on to the slopes. The money gusher was exploding again.

There had been a time when he'd loved recording as he'd played with his voice, going from one style to another; from r and b, to country, to gentle falsetto, Italian operetta, and on to his Ink Spots impersonations. Back then he could do it all, had always arrived at recording sessions fully prepared and been happy to labour over his interpretation of a song for hours; and then, when not satisfied, put it aside and come back to it at another session.

By 1976, however, RCA couldn't drag him into a studio. There was always an excuse, usually ill health. So, if Elvis wouldn't go to the studio, they would bring a studio to him. And in February a mobile recording truck was dispatched to Graceland, and the jungle room stripped of its 'ugly' furniture, to be replaced with microphones, drums, acoustic boards, guitars and lots of wires. It wasn't ideal, but at least it would be Elvis making some new records. Which he did, although not every day, and even then he sometimes disappeared back upstairs to his bedroom to play some gospel music or do whatever he found to do in his bathroom.

But he tried. After warming up on the Platters' 'Only You', a song he'd sung sometimes on the road when he'd been at Sun, he turned 'Moody Blue' into a top ten UK hit – a market where his last two hits had been re-releases of early sixties recordings 'Girl of My Best Friend' and 'Suspicion', as RCA took advantage of their royalty buy-out. Then there was 'Hurt', on which he did a Roy Hamilton impersonation and which he enjoyed singing on stage. The best tracks, though, were the rocker 'For the Heart', from Dennis Linde, the writer of 'Burning Love' – which, by being on the flip side of 'Hurt', went largely unnoticed – and 'Danny Boy'.

This was the kind of song which, sitting at the piano, he'd been singing all his life. When he turned to it now, however, he was disappointed when he couldn't reach the high notes any more, and had to settle for singing it in a lower key. He still produced a moving recording, but he was disappointed with himself. He'd always had pride in his voice and now it was failing him. As a young man he'd been a tenor who sang the blues: at forty-one he was a baritone, and when he sang some of his earlier hits on stage, such as 'Trying to Get to You' and 'Lawdy Miss Clawdy', they were pitched much lower than when he'd first recorded them, and he knew they didn't sound as good. He would even apologise on stage for not being able to sing as high as he used to.

He didn't come down from his bedroom at Graceland on the last day scheduled for recording, leaving RCA to cobble together a new album and a couple of singles as best they could. Then, within a couple of weeks, he was back on the road.

That was his life now. One week on the road, as, in separate tours, he flew his way around America, from Johnson City in Tennessee to Charlotte, North Carolina, Cincinnati, Kansas City, Denver, Long Beach, Seattle, Spokane, Oklahoma City, Lubbock, Tucson, El Paso,

Duluth, Wichita, Kalamazoo, Roanoke, Abilene and many other places; and then two weeks off to recover during which time he rarely left his bedroom. The money was great, but the reviews now were rarely forgiving. It was as though his life was going backwards as he forgot the words of some of his most famous records, had to sit others out while the Sweet Inspirations or the Stamps sang and gave him time to recover, and generally struggled to keep going from one concert to the next. But he was still Elvis, still welcomed rapturously wherever he went, patriotically singing 'America the Beautiful' without any mock irony in that bicentennial year.

In other circumstances, in better health and with a better manager, he could have been singing in London, Paris, Rome, Amsterdam, Madrid and Berlin. Then there was Tokyo, Manila, Sydney, Seoul, Hong Kong . . . He was wanted everywhere. But the ambition that he would one day tour the world was gone for ever now.

He'd never shown any interest in any kind of investment, nor in any business outside entertainment, but when it was put to him by Dr Nick, a racquetball enthusiast, that he could be in for 25 per cent of the profits if he put his name to a company that made racquetball courts he saw it as an opportunity. He'd already had a court installed at Graceland, and when his top man Joe Esposito became involved, too, he signed up for the deal.

But like his karate film, the scheme never came to fruition, and by August 1976 he wanted to take his name off the project, fearful that instead of 25 per cent of the profits he would be liable for 25 per cent of any losses.

Seeing his son's sudden fear that he might have to come up with a million dollars for the venture, Vernon couldn't resist the temptation to talk to him about money and his other liabilities. Although money was flooding in from the tours, because of the cost of the planes, the pilots' salaries, the sheer expense of running Graceland, the payments due on the loans from the bank and Elvis's constant profligacy – the previous Christmas he'd given nearly sixty thousand dollars to various Memphis charities – it really was, Daddy said, time to start making some budget cuts.

Vernon chose his moment well. For months, bubbling worryingly in the background was a lawsuit against Elvis by a male fan who claimed to have been roughed up by the guys, bodyguards Red and

Sonny West and karate expert Dave Hebler. Who knew how expensive that could turn out to be, Vernon would repeatedly ask. This was not the first time that Red had been accused of having hurt someone while doing his duties. He and the others would, perhaps reasonably, justify their actions by saying that force was sometimes necessary in their job of protecting the boss, and that Elvis had encouraged them to be forceful. But, whether fair or not, in Vernon's opinion – or perhaps just because it had become convenient for him – the three had become a liability.

'I'm going to make some changes. The Memphis Mafia embarrass me,' Elvis had admitted to spiritual adviser Larry Geller one night.

The changes came on 13 August 1976, when Vernon telephoned Red, Sonny West and Dave Hebler individually, and fired them, giving them just one week's notice each. For Vernon it was a coup. He'd always hated the mob of young men that surrounded his son. His excuse to them was that the entourage had become too expensive, but the lie to that was given immediately when a couple of ex-cops, including Linda's brother Sam Thompson, and karate friend Ed Parker, were hired as replacement bodyguards. Dee Stanley's elder sons, Elvis's half-brothers Ricky and David, were already on the payroll. Only Joe and Charlie Hodge remained of the original Memphis Mafia, together with Billy Smith, and he was family.

The guys who'd been fired were more than stunned. Red, the longest serving, was devastated – for a second time. What made it worse was that Elvis hadn't told him himself. Though all three of them tried to call him over the next few days, Elvis made himself unavailable, secreting himself in Dr Ghanem's home clinic in Las Vegas and not taking their calls. As they'd seen so many times, Elvis would always go missing when there was any confrontation.

'Even coolies get two weeks' notice,' Red, who'd been with Elvis for twenty years, would later say bitterly.

Letting go of Red and Sonny wasn't Elvis's finest moment.

40

'I get carried away very easily.'

On reflection, Elvis soon regretted the decision Vernon had talked him into. For almost all his professional life, Red had been there, just a few paces behind, or, while on tour, in front, clearing the way, putting himself in the path of any potential threat. He'd fired guys before and usually had them back, and that thought was still lingering in his head when, a few weeks later, rumours began to circulate that the ex-employees were planning to write a book about their years with him. That panicked him. Red and Sonny knew everything.

Publicly he pretended to be unconcerned, but privately he worried to Linda and Charlie about what the book might reveal. In October, through his lawyer, he offered Red, Sonny and Dave Hebler $50,000 each and financial help in training them for some other kind of employment if they cancelled the book. They turned the money down. They'd already agreed a deal with an Australian ghostwriter, journalist Steve Dunleavy, and Ballantine Books.

He was getting desperate, so when he was told that Red had called, he phoned him back. It was a difficult conversation in which Elvis tried at first to explain how he'd been distracted at the time of their firing by the problems of the racquetball venture.

They were soon both laughing with indignation like old friends again, until finally Red got to the point. 'I guess all that pressure and everything . . . led up to our demise . . . But it was a shock to all of us . . . We're all broke. I had some property and stuff. I sold everything. I sold my house. I hated to do that . . .'

'You sold your house?' Elvis was surprised.

'Oh yes. I sold my house, both cars and everything . . . It was just a bad time by all, I'll tell you.'

'Hell! I guess there's never really a good time,' Elvis replied. 'It was bad for me, too . . . I hadn't been out of hospital long enough to start rolling . . .'

'Yes, but . . .'

'My Daddy. I almost lost him. He's my Daddy, regardless of anything else.'

'Oh yeah . . . I understand,' said Red. 'It's just, I wish we'd been able to talk . . . if I'd just heard from you . . .'

At which point the Colonel's mantra came in useful. Elvis didn't do things connected with business, he told Red.

The conversation wandered on, with Elvis apologising that Red hadn't been invited to his and Priscilla's wedding nine years earlier, and Red trying to get him to talk about the last couple of years when Elvis had been 'pretty fucked up'.

Elvis wasn't having that. 'I am not fucked up. By no means. On the contrary, I've never been in better condition in my life,' adding that insurers Lloyd's of London would vouch for that.

Red didn't even bother disputing it. It didn't matter what Lloyd's of London said, he knew the state Elvis was in. It seemed to him that one of the reasons he'd been chosen for firing was because he'd been too outspoken about the drugs Elvis was taking.

On they went, mainly Elvis doing the talking . . . about his health, his intestinal blockage, his being overweight, how he didn't even like racquetball particularly and the 'negative vibes' he'd felt within the entire group. It had all been 'a failure to communicate', he decided, quoting, as he so often did in conversation, from song lyrics. It was there in Roy Hamilton's song. 'Understanding solves all problems . . .' he said, referring to 'One-Sided Love Affair', which he'd covered on his first album.

They agreed on that.

There'd been 'a failure to communicate, too many suspicious minds, just like in that song we did. "We can't go on together with suspicious minds".'

The conversation was drawing to a close when Elvis said, 'Well, look, you take care of yourself and your family, and if you need me for anything, I'd be more than happy to help out . . .'

'If everybody's worried about the book . . . ?' came in Red, seeking to prolong the conversation and reassure.

'Oh, they aren't,' Elvis brushed it off casually. 'Not on my part.'

It seemed Red wanted to explain: ''Cause I was broke. I was made an offer to write the book. I said, I'll write it if I can [include] all that [happened] from day one . . . We're writing the good days . . .'

'You do whatever you have to,' Elvis interrupted. 'I just want to let you and Pat know I'm still here.'

And with that, wishing each other well, they hung up. Elvis felt better that he and Red had finally talked. What he didn't know was that the conversation had been recorded, and that excerpts from it would soon be published in magazines across the world and then in the book *Elvis: What Happened?*, as well as an account of how he had tried to buy the two Wests and Hebler off with $150,000.

Too late he realised he'd been the victim of a set-up, planned by a clever tabloid journalist. He was bitter. But Red probably didn't feel too good about his part in the phone call either. Red would later say that it had been necessary to provide evidence to support what he and the other fired bodyguards had written, and that he considered the book a warning to Elvis. But he would have his regrets, too.

For a man who had guarded his image so carefully for so long, it was like waiting for a time bomb to go off. It would bring him to tears, as he fretted about what Lisa Marie would think of her father when she read it. And even though Frank Sinatra called to sympathise, and, in a fit of bravado, ask if Elvis wanted any 'help', he knew there was nothing he could do but go back on tour and sing. And worry.

RCA were worrying, too. They needed more tracks to complete the new album, and as soon as Elvis got back from appearing in South Dakota and Wisconsin, their mobile recording truck was once more pulling through the Graceland gates.

In some ways, the two-night session which followed would, in just four songs, define the new limits of Elvis's current musical interest. There was a rock song, 'Way Down', which Felton Jarvis pushed on him; a country and western cover that Jim Reeves had made his own, 'He'll Have to Go'; and a late, great Johnny Ace hit from 1954, 'Pledging My Love'. Elvis never stopped returning to those r and b songs from the days just before he became famous. The fourth song he recorded was a ballad soaked in regret about a man who left his wife and children for a new girlfriend who no longer wants him – and now the guy can't go home again.

'And now you tell me . . . I should go back again, what do you think I should say?' he sang.

Written with Elvis's situation in mind by the English team of Tim Rice and Andrew Lloyd Webber, it had been sent to him from London by Freddy Bienstock. The lyric obviously struck a nerve. 'I get carried away very easily . . . emotional son of a bitch,' he said, just before the first take.

Producer Felton Jarvis had expected to record more songs, but Elvis quickly lost interest, sending those singers and musicians from California back to Los Angeles in his *Lisa Marie* plane instead of having them take a regular airline. And, since bass singer J.D. Sumner lived in Tennessee, Elvis gave him his white Lincoln as a gift to drive the Stamps and himself home. He didn't need it, he said. He had lots of other cars.

His giving had long ago reached a pathological level. He was clearly unwell, yet he worked ceaselessly, having to earn enormous amounts of money simply to pay his staff, service his debts and divorce agreement, buy himself whatever he wanted and then give the rest away. Saving was an alien concept to him. He'd never saved a penny in his life. Caught in a cycle of extravagance of his own making, no matter how out of it he might have been, or how bad his body might feel, he just had to carry on touring in order to keep earning so that he could go on spending and giving . . . But all to what end?

A manager other than Tom Parker might have recognised the state he was in, cancelled all future tours and recording sessions, and booked him into a hospital until his health was improved and his body fully detoxified. Like it or not, faced with the possibility that he would have no income if the Colonel hadn't booked him anywhere, Elvis would have had no choice but to agree. But Parker didn't do that. Instead, when he became embarrassed about how bad some of Elvis's performances were, he simply shouted at him, repeating that he must pull himself together or 'you're going to lose your home, your fans and everything . . .' He would then book him for another tour.

He had to. He had his own agenda. He had to feed his gambling habit and pay those gambling debts. And the only way he could do that was by keeping Elvis working.

So, for the rest of 1976, tour followed tour. Shows at Fayetteville, North Carolina and Pine Bluff, Arkansas might not have had the prestige or excitement of appearances at Madison Square Garden, but the money was as good there as anywhere else. It may even have been better. Living costs for the musicians, singers and road crew were considerably lower in the South than in Manhattan.

So, there they were, mutually dependent, locked together, Elvis and the Colonel flying around America, two quite different people with the same desperate need for money, but each with his own problems.

41

'I have thirty-nine employees depending on me.
If I took a year off what would happen to them?'

Things had been shaky with Linda for months. He couldn't blame her and he didn't, except when, with good reason one might think, she nagged him about the other girls. He usually denied there was anyone else, or apologised when he was caught out, but there always *were* other girls. It wasn't that he was obsessed with sex. He wasn't. Some girls said that being with Elvis was like dating a teenage boy, even though he was in his forties. He didn't mind that. In some respects it was as though he'd become frozen as a boy/man at the moment his extraordinary fame had arrived. Nothing had ever been the same again. Those exciting, innocent, final years of late adolescence before stardom with Mama and Dixie still played on his mind, along with the songs of that time. And, as he would so frequently say, despite everything that was always going on around him, he was still Elvis inside.

So, although he was technically committed to Linda, the remaining guys still kept their eyes open for pretty young women they thought he might like. And that was how, in a ritual that was almost medieval, his replacement consort in the shape of Ginger Alden was found and presented to him for consideration.

It began when old school friend George Klein, who was now working as a Memphis disc jockey, invited Ginger's elder sister, local beauty queen Terry Alden, out to Graceland one evening in November 1976. Ginger, who was twenty years old, an assistant in a dress shop and currently Miss Mid-South Fair, tagged along too, as well as the youngest Alden girl, Rosemary.

Upstairs in his bedroom, Elvis was secretly watching on his

closed-circuit TV system as the three young women arrived at Graceland, and were shown by Klein into the jungle room, where cousin Patsy Presley, who worked as a secretary for Vernon, and her husband GeeGee were playing cards with Billy and Jo Smith. Only after being given a tour of the house by Charlie Hodge, passing other CCTV cameras along the way, were the three girls summoned up the red-carpeted staircase to Elvis's top-floor office.

After another delay, at last he appeared, chatted and made his choice. It was Ginger. And, as Charlie led the other two sisters back down the stairs to be eventually sent home, Ginger followed Elvis through into his bedroom, with its vast square bed and the photographs of Linda on the walls.

Whatever Ginger was expecting, wasn't what happened. Getting out a copy of Cheiro's *Book of Numbers*, Elvis sat on the bed, indicated she should join him and then asked her for her birth date. From that, she was, he calculated, a number four, which suggested she would be a loyal and sensitive person. He was a number eight, which made him one of the misunderstood and lonely, either a great success or a complete failure. A religious book came next, and the two sat side by side on the bed reading to each other until deep into the night, when he asked for a car to take her home. He kissed her just once, she would later say, before she left.

She'd passed the first tests, so the next night he sent George Klein to pick her up. Again she was taken to his bedroom, where this time he sang a hymn for her, before taking her to Memphis Aero, a private airstrip, where his Lockheed JetStar was waiting. He'd planned a flight to show her Memphis by night, but then suddenly decided that, along with Patsy and GeeGee and a couple of bodyguards, they should all go to Las Vegas for the night – fifteen hundred miles away. Being Elvis, he could do things like that. In mid-air he gave her a first gift of a gold bracelet with diamonds. More would follow.

She'd never been to Vegas before. In fact, it was only her second time in a plane. But there was no time for sightseeing. After taking her to the Hilton, where Dr Ghanem arrived and gave them both vitamin shots, Elvis passed her a pair of blue pyjamas to match his own, called her mother to say that she was quite safe with him, then fell asleep in bed holding her hand. The next day they flew back to Memphis, and then, before they could get to know each other any better, steady girlfriend Linda was back at his side for a tour of the Pacific Northwest.

For four and a half years Linda had been part girlfriend and part carer, putting on a brave face in public, falling out with Elvis in private. The excitement of being with him had long since palled. Her life with him had become like that of 'a vampire', she would complain, sleeping all day and being up all night, hiding out at Graceland to keep out of the public eye, then waiting for the cook to bring breakfast at nine in the evening. Then maybe Elvis would go out driving in the dead of night when no one would see him.

He'd recently rented her an apartment in Los Angeles, where she hoped she could make a career as an actress, so she was gradually becoming more independent of him. But there was something else. She'd begun seeing David Briggs, a pianist who'd played on several Elvis sessions, the last as recently as two weeks earlier. Now Elvis had met someone else, too.

The end of their relationship came when the tour reached San Francisco, and Elvis suggested that, as his JetStar had just arrived from Memphis, it might be an idea if Linda took a ride back there for a few days. She read the obvious between the lines. Her replacement must have arrived on the plane. She had. Ginger was already waiting in a room on the floor below. After delaying for a day, Linda decided it was time to take her leave with as much dignity as possible. Elvis's final words to her were: 'No matter what you hear, there's no one else. It's you I love.' She didn't believe him.

Calling one of the guys, he had her driven to the airport, and although they spoke on the phone a couple of times, he never saw her again. Immediately Ginger was summoned from her hotel room, where she had been waiting for nearly twenty-four hours, and took her place at Elvis's side as she met his entourage of six guys and two stepbrothers. Also there was Dr Nick, who routinely injected him before that night's show. Then she sat with him as they were driven to the Cow Palace for the concert.

With a new woman in his life, Elvis's spirits, and his performance on stage, rose for a brief moment as the tour moved down to Anaheim and then on to Las Vegas for two weeks. But he was needy. When Ginger said she would like to go home for a break, he flew her parents out to join her instead, and had his driver buy her a Lincoln Continental. Depression was never far away, and, after spraining an ankle, he threw a microphone into the perturbed audience one night, shouting, 'Does anybody want this tinny sonofabitch? I hate Las Vegas.'

The solace that Ginger brought to his life was never more than temporary. Deep into one December night, sitting alone in his penthouse suite as she slept, he scribbled notes to himself on Hilton stationery, to be later found by a cleaner and sold at auction.

One read: 'I feel so alone now. The night is quiet for me . . . I will probably not rest tonight.'

While another said: 'I wish there was someone who I could trust and talk to . . . I feel lost sometimes.'

And a third: 'I don't know who to talk to anymore . . . Help me, Lord, to know the right thing.'

The following night he asked TV evangelist Reverend Rex Humbard to come to the show, after which the two sat together in his dressing room as Elvis asked about Armageddon and the Second Coming. When did Humbard think Jesus Christ was coming back, he wanted to know.

'I think very soon,' Humbard told him.

'I think so, too,' said Elvis. Then they prayed together.

For two decades he'd taken Christmas week off to enjoy Graceland with its life-sized crib of the Holy Family in the garden, and then later to play football with his gang. But his increasing health problems and weight meant those times were over. And, with discouraging rumours that the Colonel had lost a million dollars at the roulette table in Vegas, he went back to work two days after Christmas on a five-city tour, culminating on New Year's Eve singing 'Auld Lang Syne' on stage in Pittsburgh, Pennsylvania. As a year, 1976 had been difficult. But despite his hospitalisations and drugs problems, including the seasons in Las Vegas, he had sung on stage for at least an hour in a hundred and twenty-seven shows in seventy-seven US cities. The work load never let up.

Since the age of twenty every relationship he'd had with a woman had been on his terms. Ginger Alden, whom he called Gingerbread, was different. More than two decades his junior, a fun night for her

(*above*) From his youth Elvis had bought Mahalia Jackson records, even recording her gospel hit 'Take My Hand', 'Precious Lord'. Here he has just been introduced to her by actress Barbara McNair on the set of *Change of Habit*.

(*left*) 'I heard the rumour that Elvis slept with all his co-stars except one. Well, I know who the one was …! And what was I thinking?' joked Mary Tyler Moore after co-starring in *Change of Habit*.

The Memphis Mafia and other friends. All dressed up with their deputy sheriff badges for Sonny West's wedding in December 1970, they are (standing, left to right) cousin Billy Smith, former sheriff Bill Morris, Lamar Fike, Jerry Schilling, Sheriff Roy Nixon, father Vernon Presley, Charlie Hodge, Sonny West, George Klein and Marty Lacker. And, at the front, are Dr Nichopoulos, Elvis and Red West.

Elvis first heard Jackie Wilson when, during his unsuccessful engagement in Las Vegas in 1956, he went to see Billie Ward and his Dominoes. Wilson was their lead singer who, Elvis thought, sang 'Don't Be Cruel' better than he did on the record. Here, in the early Seventies, he is backstage with the singer after seeing another Jackie Wilson show.

The culmination of a family row that led a runaway Elvis to call in on President Nixon in the White House in December 1970. Amazing but true.

Elvis always imagined having a happy family life. This photograph taken of him, Priscilla and Lisa Marie around 1970 was probably as close to that as he ever got.

Elvis chose the Sweet Inspirations for his onstage backing singers after hearing them on Aretha Franklin, Wilson Pickett and Dusty Springfield albums. Left to right they are Myrna Smith, Sylvia Shemwell, Estelle Brown and Cissy Houston – Whitney Houston's mother.

Priscilla didn't care for the increasingly ornate rhinestone-studded outfits Elvis wore on stage, but he had learned from Liberace. It was, he believed, important to give the audience a spectacle – which is what a world audience of an estimated billion saw in the satellite TV show *Elvis: Aloha from Hawaii* in 1973.

'Elvis has left the building', the announcement would ring out at the end of every show, as Elvis would be rushed off stage to his car by his minders – including, in this image, his right-hand man Joe Esposito.

Of all Elvis's later girlfriends, none was as popular among the Memphis Mafia as the former Miss Tennessee, Linda Thompson. But, like Priscilla before her, she rarely had the singer to herself. Here in 1974 the two are accompanied by Elvis's longtime minder Red West.

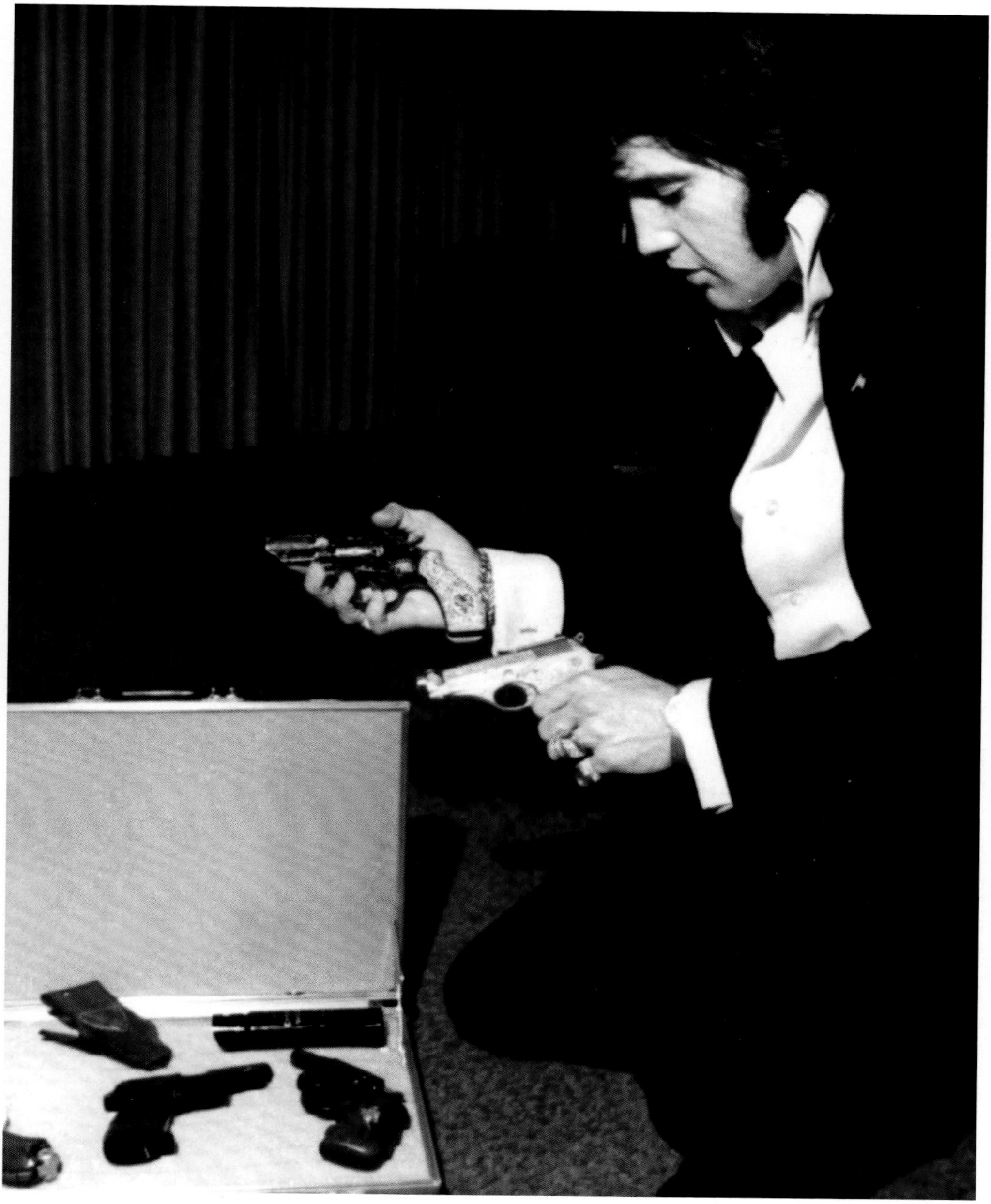

Kidnap threats to his family and worries about security dogged Elvis's last few years and he lavished money on a small armoury for himself and his entourage. He even went on stage with a handgun in each boot.

Elvis and his girlfriend, twenty-year-old Ginger Alden, on his last holiday in Hawaii in March 1977.

wasn't sitting round in his bedroom wearing pyjamas and discussing books on religion, or watching the *Monty Python* TV shows he loved so much. It wouldn't have been for any girl of her generation. And therein lay a problem.

He wanted her with him all the time. It was as simple as that. Infatuation can be cruel and humbling when an older rich man becomes obsessed with a beautiful young girl. He couldn't be her age, nor want to do the things she wanted to do, which was spend more time in normality with her friends and sisters. So, instead, he threw money at her in the shape of mink coats, ball gowns, diamond rings and bracelets, a car for her and another for her parents. He even offered to buy them a new house closer to Graceland. In public he wanted her at his side; in private his behaviour swung wildly between the adoring, the pleading, the dictatorial and the scary. He became angry when she refused to call her old boyfriend in front of him and explain that the guy was out of her life for ever. Then, after taking her and her sister, Rosemary, to Palm Springs to celebrate his forty-second birthday, he terrified her by firing a bullet into the wall above their bed, because she didn't fetch him the carton of yoghurt he'd requested. She'd thought he'd already had enough yoghurt and was concerned about his overeating. He apologised, of course, but every day she was making it apparent to him that he wasn't going to get his way all the time with this girl.

To make up for the disappointing recording session at Graceland in November, he agreed that all the regular musicians and singers should congregate in Nashville at the end of January 1977, only to not turn up himself. Ginger didn't like Nashville, and had simply refused to go. Not many previous girlfriends would have eschewed the opportunity of being at one of his recording sessions, but Ginger wasn't like the others. At Felton's urging, Elvis did eventually arrive in Nashville, a day late, but then wouldn't leave his motel, complaining of a sore throat, before getting a doctor to write him a sick note to send to RCA. Then he flew back to Memphis and Ginger, where he gave her an engagement ring. A report in a Nashville newspaper saying that his new girlfriend was 'running him ragged', a tip-off which had clearly emanated from someone at the aborted session, didn't ease his mood. Only when they were on tour could he be sure that Ginger wasn't about to slip off to see her sisters and friends, so it was a relief for everyone around him when she agreed to accompany him on a ten-day tour of the south-eastern states. Even so, halfway through, he had to fly her entire family in to join the tour, when she got homesick.

The guys, whose job was to keep him happy, weren't amused, but perhaps he wasn't entirely love blind. Although Ginger was one of the witnesses to the signing of his will in February, she wasn't made aware that neither she nor, indeed, anyone else other than Lisa Marie and Vernon was mentioned in it. Lisa Marie would inherit his entire estate at the age of twenty-five, until which time Vernon was charged with taking care of everything for her and Grandma.

All through the spring and early summer of 1977, Elvis toured. Already a very sick man, looking fat, sleepy, bloated and drugged, his speech was slurred and often incomprehensible, his movements and karate stances clumsy and his voice uneven, and almost everywhere he went the newspaper reviews the following day were damning. But the fans still came. It was as if they were thinking that if he couldn't accept how ill he was, they were determined not to see it either. When Ginger was with him, he made an effort; when she wasn't, he was distraught. And in Baton Rouge, Louisiana, he was so zonked out by showtime he just couldn't go on, and was flown home to hospital in Memphis, with the rest of the tour cancelled.

He didn't stay in hospital long, although he had innumerable problems. When it was suggested, as it often was by those other than the Colonel, that he should take a complete year off to convalesce, his response was: 'I have thirty-nine employees depending on me. If I took a year off what would happen to them?'

It was a variation of the answer he'd given to Dixie Locke in 1958 after his mother had died. 'I'm in too far to get out now.'

Nor were all his problems physical. Emotionally he was wretched. Cousin Billy Smith and his wife Jo had now become his closest confidants and he would fret ceaselessly to them that he didn't think Ginger loved him, something they could very well judge for themselves. And, after another row with Ginger, as if to break his dependence on her he invited another twenty-year-old girl he'd met called Alicia to go with him to Las Vegas along with Billy and Jo. It wasn't about sex, because there wasn't any. He just wanted her to be near, to sleep alongside him, and for her to hold his hand and talk to him until the Placidyls did their job and he nodded off. It had been the same with Linda, Sheila and Ginger – almost as if he was regressing to childhood with a little voice to 'sleep with me a little while'. After Vegas he moved on with Alicia, Billy and Jo to spend a few days in his house in Palm Springs, where he once again woke up with breathing troubles, and Dr Ghanem had to be flown out to minister to him. When they got back to Memphis, he bought Alicia a car as a thank you present.

Then it was back to work on tour again during April in Chicago, Duluth, Detroit, Milwaukee and other places, with Ginger at his side, their relationship patched up for a while. So many concerts; so many small cities to visit. In May it was the turn of Louisville then Providence, Rhode Island and twelve other towns until, in Binghamton, New York, Ginger got fed up and left, leaving him floundering in such emotional turmoil that backing singer Kathy Westmoreland, whom he'd so recently insulted on stage, was sent for.

Kathy was a good friend who had been sadly watching his descent from just ten feet away, night after night. Now she became his nurse and comfort as, at her side and unable to sleep, he rambled on through the night about his mother and Ginger and his career, even asking Kathy how she thought he would be remembered after he was dead. He hadn't made a classic film, he told her. Despite everything he'd done, his failed ambition to become a real movie star still lingered. And he was now talking about himself in the past tense, as though he couldn't see a future. He even jokingly told her to wear white at his funeral. Quietly Kathy consoled him. He wasn't going to die, she told him. And she held his hand until he fell asleep.

When the tour was over he bought Kathy a car, too, as a reward for her loyalty. It wasn't necessary. She loved him. But it fitted a pattern. Whenever anyone did something kind he felt he had to reward them with an expensive gift. He was so used to giving he couldn't comprehend that kindness and affection didn't demand a gift in return.

Everywhere he looked there were problems. In Memphis he was being sued over the Elvis Presley Racquetball Center fiasco, Priscilla was enquiring about the almost $500,000 due to her in the divorce settlement, Daddy's heart was sporadically giving cause for concern, and a psychic in Boston predicted on the radio, an item quickly picked up by newspapers, that Elvis would soon die. Then in the middle of all of this there was a rumour in a Nashville newspaper that the Colonel wanted to sell Elvis's contract. It was denied, of course. Though they rarely spoke any more, the Colonel still needed to milk his prize cash cow. It was too late, anyway, far too late, for either of them to withdraw from what had become a twosome of a *danse macabre*.

Then at the end of May came the moment Elvis had most dreaded. A tabloid newspaper in Britain began publishing extracts from *Elvis: What Happened?* It was worse than he'd expected. The section chosen for serialisation was a lurid account of how, off his head on drugs and anger, he'd asked Red and Sonny to murder Priscilla's lover, Mike Stone.

'What's Lisa going to think about her daddy when she grows up and reads things like this about me?' he sobbed to Billy and Jo.

The Colonel didn't believe in tears. 'Don't worry about it,' he told him. 'It'll sell tickets.'

And then, as if to cap his indifference to what the world thought, Parker announced that a film crew from CBS TV would be accompanying Elvis on tour during June to make a one-hour special, *Elvis in Concert*. The news was greeted with dismay among the musicians, singers and entourage. Parker, more than anyone, knew that Elvis was in no state to be filmed in close-up. Obese and ill, some nights it seemed a miracle of mind over a failing body that he got through a show at all. But CBS were paying $750,000 for the show. Split 50–50 between Elvis and himself, with money like that there was no way Parker was going to turn CBS down. Perhaps Vernon could and should have intervened to protect his son. But Vernon challenged the Colonel even less than Elvis.

For weeks Elvis worried about how to address audiences about the newspaper allegations. Should he throw himself on their mercy, admit he had a problem, and say he was going to get help? Or should he deny everything? But if he was still unable to admit to his entourage and himself that his addiction was dangerously out of control, there was no chance that he was going to admit it to the fans. On the second night of the new tour in Kansas City he went on the attack.

'I just want to say that in spite of what you might hear or what you may read, we're here, and we're healthy, and we're doing what we enjoy doing,' he told the audience, who applauded.

He might have been *there* the following night in Omaha, too, when the CBS cameras went to work, but he appeared to be neither healthy nor enjoying what he was doing. Only three songs could be salvaged for the TV show.

Not much was left of the once glorious confidence and vitality, but, in his Aztec cream stage suit, the only one that now fitted, he still had his charm and his pride, and he rallied for the filming at Rapid City, South Dakota, giving CBS enough to cut some sort of show together. Whether it would be kind to show it to the wider public was another matter. Perhaps the most telling moment of the resulting documentary would be when he introduced his song 'Are You Lonesome Tonight?'. As he did, he broke off and answered his own question: 'I was . . . and I am . . .' Just as he'd always been.

The tour drew towards its close in an incident of typical Elvis impulsive eccentricity. After arriving at Madison, Wisconsin, in the early hours of the morning he was being driven to his hotel when, passing a gas station, he spotted a couple of youths harassing the attendant. Ordering the limo to stop, he got out and went to intervene on the side of the attendant, ready with his karate chops. But, upon seeing who the newcomer was, the assailants and the attendant immediately broke off from their rowing and stared in astonishment – eventually even agreeing to have their photographs taken with him with everyone smiling. That was what it was like being Elvis. Then, as quickly as he had arrived, he was driven off into the night.

His last public appearance was two nights later in Indianapolis, on 25 June 1977.

42

'I'm just so tired of being Elvis Presley.'

He was weary when he got home to Graceland and spent much of the following few weeks recuperating and rarely leaving his room. Another tour had been planned for the second half of August, but at first he just wanted to rest in bed, talk occasionally to Charlie who still lived in the basement, or to Billy and Jo, watch television and read. Sometimes he would call Priscilla to plan Lisa Marie's next stay, or just to while away the loneliness. He called Kathy Westmoreland, too, and Larry Geller, who was promising to bring him some new religious books. His family was there, of course, Grandma in her room at the back of the house watching *Hee-Haw* on TV, and Aunt Delta marching around shouting at her dog, and naturally Daddy would call in. But whenever old friends, maybe George Klein or Lamar Fike, stopped by, they weren't encouraged to come upstairs.

'I'm just so tired of being Elvis Presley,' he'd said to Felton Jarvis one night after a show. He didn't feel that way all the time, on other days he just loved being Elvis. But when blackness overtook him it was difficult to find consolation anywhere, and his swollen body, hands, face and ankles would upset him. They didn't belong with how he'd always seen himself.

Hours were spent wondering where Ginger was when she wasn't with him, why she didn't want to move in with him, and whether the new Triumph sports car he'd bought her would endear him to her. And then fearful, sleepless nights would pass as he worried about how the fans would react to the publication of *Elvis: What Happened?* Lurid articles in tabloid newspapers could be dismissed as spiteful gossip, but people took a book more seriously, and he would bubble up in anger at Red and Sonny.

Only very occasionally did he summon the energy to go out through the prison gates of Graceland and drive off down Elvis Presley Boulevard. That was at night when the gates were less likely to be under siege from that small group of fans who daily congregated there. But once through the gates, there was really nowhere he had to go any more, nowhere he wanted to go. Years earlier he'd been able to call in on Sam Phillips at Sun Records at 706 Union Avenue once in a while. But, though he would still always glance at the building as he drove past, the studio wasn't there any more, the microphones and mixing desk having been ripped out when the place had been turned into a motorcycle repair shop. Only the next-door Taylor's café remained. He knew that Sam was only a few blocks away in a new, purpose-built studio, but that wouldn't have refreshed his happy memories of Sun, so it didn't draw him. Laskys was still there on Beale Street, but it was twenty years since he'd been able to go there without drawing a mob. And clothes were always brought to him to choose, either at Graceland or at his house in California, then tailored to fit. A church service would have done him good, he knew, but the only services he attended were when he watched the television evangelists on a Sunday morning and listened to the hymn singing, as, lying in bed, he remembered his mother.

Dr Nick still called by, of course. He had need of him.

He and the Colonel rarely spoke for very long these days, and only ever about business, so his manager's calls weren't welcomed. He was intrigued by a story in one of the fan club magazines that Parker might not be American, but Dutch, and an illegal alien at that. He'd heard a similar rumour a few years before, and dismissed it, but if it was true it would explain the slightly odd accent that Bill and Scotty used to puzzle about and imitate all those years ago, but which he'd just got used to. He'd never asked about it, like so much to do with the Colonel, simply putting his manager's gruff accent and manner down to the time he'd spent in the army, where he'd seen how things were done and learned how to bark out orders.

If he thought about it, though, he probably didn't care if the Colonel wasn't who he said he was or if he'd invented his childhood in that Pony Circus he used to talk about. Back on those little tours around the South that Elvis had done in the mid-fifties, there'd been a comedian who called himself the Duke of Paducah, but who was really Whitey Ford from Missouri. Nobody had minded. What was in a name? Lots of singers didn't use the name they were given when they were baptised, although he always had. Some people had found it unusual and spelled it wrongly at first, but he'd always been proud to be Elvis Presley from Tupelo, Mississippi.

Of course, if the Colonel was an illegal, without a passport, it would explain why he'd never wanted to leave the US and have Elvis tour the world. Once out of the US they might not have let the old man back in again.

A world tour? Elvis had promised it so often. What about now? He could still do it, he supposed, get a new manager and go to England and Germany and all those places where people bought his records. But . . . it just didn't appeal in the way it used to. He enjoyed his home comforts too much now. And then there was his health problems and his doctors. Maybe when he got himself straightened out . . .

So he lay in bed, rarely got out of his pyjamas, smoked the occasional Tiparillo as he watched all of the three televisions facing him and reflected on things. A lot of the time he was morose, but not quite always, because it wasn't all bad news. His part in the Elvis Presley Racquetball Court problem had been suddenly resolved, and the damage hadn't been too great, his latest single, 'Way Down', was at least on the *Billboard* Top Forty, while the flip side, 'Pledging My Love', was top of the country chart, and soon Lisa Marie would be coming to stay. He always looked forward to that, and this would be her longest visit since Priscilla and he had broken up. Having a child around the house always lightened up Graceland. It was the only place he wanted to be, but sometimes, with its trophy room of gold records and guards at the gates, it felt more like a museum than a home. And museums were there to celebrate the past, not the present or the future.

He liked to think he was a good father to Lisa Marie, who everyone now called Lisa, and who at nine was growing into a holy terror when she chose to be. She'd become quite close to Linda before they'd parted, and many were the times he'd wished the little girl could have had a family where her father and mother were still together. That didn't seem as easy as it had been when he'd been growing up. Daddy was now, thankfully, separated from Dee, but although his two elder stepbrothers now worked for him, he didn't feel close to them.

So, during that hot Memphis July, entombed in the Frigidaire cool of his air-conditioned bedroom, he lay and thought and read, and consulted his book of numbers and his Bible. He craved sleep, yet feared it, too, lest it brought that dream he'd had for so long, the one where he'd lost everything, his home, his fans, his fame and his money.

Lisa arrived on the plane he'd named after her on the last day of July and right away she was racing her miniature electric golf cart around the grounds, Elvis sometimes in another. Luckily Ginger's elder brother had a little girl called Amber of around the same age, and Lisa and Amber played together. It was a few years since Elvis had imagined himself a cowboy on a ranch, or done any horse riding, but on a whim he bought Lisa a pony from a cousin. Then, with Lisa riding it, he walked it into the house to show Grandma and Aunt Delta. On another day he was disappointed when not even he could get a print of *Star Wars* for Lisa to see again. Like any dad he wanted to please his daughter.

When he wasn't worrying that she might be kidnapped he enjoyed the ordinary fatherly pleasures of the child's presence. But the joys had to run in daily parallel with his regimen of drugs. They were a mixture of uppers, downers, sleeping pills and the heavy-duty pain-killer Dilaudid – with Dr Nick's chief nurse, Trish Henley, on hand, living in one of the trailer houses at the back of Graceland, just in case.

And, though his mood was generally good when Lisa was around, his behaviour was often unpredictable. Having promised to take the children and a party of adults to Libertyland, the renamed old Fair-grounds he'd always loved, he suddenly changed his mind, only for Ginger, who wasn't long out of childhood herself, to make sure he changed it back again. He couldn't disappoint the children like that, she protested. He gave in, and the outing took place right through one night with Lisa and Amber adjusting to his sleeping cycle.

The sticky dog days of August wore on. He had his hair washed and coloured by Charlie, blacking out his white roots, and Joe Esposito and some of the guys began to assemble as usual at Howard Johnson's Motor Lodge down the road, in preparation for the next tour due to start on 17 August in Portland, Maine. One or two of the guys sometimes suggested he should let his hair return to its natural colour, but he was insistent that the fans wanted him to look like the Elvis of legend. So the hair dye always came out before every tour, together with the costumes, as an essential part of the Elvis mask.

All the time his moods flipped and flopped. One minute he was positive, asking for six new songs to be included in the tour, and demanding that music scores be found for the orchestra and singers, then at another he talked about possibly announcing his engagement to Ginger on stage. Then, when she told him she wouldn't be with him for the start of the tour, he was instantly miserable, asking for another girl to be invited along in her place.

His attitude to his weight was contradictory, too. He now weighed over seventeen stone, and hardly any of his stage suits fitted without being let out, but, although he hated being fat, he didn't do much about it. A few days of a liquid diet and five minutes on an exercise bike weren't going to make much difference.

And all the time his mind kept returning to *Elvis: What Happened?* He told Ginger that it was fictional, but he knew that wasn't true. Colourfully written it may have been, but the basic facts weren't lies.

Although no one in his circle believed him, he still maintained that he didn't have a drugs problem, even wearing a federal DEA (Drugs Enforcement Administration) jacket. But he wasn't a fool. He knew he was an addict. He just didn't recognise how serious his addiction had become. And he liked the high that Dilaudid gave him.

There had always been something to help. Twenty years earlier there'd been the innocent little NoDoz to keep him awake when driving through the night from town to town with Scotty and Bill, and, when he was in the army amphetamines had been handed out routinely to keep him and the other guys alert on night patrol in Germany. He'd liked the effect they'd had on him, to the extent that he'd set up his own private supply line, just as he'd enjoyed it when he and the guys had filled their Hollywood days with fun and games on Dexedrine and never felt tired. He knew Dr Nick was attempting to control his habit, which involved Nick or the guys sometimes opening some pills, emptying the contents and then closing them again to turn them into placebos, but he wasn't fooled. He knew what his body told him it needed, and one way or another, from doctors in Memphis, Los Angeles and Las Vegas, he made sure it got it.

The fifteenth of August 1977 was wet and dull in Memphis, and the day started as usual in mid-afternoon for Elvis, when he played with Lisa in the grounds for a while. She would be returning to Los Angeles the following day, when he would set off on tour. He'd been hoping to see the Gregory Peck movie *MacArthur* once again, but when no projectionist could be found to work after hours, he had someone call his dentist instead for an appointment at 10.30 that night. Being Elvis made that possible. Ginger had arrived by then, and went with him in his favourite car, the black Stutz Blackhawk, together with Charlie and Billy. Elvis drove, two handguns tucked in his belt.

He was in a cheerful mood, offering the dentist a ride out to California in the *Lisa Marie* sometime, getting a couple of minor cavities filled and his and Ginger's teeth cleaned, while picking up a prescription for codeine.

Back at Graceland after midnight, he enquired about arrangements for the tour, and then asked to see the new religious books that Larry had brought from Los Angeles that day. *A Scientific Search for the Face of Jesus*, a study of the Shroud of Turin, intrigued him. He was hoping that Ginger would change her mind and be going with him on tour, but when she still baulked, saying that she didn't feel well because it was her period, he was disappointed and cross.

Claiming that one of the teeth that had just been filled was troubling him he called Dr Nick at around a quarter past two in the morning, and was prescribed six Dilaudid tablets. As one of his staff was always on duty twenty-four hours a day for whatever was needed, his stepbrother, Ricky Stanley, ran the errand to collect the pills at the Baptist Memorial Hospital all-night pharmacy.

Then he and Ginger chatted on until, at some time after four in the morning, he woke Billy and Jo in their trailer home and demanded they join him and Ginger on the racquetball court. Getting his cousin and his wife out of bed to play with him was also something that, being Elvis, he could do.

They didn't play seriously, or for very long, mainly it was just a knock up. After which he had a few minutes on his exercise bicycle, before, sitting down at the piano, he amused himself by singing the Willie Nelson country hit 'Blue Eyes Crying in the Rain'. Then Billy washed and dried his hair, before stepbrother Ricky brought him a packet of pills, mainly depressants, sleeping pills and placebos – part of an established routine that Dr Nick had devised to help get his patient some sleep.

They didn't work. Elvis was now on edge. He had to fly to Maine that afternoon. He just had to get some rest. So, a couple of hours later, sitting wide awake in bed, Ginger asleep at his side, Elvis called down to Ricky for the second packet of pills in the routine.

They didn't work either. At around eight in the morning he tried to reach Trish, the nurse who lived in a trailer behind Graceland, but she'd already gone to work. So Aunt Delta was asked to phone Dr Nick's office, where, after talking to her boss, Trish gave instructions that Delta could give Elvis a third packet of drugs.

Thanking Delta, he then told Ginger, who had woken, that he was going into his private bathroom to read.

'Don't fall asleep,' Ginger told him.

'Okay, I won't,' he replied. Then he smiled and pulled the door closed behind him.

43

'A lonely life ends on Elvis Presley Boulevard.'

Memphis Press-Scimitar

His body was face down in the red shag carpet in the middle of the bathroom, as though he'd been reaching for the phone which was attached to the wall. A book about sex and psychic energy lay close by.

It was some time after one thirty in the afternoon. Ginger had woken earlier, and, not finding him at her side, had phoned to chat to her mother. Then, after going to the guest's dressing room to wash, and wondering where Elvis was, she tapped on his bathroom door. Getting no answer, she pushed it open slightly. There were no locks on any of the doors in his private quarters.

Nancy Rooks, one of the maids, was in the kitchen taking a break from her job and watching TV when the intercom rang. It was Ginger, breathless and sobbing, saying there was something wrong with Elvis. Nancy hurried upstairs, peeped into the bathroom and then ran down again to tell Al Strada, a wardrobe assistant who was checking Elvis's stage suits for the coming tour. By now Ginger had also phoned the office behind the house where Patsy Presley and Joe Esposito had been talking to Vernon. Joe raced into the house and up the stairs to find Strada trying to turn Elvis's body over. Strada had assumed Elvis had overdosed. One side of Elvis's face was swollen and purple, his tongue discoloured. He had been sick on the carpet.

As the news spread around the house and 911 calls were made, Vernon was being helped up the stairs by Patsy. Soon, hearing the commotion, Lisa was trying to get into the bathroom, asking what was wrong with her daddy. Ginger kept her out.

A Memphis Fire Department ambulance was there within minutes as more and more people crowded into the bathroom where Joe and Charlie Hodge were trying to give artificial respiration. Vernon was hysterical. 'I'm coming soon, son. Wait for me. I'm coming,' he wailed.

It was already clear to the ambulance attendants and those present that Elvis was dead. But, as his body was carried down the stairs on a stretcher, Dr Nick drew up in his car, and leapt into the back of the ambulance with Charlie and Joe.

'Breathe, Presley. Come on, breathe,' he pleaded, as he began working on the body.

It took seven minutes to drive to the Baptist Memorial Hospital in Memphis, but there was nothing that could be done. The formal words would be 'dead on arrival'. Elvis had been dead for some hours.

At a little after 3.30 Joe managed to compose himself enough to begin making the inevitable calls. The first was to the Colonel, who was already at a hotel in Portland, Maine, preparing for the tour.

After the initial silence of shock, and then a murmured 'Oh, dear God', Parker immediately turned to business. People had to be told that the next night's show was cancelled; the musicians and back-up singers were already on the plane. They had to be turned back.

Joe's second call was to Priscilla in California. Her immediate worry was for Lisa. Joe reassured her that the child was being taken care of.

Already reporters, tipped off by hospital staff, were gathering outside the hospital. It should have been Joe's job to announce the death, but he was too upset. In the end the hospital administrator did it.

Back at Graceland, knowing that there would be a police investigation, Elvis's private rooms were already being cleared of any drugs or drugs paraphernalia by Aunt Delta, helped by maid Nancy Rooks. Those drugs that weren't immediately flushed down the toilet were buried in a hole in the garden. When the police, accompanied by a medical investigator, arrived, there wasn't so much as an aspirin in the bathroom medicine cabinet, and the black leather bag which Elvis always took around with him to carry his pharmaceutical supplies was also empty. Only two empty syringes had been missed in the clean-up. The medical investigator later commented upon how extremely unusual it was to enter a bathroom so devoid of any of the usual medicines. He could see what had been done. Questions would normally have been asked of the staff and relatives. They weren't. Being Elvis meant that even in death he was protected.

As the crowds now grew outside Graceland and the world's media began to descend on Memphis, an autopsy was started. Before it was completed, however, at eight o'clock that night, Dr Jerry Francisco, the chief medical examiner for Shelby County, announced to the press that the cause of death was due to cardiac arrhythmia; in other words, a heart attack. The hospital's pathologists were embarrassed. They knew it was more complicated than that. What had caused the heart attack?

Over the next several hours, more information was released. Yes, Elvis's health had been bad. His heart had been massively enlarged, his arteries and veins were corroded, his liver showed considerable damage and his large intestine was blocked. He also had an ulcerated larynx, glaucoma and an ear infection. But only when the laboratory reports on his blood and the contents of his stomach were released two months later did a clearer picture emerge. Fourteen drugs were found in his body; ten, including codeine and Quaaludes, in significant, toxic quantities. All the drugs had been legally obtained with a prescription signed by a doctor, so there were none of the street drugs of which Elvis was so afraid. But questions needed to be answered.

Was his heart attack brought on by the drugs he'd taken during that last night? Had they reacted violently and fatally with each other, as the Memphis pathologists believed might have happened? Or did the heart attack occur because its functions and those of his arteries, liver and large intestine had been impaired by years of his abusing his body with phenomenal amounts of a wide array of drugs? The questions were never satisfactorily answered because most of the autopsy, which was a private matter, was kept secret. Either way, though, it seems fair to say that Elvis's death was as a result of drug abuse.

What those close to him did know was that although his death came as a shock, on reflection it wasn't a surprise. Red and Sonny West had predicted it in their book, which had been published just ten days earlier and which would now go on to sell three million copies. Another long-time friend, Lamar Fike, had summed up his opinion of Elvis's health two months earlier when he'd said 'He'll never see the snow fly', and even Aunt Delta had remarked to maid Nancy Rooks: 'Elvis is going to kill himself with all those drugs.'

When Gladys had died, her husband and son had been talked out of having the funeral service at Graceland. But this time Vernon wouldn't be dissuaded. Nor did he back down when he was advised not to let the fans file past the body and pay their last respects. Elvis had always loved his fans, he insisted. He would want them to see him. So, after Larry Geller and Charlie Hodge did Elvis's hair for the last time, his body was dressed in a white suit, shirt and tie and returned in his coffin to Graceland by the back entrance.

Then, with a police guard, and ambulances on hand in case of hysteria or faintings in the heavy August heat, the Graceland gates were opened and fans, who had been queuing since the previous afternoon, wound their way up the drive and into the music room of the house where the body had been laid out. Inevitably thousands were still waiting, disappointed, when the gates had to be closed after three and a half hours.

Meanwhile, as the flags on all public buildings in Memphis were lowered to half-mast, messages of condolence flooded towards Graceland from all parts of the world. President Carter, who had spoken to Elvis on the phone just a few months earlier, said his death 'deprives our country of a part of itself', adding that Elvis had been 'unique and irreplaceable'.

The funeral was held on 18 August in the living room at Graceland. It was not a celebrity affair. Elvis had never moved in starry circles. Before the ceremony, Priscilla, Lisa and Aunt Delta assembled in Grandma's room at the back of the house as family and friends arrived. Linda Thompson was there, together with Ginger, Kathy Westmoreland and Ann-Margret, who was accompanied by her husband, Roger Smith. Then there was the governor of Tennessee, Raymond Blanton, guitarist Chet Atkins and several RCA Records executives. The TV evangelist Rex Humbard, who had recently prayed with Elvis in his Las Vegas dressing room, gave a short sermon, then 'Danny Boy', followed by several hymns, including 'How Great Thou Art', was sung by J.D. Sumner and the Stamps. James Blackwood and Kathy Westmoreland, wearing white as she'd promised, sang other hymns. The entourage who had been closest to Elvis – Joe

Esposito, Lamar Fike, George Klein, Jerry Schilling, Charlie Hodge, cousins Billy and Gene Smith, and, a surprise to some mourners, Dr Nick – were the pallbearers. The Graceland staff watched from a doorway. Red and Sonny West and Dave Hebler weren't, of course, invited. For Red, who had been so faithful for so long, it must have been the most painful of days.

The Colonel was there, of course. Wearing a patterned, short-sleeved blue shirt, no tie, crumpled baggy trousers and a baseball cap, a solitary, unreadable, eccentric figure among the dark suits, he stood in the hall watching. Perhaps he didn't know how to show grief. He'd been busy, though, and had brought with him some contracts he wanted Vernon to sign which gave control of all Elvis Presley merchandising to a company called Factors Etc. . . . from which he would draw a slightly larger royalty than the Elvis estate. A few days later, Vernon signed.

After the ceremony the coffin was placed in a white hearse, and, with seventeen white limousines carrying the mourners, the cortège was driven three miles past thousands of silent fans to a mausoleum at Forest Hill Cemetery. All the flowers sent for the day were distributed among the fans.

As the headline on the front page of the *Memphis Press-Scimitar* put it so brilliantly:

'A lonely life ends on Elvis Presley Boulevard.'

AFTERWORD

He'd been right to worry about money. While he was by no means poor, when auditors looked into Elvis's finances after his death and added up his assets, they were surprised. Including his home, cars and aeroplanes, they reckoned that despite the hundreds of millions of dollars he'd generated in his career, his total worth was less than ten million dollars. At the rate Elvis spent and gave, and considering the financial obligations he had to family and staff, that wouldn't have lasted very long had he stopped touring. By way of comparison, John Lennon, who was to be murdered just over three years later, is believed to have left over a hundred and fifty million dollars. But then Lennon's finances were being overseen by Yoko Ono, the daughter of a Japanese banker. Elvis's money was managed by his self-educated father Vernon and Colonel Tom Parker.

He couldn't have been more wrong about one thing, however. Afraid that he would be forgotten after his death, the reverse happened. He has been more honoured and is more respected in death than he ever was in his lifetime. The immediate surge in record sales in 1977 might have been expected, but the continuing interest in him, which, since then, has doubled the number of his records sold to an estimated billion-plus, couldn't have been anticipated. RCA's buying of his back catalogue from him in 1973 proved a shrewder move than they could have guessed: half a billion more records and no artist royalty to pay. That being said, having taken over the management of the catalogue, RCA finally gave the recordings the respect they deserved, repackaging them in multiple themes – Fifties, Sixties, Seventies, Blues, Country, Rock, Movies, Religious, Romance, Ballads, etc. On top of that, virtually all the surviving out-takes of hundreds of his recordings have now also been made available, while in 2016 a new album, *If I Can Dream*, on which his voice is backed by London's Royal Philharmonic Orchestra, sold over a million copies.

As shocked and upset as the fans were at the time of his death, there was quickly a corresponding emotional reaction among a generation of musicians, many of whom had been drawn to music by Elvis. Soon, some would be writing songs about him, with the result that detractors, who had listened with their ears tightly shut, were given a lesson in cultural appreciation by Neil Young, Bob Dylan, Mark Knopfler, Bryan Adams, Elton John, Frank Zappa and many others. Bruce Springsteen, a big fan, was at the time of Elvis's death trying to get a new song he'd written especially for him to Graceland for consideration. He's never known whether it ever reached Elvis. It was called 'Fire' and it became a million-selling hit for the Pointer Sisters the following year. Elvis may never have understood how or why he sang the way he did. But those who followed him knew that he had been unique and inspiring.

Mercifully, although many of those sixties films which he so despised played for decades on afternoon television, that part of his career seems, in recent years, to have been all but wiped from the public memory. Today *Spinout, Fun in Acapulco, Tickle Me* and the rest might just as well have never been made; but nothing, not even some of the most dire Elvis impersonators, of whom there are tens of thousands around the world, can seemingly kill the continuing popularity of 'Suspicious Minds' and 'Don't Be Cruel'.

Obviously Elvis's looks have helped the continuing mystique, as they helped throughout his career, with an image of him as a young man appearing on US Mail postage stamps in 1992 and again in 2015. The careful marketing of Graceland as a tourist attraction, and the prudent licensing of his recordings to movies like *Ocean's Eleven* and *Men in Black*, as well as to commercials for telephones, supermarkets and sportswear, have also helped keep his memory fresh.

But none of this fully explains why, forty years after his death, he remains one of the most recognised figures of recent history, with his estate now earning an estimated $55 million a year, according to *Forbes* business magazine. Shrewd marketing can only go so far. There has to be something else. It is, of course, his voice – or, should we say, his voices, because he used a multiplicity of styles for different songs.

'I didn't copy my style from anyone,' he often said early in his career.

Actually, he did. He copied it from everyone, his own voice being the result of a collision between all the different styles he loved. And, in the barrage of sound that popular music constantly throws at us, it is the tonality of that voice which still connects, for some indefinable reason and in some subliminal sense, with millions of people, whether or not they speak English.

He wasn't a trained singer, he listened and he learned; and the songs he sang weren't sophisticated in their construction. But when, not much more than a youth, he would seamlessly soar into his falsetto of pleading and yearning, or as a lonely middle-aged man his singing would break with regret, millions recognised the emotion. Capable of going from bass to baritone and on to tenor and falsetto in the same song, his voice was the most pliable of instruments. Consummately versatile, it didn't matter if it was urgent rock and roll, pop operetta or a spiritual, at his best he sang as though he truly believed in the feelings he was expressing.

That was his gift and that was his appeal. He could communicate in song like very, very few others. Whether he could be classed as a *great* singer has to be a personal opinion. For me, I've always liked what Bob Dylan had to say about his liberating effect.

'Hearing Elvis for the first time,' said Dylan, 'was like busting out of jail. I thank God for Elvis Presley.'

After Elvis Died What Happened to . . . ?

LISA MARIE PRESLEY: The sole heir to her father's estate. During a career as a singer/songwriter she has been married four times, and is the mother of four children. Recently she lived mainly in Sussex in southern England with her fourth husband, music producer Michael Lockwood, and their twin girls. Earlier husbands were musician Danny Keough, Nicolas Cage and Michael Jackson. The owner of Graceland, she is the chairperson of the Elvis Presley Charitable Foundation, and, like her mother, is a Scientologist.

PRISCILLA PRESLEY: At the suggestion of a board of advisers, which included bank officials and Elvis's accountant, all of whom were acting on behalf of daughter Lisa Marie, she agreed in 1982 that rather than sell Graceland to pay inheritance taxes, she would open it as a tourist attraction. As such it has been wildly successful and is now the second most visited home in the USA, after the White House, with half a million visitors a year.

For fifteen years she was also an actress, most successfully on TV in *Dallas*, while also, showing a touch for comedy, in the *Naked Gun* movies. In recent years she has appeared in Christmas pantomimes in the UK. Never remarrying, she had a twenty-two-year relationship with Italian screenwriter/director Marco Garibaldi. Their son, Lisa Marie's half-brother Navarone, is now a rock musician.

VERNON PRESLEY: Having separated from his second wife Dee Stanley and set up home with nurse and mother of three Sandy Miller, he and Dee were divorced in November 1977. He died in June 1979. Grandma died in 1980, while Aunt Delta lived on at Graceland until her death in 1993.

'COLONEL' TOM PARKER: The rumours that he wasn't who he said he was were finally confirmed in 1981, when biographer Albert Goldman, with the help of an astonished Lamar Fike, discovered that his real name was Andreas Cornelius van Kuijk and that he had been born in Breda, Holland. Probably an illegal immigrant into the USA in 1929 (when he was twenty), he didn't have a passport, so he was, it is now widely assumed, afraid that if he ever left the US he wouldn't be allowed back in again. This would explain why he didn't allow Elvis to tour abroad. The agreement he'd quickly set up after Elvis's death with Factors Etc. to control memorabilia gave him a steady income. But in 1983 a Tennessee court investigated his management of Elvis, alleging that his share of sometimes over 50 per cent of income had been extortionate, and that he had not always acted in his client's best interests. At that point his connection with the Elvis Presley Estate was terminated. He continued to live at the Las Vegas Hilton Hotel, keeping the same free suite he'd always had while he worked as a 'consultant' to pay off his gambling debts, but in 1984 he was evicted, and lived in a modest home in a Las Vegas suburb. After his wife, Marie, died in 1986, he married his long-term secretary, Loanne Miller. Although he earned many millions of dollars during his management of Elvis, when he died of a heart attack in 1990 his estate was valued at just one million dollars.

LAMAR FIKE: As he said of himself and other members of the entourage: 'Essentially, Elvis's death fucked up everybody's life. Most of us weren't trained to do anything but look after him.' At first Fike set up a van conversion plant in Waco, Texas, but when it went bankrupt he returned to Nashville to work in the music business again. He died in 2011.

RED WEST: After his songwriting and bodyguard career with Elvis was cut short by Vernon, he made a new career for himself in Hollywood as a stunt man and then actor, appearing in the TV series *The Wild Wild West* and the movies *Road House* and, most recently, *Safe Haven*. Later he set up an acting school in Memphis.

SONNY WEST: Raised Arabian horses for a while in California, but then moved to Nashville, where he worked as a road manager for rock band Alabama and became a born-again Christian.

GEORGE KLEIN: Continued to work as a disc jockey on Sirius XM Elvis Radio, and occasionally for Elvis Presley Enterprises.

CHARLIE HODGE: Stayed on in his basement apartment at Graceland where he'd lived for seventeen years, before being asked to leave by Vernon in 1978. Later he toured the world talking about Elvis. He died in 2005.

BILLY SMITH: The son of Uncle Travis, who minded the gates, he continued working at Graceland for several months, believing that the trailer home Elvis had given him was his for life. But when he and his wife wanted to leave and return to Mississippi and take the trailer with them, he was told by Vernon that the trailer didn't belong to him. Later he worked for a while as a guide at Graceland, but was eventually fired. He has since worked as a machine specialist.

JERRY SCHILLING: Wisely he'd already started a second career as a film editor, having hoped to have a career in movie or music production. Jobs in TV followed, and the position as head of creative affairs at Graceland. For a while he was tour manager for the Beach Boys and Billy Joel and managed Lisa Marie Presley.

LARRY GELLER: The spiritual adviser/healer/hairdresser who annoyed the Colonel so much has spent much of his life since 1977 writing and speaking about Elvis.

JOE ESPOSITO: The chief organiser and link between the Colonel and Elvis, he later worked as road manager for Michael Jackson, the Bee Gees, Karen Carpenter and John Denver, as well as being a partner in a limousine rental company. He has written several books on Elvis.

SAM PHILLIPS: Although he also first recorded Carl Perkins, Jerry Lee Lewis and Johnny Cash, his mojo ceased to work in the sixties.

He sold Sun Records in 1968, investing his money in several radio stations. In rock circles he is remembered as a brilliantly innovative pioneer. He died in 2003.

DR GEORGE NICHOPOULOS: Believed to have prescribed thousands of amphetamines, barbiturates, sleeping pills, tranquillisers, etc., to Elvis, he had his licence permanently revoked in 1995 by the Tennessee Board of Medical Examiners after it was revealed that he had been overprescribing to numerous patients for many years. Later he took a job evaluating medical insurance claims by FedEx employees. He died in 2016.

SCOTTY MOORE: Considered to be one of the most influential guitarists in rock history, arthritis in his hands ended his career in his sixties. He died in 2016.

Elvis Presley's Best Recordings

Elvis Presley recorded around 750 songs. Most of the best were made in a studio, although, as many of his stage shows were recorded, not quite all. This list demonstrates his wide range of styles, from straight pop to rock and roll, country, blues, spirituals, hymns and r and b.

A Fool Such as I
A Mess of Blues
After Loving You
All Shook Up
Always on My Mind
An American Trilogy
And the Grass Won't Pay No Mind
Any Day Now
Any Way You Want Me
Anything That's Part of You
Are You Lonesome Tonight?

Baby I Don't Care
Baby, Let's Play House
Big Boss Man
Blue Christmas
Blue Moon of Kentucky
Blue Suede Shoes
Bridge Over Troubled Water
Burning Love

Can't Help Falling in Love
Crawfish

Crying in the Chapel

Doin' the Best I Can
Don't
Don't Be Cruel
Don't Think Twice, It's All Right
Doncha Think It's Time

Early Morning Rain
Easy Question

Fever

Good Luck Charm
Good Rockin' Tonight
Got a Lot of Livin' to Do
Guitar Man

Heartbreak Hotel
Hi-Heel Sneakers
His Latest Flame
Hound Dog
How Great Thou Art

I Feel So Bad
I Got a Woman
I Got Stung
I Need Your Love Tonight
I'll Remember You
I'm Left, You're Right, She's Gone
If I Can Dream
In the Ghetto
It Feels So Right
It Hurts Me
It's Now or Never

Jailhouse Rock
Joshua Fit the Battle

Kentucky Rain

Lawdy Miss Clawdy
Like a Baby
Little Sister
Long Black Limousine
Love Me
Love Me Tender
Loving Arms
Loving You

Memphis, Tennessee
Merry Christmas, Baby
Milky White Way
Money Honey
My Baby Left Me
Mystery Train

Old Shep
One Night
One-Sided Love Affair
Only the Strong Survive

Paralysed
Peace in the Valley
Pieces of My Life
Polk Salad Annie
Promised Land

Reconsider Baby
Return to Sender
Run On

Santa Claus Is Back in Town
Shake, Rattle and Roll
She's Not You
So Glad You're Mine
Such a Night

Surrender
Suspicion
Suspicious Minds
Swing Low, Sweet Chariot

That's All Right, Mama
The Girl of My Best Friend
Tomorrow Is a Long Time
Too Much
Too Much Monkey Business
Treat Me Nice
Trouble
Trying to Get to You

Viva Las Vegas

We're Gonna Move
When My Blue Moon Turns to Gold Again
Wooden Heart

BIBLIOGRAPHY

There are so many books on Elvis it would be impossible for me to have read all of them, but below is a list of those I consulted. I hope I haven't forgotten to mention any.

Alden, Ginger: *Elvis and Ginger*. Berkley Press, New York, 2014

Ann-Margret: *Ann-Margret – My Story*. Orion, London, 1994

Bertrand, Michael T.: *Race, Rock and Elvis*. University of Illinois Press, Chicago, 2000

Brewer Barrett, Jonnita: *Once Upon a Time – Elvis and Anita*. BrewBar Publishing, Jackson, MS, 2012

Brown, Peter and Broeske, Pat: *Down At the End of Lonely Street*. Arrow Books, London, 1997

Chadwick, Vernon: *In Search of Elvis – Music, Race, Art, Religion*. Westview Press, Boulder, Colorado, 1997

Clayson, Alan and Leigh, Spencer: *Aspects of Elvis – Tryin' to Get to You*. Sidgwick & Jackson, London, 1994

Clayton, Rose and Heard, Dick: *Elvis: In the Words of Those Who Knew Him Best*. Virgin Publishing, London, 1994

Cortez, Diego: *Private Elvis*. FEY, Stuttgart, 1978

Curtin, Jim: *Elvis – Unknown Stories Behind the Legend*. Celebrity Books, Nashville, 1998

Dundy, Elaine: *Elvis and Gladys*. Weidenfeld & Nicolson, London, 1985

Escott, Colin with Hawkins, Martin: *Good Rockin' Tonight*. St Martin's Press, New York, 1990

Farren, Mick and Marchbank, Pearce: *Elvis in His Own Words*. Omnibus Press, London, 1997

Geller, Larry and Spector, Joel with Romanowski, Patricia: *If I Can Dream: Elvis's Own Story*. Arrow Books, London, 1989

Goldman, Albert: *Elvis*. McGraw-Hill, New York, 1981

Gregory, Neil and Gregory, Janice: *When Elvis Died*. Communications Press, Washington, DC, 1980

Guralnick, Peter: *Last Train to Memphis*. Little Brown, New York, 1994

Guralnick, Peter: *Careless Love*. Little Brown, New York, 1999

Guralnick, Peter: *Sam Phillips: The Man Who Invented Rock 'n' Roll*. Weidenfeld & Nicolson, London, 2015

Guralnick, Peter and Jorgensen, Ernst: *Elvis Day by Day*. Ballantine, New York, 1999

Harbinson, W.: *Elvis Presley – An Illustrated Biography*. Michael Joseph, London, 1975

Hirshberg, Charles and the Editors of *Life: Elvis – A Celebration in Pictures*. Warner Books, New York, 1995

Hopkins, Jerry: *Elvis*. Simon and Schuster, New York, 1971

Hopkins, Jerry: *Elvis – The Final Years*. St Martin's Press, New York, 1980

Hutchins, Chris: *Elvis – A Personal Memoir*. Neville Ness House, Richmond, Surrey, 2015

Hutchins, Chris and Thompson, Peter: *Elvis Meets the Beatles*. Smith Gryphon, London, 1994

Jorgensen, Ernst: *Elvis Presley – A Life in Music*. St Martin's Press, New York, 1998

Juanico, June: *Elvis – In the Twilight of Memory*. Little Brown, New York, 1997

Klein, George and Crisafulli, Chuck: *Elvis: My Best Man*. Virgin Books, London, 2011

Lloyd, Harold: *Elvis Presley's Graceland Gates*. Jimmy Velvet Publications, US, 1987

Mann, May: *Elvis and the Colonel*. Drake Publishers, New York, 1975

Mansfield, Rex and Mansfield, Elisabeth: *Sergeant Presley: Our Untold Story of Elvis' Missing Years*. ECW Press, Toronto, 2002

Marcus, Greil: *Dead Elvis – A Chronicle of a Cultural Obsession*. Viking, New York, 1991

Marsh, Dave: *Elvis*. Rolling Stone Press/New York Times Book Co., New York, 1982

Marsh, Dave: *Sun Records – An Oral History*. Avon Books, New York, 1998

Moore, Scotty, as told to Dickerson, James: *That's Alright, Elvis*. Shirmer Books, New York, 1997

Nash, Alanna: *Baby, Let's Play House – The Life of Elvis Presley Through the Women Who Loved Him*. Aurum Press, London, 2010

Nash, Alanna: *Elvis and the Memphis Mafia*. Aurum Press, London, 1995

Nash, Alanna: *The Colonel*. Simon and Schuster, New York, 2003

Osborne, Jerry: *Elvis Word for Word*. Harmony Books, New York, 2006

Parker, David: *Elvis for Everyone*. Abstract Sounds Publishing, London, 2002

Pierce, Patricia Jobe: *The Ultimate Elvis, Day by Day*. Simon and Schuster, New York, 1994

Presley, Dee and Billy, Rick and David Stanley: *Elvis We Love You Tender*. Delacorte Press, New York, 1980

Presley, Priscilla: *Elvis and Me*. Berkley, New York, 1985

Presley, Priscilla and Presley, Lisa Marie: *Elvis by the Presleys*. Century, London, 2005

Rooks, Nancy: *Inside Graceland – Elvis' Maid Remembers*. Xlibris, Philadelphia, 2005

Schilling, Jerry: *Me and a Guy Named Elvis*. Gotham Books, New York, 2006

Silverton, Peter: *Essential Elvis*. Chameleon Books, London, 1997

Stearn, Jess and Geller, Larry: *The Truth About Elvis*. Jove Publications, US, 1980

Sullivan, Robert (editor): *Remembering Elvis 30 Years Later*. Life Books, New York, 2007

Vellenga, Dirk with Farren, Mick: *Elvis and the Colonel*. Grafton Books, London, 1990

Wertheimer, Alfred: *Elvis 1956 – In the Beginning*. Macmillan, New York, 1979

West, Red, West, Sonny and Hebler, Dave, with Steve Dunleavy: *Elvis: What Happened?* Ballantine, New York, 1977

West, Sonny and Terrill, Marshall: *Elvis – Still Taking Care of Business*. Triumph Books, Chicago, 2008

Westmoreland, Kathy and Quinn, William G. *Elvis and Kathy*. Glendale House Publishing, Glendale, CA, 1987

Williamson, Joel: *Elvis Presley – A Southern Life*. Oxford University Press, New York, 2014 (USA)

Elvis Information Network
Elvis Australia – Official Elvis Presley Fan Club

NOTES

Author's Note:

p.xv 'You were there? How was he?' Bob Dylan in telephone conversation with this author, August 1969, following Elvis's opening in Las Vegas.

p.xvi 'Was Scotty Moore with him? And the Jordanaires?' John Lennon in telephone conversation with this author, August 1969.

Foreword:

p.xvii 'How are people going to remember me when I'm gone?' Elvis to Kathy Westmoreland, from *Elvis and Kathy* by Kathy Westmoreland and William G. Quinn.

p.xix 'Those people don't love me in a personal way. They don't know what's inside me.' Elvis quoted by hairdresser Larry Geller in *If I Can Dream – Elvis's Own Story.*

p.xxi 'I'm so tired of being Elvis Presley.' As remembered by record producer Felton Jarvis.

Chapter One:

pp.1-5 Details of Elvis's birth and childhood in Tupelo mainly from relatives, great aunt Christine Roberts Presley, cousins Wayne E. Presley, Harold Lloyd, Annie Cloyd Presley, uncle Vester Presley, and neighbours Elois Bedford, Corene Randle Smith, and Odell Clark, from *Elvis: In the Words of Those Who Knew Him Best* by Rose Clayton and Dick Heard.

p.1 Elvis tried to find out where Jesse was buried . . . classmate Joe Savery, *Ibid.*

p.5 'Yes, we was poor . . . but we weren't trash.' Vernon Presley quoted in *Good Housekeeping*, 1978.

p.5 'We'd have pork chops or country ham and cream potatoes. Stuff like that, with red eyed gravy.' Elvis interviewed by author and journalist Robert Carlton Brown, *Personally Elvis LP.*

p.6 'I remember when I was little, people would listen to me singing around the housing project where we lived.' Unused Elvis interview with Pierre

Adidge and Robert Abel for *Elvis On Tour* movie, 1972.

p.6 'Since I was two years old all I knew was gospel music.' *Ibid.*

p.7 'When I was little she never let me out of her sight.' *Ibid.*

Chapter Two:

p.9 He'd always been taught to be polite and courteous and say 'yes, ma'am' and 'no, ma'am'. Becky Martin, classmate, from *Elvis: In the Words of Those Who Knew Him Best.*

p.9 At seven, Elvis sang a duet of 'You Are My Sunshine' with a little girl called Shirley. Becky Martin, *Ibid.*

p.10 At ten, Elvis sang 'Old Shep' at the Mississippi-Alabama Fair and Dairy Show. Shirley Jane Jones, classmate, *Ibid*. Elvis would say that the song reminded him of the dog he had as a boy Rex.

p.10 'Mama gave me a whipping that day, and I thought she didn't love me.' Unused Elvis interview in *Elvis On Tour*, 1972.

p.11 'You could play it when you sing . . . and you know people like to hear your singing.' Gladys to Elvis on buying his first Gene Autry-type guitar – quoted in *TV-Radio Mirror*.

p.13 'Don't you worry none, Mama. When I grow up I'm going to buy you a fine house and pay everything you owe at the grocery store, and buy two Cadillacs, one for you and Daddy and one for me.' Recalled by Gladys Presley in 'The Boy With The Big Beat', *Celebrity*, 1958, and later by Vernon Presley in other interviews.

Chapter Three:

p.16/18 Elvis liked 'the real low down Mississippi singers' and gospel groups like the Blackwood Brothers. From the *Elvis On Tour* interview, 1972.

p.18 'I never knew a guitar player who ever made a dollar', or sometimes, '. . . who was worth a damn'. Vernon Presley remembered by Elvis in *Elvis On Tour* interview.

p.19 According to the records Elvis gave Scotty Moore to transfer to tape in 1969, at least two thirds of his collection was by black artists.

p.20 'When I started out I had terminal acne . . .' Elvis reminiscing on stage in Las Vegas, 1972.

p.20 Elvis would go down to the Tiger Shop in Memphis where the black musicians bought clothes. Classmate Bill Perry, *In the Words of Those Who Knew Him Best.*

p.20 Rubbed pomade into his quiff and whipped out his comb whenever he thought it might be messed up. From *Elvis: My Best Man* by George Klein and Chuck Crisafulli.

p.21 Red West's early friendship with Elvis mainly from *Elvis: What Happened?* by Red West, Sonny West, Dave Hebler and Steve Dunleavy.

p.21 Elvis attending classical concerts in Overton Park, Memphis. 'The orchestra could play for hours, and . . . most of the time the conductor wouldn't even look at his sheet.' From the *Elvis On Tour* interview, 1972.

p.21 'It was amazing how popular I became' after the Humes High Minstrel Show when he sang the Teresa Brewer hit 'Till I Waltz Again With You'. From the *Elvis On Tour* interview, 1972.

p.22 'Truthfully, I don't really know why they gave me a diploma . . . I would just sit there in class . . . thinking about Tony Curtis and Marlon Brando and being a star and singing.' Elvis quoted by Larry Geller in *If I Can Dream: Elvis's Own Story.*

p.22 'I'd like to have gone to college . . . didn't have the money.' Elvis to reporter Lloyd Shearer writing as Walter Scott in *Parade* magazine.

Chapter Four:

p.24 Elvis: 'I don't sound like nobody.' Marion Keisker's interview with this author, 1973.

p.26 'So he sat in with the family and played Monopoly.' Dixie Locke interview on *Elvis Australia's Elvis Presley News (EPN).*

p.26 Elvis's visits to the black Baptist church on East Trigg Avenue, Memphis. The Rev. Herbert Brewster's interview with the author, 1986.

p.28 'I was driving a truck and fell into this crazy music business'. Elvis's account of his career as told frequently on stage in Las Vegas from 1969.

p.28 He had 'the same intimidated expression that some of the blues singers had when they first went into Sun . . .' Sam Phillips' interview with the author, 1973.

p.29 'Sing me something that means something to you.' *Ibid.*

Chapter Five:

p.32 'I don't think anyone was real impressed' – Scotty Moore when he and Bill Black first heard Elvis. 'He had a good voice and he could sing. But the type of stuff he was singing he was just like everybody else – *That's Alright, Elvis* by Scotty Moore and James Dickerson.

p.32 'We were all below average musicians'. Scotty Moore, *Ibid.*

pp.33-4 Details of the recording of 'That's All Right'. *Ibid.*

pp.34-5 Elvis on WHBQ with Dewey Phillips – 'Just don't say nothing dirty.' From many sources, including Stanley Boothe's article 'A Hound Dog to the Mansion Born', *Esquire*, 1968.

p.33 'Don't complicate it, Scotty. If we'd wanted Chet Atkins, we'd have brought him over from Nashville.' Sam Phillips' voice on a take of 'Blue Moon of Kentucky'.

p.36 'Hell, now that's different. That's a pop song now, nearly 'bout, little boy.' *Ibid.*

Chapter Six:

p.40 'What happened? What happened?' After Elvis's first time on stage. Many sources, including his own recollections in *Elvis On Tour*, 1972.

p.40 Elvis was paid $32.50 at the opening of Katz drugstore and sang to a racially mixed audience. Scotty Moore's brother, Ralph, in *That's Alright, Elvis*.

p.42 Recording 'I Don't Care If the Sun Don't Shine'. Marion Keisker's interview with the author, 1973.

p.43 The Presleys didn't own a suitcase, so Marion Keisker lent Elvis one. *Ibid.*

p.43 The appearance at the Grand Ole Opry. Mainly from *That's Alright, Elvis*.

p.44 Elvis leaves bar in Nashville. It wasn't the type of place his parents would want him to be in. *Ibid.*

Chapter Seven:

p.47 'The closest I ever came to getting married was just before I started singing. In fact, my first record saved my neck.' US Army press conference, Brooklyn, New York, 1958.

p.48 'There's no point in you covering songs that are already in the damn charts by other singers. You have to be different.' Sam Phillips in an interview with this author, 1973.

p.48 'I couldn't write a song.' Elvis to radio reporter Jim Stewart in New Orleans.

p.49 D.J. Fontana had played in many strip joints so he was familiar with playing by watching the bumps and jerks of a backside – 'but not one like Elvis's'. Interview on YouTube.

p.50 'Hi Babies, Here's the money to pay the bills.' Western Union telegram from Houston to Elvis's parents, November 1954.

Chapter Eight:

p.55 'Don't you have a hobby or anything else to do?' To which Parker is said to have replied: 'You're my hobby.' Eddy Arnold quoted in *Elvis* by Albert Goldman.

p.57 'Okay, girls, I'll see y'all backstage.' Elvis to the fans in Florida, 1955, as remembered by Mae Axton in *Elvis: In the Words of Those Who Knew Him Best*.

p.57 'I'd give anything in the world . . .' Elvis to Mae Axton, *Ibid.*

p.58 '. . . you'll either have to marry the girl or leave the damned town real quick.' Bill Black's advice to Elvis when a condom burst. From *That's Alright, Elvis*.

p.58 'Roses are red, violets are pink.' Elvis and Bill Black joking on stage. *Ibid*.

p.61 'I've agreed in principle with Tom Parker to sell your record contract to RCA.' From *Sam Phillips: The Man Who Invented Rock 'n' Roll* by Peter Guralnick.

p.61 'Go over there to RCA in Nashville and don't let anybody tell you what to do . . .' *Ibid*.

pp.61-2 Details of Elvis's contract with RCA and Hill and Range from *Last Train to Memphis* by Peter Guralnick and *Elvis* by Albert Goldman.

p.62 'Elvis was one of the most introspective people I ever met'. Sam Phillips' interview with this author, 1973.

Chapter Nine:

p.64 'Earned $25,240' during 1955. US Internal Revenue Service figure.

p.65 'Hot dog, Mae, play it again.' Elvis's reaction when he first heard the song 'Heartbreak Hotel'. Mae Axton in *Elvis: In the Words of Those Who Knew Him Best*.

p.68 'Heartbreak Hotel' . . . 'a morbid, melodramatic mess'. Sam Phillips to this author, 1973.

p.68 'We think tonight he's going to make television history for you. Ladies and gentlemen . . . Elvis Presley.' Bill Randle's introduction on CBS TV's *Stage Show*.

p.72 'Don't hide. Walk the streets, go to restaurants, but don't hide. Because, if you do, you're going to be the loneliest guy in the world.' Jackie Gleason to Elvis as told later by Gleason to CNN's Larry King. (Part of King's interview with Linda Thompson.)

p.72 'You are the best, most wonderful person I could ever hope to work with.' Elvis's telegram to Colonel Parker, 1956.

Chapter Ten:

p.75 'Mr Phillips, I believe I might have syphilis.' Sam Phillips to this author, 1973.

p.78 'One day go out like a light . . . just like it came on'. Elvis to many journalists during 1956/57.

p.79 'I know right from wrong but it's so easy to get into trouble. You can get trapped into something maybe you didn't think to do . . . The worst kind of trouble I've ever been in was stealing eggs when I was real little.' Elvis in an interview with Robert Carlton Brown, 1956.

p.80 'Why should music contribute to juvenile delinquency? If people are going to be juvenile delinquents they'll be juvenile delinquents if they listen to Mother Goose rhymes.' Elvis to radio reporter Lou Irwin, Los Angeles, 1956.

p.81 On Elvis the Pelvis: 'That seems to me the most stupid thing an adult person can say.' Elvis to Paul Wilder for *TV Guide*, 1956.

Chapter Eleven:

pp.82-3 Account of the scare when flying to Nashville. From Elvis talking to reporter Ray Green in Little Rock, Arkansas.

p.84 'Get out of the stable, Grandma, you're too old to be horsing around.' Elvis on stage at the Frontier Hotel in Las Vegas, 1956.

p.86 'She'd had feathers on her behind where they wiggle most and she'd bumped and pushed all over the place. I never saw anything like it. I was like Little Boy Blue in comparison. But who did the newspapers say was obscene? Me!' Elvis to a reporter on the *Charlotte Observer*, Charlotte, North Carolina.

p.86 'The coloured folks have been singing and playing it just like I do now, man, for more years than I know.' *Ibid.*

p.86 'When I sing hymns with my parents back home I stand still and look like you feel when you sing hymns.' *Ibid.*

p.86 'No matter what people say, you know who you are. That's all that matters.' Gladys Presley, as quoted by cousin Harold Lloyd in *Elvis Presley's Graceland Gates*.

p.87 'Rock and roll is a healthy thing. You don't have to be doped up to do it.' Elvis to radio reporter Lou Irwin, 1956.

Chapter Twelve:

p.93 'I was totally green about movie production.' Elvis on stage in Las Vegas, 1969.

p.94 'Music hath charms to soothe a savage breast . . .' Charles Laughton introducing Elvis while standing in for Ed Sullivan on *The Ed Sullivan Show*, 1956.

p.95 'It makes me feel bad coming back here like this to remember how poor we was.' Gladys to friends and relatives in Tupelo when Elvis returned there for an appearance at the Mississippi-Alabama Fair and Dairy Show.

p.95 'The Lord giveth and the Lord taketh away. I might be herding sheep next year.' Elvis to a reporter in Dallas, Texas, 1956.

pp.97-8 'Son, you gonna spend us all bankrupt. You're just a-wasting money.' Vernon to Elvis. Cousin Harold Lloyd in *Elvis: In the Words of Those Who Knew Him Best*.

Chapter Thirteen:

p.99 'a 172 pound six foot tall sausage'. From the *Time* review of *Love Me Tender*.

p.100 'playing a part so far from me it wasn't even funny'. Elvis to an unknown radio interviewer after the criticism he received for his part in *Love Me Tender*.

p.100 Cadillacs parked outside Sun 'like nothing so much as a row of roosters perched on a fence'. Marion Keisker to the author, 1973.

p.101 'I hate to get started in these jam sessions because I'm always the last one to leave.' From the recording of Elvis's visit to Sun Records on 4 December 1956 – *The Million Dollar Quartet*.

p.102 'It was either hit or be hit. I can stand slander and ridicule, but . . .' Elvis to Red Robinson and other journalists in Vancouver in August 1957.

p.103 An ugly rumour had begun going around that Elvis had said 'the only thing Negroes can do for me is buy my records and shine my shoes'. He'd been upset by it. 'People who know me, know I wouldn't have said that,' he told Louie Robinson in 'The Truth About The Elvis Presley Rumour', *Jet* magazine, 1956.

Chapter Fourteen:

p.105 'We've never had a pleasanter experience with a big name than we've had with you.' Ed Sullivan eating his words on his show, October 1956.

p.110 Hollywood director Philip Dunne, who made *Wild in the Country,* would later describe the Memphis Mafia as 'fart catchers'.

Chapter Fifteen:

p.114 'What doth it profit a man if he gain the whole world, and loses his soul?' A Gladys stand-by from the Bible that Elvis liked to repeat.

p.115 'What's going on?' Elvis asked when the MGM executive stopped the Jordanaires singing with him. Scotty Moore in *That's Alright, Elvis.*

p.116 'You know, I'd love for you to write me a real pretty love song.' The writing of 'Don't', as told by Mike Stoller to this author, 1985.

p.116 'Hang up your pretty stocking, turn out the lights, Santa Claus he's coming down your chimney tonight . . .' *Ibid.*

p.117 'Just give it here . . .' Account of the row over Bill Black's failure to play the Fender bass from a Gordon Stoker interview quoted in *Last Train to Memphis* by Peter Guralnick.

p.117 Elvis's apology for berating the Jordanaires – *Ibid.*

Chapter Sixteen:

p.124 'This rancid-smelling aphrodisiac, rock and roll, smells phony and false . . .' Frank Sinatra's barely disguised attack on Elvis, *Western World* magazine, 1957.

p.125 'There are gonna be people who like you and people who don't like you.' Elvis talking to disc jockey Jim Stewart, New Orleans, 1956.

p.125 'My movements, ma'am, are all leg movements. I don't do nothin' with my body.' Elvis to a reporter after a Los Angeles concert, 1958.

Chapter Seventeen:

p.127 'Son, I don't rightly know the answers to your problems . . .' Harold Lloyd quoting Gladys in *Elvis: In the Words of Those Who Knew Him Best.*

p.127 Christmas cards with the message 'from Elvis and the Colonel' in 1957 – already theirs is a joint enterprise.

p.130 'I never was very good at arithmetic.' Elvis when he failed to be selected as officer material in the army, 1958.

Chapter Eighteen:

p.132 'A lot of times I feel miserable. And I don't know which-away to turn. Even though I'm surrounded by people I get lonely and stare at the wall.' Elvis to Joe Hyams in the *Herald Tribune*, 1957.

p.133 'He was very sad, very low, very depressed.' Based mainly on Eddie Fadal's account in *Elvis: In the Words of Those Who Knew Him Best.*

p.133 'It's all over . . .' Elvis to Eddie Fadal, *Ibid.*

p.136 'I knew what it was before I even answered the phone.' Elvis to his friends on hearing of his mother's death.

p.136 'She was all we lived for . . . When Mama was feeling bad we used to walk her up and down the driveway here to help her feel better.' Elvis to Memphis reporters outside Graceland the morning after his mother died.

pp.136-8 The death of Gladys. From accounts by Eddie Fadal, Red West and Lamar Fike.

p.137 'Mama, you never would dress up for me and now here you are dressed up in the most beautiful gown . . .' From Eddie Fadal's account.

p.137 'Mama, here's Eddie. You know Eddie. You met him in Killeen . . . Wake up, Mama. Wake up, Baby, and talk to Elvis.' *Ibid.*

p.137 'I never seen a man suffer as much or grieve as much as Elvis did over the loss of his mother.' J. D. Sumner to Peter Guralnick in *Last Train to Memphis.*

p.138 'People are watching you.' From Lamar Fike's account of Elvis's hysteria at the graveside.

p.138 'There are too many people that depend on me now.' Elvis to Dixie Locke. Interviewed by Peter Guralnick in *Last Train to Memphis.*

p.139 'Since I was an only child we might have been a little closer . . .' Elvis talking about his mother in an army press conference at Brooklyn, New York, before leaving for Europe, 1958.

Chapter Nineteen:

p.141 'I gotta act like one of the guys, but it ain't easy being one of the guys. I ain't never been one of the guys and I never will be one of the guys.' Elvis to Lamar Fike in *Elvis* by Albert Goldman.

p.143 'I guess I got in more singing in the army than I would if I'd been working on it.' Elvis at a Memphis press conference in 1960.

p.144 'clean and wholesome', that being the thing that could 'determine our lives and happiness together'. Fragment of a letter from Elvis in Germany to Anita Wood.

p.144 Elvis was seeing a little German 'chuckaloid' who looked a lot like Brigitte Bardot, and with whom it was 'grind city'. Parts of a letter from Elvis in Germany to his friend Alan Fortas in Memphis.

p.145 'That woman is just a gold digger, and other things.' Grandma on Vernon's new girlfriend Dee Stanley. From *Sergeant Presley: Our Untold Story of Elvis' Missing Years* by Rex and Elisabeth Mansfield.

p.145 'I heard about that woman Vernon was with. The Presleys was all bad about such as that.' Elvis's great aunt Christine Roberts Presley in *Elvis: In the Words of Those Who Knew Him Best.*

p.147 'Benzedrine . . . no side effects.' Elvis to Rex Mansfield in *Sergeant Presley: Our Untold Story.*

p.148 'The world is more alive at night. It's like God isn't looking.' A favourite Elvis saying.

p.148 'the old coloured spirituals from years back' – Elvis's first love in music. Talking to reporter Red Robinson in Vancouver, August 1957.

p.148 'Marion! I don't know whether to kiss you or salute you.' Marion Keisker's interview with this author.

Chapter Twenty:

p.151 re. Gladys. 'I don't believe that death is the end. I just don't.' To a Memphis reporter.

p.153 'We were all surprised. We knew he could sing. But we didn't know he could sing that well.' Gordon Stoker of the Jordanaires after making Elvis's record 'It's Now or Never' with him.

p.154 'Elvis really got into his Ink Spots routine on that one.' Songwriter Mort Shuman in conversation with this author about Elvis's version of 'Doin' the Best I Can', 1989.

p.154 'Hell, what could he say? I'm locked into this thing.' Elvis in Hollywood on the phone to Priscilla. From *Elvis and Me* by Priscilla Presley.

p.155 'The army makes men out of boys.' Favourite Elvis saying.

p.156 'She seems pretty nice. But I only had one mother, and that's it . . . As long as she understands that, there won't be any trouble.' Elvis to a reporter from the *Memphis Press-Scimitar.*

p.156 re. Vernon. 'He's all I've got left in the world. I'll never go against him or stand in his way.' *Ibid.*

Chapter Twenty-One:

p.158 'I think of [mother] nearly every single day. If I never do anything really wrong, it's all because of her. She wouldn't let me do anything wrong.' *Ibid.*

p.158 'Rock and roll is basically just gospel music, or gospel music mixed with rhythm and blues . . . Gospel music is the purest thing on this earth.' Elvis's frequent explanation of his music.

Chapter Twenty-Two:

p.166 On movies. 'I didn't have any say-so in it all, so I did it like it was a job.' Unused interview for *Elvis On Tour,* 1972.

p.167 'Not all the films were bad. Some were quite funny . . . entertaining.' *Ibid.*

p.168 'It's nobody's fault except my own.' *Ibid.*

p.168 'What am I supposed to do with this piece of shit?' Elvis to Gordon Stoker of the Jordanaires talking about one of the many bad film songs he had to sing. From *Careless Love* by Peter Guralnick.

p.169 'I felt obligated to do things I didn't believe in. I was locked in.' Elvis in the *Elvis On Tour* interview.

p.170 'If she thinks she's going to just take over Graceland, she has another think coming.' Elvis comments, probably to the Graceland staff, about Vernon's new wife, Dee. Vernon got the message.

Chapter Twenty-Three:

p.173 'I kept a ribbon from your hair . . . a breath of perfume lingers there . . .' Lyrics to *Anything That's Part of You* by Don Robertson.

p.174 'I was ready. He wasn't.' Priscilla Presley in *Elvis and Me.*

p.175 'Don't tell me how to do my job.' Elvis to Priscilla, *Ibid.*

p.175-6 'If I can entertain people with the things I'm doing, I'd be a fool to tamper with it.' To Lloyd Shearer, *Parade* magazine, 1962.

p.177-8 Sexy Polaroid photos of Priscilla. From *Elvis and Me* by Priscilla Presley.

p.198 Re. *To Kill a Mockingbird*. 'That's a wonderful movie,' Elvis said to a reporter from the Memphis *Commercial Appeal.*

p.179 'She comes round here on weekends on her motorcycle.' Elvis on the phone to Priscilla about Ann-Margret. From *Elvis and Me* by Priscilla Presley.

p.180 'I want a woman who is going to understand that things like this might happen. Are you going to be her, or not?' *Ibid.*

Chapter Twenty-Four:

p.182 'Congratulations on your appearance on The Ed Sullivan Show . . . Elvis and the Colonel.' Diplomatic, lukewarm telegram welcoming the Beatles to the US in 1964, read out by Sullivan on the show.

p.185 'I just happened to come along in the music business when there was no trend.' Elvis at the army press conference in Brooklyn, New York, 1958.

p.187 'If we can control sex, then we can control all other desires.' Elvis to Priscilla. From *Elvis and Me* by Priscilla Presley.

Chapter Twenty-Five:

p.189 'When the script arrived for the next film I would just read a few pages and know that it was pretty well the same plot as the last time . . .' Elvis in the *Elvis On Tour* interview, 1972.

p.193 'In order to do the artistic pictures it is necessary to make the commercial Presley pictures.' Syndicated interview with Hal Wallis, 1964.

p.193 'Elvis Presley movies won't win any Academy Awards. All they're good for is making money.' Colonel Parker quoted in the *Los Angeles Times,* 1964.

p.193 'The only thing worse than watching a bad movie, is being in one.' Elvis, repeatedly, to his friends.

p.194 Elvis 'saw Hollywood as the home of phonies'. Priscilla Presley in *Elvis and Me.*

p.195 'He wanted my skirts shorter, my eyeliner darker . . . I was his doll whom he loved to dress.' *Ibid.*

Chapter Twenty-Six:

pp.196-9 The account of the Beatles visiting Elvis at his home in Beverly Hills is based on the author's conversations with John Lennon, Paul McCartney, Ringo Starr and Chris Hutchins, who organised the meeting.

p.200 'Bill [Black] was a very great man . . .' Elvis to the Memphis *Commercial Appeal.*

Chapter Twenty-Seven:

p.203 'Green, Green Grass of Home'. Elvis said it was 'too country' for him. Red West in *Elvis: What Happened?*

p.203 'You tell me just how I can take this yoga serious . . .' Lyrics to 'Yoga Is As Yoga Does' by Gerald Nelson and Fred Burns from the film *Easy Come, Easy Go.* According to Larry Geller, Elvis went into a rage about having to sing this song.

p.204 'I'd rather try and close a deal with the Devil.' What Hollywood producer Hal Wallis would privately say of Parker's negotiating tactics.

p.204 'A Presley movie is the only one sure thing in show business.' What Hal Wallis would say in public.

p.204 'Hollywood . . . are a lot of fancy talkers who like to pigeon-hole you.' Elvis in an unused interview for *Elvis On Tour,* 1972.

Chapter Twenty-Eight:

p.206 The Circle G Ranch: 'picture postcard perfect . . . a hundred and sixty acres of paradise'. Priscilla in *Elvis and Me.*

p.207 'We would go out and look at a three hundred dollar horse. But when the people found that it was maybe for Elvis it became a three thousand dollar horse.' Dr E.O. Franklin, veterinarian, in *Elvis: In the Words of Those Who Knew Him Best.*

p.207 'One day he bought eight pick-up trucks for all the guys in his entourage . . . Then he bought house trailers so the guys could have someplace to stay.' *Ibid.*

p.208 'Some of you maybe think that Elvis is Jesus Christ who should wear robes and walk down the street helping people . . .' Colonel Parker to the Memphis Mafia, as told by Larry Geller in *The Truth About Elvis* by Larry Geller and Jess Stearn.

Chapter Twenty-Nine:

p.213 'Why didn't you tell me this before I come here?' Jerry Reed to Freddy Bienstock. The studio row over the publishing rights to 'Guitar Man' mainly from *Careless Love* by Peter Guralnick.

p.215 'I haven't been in front of an audience in eight years . . . What if they laugh at me?' Recalled by TV director Steve Binder in various press interviews.

p.216 'That ain't an Elvis kind of song' – Colonel Parker when he first heard 'If I Can Dream'. Songwriter W. Earl Brown in interviews. The song used a direct quotation from Martin Luther King, who had been assassinated in Memphis earlier that year, 1968.

p.216 'Play it again.' *Ibid.*

p.216 'My boy, my boy, this could be the one.' Scribbled by Elvis on the lyric sheet of 'If I Can Dream'. By this time he was desperate for a big hit.

p.217 'I'm never going to sing another song I don't believe in. And I'm never going to make another picture I don't believe in.' Elvis to Steve Binder, who repeated the remark in interviews.

Chapter Thirty:

p.221 'I want to hear every song I can get my hands on . . .' Marty Lacker in *Elvis and the Memphis Mafia* by Alanna Nash.

p.221 '. . . consider this the most expensive demo session in history.' Producer Chips Moman, *Ibid.*

p.221 'This boy's right. We're gonna stay here and we're gonna do the sessions his way.' Harold Jenkins from RCA supporting Chips Moman over 'Suspicious Minds'. *Ibid,*

p.222 'let him fall on his ass'. Colonel Parker about Elvis when he insisted on recording 'Suspicious Minds'. Marty Lacker in *Elvis and the Memphis Mafia.*

Chapter Thirty-One:

p.224 'Elvis was never the same after Las Vegas. It was as though he'd lost his family.' Gordon Stoker of the Jordanaires in *Elvis: In the Words of Those Who Knew Him Best.*

p.225 'I want musicians who can play every kind of music.' Elvis said this in the *Elvis On Tour* interview, 1972.

p.225 'All the musicians around me were handpicked. We auditioned for days and days.' *Ibid.*

p.227 'I sure got into a rut with those films.' Elvis on stage in Las Vegas, 1969.

p.227 'I know I keep saying I'll come to England one day, but I will.' Elvis to this author, 1969.

p.228 'I wouldn't be being honest with you if I said I wasn't ashamed of some of the movies I've been in . . .' *Ibid.*

p.228 'I've no idea about the money. I don't want to know. You can stuff it.' *Ibid.*

p.228 'The Colonel has nothing to do with Mr Presley's finances. That's all done by his father, Mr Vernon Presley, and his accountant. He can flush all his money away, if he wants to. I won't care.' Colonel Parker, *Ibid.*

Chapter Thirty-Two:

p.236 'some sonofabitch crazy bastard pictured sneering in the newspapers about having killed Elvis Presley'. To members of his bodyguard as, back on tour, Elvis worried about his safety and that of his family.

p.237 'I never did like that toilet.' Nancy Rooks in *Inside Graceland – Elvis' Maid Remembers.*

pp.237-8 Vernon rows with Elvis about his spending. From *Elvis and Me* by Priscilla Presley.

Chapter Thirty-Three:

p.243 'You dress kind of wild, don't you.' President Nixon to Elvis from notes made at the meeting by Egil 'Bud' Krogh, deputy counsel to the president.

p.243 'Mr President, you got your show to run and I got mine.' *Ibid.*

p.243 'filthy, unkempt appearance and suggestive music of the Beatles'. *Ibid.*

p.243 'Sir, they have wives, too.' From Jerry Schilling's book *Me and a Guy Named Elvis.*

Chapter Thirty-Four:

p.246 'When I was a child, ladies and gentlemen . . .' Elvis's speech at the Jaycee Awards as reported by the Memphis *Commercial Appeal.*

p.246 'She's the one I told you about, who made it all possible,' Elvis told Priscilla. Marion Keisker to this author.

p.248 'Well, at least it's Elvis.' Billy Swann, quoting Kris Kristofferson, to this author.

Chapter Thirty-Five:

p.250 'If I made you feel second best, I'm so sorry, I was blind . . . You were always on my mind . . .' Lyrics of regret in 'Always on My Mind', written by Wayne Carson, Johnny Christopher and Mark James.

p.252 'I'd thought that they would give me a chance to show some kind of acting or do a very interesting story . . .' Unused interview in *Elvis On Tour*, 1972.

p.252 'They couldn't have paid me no amount of money in the world to make me feel self-satisfaction inside.' *Ibid.*

p.254 'lardass, bad tempered sonofabitch'. Elvis telling his entourage what he really thought about Colonel Parker in later years. From *Elvis and the Memphis Mafia* by Alanna Nash.

p.255 'I get mean when I drink.' Colonel Parker admitted this to Joe Esposito, explaining why he didn't drink.

Chapter Thirty-Six:

p.259 It's very hard to comprehend, but it's my favourite part of the business, a live concert.' Elvis to a press conference announcing the satellite TV concert *Elvis: Aloha from Hawaii*.

p.259 'I want you to go on a diet. I want you to lose some weight.' Director Marty Pasetta in press interviews.

p.259 '. . . it's one of the first times anyone has been honest with me. I'll go on a diet for you.' Marty Pasetta quoting Elvis, *Ibid*.

p.262 'keep the spotlight on her, man, she's beautiful, I want to look at her'. Elvis on stage in Las Vegas after spotting Ann-Margret in the audience, 1973.

pp.263-4 'The man has to go . . . Find someone who can wipe the sonofabitch out. He has no right to live.' Red West in *Elvis: What Happened?*

p.264 'Maybe that's a little heavy. Just leave it for now.' *Ibid.*

p.265 'I would sit there with him in Vegas and I was going nuts, too.' *Ibid.*

Chapter Thirty-Seven:

p.269 'It is tragic, disheartening and absolutely depressing to see Elvis in such diminishing stature.' *Hollywood Reporter* critic on Elvis's opening night at the Las Vegas Hilton, August 1973.

p.269 'You can't fire me. I've already resigned . . .' Elvis's row with Colonel Parker was witnessed and later written about by several of the entourage, including Jerry Schilling, Lamar Fike and Joe Esposito.

p.271 'Daddy, I just want you to know I've finally got my own group.' Mainly from Shaun Nielsen in *Elvis: In the Words of Those Who Knew Him Best*.

Chapter Thirty-Eight:

p.277 'That's the weirdest furniture I ever saw . . .' Vernon Presley in *Good Housekeeping*, 1978.

p.278 'Well, by God, I'll tell you something. I have never been strung out in my life, except on music . . .' Elvis on stage, Las Vegas Hilton, 1974.

p.280 'And you worried your Mama right into her grave.' Vernon to Elvis when both were in hospital and Billy Smith was visiting. Smith quoted in *Elvis and the Memphis Mafia* by Alanna Nash.

Chapter Thirty-Nine:

p.286 'all you sons of bitches . . . just want his damn money'. Aunt Delta on board Elvis's plane, to his entourage. Billy Smith quoted in *Elvis Aaron Presley* by Alanna Nash.

Chapter Forty:

pp.290-2 'It started out kind of innocent . . .' These pages are based on the taped telephone conversation between Elvis and Red West, later published in *Elvis: What Happened?*

p.293 'I get carried away very easily . . .' Elvis as he is about to record 'It's Easy for You', October 1976.

Chapter Forty-One:

p.297 'No matter what you hear, there's no one else. It's you I love.' Elvis's goodbye to Linda Thompson, recounted by her to Larry Page on CNN.

p.302 'What's Lisa going to think about her daddy when she grows up and reads things like this about me?' Elvis to Billy Smith in *Elvis Aaron Presley* by Alanna Nash.

p.303 '. . . in spite of what you might hear or what you may read, we're here, and we're healthy . . .' Elvis to the audience on his final tour, June 1977.

p.303 'I was . . . and I am . . .' Elvis answering the question 'Are You Lonesome Tonight?' in Rapid City, South Dakota, June 1977.

Chapter Forty-Two:

p.310 'Don't fall asleep,' Ginger told him. From *Elvis and Ginger* by Ginger Alden.

p.310 'Okay, I won't.' *Ibid.*

Chapter Forty-Three:

pp.313-14 'He'll never see the snow fly.' Lamar Fike's prediction, in *Elvis* by Albert Goldman.

p.314 'Elvis is going to kill himself with all those drugs.' Aunt Delta to Nancy Rooks, *Inside Graceland – Elvis' Maid Remembers.*

p.314 'deprives our country of a part of itself'. President Carter statement.

Song Credits

Peace In The Valley written by Thomas A. Dorsey
Flip, Flop And Fly written by Charles E. Calhoun and Lou Willie Turner
Shake Rattle And Roll written by Charles E. Calhoun
That's All Right written by Arthur Crudup
Heartbreak Hotel written by Mae Boren Axton, Thomas R. Durden and Elvis Presley
Promised Land written by Chuck Berry
Hound Dog written by Jerry Leiber and Mike Stoller
One Night (of Sin) written by Dave Bartholomew, Pearl King and Anita Steiman
Santa Claus Is Back In Town written by Jerry Leiber and Mike Stoller
Don't written by Jerry Leiber and Mike Stoller
You Are My Sunshine written by Jimmie Davis
Anything That's Part Of You written by Don Robertson
I Saw Her Standing There written by John Lennon and Paul McCartney
Run On traditional, arranged by Elvis Presley
Yoga Is As Yoga Does written by Gerald Nelson and Fred Burch
Without A Song written by Ken Rose
Long Black Limousine written by Bobby George and Vern Stovall
Always On My Mind written by Wayne Carson, Johnny Christopher and Mark James
Loving Arms written by Tom Jans
Pieces of My Life written by Troy Seals
It's Easy For You written by Tim Rice and Andrew Lloyd Webber
One Sided Love Affair written by Bill Campbell

Index